SOVIET NAVAL THEORY AND POLICY

SOVIET NAVAL THEORY AND POLICY

Gorshkov's Inheritance

Robert Waring Herrick

NAVAL INSTITUTE PRESS
Annapolis, Maryland

Originally published by the Naval War College Press, Newport, Rhode Island, 1988.

Copyright © 1988 by Robert Waring Herrick

First printing of the Naval Institute Press edition, 1989

Library of Congress Cataloging-in-Publication Data

Herrick, Robert Waring.
  Soviet naval theory and policy.

  Bibliography: p.
  Includes index.
  1. Naval art and science—History—20th century. 2. Soviet Union. Voenno-Morskoi Flot.
3. Naval strategy—History—20th century. 4. Gorshkov, Sergeĭ Georgievich, 1910–
  . I. Title.
V55.S65H47   1988   359′.00947   88-19563

ISBN 0-87021-677-5

Printed in the United States of America

Dedication and Acknowledgements

This book is gratefully dedicated to Richard Rockingham-Gill and to the late James E. King, Jr.: to Rocky Gill for persuading the shoemaker to stick to his last by continuing to study and write about the Soviet Navy; and to Jim King who, while Director of Advanced Research at the Naval War College, provided the initial encouragement and funding that made this work possible.

Deep appreciation for their assistance must go to Ervin Kapos who, as Director of Washington Operations of Ketron, Inc., put his job on the line several times to continue unfunded work on a project which he believed would be of value to the U.S. Navy; and to Frank Uhlig, Jr. who, as Senior Editor of the Naval Institute Press, published my doctoral dissertation as *Soviet Naval Strategy: Fifty Years of Theory and Practice* in 1968 and who, as the current publisher of the Naval War College Press, decided to publish this study as a contribution to a better understanding of the nature of Soviet thought on the naval side of any third world war. The author is indebted to Ms. Winfield Swanson for the initial copy editing and for adapting a clear and simple method of footnoting. Robert M. Laske reviewed this study and steered it through publication amidst the incessant demands on him as Editor of the *Naval War College Review*. For this he has my admiration and gratitude along with his esteemed associates from the NWC Publications Department, who were responsible in getting this into publishable form.

Finally, heartfelt thanks go to my younger son Olaf and daughter Nicole for patiently putting up with their Dad's preoccupation with this study for ten years; to Laura Drago and Elizabeth Stewart, and to Vernon Freeman, that Great Extinguisher of Texas oilfield (and other) fires, for their special contributions to the author's well-being.

Contents

Foreword

The 1960s and 1970s brought a significant expansion in the role, missions, and forces of the Soviet Navy. The form, pace, and extent of that expansion were determined by an evolving doctrinal consensus, resulting from a continuing debate within the Navy and between the Navy and higher authority. That debate was reflected in Soviet writings over the period and was followed with interest by Western naval professionals and analysts seeking to understand the development of Soviet naval intentions and capabilities.

Most Western readers, like myself, received their introduction to such Soviet terms and concepts as "command of the sea," "combat stability," "balanced forces" and others from these writings. To us the debate and evolving consensus seemed to indicate a new direction in Soviet naval development and to mark Admiral Gorshkov as a unique naval thinker in setting that course. To a knowledgeable Soviet reader or experienced observer such as Robert Herrick, however, there must have been a strong sense of *deja vu*.

This book reveals the continuity of Soviet naval thought over the years. It clearly shows that the debate and resultant doctrinal formulations that shaped the Navy during the 1960s and 1970s had their origins in the initial attempts to begin the development of a new Soviet Navy in the 1920s and 1930s. Admiral Gorshkov stands out as a lineal descendant of the distinctive "Soviet School" that emerged from the bitter arguments of that earlier period.

This historical perspective contributes immensely to our understanding of why and how the Soviet Navy developed as it has. It should also cause many to revise, but not reduce, their high opinion of Admiral Gorshkov as an original naval thinker and master political operator, and to place less emphasis on the former and more on the latter. Most importantly it can help us to understand the future direction and scope of Soviet naval development.

Indeed, from this historical perspective, the 1960s and 1970s are not an unusual era in Soviet naval development springing from the conceptual thinking of one unique leader. Rather, the development that we have observed has been a resumption of the evolution of the Soviet Navy underway since the beginning of the Soviet state and only interrupted by the outbreak of World War II. It clearly owes its form to a whole line of brave naval thinkers.

Thus, we should not expect either a termination or sudden reversal in the current trends of Soviet naval development. Rather, from a new historical viewpoint, we should look for a continuing development of the Soviet Navy in accordance with the continued evolution of the doctrinal concepts that have been in formulation since the creation of a Soviet Navy.

William Manthorpe

Preface

Every navy's strategy is a national strategy, oriented around problems which are peculiarly its own . . . . The idea that a navy can consistently support army operations and carry out regular escort work in areas where it has not previously gained mastery of the sea has been proved by history to be clearly wrong.

Bernard Brodie, *A Guide to Naval Strategy*, 5th revised edition, 1965, pp. 114–115.

This study attempts to provide as full an account of Soviet strategic thought on naval warfare from 1917 until 1956 (when Admiral Gorshkov became the Navy CINC) as the available Soviet professional writings make possible. For those with an interest in *what* the Soviets think on this subject, the following account can provide a number of insights as well as a general understanding of *how* they think about such matters.

The problem of "mirror-imaging" the Soviet Navy as basically like the US and other big Free World navies has often been noted to be a severe one for officers of large Free World navies. I hope that this study may help alleviate this problem for those who take the time to read and think about the first nearly 40 years of the Soviet experience in solving one of the still-central problems of the Soviet Union, how to ensure the security of the homeland against the seaborne strikes of the "strong and experienced" naval adversaries that they continue to perceive us to be.

Much of current relevance is to be found in the early views of Soviet naval leaders and "official theoreticians" as set out in the subsequent pages. Of particular interest and importance for understanding Soviet naval strategy today are the strategies and stratagems resorted to by a navy weaker than those of its probable opponents.

While the weapons systems involved have been transformed almost beyond recognition since the end of World War II and the advent of nuclear power and missiles, the strategic problems remain amazingly similar. Gaining control of the critical sea and ocean areas and maintaining that control despite enemy opposition—so as to be able to make use of sea communications for one's own merchant shipping and naval operations while denying such uses to the adversary—is still the name of the game in war at sea.

Even in the 1920s and 1930s the issue of building aircraft carriers and determining which missions they should perform to ensure sea control in Soviet home waters was a hotly debated one. That issue and the degree of "command of the sea" required has continued to be debated. The similarity of the pros and cons of the debate then, with the extensive discussion of the same issue in contemporary Soviet naval writings, is striking indeed.

A follow-on study to examine the developments under Gorshkov's aegis in Soviet thinking on naval warfare in the nearly three decades of the Khrushchev and Brezhnev eras is well underway and is expected to be published in the not too distant future.

Robert Waring Herrick

Annandale, Virginia
15 June 1988

Editorial Method

This book rests exclusively on available Soviet source material. The author discusses the literature in chronological order and each work cited is completely referenced. Within the following discussion, quotations drawn from the foregoing reference are cited only by a page number in parentheses to indicate the location of the source.

A glance at the index entries on command-of-the-sea and naval strategy will provide the reader with an appreciation of the subject matter of this study, and of the scope and depth of the inquiry.

Readers will note that throughout the text and footnoting the terms *Naval Digest* and *Morskoi sbornik* are used interchangeably. The Military Press of the Soviet Ministry of Defense published most of the books cited herein and may be assumed to have been the publisher of all books footnoted except where another publisher is cited.

Prologue: The Tsarist Legacy

At least as early as 1907-1908 there was a debate within the top echelons of the Tsarist Russian Navy over the force structure of the primarily capital ship fleets of battleships and battle cruisers that were being built in Russia. The ship construction programs had been based on the dominant views of Mahan and Colomb that only big-ship navies could successfully contest for command of the sea so as to be free to carry out their own shipping and naval missions while preventing a naval adversary from doing the same. Yet some senior Russian military and naval officers and theoreticians advocated giving up any further construction of capital ships in favor of building only the much cheaper submarines.[1]

In effect these exponents of the French *Jeune École* of naval strategy in the Soviet Navy advocated building only cheap, light, fast naval forces for the sole purpose of deterring or defending continental powers against seaborne assault. These Tsarist Young School adherents were unsuccessful in their advocacy of merely building submarines, and the construction of capital ships continued.

What by 1928 became known in the Soviet Union as the Old School of naval strategy prevailed in the 1907-1908 debate. That school's adherents supported the predominant command-of-the-sea doctrine and fleets of capital ships. They not only won the day for continuation of capital-ship construction but also persisted in their conviction that submarines were only useful for carrying out secondary or auxiliary tasks such as reconnaissance and picket duty.

In commenting on the immediate prewar naval construction program of Tsarist Russia, the Naval Minister in 1911 insisted that the 1911-1916 shipbuilding program could only have as its aim the development of the naval forces necessary to put an end to the German Navy's unconditional command of the sea in Russia's most important sea theater, the Baltic, and instead place that command in dispute[2] (so that the *Hochseeflotte* would be deterred or prevented from carrying out its missions for fear of losing some of its irreplaceable battleships). This could not be done, the Minister remarked pointedly, if the Baltic Fleet were limited to the mission of supporting the Army's coastal flank. Once Germany had lost her formerly undisputed command, the Naval Minister was quoted as having implied, she would also lose her freedom to continue her Baltic shipping, "the most important line of communications in the military sense."

In the same 1911 document the Tsarist Naval Minister justified the need for a battleship navy in the Baltic by saying that "unless the characteristics of the theater exclude the possibilities of operations by the line fleet [i.e., line-of-battle fleets or battleships and battle cruisers] of the enemy in the particular region, then combat with him is only possible with the same type of forces, that is, with a line fleet." (p. 36)

The opponents of a battleship navy—who ostensibly were arguing that the Baltic was too confined for operations of battleships, largely because of the developing threat from submarines and aircraft—seemingly were silenced by the rationale of the Naval Minister. At any rate, by 1914 Tsarist Russia had seven battleships under construction and an eighth scheduled to be laid down.[3]

Thus, it seems clear that the Tsarist naval legacy rested upon the building of big-ship fleets to implement the command of the sea strategy favored by the major naval powers of the time. As will be seen in the following chapter, this Tsarist Old School inheritance, although clearly beyond Soviet Russia's immediate industrial capacity to live up to, was to prove exceptionally difficult to renounce. It was to require well over a decade and some truly Procrustean measures to accomplish, and even then the repudiation lasted for only a few years.

Two other legacies of Tsarist times that were equally difficult to overcome were those for an independent naval ministry and for mission assignments largely independent of the Army. In 1968 a leading Army strategist, Professor (Major General) N. Lomov, noted that the long-standing friction between the Army and Navy was caused in part by the desire of some naval officers for independence from the Army.[4] The continuing existence of this ambition was acknowledged in the late 1920s by the then Naval Commissar of "the Naval Forces of the Red Army," Ivan Ludri.[5]

This longing of some senior Soviet naval officers was to be met briefly in the interwar period when Stalin established an independent naval ministry in late 1937. But the ministry was promptly disestablished in 1941 when Nazi Germany invaded the Soviet Union and the Soviet Navy, losing its newly independent missions, was again reduced to being merely the Army's faithful assistant.

Notes

1. N. V'yunenko, "Deistviya podvodnykh lodok v pervoi mirovoi voine" ["Submarine Operations in the First World War"], *Military Historical Journal*, November 1975, p. 87.
2. Doc. no. 1535 from the Soviet Central Archives' section, "Affairs of the Naval General Staff." Cited and quoted from at length in *Morskoi sbornik*, April 1930, pp. 36-37.
3. S.E. Zakharov, ed., *Istoriya voenno-morskogo iskusstva [History of Naval Art]* (Moscow: Military Publishing House, 1969), p. 104. Only two of the eight battleships programmed in 1911 were even approaching completion at the outbreak of war, so Russia entered the war with only the four battleships in the Baltic which had been built earlier; Mairin Mitchell, *The Maritime History of Russia 1848-1948* (London: Sedgwick and Jackson, 1949), p. 323.
4. N. Lomov, "Sbornik trudov o razvitii teorii Sovetskogo voennogo iskusstva v mezhvoennyi period," [A Digest of Works on the Development of Soviet Military Art in the Interwar Period]. *Military Historical Journal*, January 1968, p. 105.
5. I. Ludri, "Krasnyi flot v sostave vooruzhennykh sil respubliki" [The Red Navy in the Composition of the Armed Forces of the Republic], MS No. 10, October 1927, p. 27.

SOVIET NAVAL THEORY AND POLICY

I
The Dominant Old School Versus the Young School, 1917-1927

The Evidence and Some Partial Analysis

Professor Gervais Propounds Classical Sea Power Theory. The first systematic expression of post-1917 views on naval warfare were those set out in a lecture course for naval officers during 1919-1921 by a former Tsarist naval officer, Boris B. Gervais.[1] Professor Gervais expounded a classical Mahanist theory that war at sea was essentially a contest for control of the maritime shipping lanes. This control was to be gained either by destroying the enemy navy's main forces of capital ships in one or more major naval engagements for gaining full command of the sea, or by neutralizing them by keeping them blockaded in port.[2]

Achieving such mastery of the sea communications, Gervais asserted, permitted the victor to use the seas for his own purposes while denying its use to the vanquished. This constituted full or general command of the sea. The old (Tsarist naval) specialists or "spetsy" who advocated gaining such general command of the sea by first eliminating or neutralizing an adversary's navy were soon to become known as the "Old School" of naval warfare. Gervais was to be its leading advocate until his purge in 1932.

Sinking the enemy's fleet was to be accomplished by ships' artillery. The larger the gun, the more powerful, so battleships with their bigger guns should constitute the main force of any proper navy. A weaker navy was supposed to hold its capital ships in port, except for prudent sallies when circumstances made it safe to put to sea briefly. This strategy avoided risking the loss of the weaker side's main combat capability, thereby leaving the enemy force free to ravage his trade and bombard his coastal cities at will. The light cruisers and destroyers should, at the same time, be used in an effort to maintain free access to the open sea, even against a blockading force.[3]

By including the right types and numbers of ships in one's naval forces, by employing those forces in accordance with a suitable strategy, and by operating from well-defended, nearby bases and offshore mine artillery positions, one could hope to successfully keep command of the sea in dispute.[4] Through such accomplishments one could prevent even significantly stronger enemy forces from completion of such missions as cutting one's own coastal sea communications, conducting seaborne landings, and supporting the coastal flanks of their ground forces. Gervais clearly was describing the Soviet situation, indicating that the weak Baltic Fleet could retreat to the safety of its bases to prevent its destruction. The consequence of such action would be the gaining of command of the sea by the adversary and the unhindered freedom to carry out his missions against Soviet coasts, coastal ground forces, and coastal shipping.

Stating what he considered the minimum, normal composition of a fleet faced with strong opposition, but obviously having in mind again the Soviet Baltic Fleet confronted with the stronger British Baltic squadron (with the rest of the Royal Navy available if necessary), Gervais recommended a force composed of 8 battleships, 4 heavy and 16 light cruisers, and 32 destroyers. Notably, no submarines were deemed necessary for inclusion.

Thus, it is clear that the command-of-the-sea doctrine bequeathed the Soviet regime by Tsarist Russia continued to dominate naval theoretical thought in the early postwar period. This is understandable given that there were no Soviet-trained naval officers to teach naval strategy. The regime had no real choice but to continue to use former Tsarist officers for whom the views of Vice Adm. Philip Colomb, Royal Navy, and Rear Adm. Alfred Mahan, US Navy, on the need to exercise an overall command of the sea with big battleship navies, were articles of faith.

With the Soviet regime literally fighting for its life, it is not surprising that no Party leader concerned himself with what was being taught at the Naval War College in Leningrad. Nor had there been time to analyze and assimilate the lessons which World War I held for naval strategy. Consequently, the inertia of tradition prevailed and the same command-of-the-sea theory was propounded by Professor Gervais and others, including Professor Nikolai Klado who taught before World War I and the Russian Revolution. Klado continued to advocate Old School views until his death in 1919.

The Navy's need for ship-based aviation to take airpower further out to sea than was then feasible with shore-based aviation was made apparent as early as November 1922 by an article in the Navy's professional journal. This article asserted that "the urgent requirement of the Navy for aviation . . . must be satisfied . . . . Aviation must exist in the fleet itself." It was added that aircraft carriers were task-specific ships "of special purpose" required by the Soviet Union to protect and support the fleets. It was noted, too, that both the United States and Japan already had undertaken construction of aircraft carriers of the maximum size (27,000 tons) set by the Washington Naval Conference earlier that year.[5]

Professor Gervais published an article at the end of 1922 setting out his views on the nature of the study of naval strategy that should be conducted at the Naval War College where he was teaching. He acknowledged that it would be unrealistic to elaborate a concept for "an oceanic war between two big navies" and noted that the Naval Command of the Republic was interested in development of the theory for "a small war" in the naval theaters contiguous to Russian territory.[6]

According to the 1965 selection of excerpts from lectures which Gervais delivered at the Naval War College from 1919 to 1921, he had held that, while the stronger naval power would attempt to gain full command of the sea by destruction or blockade of his adversary, the weaker belligerent should try to hold command of the sea in dispute and thereby prevent the stronger side from carrying out his assigned missions. These were formulated by Gervais as cutting the enemy's sea lines of communication (anti-SLOC), amphibious invasion, and support for the Army's coastal flank.

By June 1923, Gervais had somewhat reformulated and broadened these missions. In a Navy meeting with officers of the Ground and Air Forces, Gervais stated his revised missions for the Soviet Navy as: warfare on sea communications (i.e., SLOC protection as well as anti-SLOC); warfare for the seacoast (defense of one's own and taking the enemy's); and cooperation with the Army.[7] All three of these missions were described by Gervais as of vast importance—a way, it would seem, to imply his belief that gaining command of the sea by SLOC warfare was at least as important as cooperation with the Army. Gervais insisted that gaining command of the sea was an absolute prerequisite to carrying out any of these three missions.

In the same article Gervais derided the alleged capability of 100 carrier aircraft to sink a battleship. He argued that it would require all 100 planes to drop their bombs simultaneously to have a good chance of success and this, he maintained, would be tactically impossible. Moreover, he further asserted, it would require two aircraft carriers to carry the 100 planes, with each one costing as much as the battleship. Accordingly, he concluded, the aircraft carrier would not be a suitable replacement for the battleship but instead should be considered to be a new variant of the capital ship. He added that the correct view was the one held by the Americans. The aircraft carrier was in fact a capital ship, but one in which the big guns (artillery) had been replaced as the main weapons systems by the airplane. Here Gervais was taking issue with the generally accepted Soviet view that the aircraft carrier was a special-purpose ship just for reconnaissance and scouting and providing air cover for the surface forces of a fleet. By taking exception to this prevailing view of the aircraft carrier, Gervais made it clear that he recognized the potential of attack carriers for air warfare at sea beyond the range of land-based fighter planes. One gained the distinct impression that Gervais was not opposed to the construction of aircraft carriers per se, but rather was primarily concerned with preventing them from being considered as suitable candidates for construction in lieu of battleships.

In Gervais' view, command of the sea was of three kinds. First, it could be absolute to the degree that the enemy could carry out no hostile operations.[8] Or, second, when the enemy naval forces were blockaded in port, command of the sea was conditional since there was always the possibility, however remote, that he might break out to fight again.[9] Third, command of the sea might be in dispute when two hostile navies could operate in the same sea area but neither could protect his sea communications against the other.[10]

Attempting to hold command of the sea in dispute, Gervais asserted, remained the correct aim of even a weaker navy blockaded in port. It should conduct a small war against the blockading forces through offensive mining and aggressive torpedo attacks until such time as the enemy's blockading force could be cut down to a size that would permit the blockaded force to leave port and seek an engagement at sea.[11] When a weaker navy was charged with protecting sectors of the coast of strategic importance for ground force operations, a "positional war" strategy was in order. Gervais noted that this type of warfare had already been accurately described by Professor Petrov, an Old School colleague at the Naval War College.

Petrov, 1919-1924. Positional war was described by Professor Petrov as combat conducted from a position in the waters off the coast that could be defended by coastal artillery as well as by minefields, antisubmarine nets, and other naval positional means.[12] Petrov explained that such fortified positions offshore were not intended to be impenetrable. Rather, they were to allow a weaker navy the opportunity to so weaken and disorganize the enemy that it would permit the weaker side to equalize its chances in the battle which would ensue.

From his writings it is clear that Petrov considered the only theoretical alternative to positional war to be battle in the open sea (p. 179), characterized as a general naval engagement (p. 182). Such classical Mahanist command-of-the-sea general engagements on the high seas could be fought only between naval forces whose main combat strength lay in battleships; so such an option would not be open to the Soviet Union for as long as it would take it to build up a big navy—that is, one composed of balanced surface forces, including battleships, battle and light cruisers, and destroyers. Since construction of such a navy was unlikely for some years, Petrov professedly had submerged his Old School views and was devoting himself to working out the tactics for a "small war" by a "small navy."[13]

Accordingly, in 1924 Petrov affirmed the continuing validity for the Soviet Union of the positional-war strategy.[14] However, he held that there were several important considerations in conducting a small war from one or more naval positions. For one thing, such positions were not to be considered as an end in themselves but as a means for the most effective conduct of a small war.[15] Naval positions were to be selected to lie "in the main direction" of the expected enemy attack and should be far enough forward to constitute a threat to the enemy's operation areas and bases.

Since the initiative for major offensives would always lie with the stronger navy, and since the locations of established naval positions were basically fixed, dependence on the defensive alone in positional war would ensure eventual defeat. Consequently, the weaker navy must "search out other possibilities, and above all for taking the offensive." In general, this required determining when and where the enemy was weaker or could be caught by surprise when unprepared.

Petrov made no secret of the difficult position of the weaker navy. He pointed out that the spectrum of missions which the weaker force could hope to accomplish was very limited. Even for them, he observed, success would depend on the occurrence of favorable circumstances, such as the chance to concentrate one's forces against a weaker part of the enemy's forces in a surprise attack.

Moreover, Petrov noted that the enemy might choose to blockade rather than penetrate the Soviet Union's naval positions. To make this as difficult as possible, he recommended that naval positions should be created to maximize the time required to impose an effective blockade and also to maximize the distance factors, thereby placing added geographic constraints on enemy transit in establishing an effective blockade.[16]

Obviously, there is no panacea for strategic inferiority and Petrov offered none. He elaborated on the tactics that were suitable for the weaker navy, such as attacks at night or in fog, or use of smokescreens over the whole field of battle so that the enemy's battleships could not see their targets.[17] He also stressed the importance of full intelligence on enemy movements, and the study of his routine operational procedures and tactics to identify any vulnerable points.[18]

Concurrently in 1924 when he published his thesis on "naval positions," Professor Petrov also declared himself on the alleged nonutility of aircraft carriers. Perhaps because aircraft carriers did not fit into his strategy of naval positions, Petrov professed to see little use for them in the defensive strategy at sea, one that the Soviet Union would of necessity be forced to follow for the foreseeable future. As Marshal Voroshilov was to allege in 1934 and Marshal Zhukov again in 1956—when they were faced by a roughly comparable situation of great naval inferiority and unwillingness to spend their limited funds on remedying that inferiority—Petrov denounced the aircraft carrier as a weapons system employed only for an offensive strategy by states with aggressive aims. He strongly argued against blindly following the practice of foreign powers in naval aviation matters and claimed, with obvious exaggeration, that shore-based naval air could range fully over coastal waters out to a distance of 500-600 miles and that this was quite adequate for Soviet military requirements.

Petrov also opined that "as a general rule, naval aviation has a coastal character and may be employed in distant oceanic theaters only as an exception." He also further maintained that the role of aircraft carriers in naval battle would be limited to reconnaissance and scouting. He concluded his argument with the imaginative claim (perhaps drawn from Douhet's then popular thesis on the overriding importance for future warfare of strategic bombing by massive air fleets) that whole squadrons of aircraft carriers would be required to be effective in naval warfare on the high seas but that no country would be able to afford to build the large numbers that would be required.[19]

Petrov's 1924 article, resorting to hyperbole in derogating aircraft carriers and unduly crediting the capabilities of shore-based naval aviation, may have been prompted by concern in the Party over procarrier views such as those aired not long before in a pseudonymous book review in the Army journal *Military Herald*.[20] The review included the claims that World War I had demonstrated the enormous importance of sea-based aviation and that two of the basic components of armed forces, seapower and airpower, had found their organic union and clear realization in the aircraft carrier. The implication was clear—any navy worth its salt would have aircraft carriers. For this view to have appeared in an *Army* journal was notable, particularly in view of several later indications that carrier construction had a few prominent supporters in the Army, including Svechin, Frunze, and Tukhachevskiy. That an Army journal would support the construction of aircraft carriers for the Navy further suggested that there were carrier enthusiasts in the Army as well as in the Navy.

Developments in 1924-1925. A less negative Old School view on the utility of the aircraft carrier than that expressed by Professor Petrov in his April 1924 *Red Fleet* article had been voiced in February 1924 in a *Red Fleet* editorial. It acknowledged that the carrier had the potential for achieving great results under certain circumstances, especially in a battle between ships. In general, however, the value of such ships was portrayed as limited to acting as a fine assistant to a battleship force. It was added that the aircraft carrier could in no case replace the battleship. In an equally poor appreciation of the potential employment of such ships, the editorial also alleged that aircraft carriers "could not by themselves insure continuing control over the world ocean or any part of it."[21] Like the 1923 Gervais article and the 1924 Petrov article, the *Red Fleet* editorial seemed to be part of an Old School effort to hold the line against the incursions of the airpower/aircraft carrier enthusiasts.

A rundown of the naval forces considered appropriate for a modern navy was given in the October 1924 issue of the *Naval Digest*. It listed aircraft carriers after not only battleships and cruisers, but in fifth place following destroyers and submarines and just ahead of minesweepers. Gervais' plea to reclassify aircraft carriers as capital ships instead of ones of special purpose had gone unheeded. That there was no tactically offensive role for the carrier against an adversary's ships or bases was made clear by a subsequent sentence that specified the role of a modern aircraft carrier was to protect those "ships which are incapable of withstanding air attacks."[22]

All of the foregoing discussion about aircraft carriers apparently was considered counterproductive by Party and military policymakers in Moscow. In early 1925 the Navy chief, Admiral Zof,[23] made the trip up to Leningrad to confront the procarrier lions in their Naval War College den. He laid down the law in the following terms:

> You speak of aircraft carriers and the construction of new types of ships . . . while at the same time completely ignoring the economic situation of our country and the corresponding conditions of our technical means—and completely ignoring the fact that perhaps tomorrow or the day after we will be called on to fight. And with what shall we fight? We will fight with those ships and personnel that we have already. (p. 16)

A possible *sotto voce* protest to this order to cease and desist on public discussion of aircraft carrier construction for the Navy appeared six months later in the same source as Zof's statement. An article entitled "Modern Trends in Naval Aviation" appeared to constitute implicit endorsement of a command of the sea strategy to be executed with aircraft carriers playing the leading role. The article discussed the differing requirements for sea-based airpower in the various fleets and concluded that in a war at sea the Soviet Union's "few coastal garrisons and mine positions" would not be adequate to enable the Navy to maintain any command of the sea.[24]

In a March 1924 *Naval Digest* article Professor Petrov had conceded that while circumstances might arise under which either aircraft or submarines might be designated for making the decisive (i.e., main) attack, normally the conduct of this most critical maneuver of a battle would be assigned to the battleship force. When that force was designated to conduct the main attack maneuver, the aircraft (i.e., both ship and shore-based), as well as submarines and the smaller surface ships, must give full support to the battleship force rather than act independently.[25]

Lessons from World War I. This matter of support for the main striking forces in any operation by the other types of naval forces—whether the battleships as in the 1920s or the submarines today—often is portrayed in terms that make it apparent that such support is a Soviet alternative to gaining command of the sea beyond home waters. The importance with which the subject was viewed in the midtwenties was well illustrated by a May 1926 review in *Naval Digest* of Volume I of *The War at Sea*, the official German history of the war at sea from 1914 to 1918. The author of the history, Otto Groos, was said to have harped on the single thought with regard to almost all of the German naval operations in 1914 (to which the first volume was limited) that the support provided for operations was inadequate.[26] This is a subject to which this study will return now and again as it becomes possible to establish more explicitly the Soviet correlation of support with gaining or disputing command of the sea.

This same *Naval Digest* article of May 1926 noted that the red thread that ran through all of Groos' history of German naval operations in 1914 was that the German Navy did not have enough of the right kinds of naval forces to conduct a small war against the distant blockade established by Great Britain.[27] This view was said to be unquestionably correct, showing a marked interest in demonstrating that the small war tactics (of the fleet-in-being strategy) had not been invalidated per se by the German experience. To have carried out force-equalization by attrition, the heart of the German fleet-in-being strategy, the German Navy would have required a balanced fleet. Given this, the ship types, armaments, cruising radius, and speed would not only differ—suitable to counter the distant blockade actually imposed by Great Britain rather than the anticipated close blockade on which the German Navy's war plans were based—but also the balance between the types of ships would have had to correspond to the war plans. (p. 104)

A month later, the *Naval Digest* carried its discussion further, still appearing to be intent on convincing the naval profession and any military or Party readers of the naval journal that there was nothing inherently wrong with a small war strategy for the U.S.S.R. In the June 1926 issue, an article made the argument that the German Navy never really gave the small war strategy a fair try and that the capital ships had been held in port rather than undertaking the "active" (tactically offensive) operations essential to successful force-equalization.[28] Most interesting here was the rationale said to have underlain this alleged withholding in port of the German Navy's capital ships. It was that just the presence of the German Navy, the very fact of its existence, would protect the German coast against amphibious landings and enable it to maintain command of the Baltic Sea, i.e., the fleet-in-being concept. This same article also analyzed German submarine warfare in a way that may well still hold conceptual relevance for the Soviets today as "a combination of the method of blockade [warfare against the sea lines of communication] and the method of a small war at sea [warfare against the military fleet of England with the aim of weakening it]." (p. 8)

In July 1927, yet another article on the German Navy's small war strategy in the *Naval Digest* finally made it explicit that the reasons for the failure of the strategy did not lie in the strategy itself. Rather, the article claimed, neither the composition of the German Navy suited the strategy nor were adequate bases available.[29] In keeping with this were the conclusions of the article which included a finding that it would have been "more advantageous" to Germany for its Navy to "have operated more offensively at sea." This, of course, amounted to a combination and summary of the arguments of the previously considered articles from the May and June 1926 issues of the same journal.

In the same month Professor Petrov weathervaned 180 degrees from his very negative views about aircraft carriers of three years earlier, and touted them as about to replace the battleships completely. The advent of the aircraft carrier, Petrov asserted in an article in the *Military Herald*, had caused both a crisis in shipbuilding and a radical transformation in naval warfare. Petrov's reversal seemed most likely to have been the result of pressure from the advocates of ship-based airpower such as Yakimychev. Petrov took an opposite tack from his earlier views by advocating the construction of carriers as "*the* future means of sea power" whose construction would secure for the Soviet Union "a fitting place" among the big naval powers.[30]

Command of the Sea. In the final two and a half years of the decade under scrutiny in this chapter, there were four significant statements about command of the sea in addition to those already considered. The first two of them concerned command of the sea in a particular theater and represent a practical limitation on the world view of Soviet naval thinking that remained pronounced until recently. This should come as no surprise when one considers that the NATO naval coalition certainly has been one of the most formidable naval forces that the world has ever seen.

The first of these two references to command of the sea limited to a single theater appeared in the *Naval Digest* in February 1925 in an article titled "Uniting All Means for Naval Defense." It stated that "The mission of a fleet in a given sea is to maintain the command in that sea."[31]

The second reference to command of the sea limited to a single sea theater came in February 1926 by a young naval officer, Vladimir Belli, who was to become a leading official naval theoretician by 1938 and who is still being cited as authoritative by Soviet naval writers. Writing in the Army journal *Military Herald* on Italy's naval maneuvers of the previous August, Belli merely mentioned that in an earlier era the Austrian Navy had long commanded the Adriatic.[32] Neither of these passages are definitive but are quoted here to illustrate the early indications of a state of mind that would lead Gorshkov in his 1976 and 1979 editions of *Sea Power of the State* to define "strategic command of the sea" as that restricted to a given theater and "operational command of the sea" as embracing only a region of a given theater.

Two other comments concerning command of the sea appeared in 1927 in the *Naval Digest*. They were notable for taking flatly contradictory positions on the intrinsic value of command of the sea. The first, by some little-known author in the July issue, credited command of the sea with having put the United Kingdom in a position to "slowly but surely strangle Germany."[33] Perhaps this article was just a topical Naval War College term paper, but one suspects that its author was a student of Professors Gervais and Petrov and, hence, a disciple of Colomb, Mahan, and Corbett.

This suspicion is substantiated by the fact that the Naval Commissar himself effectively contradicted this sign of approbation for a command of the sea doctrine in the second *Naval Digest* article which appeared in the October 1927 issue. Summing up the first decade of the Soviet Navy's existence—still the Naval Forces of the Red Army—the article included a statement attributed to a British general that "Our command of the sea is as effective a weapon against the Russian method for war-fighting as is a piledriver against a radio wave."[34] The Naval Commissar went on to note the pervasiveness of classical command of the sea theory and to warn his readers that such theory was not suitable for a small navy like the Soviet Union's without battleships or Washington cruisers:

> We often . . . identify with the classical sea powers and try to operate like they do. The Battle of Jutland is our model which we study and attempt to imitate. Admirals Beatty and Spee—they are our role models. That which we learn from foreigners is good. To study and learn the tactics of a foreign navy is also necessary. But to try to transplant all that directly into our conditions is not correct. We have other forces, other means, and we operate under different conditions. Consequently, it is necessary to work out the tactics for a small navy which acts together with the Army according to a single strategic plan. (pp. 10-11)

Even more indicative of the Soviet Union's actual strategy—near the end of its first decade as the period of the New Economic Policy closed and that of the First Five-Year Plan was about to open—was an article in the journal *Red Fleet*. It carried a report that Professor Gervais had delivered to a plenary meeting of the Leningrad-Baltic filial of the Military Scientific Society. Entitled "Defense of the Sea Borders of the Soviet Union," Gervais' thesis was nothing more ambitious than to build the naval forces required to cooperate with Coastal Defense on the naval positions to make difficult any amphibious assaults on Soviet territory.[36] This, in fact, was the extent of naval development in its first decade. And as a strategy for employment—as it was again to be for a decade after the devastation of World War II—the Soviet Navy would be able to look no further than to the limits of coastal waters and prepare as best it could with the limited means made available to counter the "imperialist" amphibious invasion that seemed inevitable.

Some Army Support for Carrier Construction Indicated by Ludri. The last item of note published in the 1917-1927 decade also appeared in the October 1927 issue of the *Naval Digest*.[37] Signed by recent Naval War College graduate and soon to be Deputy Naval Commissar, Ivan Ludri, it addressed the much debated question as to whether or not battleships could and should be replaced by aviation, including aircraft carriers. The article suggested the possibility that there were some important nonnaval supporters of building attack aircraft carriers for the Navy. Most likely this support came from the Army, in view of the advocacy of carrier construction in the March 1924 issue of the Army journal *Military Herald* and later evidence was to show that the prominent military theorists and practitioners General Svechin, Marshal Tukhachevskiy, and Defense Commissar Frunze did support the construction of at least light carriers. Ludri further stated "On this question [of aircraft carriers as the replacement for battleships], the partisans of several circles favoring the creation in our naval theaters of attack aircraft carriers are according warm even fervid moral support."

An Army View of the Young and Old Schools. An Army view of the development of naval theory in this initial period was set forth in the 1981 book *A History of Soviet Military Thought*:[38]

> The development of naval theory in the interwar years evolved in a struggle of ideas and views on the construction of the Navy and its employment in future war.
>
> Two disparate views were worked out in theory and practice. One, basing itself on the materiel capacity of the country, advocated the construction of a small (mosquito) surface fleet and submarines with the aim of employing it for joint actions, mainly in coastal sectors.
>
> The other, considering big ships the basic striking force of the Navy, advocated the construction of such large surface ships for the mission of the defense of the Soviet Union's very long oceanic and sea boundaries and also for the protection of state interests. Representatives of this persuasion did not always take into account the economic capacity of the country for building a big surface navy.
>
> The partisans of the first [Young School] course more accurately estimated the requirements for the Navy in a future war. They oriented themselves on a joint struggle with the Ground Forces in a likely continental war. These views were supported [only] in individual years by the official representatives of the Naval Command. R.A. Muklevich, Chief of the Naval Forces of the Red Army from August 1926 through 1928, opposed both the theory of setting the Navy apart from the general system of the Armed Forces of the country [by favoring an independent naval ministry or any naval missions independent of the Army] and also the efforts of individual Army chiefs to mechanically subordinate the Navy to the Ground Force command. Taking into account the economic capacity of the country, Muklevich did not consider it possible, for example, to accomplish the mission of [gaining and maintaining] command of the sea and consequently opposed the construction of battleships and cruisers. (pp. 178-179)

It should be added to the above that Muklevich probably had not only opposed the construction of battleships and cruisers, but also of aircraft carriers. He likely was under the same Party-Army constraints against big-ship naval programs as his predecessor, Admiral Zof, who had explicitly reprimanded the advocates of building aircraft carriers, in his previously quoted address at the Naval War College in 1925.

Gorshkov Tells It Like It Was. It is particularly interesting to note Admiral Gorshkov's description of the naval strategy adopted in this initial period of extremely limited means. Writing in his long series of articles on "Navies in Wars and in Peacetime" in 1972-73, he gave what seems to be a largely accurate description of what actually transpired:

Simultaneously, creative military-theoretical work was conducted. The small number of combatant ships available necessitated research on the strategy and tactics for carrying on the mission for defense of our maritime borders with the forces of a "small" navy in cooperation with the ground forces. In the process of this research was born the theory of "the small war" which, stemming from the specific circumstances, determined the rational strategy, tactics, and forms of struggle with a stronger naval opponent.

Its essence—the delivering of quick strikes on the main objective of the enemy without being separated from one's base, with all types of forces secretly concentrated and jointly operating from various directions. In the capacity of the basic form of joint operations was proposed the concentrated (combined) strike of surface ships, torpedo boats, submarines, aviation, and coastal artillery organized on mine-artillery positions. Such strategy and tactics for the employment of forces of our Navy at this time was in the closest approximation to its actual combat capabilities and was consonant with the essential missions of defense and the economic possibilities of the Soviet state.[39]

These observations by Gorshkov will be commented on in the analyses and interpretation of the foregoing evidence for the 1917-1927 period to which we now turn.

Further Analysis and Interpretation of the Evidence, 1917-1927

It is the author's conclusion that the leading Soviet naval theoretician of the period, Professor Gervais, continued the Tsarist advocacy of the classical Mahanist command-of-the-sea strategy for a weaker of two battleship navies—by attempting to hold command of the sea in dispute. Although his views recognized the need for naval cooperation with the Army, he basically advocated a big-ship navy sufficient for holding command of the sea in dispute in the areas through which the key Soviet SLOC passed. He conceded that the correct strategy for the Soviet Union to deter or defeat the much-feared amphibious invasion of the homeland, was for the Navy to cooperate in providing Soviet coastal defenses on coastal naval positions.[40]

Gervais further argued that the correct strategy for a weaker navy blockaded in port was the small war which would exploit every possible opportunity to attack elements of the blockading force with mines and torpedoes. This action would be continued by the light forces until the enemy's navy had been sufficiently attrited as to permit one's own battleships and heavy cruisers to leave the protection of their ports or naval positions and defeat the enemy in a decisive general engagement. This was advocacy of an *active* fleet-in-being strategy—one which envisioned achieving force-equilization by reducing the adversary's forces through attrition so as to make seeking out a general engagement feasible. Gervais' partisanship for battleships caused him to underestimate the potential of aircraft carriers as *the* future ship type for executing a command-of-the-sea strategy.

It may also be noted that Gervais' prominent colleague at the Naval War College, Professor Petrov, shared Gervais' views in all essentials even though he expressed them in the context of a positional war strategy, one that would be adapted to Soviet circumstances. Unlike Gervais, however, Petrov proved himself more politically adaptable by acknowledging that it would be a considerable time before Soviet Russia could develop a navy that would be capable of even holding command of the sea in dispute in Russia's peripheral seas.

Accordingly, Petrov turned his efforts to developing tactics for a small war by a small navy. This was the most favorable situation that Soviet naval officers could look forward to for the foreseeable future. Nevertheless, Petrov refrained from any attestation that such a navy would secure Soviet Russia's defense to seaward. Rather, by implication he made it clear that the small war strategy was a poor substitute for a command of the sea strategy. The implication was that the sooner a big navy could be built, the better for Soviet security. Basically, Petrov left himself as open as Gervais to the charges that would follow in 1928 of being defeatist and reactionary; that is, of recommending a naval building policy that the regime considered beyond its productive capacity and more urgent priorities in light of what were considered more pressing needs.

Contrary to Petrov's implication that the small-war strategy was a poor substitute for a command-of-the-sea strategy—at least for one following the Mahanian prescription for a smaller navy of attempting to hold command of the sea in dispute—1926-27 witnessed a concerted effort to show that the small-war strategy had not been proven unworkable by the events of the World War. The final consensus was that the German strategy failed simply because the German Navy and the naval basing system had not been conceived for a distant blockade but for a close blockade. The implication was manifestly clear that, used intelligently, the small war strategy could serve the Soviet Union well.

Although the small-war theory *per se* was not the original product of Soviet thought as Gorshkov claimed, the term small war had been used by Young School writers to mean guerrilla warfare by mosquito-fleet forces. For the Old School theoreticians, it implied a strategy of force-equalization by attrition prior to a general engagement by a weaker fleet, but one whose main force was composed of battleships that did not suffer too great a disparity in strength. As used by Gorshkov, the small-war strategy implied something more than guerrilla warfare by light, fast forces and much less than the force-equalization strategy by a strong but inferior battleship fleet. The mine-artillery positions (or simply "naval positions") could accomplish a force-equalization if the enemy should try to penetrate them. Yet, the Soviet disparity in battleships precluded open sea operations to search out and attack weaker parts of an enemy fleet. Consequently, there were no realistic prospects that a general engagement could be forced on an enemy under circumstances likely to bring a favorable outcome, one that would gain a general command of the sea.

Until Soviet industry could be developed sufficiently to build the battleships and armored cruisers required to make possible a strategy of holding the seas peripheral to the Soviet Union in dispute against the powerful British Fleet of capital ships, a small-war coastal-defensive strategy would be employed. Soviet naval forces would largely be used in mine-artillery positions, as in the World War, where these forces could be supported by defensive minefields, shore batteries of the Coastal Defense Service, as well as by land-based airplanes. And all of this, as Professor Gervais made clear in his 1926 report to the Leningrad branch of the Military Scientific Society, was not done with any real expectation of successfully repelling an amphibious invasion. It was done merely to make the landings difficult so that the Army ground forces on the beaches might find it possible to defeat any such invasion attempt.[41]

One is struck with the thought that even in the final years of the first decade of the Soviet Navy, there was not the slightest notion of any command of the sea beyond the confines of individual sea theaters littoral to the Soviet homeland. Any thought of someday aspiring to even hold in dispute command of the sea in broad ocean areas was simply alien, and understandably so, to the top naval officers and leading naval theoreticians. It is worth noting that shortly after one Soviet writer spoke of British command of the sea in the World War as having put Great Britain in a fair way to strangling the economic and military life of Germany, Naval Commissar Muklevich made a striking rebuttal. He quoted a British general to the effect that British command-of-the-sea would be no more effective against the Soviet Union's tactics for war at sea than a pile-driver against a radio wave.

One might suspect that the obscure individual who spoke well of command of the sea was a stalking horse, wittingly or otherwise, for Professors Gervais, Petrov, and the senior naval officers. Their goal was to secure a larger share of the defense budget so as to overhaul more of the old battleships and to speed up the day that a small-war or force-equalization strategy could be put into effect. At any rate, the Naval Commissar's denigration of the utility of command of the sea for the Soviet Navy in his October 1927 article in *Naval Digest* may be seen in retrospect as a harbinger of the uncompromising attacks on the classical command of the sea strategy of Professor Gervais and his Old School that 1928 was to bring.

Starting in late 1922, a discussion ensued in Soviet naval and military writings on the merits of constructing aircraft carriers for the Navy to implement a command-of-the-sea strategy. In November 1922 an article in the *Naval Digest* asserted that the Navy had an urgent requirement for such special-purpose ships, i.e., task-specific ones for providing a fleet with scouting/reconnaissance and air cover. The article asserted that this requirement must be satisfied in order to provide the fleets with airpower further out at sea than was possible employing land-based aircraft. To bolster this argument, it was noted that both the United States and Japan had started construction of aircraft carriers of the maximum tonnage of 27,000 allowed by the Washington Naval Conference.

But in June of the following year Professor Gervais argued that aircraft carriers could never replace the battleships, although they might have utility for air warfare beyond the range of shore-based fighter planes—as a *Red Fleet* article by Yakimychev had argued at that time. Gervais also claimed that it would not be cost effective to build attack aircraft carriers primarily for sinking battleships. However, Gervais did make the case for reclassifying aircraft carriers from "special-purpose" auxiliaries to capital ships, as the United States had done. One might speculate on the motivation behind such a classification change. Could it be that the reclassification of carriers as capital ships might lessen the chances of their ever being built? A case can be made that the special-purpose designation tended to support their construction inasmuch as they could have been part of building programs for the light surface forces then in favor.

In early 1924 two more articles appeared that supported Gervais' position that, while aircraft carriers might have their uses, they could never replace battleships. In February *Red Fleet* carried an unsigned editorial which asserted that the carrier could in no case replace the battleship. The rationale for this claim was that, while carriers might achieve great results under certain circumstances, especially in a battle between ships, they could not by themselves insure continuing control over the World Ocean or any part of it. To perform this top priority of the Old School mission, battleships were said to be required. Aircraft carriers allegedly could only play the secondary role of supporting the battleships.

Then in April 1924 Professor Petrov went to extremes in an effort to discredit carriers. He claimed to see little utility in carriers for the Soviet Union's defensive strategy since shore-based air allegedly could provide adequate air cover in home waters, to 500-600 miles radius. The role of carriers in naval battles was held to be limited to reconnaissance and scouting for the fleet. Yet with obvious inconsistency, Petrov portrayed the aircraft carrier as inherently the weapons platform of states harboring aggressive aims. Finally, he argued that so many carriers would be required to be effective in naval warfare that no country could possibly afford them.

It would appear that Petrov had set out to do a hatchet job on the aircraft carrier. Perhaps his inconsistency was the result of half-heartedness. It is quite conceivable that this had been written under Party pressure and that Petrov was a closet carrier advocate—one who was to come out only three years later singing paeans to the carrier as the bandwagon of opportunity for a golden naval future for the Soviet Union.

In the intervening month between the *Red Fleet* editorial in February and Petrov's in April, a pseudonymous article in the March 1924 issue of the Army journal *Military Herald* had portrayed the carrier as of "enormous importance" as the "organic union" of seapower and airpower. Apparently, judging from this article and Yakimychev's in 1923, there were some air enthusiasts in the Army as well as in the Navy who were strong advocates of building aircraft carriers and whose advocacy had inspired the Old School campaign to protect battleship construction from losing out to carriers. This Army advocacy of carriers in 1924 provides some substantiating evidence for the author's hypothesis that in October 1927 there were several groups, confirmed at that time by recent Naval War College graduate Ivan Ludri, that were fervid partisans of attack carrier construction including some Army air enthusiasts. Further credence is afforded for this hypothesis by the fact that General Svechin, Marshal Tukhachevskiy, and Defense Commissar Frunze, three leading military practitioners and theorists, were subsequently identified as having been supporters of building aircraft carriers for the Navy.

In March 1925 Professor Petrov, in a *Naval Digest* article "On Attack by Aviation in a Meeting Engagement at Sea," again asserted the primacy of battleships by asserting that aircraft carriers and other naval forces must provide full support for the battleships in a battle at sea rather than acting independently. At about the time that this article appeared, the Old School's rearguard action to protect the battleship against incursions by the aircraft carrier was given emphatic support by the Naval Commissar, Admiral Zof. According to the May 1925 issue of *Naval Digest*, Zof had recently adjured the procarrier advocates in Leningrad that their advocacy of the carrier was misplaced because it completely ignored the current state of the economy and the urgent need to ready the Navy to fight at any time with the ships that were operational. However, despite this official injunction to refrain from further advocacy of carrier construction, an article in the November 1925 issue of *Naval Digest*, "Modern Trends in Naval Aviation" did make an implicit case for such construction on the grounds that aircraft carriers were essential for exercising sea control outside of Soviet coastal waters.

Moreover, in July 1927, Professor Petrov effectively recanted his earlier derogation of aircraft carriers by portraying them as "the future means of sea power" and by arguing that the Soviet Union should build such ships so as to gain a fitting place among the great naval powers. The reason for Petrov's turnabout on the carriers-*versus*-battleships issue was not readily apparent but may well have been because of his already demonstrated ability to adapt to the political winds. In this case he shifted to the side of the emerging Young School with its preference for submarines and aircraft, including light carriers, over battleships.

Now let us turn to the 1928-1932 period and the exciting developments that brought about the dramatic suppression of the Old School and the rise to brief dominance of the Young School of naval warfare.

Notes

1. First publication of excerpts from Boris B. Gervais' lectures of 1919-1921 did not occur until 1965 when they appeared under their course title "Osnovy voenno-morskoi strategii" ["Fundamentals of Naval Strategy"] in *Voprosy strategii i operativnogo iskusstva v sovetskikh voennykh trudakh 1917-1940* [*Questions of Strategy and Operational Art in Soviet Military Works 1917-1940*] (Moscow: Military Press, 1965), pp. 684-688.

2. "A naval force, in the case of offensive missions, must exert itself to gain full command of the sea ['gospodstvo na more'], that is, to destroy the enemy navy or, at least, to successfully blockade him in his operating bases . . . . The first, immediate aim of operations at sea by the stronger, offensive side, in all cases, is to gain full command of the sea." pp. 685-686

3. "Conversely, in the case of defensive missions, the weaker side must try to preserve its combat capability and to maintain its free access to the sea." p. 685

4. "The mission of the defending side is to dispute the command of the sea. The correct composition of its naval forces, the right strategy, audacity on the part of its personnel, and well-defended operating bases afford the possibility even to a significantly weaker navy to successfully hold command of the sea in dispute against a stronger enemy and so prevent him from carrying out his assigned, ultimate military aims, that is, cutting the maritime communications of the defending side to the outside world, landing his army on your coast, and cooperating with his army operating in the coastal regions of the land theater of war." p. 686

5. K. Beigelin, "Sily vozdushnye i morskiye" ["Air and Naval Forces"], *Morskoi sbornik*, November 1922, pp. 57-74.

6. B. Gervais, "Ocherk 5, O Morskoi Akademii, yeye nauchnaya deyatel 'nost'" ["Essay 5, Concerning the Naval War College, Its Scientific Work"], *Morskoi sbornik*, December 1922, p. 82.

7. "Flot morskoi i flot vozdushnoi v sovremennoi voine" ["The Sea Fleet and the Air Fleet in Contemporary War"] from a report given by B. Gervais on 25 May 1923 to the Naval Scientific Society's Leningrad filial as summarized in *Morskoi sbornik*, June 1923, p. 203. At about the same time in 1923 an article in the Navy journal *Red Fleet* expressed the view that the Navy should be provided with attack aircraft carriers inasmuch as they were tantamount to "seagoing airfields" able to keep up with a fleet and provide it with "aerial means" for battles fought in the open sea. This article is of particular note for having been authored by Alexander Yakimychev, who was to play a prominent role among the young turk former students of Professors Gervais and Petrov and who by 1928 were to constitute the Young School in opposition to their recent mentors. A. Yakimychev, "Rol vozdushnogo flota v morskom boyu" ["The Role of an Air Fleet in Naval Battle"], *Krasnyi flot*, nos. 4 and 5, 1923, p. 7.

8. "Absolute command of the sea—the situation when the enemy's naval forces are denied the possibility of conducting any hostile operations at sea. This may be accomplished either by complete destruction of the naval forces of the enemy or by joint operations of the Army and Navy against the operational bases in which the enemy's naval forces are blockaded." *Morskoi sbornik*, June 1923, p. 204.

9. "The second aspect—conditional command of the sea. If we do not succeed in destroying the enemy's naval force in a naval battle so that it is sheltered in an operating base which we cannot seize, then we can only blockade it. Blockade guarantees us in large degree against actions of the enemy fleet so that we may carry out every one of the main missions of the Navy with assurance of success *providing we support them with an appropriate covering force*. Nevertheless, there will be some risk. Conditional command of the sea is accomplished by blockade." p. 204. (Emphasis supplied.) Note this early mention of the need for "support"—a requirement that became of renewed importance under Gorshkov after 1956 in connection with providing combat support by other naval forces for the basic striking force of submarines.

10. "If both hostile fleets are able to operate at sea, then neither can protect his sea communications, nor make a landing, nor protect the coastal communications of the army." Gervais described this situation as one of command of the sea being held in dispute. He added that one could not properly speak of either side having any command of the sea at all in this situation. p. 204

11. A blockaded fleet ". . . must conduct 'a small war' against the blockading force, taking advantage of his own closeness to the operating bases. It is essential to upset the enemy, sowing mines in the paths of his maneuvers, attacking him with submarines and destroyers, attempting in every way to weaken his forces and equalize them with his own, in order to shift to a decisive strike for gaining command of the sea." p. 205

12. "Vozdushnye sily v operatsiiy na more" ["Air Forces in Operations at Sea"] from a report given by Mikhail Alexandrovich Petrov on 11 May 1923 to the Naval Scientific Society, as summarized in *Morskoi sbornik*, June 1923, p. 185. Petrov had published his views on "Naval Positions and Positional Battle" as early as 1919. M. Petrov, "Morskie pozitsii i pozitsionnyi boi," *Morskoi sbornik*, May-June 1919, pp. 18-47 and September-December 1919, pp. 41-74.

13. The latter term was a euphemism for a navy weaker than its likely opponent(s) such as the Soviet Union then possessed vis-à-vis England. The small war strategy was not original with Soviet naval theoreticians but had originated in land fighting and had been applied widely to the German High Seas Fleet's strategy against the British Grand Fleet until the time of the Battle of Jutland. See especially

Petrov's two articles "Zametki taktika malogo flota" ["Notes on the Tactics for a Small Navy"] in *Morskoi sbornik*, September 1923, pp. 45-61 and January 1924, pp. 31-48.

14. "The matter of position and positional war has not at all lost its significance." M. Petrov, "Morskaya pozitsiya" ["The Naval Position"], *Morskoi sbornik*, April 1924, p. 30.

15. M. Petrov, "Zametki taktika malogo flota," p. 53.

16. Petrov, "Morskaya pozitsiya," p. 39.

17. Petrov, "Zametki taktika malogo flota," *Morskoi sbornik*, September 1923, p. 54.

18. Petrov, "Morskaya pozitsiya," p. 31.

19. M. Petrov, "Bol'she vnimaniya morskoi aviatsii" ["More Attention to Naval Aviation"], *Krasnyi flot*, April 1924, pp. 77-78. Petrov's views were to shift radically by 1927, as we shall note in due course.

20. "Zet," review of N.M. Lebedev, *Ocherki gidroaviatsii [The Story of Seaplanes]*, *Voennyi vestnik*, March 1924, p. 51.

21. Editorial, *Krasnyi flot*, February 1924, pp. 19-20.

22. A. Sobolev, "Na poroge novogo etape strotel'stva Krasnogo flota" ["On the Threshold of a New Stage in the Organization and Construction of the Red Navy"], *Morskoi sbornik*, October 1924, pp. 50-51.

23. V. Zof, "Mezhdunarodnoye polozheniye i zadachi morskoi oborony SSSR" ["The International Situation and the Missions for the Naval Defense of the U.S.S.R."], *Morskoi sbornik*, May 1925.

24. A. Algazin, "Sovremennye tendentsii morskoi aviatsii," *Morskoi sbornik*, November 1925, pp. 89-104.

25. M. Petrov, "Ob atake aviatsii v strechnom boyu na more" ["On Attack by Aviation in a Meeting Engagement at Sea"], *Morskoi sbornik*, March 1924, pp. 38-51.

26. I. Kozhanov, "Sootvetsvovali li organizatsiya i metody maloi voiny strategicheskim zadacham nemtsev i obstanovke v protsesse razvitiya ot nachala do kontsa 1914 goda?" ["Did the Organization and Methods of the Small War Correspond to the Strategic Missions of the Germans and to the Evolving Situation from the Beginning to the End of 1914?"], *Morskoi sbornik*, May 1926, p. 111.

27. "The red thread in the work by Groos was the idea, unquestionably correct, that for the conduct of a small war in those circumstances that had been created by the British (I have the distant blockade in mind), the forces at hand were insufficient and did not meet the essential requirements." p. 106

28. A.P. Aleksandrov, "Podvodnaya voina v 1915 godu" ["Submarine Warfare in 1915"], *Morskoi sbornik*, June 1926, p. 4. The author was to gain prominence in the second half of the 1920s as the most notable Young School protagonist of the Old School.

29. S. Blagodarev, "Malaya voina na Severnom more v 1914 g" ["Small War in the North Sea in 1914"], *Morskoi sbornik*, July 1927, p. 18.

30. M. Petrov, "Sovremennyi morskoi flot" ["The Modern Navy"], *Voennyi vestnik*, July 1927, pp. 12 and 14.

31. N. Henrikson, "Ob'edineniye vsekh sredstv dlya morskoi oborony" ["The Uniting of All Means for Maritime Defense"], *Morskoi sbornik*, August 1925, p. 111.

32. V. Belli, "Ital'yanskiye morskiye manevry" ["The Italian Naval Maneuvers"], *Voyennyi vestnik*, February 1926, p. 41.

33. Blagodarev, p. 24.

34. R. Muklevich, "Desyatiletiye oktyabrskoi revolyutsii i morskoi flot" ["The Tenth Year of the October Revolution and the Navy"], *Morskoi sbornik*, October 1927, p. 9.

35. In *Pravda* eight months earlier, the Naval Commissar had stated with unusual candor: "Our Navy is not big enough to seek battle in the open sea . . . ." R. Muklevich, "Krasnyi flot k 9-e godovshine RKKA" ["The Red Navy on the Ninth Anniversary of the Red Army"], *Pravda*, 24 February 1927.

36. "Nauchnye voprosy na konferentsii VNO Baltmorya" ["Scientific Questions at the Conference of the Military Scientific Society of the Baltic Sea"], A. Aleksandrov, ed., *Krasnyi flot*, February 1926, pp. 97-98.

37. I. Ludri, "Krasnyi flot v sostave vooruzhennyi sil respubliki" ["The Red Navy in the Composition of the Armed Forces of the Republic"], *Morskoi sbornik*, October 1927, pp. 25-26.

38. I.A. Korotkov, *Istoriya Sovetskoi voennoi mysli* [A History of Soviet Military Thought] (Moscow: Nauka Press, 1981).

39. S.G. Gorshkov, "Voyenno-morskiye floty v voinakh i v mirnoye vremya" ["Navies in Wars and in Peacetime"], *Morskoi sbornik*, June 1972, p. 21.

40. Or at least so he was reported to have stated, but by his arch critic A.P. Aleksandrov who edited the remarks of Gervais and others at the conference at which the then head of the Naval War College reputedly bowed to a situation he had found himself unable to alter. However, it is not at all to be ruled out that the concession was wrung out of Gervais under duress or that Aleksandrov misrepresented Gervais' remarks.

41. Gervais apparently agreed with the Italian strategist Bernotti that the inferior navy should have at least two thirds as many capital ships as the stronger enemy before a force-equalization strategy could succeed.

II
The Old School Goes Down for the Count, 1928-1932

The Evidence and Some Partial Analysis

Beginning in 1928, the views of Professors Gervais and Petrov and the Old School which they led came under increasingly strong attack from several of their former students at the Naval War College. Since the arguments advanced then have contemporary relevance, they particularly merit examination.

Gervais Attacked by Ludri, 1928. Gervais was criticized by name in 1928 by Ivan Ludri[1] who had just studied under him at the Naval War College the year before. Ludri challenged his mentor's view that the aim of Soviet naval construction must be a big (i.e., battleship) navy able to hold command of the sea in dispute.[2] Rather, he asserted, the Soviet Union would build a small navy that would eschew a strategy of holding command of the sea in dispute and, instead, should "organically fuse" with the Army "to carry out the common mission for defense of our borders against the offensive being prepared against us." Ludri raised the specter of a united front attack on the USSR by a coalition of hostile governments whose naval forces would have unconditional superiority in both the quantity and quality of its naval forces which, he mentioned specifically, could include both battleships and "line" attack aircraft carriers. Nevertheless, Ludri observed that there was no need to panic before the superior forces of the enemy since the lessons of the World War provided the best evidence that, with skillful preparation of the theater of operations, the weaker navy unquestionably could repel the attack of a stronger enemy. The USSR could compensate for its weakness, Ludri asserted, "by means of coastal defenses, air forces, capitalizing on the geographical characteristics of the theater, and so on." (pp. 20-22)

Petrov Assailed by Dushenov.[3] Within six weeks after Ludri's critique of Gervais' views, a similar critique of his close Old School colleague at the Naval War College, Professor Petrov, was published by Konstantin Dushenov,[4] a contemporary of Ludri's who had just graduated from the Naval War College earlier that year (1928). In an article entitled "On the History of the 'Small War' at Sea,'' Dushenov took issue with what he asserted to be Petrov's basic position that, by means of the small-war strategy, the weaker Soviet Navy could hope first to equalize its strength with a stronger opponent, namely England, and eventually to defeat that country in battle on the open sea (and so gain a general command of the sea).

Dushenov argued that Petrov's recommendation for unflagging offensive actions by the Soviet Navy's light forces (light cruisers, destroyers, PTs, submarines, and aircraft) was not Marxist in its denial of the utility of the defensive. The correct Marxist view, Dushenov asserted, may be formulated as follows: "Not everywhere and at all times is it advantageous to take the offensive." He added that "it is essential for us to inculcate caution in strategy and boldness in tactics." (p. 42)

By way of concluding his attack on Petrov's views, Dushenov quoted from British naval historian Julian Corbett's account of the Grand Fleet in World War I. The Royal Navy had exercised no command of the sea beyond England's coastal waters, according to a quotation from Corbett. Dushenov probably thought that he had clinched his case by also quoting Corbett against a principle that lay at the heart of Petrov's position: the view that "the first task of a navy consists of searching out and destroying the main forces of the enemy." This, according to Dushenov, was an incorrect understanding of the principles of naval strategy as formulated by Corbett. (p. 42)

Dushenov Rebutted by Petrov. Petrov issued an immediate rejoinder to what he termed Dushenov's polemical and tendentious distortion of his views. In a lengthy rebuttal he mentioned inter alia that he advocated not invariably offensive operations but increasing initiative on the part of commanders of weaker naval forces. He added that, while the war plans for land warfare of all of the great powers in the World War had been based on the strategic offensive, their plans for sea warfare, including those of England, Germany and Russia, had been based on the defensive strategy of the fleet-in-being.[5]

Ironically, by the time that Dushenov's critique of Petrov's views appeared in print in April of 1928, Petrov had already so modified his views in articles appearing in the two preceding months as to completely undercut the substance of Dushenov's arguments. In February Petrov had written that the Soviet Navy's central role would be to support Army operations in the main theater of war which would be on land. (February, p. 43) The following month (this was still a month before Dushenov's critique of Petrov appeared, but must have been too late for Dushenov to take note of, or he would have referred to it in the same footnote in which he had cited Petrov's article of the preceding month), Petrov went even further. He modified his views to the extent of acknowledging, in effect, that the command-of-the-sea doctrine was inapplicable to a weaker navy, such as the Soviet Union's, for which assignment of the basic tasks of defeating or blockading the navy of the probable enemy (i.e., England) would be "completely unrealistic." (March, p. 8)

Since the argument is very relevant to the contemporary period in connection with Admiral Gorshkov's extensive discussion of command of the sea in the 1976 and 1979 editions of his book, *Sea Power of the State*, it is worth taking particular note of a further comment made by Petrov along the same line. Petrov disagreed with a concept that always constituted an essential element of Gorshkov's position on command of the sea. "It is said," wrote Petrov, "that while a weak navy may not aspire to full command of the sea, it may command some of its regions." (March, p. 6) He argued that this view merely preserved the form of command of the sea but deprived that concept of its essential aim of destroying the enemy's navy or at least blockading it in port.[6] Petrov added that the idea of gaining command of the sea in just some regions of a theater as well as that of only *gradually* equalizing naval forces with a stronger enemy were palliatives that were in contradiction with the basic thrust of the theory of command of the sea. (March, p. 8) While this seems somewhat at odds with the small-war theory for which Professor Petrov nominally was engaged in elaborating suitable tactics, it is understandable if one recalls his antecedents as an Old School command-of-the-sea advocate who had only modified his views and elaborated the small-war theory under Party pressure to do so.

In what sounded like a plea for Army backing for assigning the Navy a command-of-the-sea mission and the commensurate forces to carry it out, Petrov associated himself with his Old School colleague at the Naval War College, Professor Gervais, in holding that the main staffs of both the naval and ground forces would have to develop a common aim for war if independent operations to gain and maintain command of the sea were to be successful. The independent operations of the German Navy in World War I were cited as a negative example of what can happen when a navy is left to go it alone without the support of the entire military establishment.

Perhaps stealing Young School thunder—or more likely succumbing to Party-Young School pressure—Petrov warned that as long as the command-of-the-sea theory was allowed to appear to be the official doctrine for the Soviet Union's small navy it would alienate naval strategy from that of the ground forces.[7] Petrov reaffirmed the validity of the full command-of-the-sea concept but observed that in the Soviet case the theory "lay outside the limits of the practical criteria" for "the small war strategy." (March, p. 9) He concluded with the flat statement: "And if we work out the theory for the small war at sea based solely on the theory of command of the sea, then we may say with surety that the problem will not be resolved." (March, p. 9) He seemed to be advising the Army and Party to either forgo a command-of-the-sea doctrine or build the capital ships to implement it.

Young School Supported by Yakimychev.[8] In September 1928, a particularly informative article appeared that summarized the different schools of thought on Soviet naval strategy in general and or command of the sea in particular. Entitled "War of a 'Small (Weak) Navy' and the 'Small War' in the Era of the Steam Navy," it had been written by a young Soviet naval aviator on the teaching staff of the Naval War College, Aleksander Yakimychev.[9]

Yakimychev wrote with obvious sympathy of what he termed the Young School opposition by the younger Soviet-trained officers to the command-of-the-sea doctrine espoused by the Old School of former Tsarist officers.[10] He related that "rather heated discussions" had taken place between the students and the staff professors over the question as to whether the British Grand Fleet had been able to exercise command of the sea in the face of German submarine warfare. He claimed that the professors were forced to acknowledge that the advent of the (supposedly unblockadable) submarine and aircraft had caused some breaches in the doctrine of command of the sea. As a result, Yakimychev observed, "in the eyes of the realistically inclined students, the official doctrine of command of the sea had been compromised and a 'search' begun for a new theory for war at sea."[11]

To describe the point of view of the Old School, which Professor Gervais was acknowledged to have most fully elaborated, Yakimychev began by citing what seems likely to have been the Naval War College's approved view under the aegis of Professors Gervais and Petrov of "the two aims of war at sea:" (a) cutting the enemy's sea lines of communications (and defending one's own), and (b) seizing the enemy's coast or threatening it (and defending one's own coast). These aims could be accomplished in full measure and in the shortest time only under conditions of absolute command of the sea, according to Yakimychev's portrayal of the Old School. To establish these conditions required either destruction of the enemy navy in decisive battle or a siege of the bases of the enemy navy. In a nice show of the land-mindedness of much of Soviet thinking, the author observed that in some wars the siege by ground warfare of the enemy's naval operating bases could be replaced by a sea blockade. Since the main means of war at sea was "artillery" and since battleships and battle cruisers had by far the most powerful guns, they were the ship types that Gervais considered should, in Yakimychev's description of Old School views, form the backbone of any correctly organized navy. Failure to build a fleet whose nucleus was composed of battleships and battle cruisers, according to his portrayal, could be fraught with fateful consequences for the Soviet Union according to the Old School, noted Yakimychev.

The Young School of Soviet naval warfare, as interpreted by Yakimychev, held that it would only play into the hands of England to build a weaker battleship navy since the USSR lacked the economic strength to build one as strong as the Royal Navy. Moreover, the Young School professed to believe that, even though England was perceived as the main enemy, the next war would be conducted primarily on land with insular England at the head of a coalition of European land powers. Accordingly, the role of the Soviet Navy would be "only auxiliary."

Since battleships and battle cruisers were so expensive to build and since the USSR lacked the industrial capacity to build them cheaply and, most importantly, quickly, their construction would have to await changed conditions. For the expedient defense of Soviet coastal cities in the meanwhile, the Soviet Union should resort to a small-war strategy supplemented by strong coastal defenses. This was to be done by relatively inexpensive weapons systems that would be least subject to blockade by England and other imperialist powers with strong navies. These should consist of "aviation, submarines, torpedo boats [i.e., destroyers and PT boats] and other fast, light forces of a surface fleet." (p. 47) In view of his advocacy, in *Red Fleet* in early 1923, of aircraft carriers as "seagoing airfields capable of keeping up with a fleet and providing it with the aerial means for battles fought in the open sea" and in view of the fact that aircraft carriers were still classified as a "special-purpose" ship type (rather than as a capital ship or "ship of the line"), it seems likely that Yakimychev had light aircraft carriers primarily in mind in the above statement where he referred to the "other fast, light forces of a surface fleet"—but he did not find it politically expedient to be explicit that the "aviation" he listed should include carrier-based as well as land-based aviation.

Yakimychev made the claim that the Young School rejected neither the command-of-the-sea theory nor battleships in principle but that the Old School had been given a severe rebuff for its mindlessly mechanical application of the theory to the manifestly unsuitable circumstances of a Soviet Union under the Damocles sword of the continuing threat of further "imperialist" intervention.

Next Yakimychev turned to a description and critique of Professor Petrov's views as most recently expressed. He summarized those views in the following points:

• In case of imperialist attack, the fate of the Soviet state would be decided in land fighting and the Navy would carry out auxiliary missions;

• In view of the dependence of the operations of the Soviet Navy on those of the Army, the irrefutable principle of the theory of command of the sea was unacceptable for our small navy;

• Despite the dependence of the operations of the Soviets' small navy on the operations of the Army, the combat activity of the Navy must not be limited to the defense of certain perimeters.[12] Put otherwise, the Soviets' small navy, even though tied to the Army by a single strategic mission, must be delegated wide initiative in its area;

• The Soviets' small navy, in the event of war, would be obliged to conduct a small war, fully exploiting the conditions of the situation in the theater;

● Since battle is the underlying rationale for combat operations of a navy, the Soviet Navy must possess the appropriate means for the conduct of battles and must learn well how to employ them. Maneuver must form the cornerstone of naval training;

● "Artillery" is the basic means of battle and is found at its most powerful on battleships and battle cruisers, hence, particular attention must be given to them; and

● Other types of naval forces, probably meaning aircraft carriers specifically, have only auxiliary significance and must not be built at the expense of battleships and heavy cruisers, he added in his continued portrayal of the Old School views of Professor Petrov.

Yakimychev went on to make the interesting assertion that, even though the command-of-the-sea doctrine could not be relevant for Soviet strategy for a long time to come because of the USSR's industrial weaknesses, it could not be brushed aside since it constituted the symbol of truth for the "imperialist" navies. There was no other solution for the USSR than a small-war strategy with light forces capable of paralyzing the stronger enemy naval forces. This conclusion held that the USSR was too weak to even build a navy capable of holding the command-of-the-sea in dispute. With these assertions Yakimychev realistically portrayed the divorce of strategy from the command-of-the-sea concept.

In a section of his article subtitled "On What the 'Young School' Agrees and Disagrees with Professor M. A. Petrov," Yakimychev began with an observation which suggests that Petrov had changed his views only under duress: "Above all we welcome the public presentation by M.A. Petrov of his courageous criticism of the doctrine of the 'Old School' ('the theory of command of the sea'), for the revision of his former basic propositions which, I dare say, could not have been made without great anguish." (p. 49) After this bit of cruel sarcasm, Petrov was subjected to attack for not having carried his repudiation of the practical significance for the USSR of the command-of-the-sea theory to the logical conclusion of also repudiating battleships and battle cruisers. To emphasize his criticism, Yakimychev wrote the sentence in italics and went on to borrow the English word "nonsense" to describe Petrov's alleged halfway position. Yakimychev based his criticism on the dubious assumption that battleship navies and the command-of-the-sea theory constituted an inseparably monolithic concept inasmuch as the theory allegedly was created as a result of the practical employment of such navies. Yakimychev's earlier advocacy of attack carriers could scarcely have been made without an awareness of that ship type's great potential for implementing a command-of-the-sea strategy.

Next Yakimychev turned to what was claimed to be the real aim of his article: to clarify the essential nature of a small-war strategy. He asserted in italicized print and with seeming officiousness: "The 'Young School' considers that M.A. Petrov tolerates with dire results the mistake of confusing two different concepts: war of 'the small (weak) Navy' and 'the small-war.'" (p. 50) He went on to say that this confusion stemmed from the fact that because Germany's High Seas Fleet (*Hochseeflotte*)—although based on battleships—had been weaker than the British Grand Fleet, the term "small war" had gained currency. However, Yakimychev argued, the term should be reserved to indicate combat just by light forces, particularly by submarines and naval aircraft. He posed the rhetorical question: "May one assert that 'the small (weak) navy' is incapable of the conduct of successful war at sea?" And he replied: "No, not at all." Four prerequisites existed, according to Yakimychev, and he elaborated them at length: proper training; good intelligence (especially by agents, aircraft, and submarines); faster ships; and a number of well-armed and defended bases.

Yakimychev proceeded to elaborate the characteristics that the Young School considered inherent in a proper small-war strategy for the USSR. With the aim of destroying either an enemy's naval forces or his economic strength, the weakest link in the enemy's armor should be chosen. This had been the enemy's merchant shipping in the two case histories from the World War that were adduced: Austria against Italy in the Adriatic (which was likened to the situation that the USSR faced in the Finnish Gulf) and Germany against England after Jutland, when it conducted its unrestricted submarine warfare against British shipping. The object of such a small-war strategy was to paralyze the enemy and force him to remain in port, as achieved by both the Austrians and the Italians. Yakimychev asserted that it was not the fault of the submarine-warfare strategy that it had not won the war for Germany, but just that it had been adopted too late and with only one-fourth of the necessary number of submarines available at the outset.

It is primarily land powers that are forced to resort to the small-war strategy at sea, Yakimychev continued, and their fate in war is determined, he asserted, on the ground front. Accordingly, the main missions for navies of land powers lie in supporting the ground forces. These missions could be divided into three categories: (1) preventing the stronger enemy from operating against one's own coasts, primarily to make landings or deliver gunfire support; (2) affording close support to the Army in carrying out its missions along the coasts, particularly by making landings on the flank or in the rear of the enemy, transporting troops and supplies, and giving gunfire support; and (3) providing indirect support for Army operations, mainly by interfering with the enemy's sea lines of communication but also by other operations to weaken the armed might of the enemy.

Another characteristic of a small war enunciated by Yakimychev was that the weaker navy should avoid battle with the enemy's main (battleship) forces and only employ auxiliary forces, that is, the submarines, aircraft and light, fast surface forces that could break through a blockade. Advances in technology had provided two types of weapon systems particularly suited for this purpose—airplanes and submarines. In view of the USSR's limited access to the open sea and the short range of submarines at the time, Yakimychev favored heavy (bomber) aircraft as the main striking force for the Soviet Navy. He observed that of all weapon systems, aircraft were the most mobile, that the probable enemy bases would be within the range of Soviet naval aircraft, and that as yet no radical antiaircraft countermeasures had been developed.

After further historical analysis of World War I, Yakimychev arrived at a definition of the small war at sea formulated as follows: "the defensive aspect of war for the weaker side in circumstances of a sharp disparity in the naval forces of the sides, conducted with the aim of paralyzing the armed forces of an enemy, using large numbers of [just] auxiliary means, and distinguished by wide initiative with flexible use of means and by progressive, continuous but small-scale operations." (p. 64)

He went on to list what he considered to be the key conditions for success with the small-war-at-sea strategy: (1) firmness and persistence of the high command in adhering to the strategy; (2) correct choice of aims including determination of the most vulnerable link in the enemy's maritime strength; (3) the auxiliary weapon systems selected for employment must be available in sufficiently large numbers;[13] and (4) naval bases for the selected weapon systems must be dispersed and defended against attack from both the sea and the air.

To conclude his paper, Yakimychev expressed the view that the then public discussion of the small-war strategy bore a direct relationship to the character of the further development of the naval forces of the USSR and that achieving a unity of views on this basic question would be the real guarantee of the successful resolution of the problem of the naval defense of the USSR.[14]

The Young School Given A Right Cross by Gervais. Three months after publication of the Yakimychev article and one month after the appearance of the last of Petrov's five-installment series on the small war at sea, Gervais entered the discussion with a notable contribution.[15] At the outset, he delivered himself of some sarcastic comments on Dushenov and Yakimychev and the Young School they represented.

Gervais charged that these two opponents of the Old School had arrived at the Naval War College with the preconceived idea that the old concepts of naval warfare should be replaced with new ones. This approach, he asserted, violated the laws of the dialectic by which history demonstrates that the old is only gradually replaced by the new.[16]

He reminded his readers that he had acknowledged as early as 1923 that the advent of the submarine and airplane had made breaches in the theory of command of the sea. Specifically, he explained, the submarine threat had forced the British Grand Fleet to largely remain in port rather than to actively exercise command of the North Sea.

Nevertheless, he argued, the very existence of that fleet(in-being) continued to exert its great influence on events. As a result, Gervais concluded, command of the sea had assumed a different character but that there were as yet insufficient facts available to determine exactly the nature of the changed content of the command-of-the-sea concept and hence of a correct strategy for warfare at sea.

Gervais went on to a lengthy discussion of the small-war strategy which first criticized Petrov mildly for lack of clarity in his views on the subject. Attention then was turned to the writings of the Italian naval strategist Romeo Bernotti; Gervais quoted with seeming approval from Bernotti's view of holding command of the sea in dispute as an appropriate strategy for a weaker navy. Holding command of the sea in dispute was defined by Bernotti (according to Gervais) as preventing a stronger enemy from using command of the sea for goals of important significance. Still quoting Bernotti, the practical effect of this denial of command was stated: "The stronger side, by force of its superiority, [normally] may carry out the movement of its military and commercial ships in comparative security. The small war has the aim of preventing these movements."(p. 16)

Seemingly letting Bernotti speak for him, Gervais, in effect, cautioned against just building the small forces suitable for use in a small war. He argued that the submarines, airplanes, and light, fast surface forces that could be used directly against a stronger enemy should not be constructed out of proportion to the battleships and battle cruisers whose existence was necessary to force the enemy to keep his main forces concentrated rather than being free to disperse them to hunt down commerce raiders. Bernotti was further quoted, without any demur, that to be strong enough to adopt a strategy of holding command of the sea in dispute, the inferior navy must have at least two-thirds as many battleships and battle cruisers as the superior navy.

Next Gervais turned directly to the professed objective of this article, as implied by its title, to define the small-war strategy. He provided two partial definitions stressing the active and passive aspects, respectively, which taken together make the Old School view less confusing:

> Operations against an enemy navy, conducted with destroyers, submarines, mines, and air forces, having as their aim in aggregate to weaken the main forces of the enemy in every way, thereby creating for oneself a more favorable correlation of forces with respect to the enemy navy, and so preparing favorable conditions for shifting to warfare for holding the command of the sea in dispute.[17] (p. 18)

> A form of warfare at sea having as its missions to hinder a stronger enemy navy from carrying out his operations against us: blockade of our naval forces, landing operations on our coast, seaborne strikes against our ground forces, and so on, and at the same time to weaken and exhaust the enemy with the aim of creating favorable conditions for the shifting over to active operations of our forces.[18] (pp. 19-20)

Professor Gervais next mentioned that his views on the small-war strategy were quite similar to those of Sir Julian Corbett as expressed in the section on "Minor Counter-attacks" in his 1911 book, *Some Principles of Maritime Strategy*. Gervais explained that he equated Corbett's concept of minor counterattacks with the small-war strategy as the form of warfare suitable for a navy with such a great disparity of forces compared to his stronger opponent that the weaker navy could have no realistic expectation of being able to carry out a force-equalization-by-attrition strategy; a strategy that eventually would enable it to force a general engagement with good prospects of gaining a victory in the battle and a general command of the sea as the laurels.

Gervais then turned to a criticism of three theses of Yakimychev's article. First, he noted that the latter had put himself in an untenable position by his misinterpretation of naval history to prove that the weaker navy had always been defeated by the stronger. Not only was this historically incorrect, as Gervais showed in detail, but if true would leave the USSR in a hopeless situation.

Secondly, he disagreed with what he described as Yakimychev's too-categorical prescription that the aim of a small war must always be the enemy's weakest link. He maintained that the enemy's merchant shipping might in some cases be the correct choice for the main object of attack but this would not invariably be so. He emphasized that the loss of even one battleship would be a serious blow to an enemy's international political standing as well as an important step in the direction of equalizing the correlation of forces. In effect, he was charging the Young School in general with having adopted the mosquito-fleet strategy of the unsuccessful French Young School (Jeune École) that had flourished at the end of the last century and, in particular, of having set up evasion of battle as a system. Gervais patently disagreed on both counts.

Thirdly, he asserted that Yakimychev's stated preference for aviation over submarines, torpedo boats, and destroyers was also too categorical for the unforeseeable contingencies of war. He further criticized the Young School adherent for ignoring mine warfare in his assessment of the conditions and weapons systems of potential use in a future war. He concluded that most of Yakimychev's characteristics for small war, such as firmness and persistence of the command and correct selection of the aims for operations, were equally applicable to all warfare.

Nevertheless, whether he believed it or was just being diplomatic, he said that Yakimychev's article had made a useful contribution to clarifying the confusion that surrounded the small-war strategy. Certainly Yakimychev's Young School views had elicited a valuable summary of the opposing views of the Old School as held by its leading exponent.

More importantly, Yakimychev's description of the small-war strategy as advocated by the Young School—of only attempting to so harass the adversary's shipping with "mosquito-fleet" forces of submarines, aircraft, and light surface forces as to "paralyze" it—did help to distinguish that version of small-war strategy from the quite different one of the Old School as presented by Gervais. The latter postulated at least holding command of the sea in dispute with more balanced forces that would include such capital ships as were available as well as the favored Young School forces of submarines, aircraft, and light, fast, surface craft. And as Gervais' extensive quoting of Bernotti implied, the Old School's goal was to eventually obtain construction of enough capital ships to meet Bernotti's standard of having at least two-thirds as many such ships as the USSR's probable opponents in a future war.

Gervais went on to advocate a force composition of surface ships, submarines, and aircraft to be employed in combined-arms operations. He also advocated the combined-strike tactic.

Old School Pummeled by Aleksandrov. The Young School returned to the attack on the Old School in the next major contribution to the continuing discussion of the command-of-the-sea concept, which appeared in a four-part series of articles in 1929-1930 appropriately titled, "A Critique of the Theory of Command of the Sea."[19] The author of this series was A. P. Aleksandrov, another young Soviet officer who was then serving at the Naval War College in a position which probably made him officially responsible, along with Dushenov, to ensure that the views of Professors Gervais and Petrov were altered to conform to the Party line on naval warfare.[20]

Noting that review and principled criticism of the theory of command of the sea was not just of academic interest for the USSR but a matter of great significance for determining the practical lines for naval construction and training, Aleksandrov started by observing that the original theory of command of the sea had been distorted into an end in itself rather than just a means to permit accomplishment of naval missions.[21] Yet, as it was originally intended, and as properly understood by its contemporary proponents, he commented that command of the sea implied destruction or blockade of the enemy's naval forces as a necessary preliminary to carrying out the appropriate naval missions.

Aleksandrov went on to note that efforts at revision of the command-of-the-sea theory had taken two directions, both of which were completely inadequate. The first, alleging that the theory did not apply to the weaker navy but was still valid for the stronger navy, was credited to Petrov.[22] The second, acknowledging that the theory had suffered several breaches but still maintaining that it remained basically valid, even for the weaker navy, was aimed at Gervais.[23]

Turning his attention to Gervais' three categories of command-of-the-sea theory (absolute, conditional, and disputed), Aleksandrov argued that the significance of all three of these categories had been eroded by contemporary developments. The World War had brought no examples of absolute command of the sea and, in fact, there had been few in all history and there were not likely to be any more under the changed circumstances in which the weaker side could continue to build ships and put them into commission during the course of a war. Destruction of the enemy's industrial power or occupation of his entire seacoast would be the only way in which absolute command of the sea could be achieved and Aleksandrov dismissed such a possibility as purely theoretical.

Aleksandrov's lengthy analysis concluded that the advent of allegedly unblockadable means, in the form of the submarine and airplane, had made Gervais' category of "conditional command of the sea" by means of blockade invalid. "Disputed command of the sea" was written off summarily as an organically defective category. His argument was that "this fallacious category presupposed achievement of no degree of command of the sea whatsoever and hence was meaningless." (November 1929, p. 26)

This, of course, was scarcely an adequate argument to dispose of the entire fleet-in-being concept of Colomb and Corbett—the concept that a strong but inferior battleship fleet could hold command of the sea in dispute and so deny use of the sea to the stronger fleet by constant harassment of its flanks or blockading forces and strikes at its ports and naval bases—all while avoiding a showdown general engagement.

In concluding the first of his four articles, Aleksandrov asserted that the appearance of two new basic factors in naval warfare had struck a crushing blow to the command-of-the-sea theory. These factors were the development of productive forces and technology that permitted construction of new naval weapon systems during the course of a war and the appearance of unblockadable or nearly unblockadable means of war at sea (the submarine and airplane). That he intended to imply that the blow had been fatal was apparent from the inclusion of "former" in his reference to command of the sea as "the former cornerstone of naval operational thought, that foundation on which was erected the whole edifice of naval science and all of the theoretical constructs of the science and art of the conduct of war at sea." (November 1929, pp. 26-27)

At the outset of his second article, which was subtitled "Problems of Material Support" (for the Soviet Navy), Aleksandrov made some illuminating comments on the Young School's attitude toward the command-of-the-sea theory and its Old School protagonists. Claiming that because the World War had shown that theory to be completely unsound, he asserted that progressive naval thought, (i.e., the Young School) had been inspired by a correct understanding of the war to a search for new strategic approaches to successful conduct of the missions which the USSR would have to carry out for the naval side of any future general war.[24]

Aleksandrov asserted further that the practice of naval warfare was still changing and that to ignore this fact and so to continue to apply command-of-the-sea doctrine would mean that development of the new theory required to give indispensable direction to naval policy would lag hopelessly far behind Soviet naval practice.[25] The current search for new strategy, he insisted, could not be successful without first extirpating the command-of-the-sea theory.[26]

In a particularly revealing observation, Aleksandrov showed deep distrust of the sincerity of Gervais and Petrov in their professed efforts to adapt command of the sea to Soviet circumstances: "One cannot tirelessly enough insist on the necessity for such exhaustive criticism [of the command-of-the-sea theory], especially at the present time when the revision of that theory, timid in form and inadequate and unsatisfactory in content, is joined with efforts at the resurrection in one form or another of the theory of command of the sea in our literature and in world literature related to the scientific elaboration of the conduct of naval warfare."[27] (February 1930, p. 33) Aleksandrov charged that these efforts at home and abroad were playing a reactionary and disorganizing role in leading Soviet naval thought down the wrong road.

Aleksandrov disclaimed any intention of working out in his series of articles the new naval theory for which he was agitating. To accomplish that goal, he said, sufficient time and a large "collective" of scientific and practical workers would be required. Rather, the aim of his four articles, he claimed, was limited to "helping to free naval scientific thought from the theoretical blinders of the method of holding command of the sea in dispute." (February 1930, p. 35)

He went on to argue against obsolescent propositions on the character of war at sea, particularly the view that such a war would be fought only with the weapon systems already produced in peacetime. He held that the World War had demonstrated the possibility of continuing and even expanding production during a war and he proceeded to give consideration to the necessary peacetime preparations of the heavy industrial base and skilled labor force that would ensure the USSR continued and expanded wartime production of the required naval materiel.

Yet, he observed, to rationally plan wartime production of naval ships, aircraft, and other equipment and supplies in the great quantities that would be expended in a protracted conflict, it was first essential to determine the strategy to be employed. Only on the basis of a specific strategy could Soviet force planners compute the types and quantities of weapons systems to produce, taking into account the probable enemy opposition and the geographic situation of the Soviet Union.[28]

Once this was worked out, Aleksandrov implied, the USSR need only maintain a small, cadre navy in peacetime, but one capable of rapid wartime expansion. The very limited budget allocations for the Navy made the most careful and detailed planning necessary, both for the requisite naval forces and for the supporting base infrastructure.

In concluding his second article, Aleksandrov called again for the elaboration of a scientific theory that would suit Soviet circumstances. Only when that had been done, he insisted, could the USSR take the practical steps necessary to overcome all of the economic, financial, and technical production difficulties that must be surmounted to put together a satisfactory naval budget.

In his third article, Aleksandrov concerned himself with matters of Soviet naval personnel, especially of determining an adequate peacetime complement and of providing them with sufficient training for their highly specialized jobs. He began by decrying the Soviet books and articles on the subject which were then extant, saying that with but few happy exceptions they were disoriented by the blinders of the theory of command of the sea. This literature, he maintained, provided an erroneous basis for determining personnel manning levels and training requirements. In what appeared to be a clear criticism of existing Soviet military policy for naval development, he indicated that there was a "trend toward uninterrupted and expanded construction of the Naval Forces," including personnel complements, which he claimed was unwarranted on the grounds that the USSR required only a small cadre navy in peacetime.

So on this basis, Aleksandrov again demanded that the USSR adopt the line of criticism of the theory of command of the sea so that the requisite practical working out of the problems of manning the naval forces could be accomplished rationally. To support this view he tabulated the imposingly large naval personnel strengths of the major navies during the World War.[29] From this he argued that a peacetime cadre navy with large reserves would be the more desirable policy.

In the final article of his four-part series, Aleksandrov turned to the subject of Soviet naval operations for a future war. He began by asserting that the World War had demonstrated the impossibility of first gaining command of the sea so as to provide secure conditions for the subsequent conduct of all necessary naval missions. He described and illustrated, with examples from World War I, the exceptional difficulty of determining the forces required as supporting and covering forces (of battleships and battle cruisers) for the light strike forces in the complicated circumstances of naval warfare. Once again, he pointed to the blinders constituted by the command-of-the-sea theory which allegedly obscured adequate conceptualization of the problems concerning the numbers and types of forces required for wartime missions that needed to be faced and resolved.

Without mentioning by name either the Old School or Professor Gervais, Aleksandrov went on to exploit the German *Hochseeflotte's* war experience.

This was an attempt to discredit what he implied to be Gervais' recommended small-war naval strategy of first equalizing forces through attrition prior to seeking decisive battle that would give the USSR command of the sea in a theater in dispute. The idea, according to Aleksandrov, had originated in the German idea of *Krafteausgleich* (force-equalization) which had been nullified by England's failure to live up to German expectations that they would be confronted by a close blockade.

When England, instead, chose to impose a distant blockade, and even kept the battleships and battle cruisers of the Grand Fleet in port, safe from submarine attack, Germany's short-ranged destroyers could not be employed to implement the *Krafteausgleich* strategy. By the time of the indecisive Battle of Jutland in 1916, the unrealism of this small-war strategy had become obvious and Germany abandoned it in favor of a submarine blockade of England utilizing unrestricted submarine warfare on British shipping.

All of this, Aleksandrov concluded, showed the unsuitability of such a *Krafteausgleich* strategy for the USSR. The main forces (i.e., battleships and battle cruisers) of both sides were employed, as a rule, only for auxiliary missions for the last half of the war, Aleksandrov observed.[30]

He also noted that, while the objective logic of past experience must be sought as an essential guide to the future, only the actual experience from the recent period of the dying off of the theory of command of the sea would be relevant. The study of the past could be used to foresee the future only if the face of history of Soviet research and writing on naval strategy could be turned around to look forward. The USSR must establish its research effort independently of existing Soviet and foreign writings. This research should not be abstract in nature but should be directed to the USSR's particular situation.

This necessary synthesizing of Russian naval experience, Aleksandrov added, had not been done under the tsars. The prewar construction program, attributed to the blinders imposed by the command-of-the-sea theory, had been the result of having had an independent Navy Ministry and Naval General Staff, and, consequently, had not corresponded at all with the missions of the Army, as Aleksandrov clearly thought it should. To support this statement he cited the Tsarist Naval General Staff document quoted in the prologue to this study to illustrate the tsarist naval legacy in which the Naval Minister commented on the 1911-1916 warship construction program. It called for building a battleship navy that would enable Russia to gain command of the sea in the Baltic despite the greatly superior German Navy or at least, that would be strong enough to hold command of the Baltic in dispute.

This had been wrong, Aleksandrov argued, even though at that time the command-of-the-sea theory was still valid and lent itself well to the tsar's imperialistic efforts to create a situation in which he could employ the Black

Sea Fleet to seize the Turkish Straits. It was wrong, he maintained, because it did not take into account Russia's industrial backwardness and geographical handicaps which had combined to make such a doctrine unsuitable for Tsarist Russia. Despite Moscow's having had one of the largest navies in Europe and the fastest growing naval budget in the immediate prewar period, the mechanical application of the command-of-the-sea doctrine had resulted in the collapse of Tsarist Russia's naval policy in both the Baltic and Black Seas.

Next Aleksandrov expressed the opinion that for a weaker navy to adopt the same strategy and weaponry as the stronger navy would ensure ultimate failure since to do so would permit what he termed the "Law of Numbers" to come into operation—to the inevitable advantage of the larger navy. He claimed that the submarine was a new weapon that by its very nature invalidated the Law of Numbers for naval warfare in which submarines were used as the primary weapon of the weaker side. He pointed out that the Allies in the World War had been forced to devote colossal means to building the great number of antisubmarine-warfare forces required to counter the relatively small number of German submarines.

In an apparent attack on Gervais' recommendation for building a Soviet Baltic Fleet with a minimum of 8 battleships, 4 heavy cruisers, and 16 light cruisers, Aleksandrov asserted that the way out of the USSR's predicament of being confronted by a stronger British Navy was not to be found in construction of a Grand Fleet-style force of 8 to 12 battleships and 16 to 20 cruisers but through a shipbuilding policy that would permit circumventing the Law of Numbers—that is, by building a Baltic Fleet whose main forces would be comprised of submarines.[31]

Aleksandrov also took occasion to inveigh against the view expressed in Professor Petrov's 1928 series of articles, "Toward the Formulation of the Question of a 'Small War,'" that balanced forces should be built to carry out all the foreseeable naval missions of any future war. Aleksandrov pointed out that this would require unrealistically large forces to be ready to conduct the nearly astronomical number of permutations and combinations of missions that would be involved. Rather than get into such a "muddle," only enough forces of the right types should be built to carry out the most probable missions.

Any future war, Aleksandrov continued, would be characterized by successive but continuous combat operations and by saturation of the limited-area sea theaters with light naval forces. In this connection, he mentioned the preferred naval forces of the Young School: light, fast destroyers, motor torpedo boats, submarines, and aircraft. He claimed that the advent of these weapon systems had shifted the offensive-defensive correlation of forces in naval warfare in favor of the latter. He advanced the thesis that the combined and concentrated strike by these forces would constitute an adequate counter to the multiple, dispersed operations of the enemy.

To accomplish this, Aleksandrov said, required potent means of intelligence to support the USSR's defense strategy as well as strong strike groups to conduct the combined strikes. These requirements were applicable to all naval operations, as, he observed, had been demonstrated by the World War, but particularly to the especially complicated sea transits and disembarkments on the beach that characterized amphibious landings.

"Completely untrue" were the words with which Aleksandrov rejected the conclusion of a Soviet war historian (and obvious candidate for the Old School) who had recently aired the view that it was absolutely essential to gain command of the sea before undertaking any amphibious landings.[32] According to Aleksandrov, such a conclusion was controverted both by history (although he offered no examples) and because he had already shown, he claimed, that it was no longer feasible to gain command of the sea in the conditions of contemporary warfare.

Rather, the necessary preliminary activities of future warfare at sea would be support operations for successfully deploying naval forces out onto the high seas. Although Aleksandrov was not explicit, it seems almost certain that he had in mind supporting operations by surface ships and aircraft to ensure safe exit and reentry into port of the main force, i.e., submarines, that he advocated. The increasing importance of such support operations needed to be taken into account in selecting and providing defenses for the USSR's main operating bases as well as its advanced (maneuvering) naval bases.

To conclude his series, Aleksandrov summed up what he thought were the most important conclusions of his four articles of 1929 and 1930:

• The command-of-the-sea theory was not in consonance with the USSR's practical requirements for war at sea, and the so-called revision as developed primarily by Professors Gervais and Petrov was unsatisfactory and inadequate. Command of the sea must be eliminated in both its theoretical and practical applications. This could only be effected through "principled criticism" adequate to "clear the way for forward movement" by Soviet naval scientific thought in order to cope with the Soviet Union's "practical requirements for a war at sea";

• The USSR could not afford to wait to work out a final, fully elaborated new theory based on all the historical material at hand and an understanding of further changes in strategy being wrought by weapons technology but must go ahead with what was already known and the material at hand;

• The utilitarian value of correct naval theory as a guide to practice was stressed as was the danger of alienation of theoretical formulations from military experience and practice, and from the existing material—technical base for naval construction;

• A necessity for giving naval scientific thought a practical orientation was claimed; and

● Collaboration of the naval theoreticians with the naval practitioners was urged in order to get better results.

Asserting that he had not exhausted all the potentially relevant arguments against the command-of-the-sea doctrine, Aleksandrov commented that he had aimed rather at voicing a definitive disavowal of the still dominant theory of the command-of-the-sea.[33]

The effort to discredit the command-of-the-sea theory and to find a substitute theory was continued in 1931 at a conference at the Naval War College from which Professors Gervais and Petrov apparently were barred. The main speakers were the same Yakimychev and Aleksandrov from whom so much had already been heard.

A Command-of-the-Sea Strategy Found Unsuitable by Yakimychev.[34] Speaking first, Yakimychev stated the aim of his report was to show, by use of specific historical material, the "time, place and circumstances of the downfall of the notorious theory of 'command of the sea.'" He prefaced his remarks with the assertion: "We must research all aspects of the question of to what degree this theory corresponds to our conditions and, in general, is it practical at the present time?" He added that, although the theory had been doctrine for every naval general staff in the World War, it had become impractical even for the capitalist states.

The Russo-Japanese War of 1904-1905 had seen the command-of-the-sea theory at its zenith, Yakimychev observed, but now it was in an irreversible dialectical decline. Even in that war, 7 Russian and 11 Japanese surface ships had been lost to mines, he pointed out in reference to the earliest weapon considered by the Soviet Young School to have breached the classical command-of-the-sea theory. The Battle of Tsushima had evidenced the danger of making the fate of a state dependent on a main force of battleships that could be sunk in a few hours. Considering the years it takes to build such a naval force, the speaker continued, it should have come as no surprise that the decision to engage in a naval battle was considered too important by all the governments involved to be left up to the fleet commander but instead had been decided from the land. This land-based command has been characterized by an avoidance of decisive battle that was abnormal and contradicted the doctrinal conception of an independent battleship fleet.

The advent of the diesel engine to replace kerosene motors in 1910 had made submarines capable of moving out of their coastal positions to fight in the open sea. This had led the British Admiralty in 1912 to change its war plans, vis-à-vis Germany, to a strategy of distant blockade instead of close-in blockade which, along with the general engagement of line fleets, was one of the two primary methods of implementing that theory. When the British subsequently shut up the Grand Fleet in harbor behind antisubmarine nets rather than actively and unremittingly seeking a general engagement, the second and final phase of the downfall of the command-of-the-sea theory had begun, according to Yakimychev's viewpoint.

England then further violated the command-of-the-sea theory by not sending out the Grand Fleet to seek battle with the German *Hochseeflotte*. Similarly, the Germans did not send a strong fleet to the Finnish Gulf to destroy the Russian Baltic Fleet. In both cases, Yakimychev noted, the plans of the weaker navies for positional defense were upset by the failure of their stronger opponents to apply the accepted method of close blockade to their strategy at the outset of the war. Moreover, the Russian Baltic Fleet, like the British and German Navies, was unprepared to fight against submarines and so was shut up in its bases. This led to a tsarist view that all hopes had to be placed on submarines, but construction of the first Russian type capable of putting to sea was just starting. "What to do under such circumstances?" Yakimychev asked rhetorically and commented: "The textbooks on command-of-the-sea theory didn't give any answer to this question." The answer for the Russian Baltic Fleet, Yakimychev went on to relate, came in the form of three British submarines sent into the southeastern Baltic. Their mere presence, he implied clearly, sufficed to deter any further German offensive operations against the Russian Baltic Fleet which never once during the whole war ventured into the southern Baltic.

He noted sarcastically that by the end of 1914 the Baltic Fleet command belatedly realized that submarines and mines had become of major importance for carrying out a small-war strategy. Accordingly, the fleet commander had proposed that two of the Baltic Fleet battleships be employed to give support to the light forces at sea and recommended cancellation of the battleship-building program in favor of building 85 sea-capable submarines and a number of fast minelayers. According to Yakimychev, the main reason these recommendations were not adopted was that the battleship-building program was too inflexible to change.

From his study of the World War, Yakimychev drew a number of conclusions. The advent of new technology such as submarines, mass mining and aircraft had made impractical the two most characteristic methods of a command-of-the-sea strategy: close-in blockade and the general engagement of the line fleets in the open sea. He argued further that the new means of warfare had not been used extensively or consistently enough to prove their utility. In the case of mines, whose laying off the entrances to ports and along the shipping lanes could be effective, Russia had lacked enough minelayers. Another conclusion reached by Yakimychev was that the conduct of active (i.e., tactically offensive) operations by the light surface forces of a fleet required the support of the heavy ships, including battleships. Also, he observed that the command-of-the-sea strategy had been overrated before the war. The question being asked in the postwar period, when there were no "established views on the character of a future war at sea," was, "A battleship navy or . . . ?" Yakimychev, a partisan of aircraft instead of battleships, closed with a profession of faith in Marxist-Leninist methodology as the scientific key to victory in future war.

Old School Denounced and Substitutes Recommended by Aleksandrov.[35] When his turn came to speak at the conference, Aleksandrov began his report by remarking that it was not by chance that, although buried long ago, the theory of command of the sea was still a topic of discussion. This, he stated, was due to the fact that certain instructors and professors at the Soviet Naval War College were still protagonists of the theory and were propagating it to the young Soviet student officers. Despite the criticism of the theory, these people persisted. Hence, it would be necessary to criticize it again. Aleksandrov observed with obvious annoyance that when the bourgeois imperialist theory was put out the door, it came back in through the window. He expressed his satisfaction that none of the supporters of the theory were in his audience or at least none were scheduled to speak. He also claimed that the injection of command-of-the-sea principles into a recent war game at the Naval War College had caused a whole series of errors.

Aleksandrov then launched into the substance of his report, observing that command of the sea had to be viewed from two aspects, the political and the operational. The political side, he held, was that the theory was the operational expression of the imperialist policy of expansionism in a struggle for control of the shipping lanes. He called for giving a "decisive rebuff to those people who were trying to transplant onto Soviet soil the imperialist theory of command of the sea."

The operational aspect of the theory, Aleksandrov continued, lay in warfare for control of the sea lanes, the so-called independent missions of naval forces, and in that not a single operational mission of naval forces could be carried out without the essential preliminary of gaining command of the sea. The speaker went on to quote Professor Gervais on the essence of the theory as requiring gaining of command as a preliminary to carrying out assigned naval missions and as having three phases: *absolute command, conditional command,* and *disputed command.* He referred his audience to his series of four articles published in *Morskoi sbornik* in 1929-1930 (treated above) and passed on to consideration of what he termed "two new basic factors" resulting from the contemporary development of productive forces. The first of these, he stated, was the increased production during the course of a war of naval materiel (including warships). The second was said to be the appearance of new means of warfare at sea that were difficult or impossible to blockade, that is, submarines and naval aircraft.[36] These two new basic factors of course were the same old ones that Aleksandrov had discussed in his November 1928 *Naval Digest* article on "Criticism of the Theory of Command of the Sea."

However, on this occasion he went on to note that the answer given to the second factor by the command-of-the-sea proponents was to concede that submarines and aircraft could not be blockaded but that the main forces, particularly the battleships, could still be blockaded in port and the blockading force would thereby gain conditional command of the sea. He added, with marked peevishness, that no study had yet been made to deprive this creeping theory of its latest refuge.

Next Aleksandrov argued in rebuttal that longer-range coastal artillery, improved mining, and better smoke screens had made it easier for the main forces to break through a blockade. These developments had made the task of a blockading force more difficult and would require naval forces three times as strong as the force being blockaded in order to cover the line of blockade adequately to ensure interception and defeat of the blockaded force. This new situation, Aleksandrov argued, invalidated blockade as a means of gaining command of the sea even in daylight, let alone during periods of darkness or low visibility. Claiming that his argument had served adequately to dispose of the latest position taken by the command-of-the-sea adherents, the speaker noted that a new strategic theory was needed to replace the old one.

As a contribution to this end, he suggested that the principle of the general naval engagement characteristic of the old theory could be replaced with one well known to the Red Army, that of successive operations as a means of winning victory (as opposed to one single all or nothing battle). He added that "the ideologues of command of the sea at the Naval War College showed a tendency to ignore and remain mute about the experience of the Red Army with respect to this theory of successive operations of which they are scornful." Aleksandrov called on his audience to join him in "propagandizing and developing this theory, adapting it to specific circumstances of our naval theaters and to the particularities of the conduct of war at sea." (p. 34)

Another contribution proffered by Aleksandrov toward replacement of the old theory was the method of giving direct support to individual operations. This was to be accomplished by employing covering forces assigned to ensure mission accomplishment rather than first undertaking to gain command of the sea as held necessary by the old theory. Asserting that gaining such command of the sea was impossible under contemporary conditions and that acceptance of the theory would lead to passivity and defeat, Aleksandrov said it was necessary "to activate our creative naval thought along the line of working out methods for direct combat support, along the line of searching for new methods and means for providing support for the operations of our naval forces."[37] (p. 35)

A third contribution toward a replacement theory for command of the sea given by the speaker was to oppose the enemy with naval forces of different types (from his battleship squadrons) in order to invalidate the Law of Numbers that applies to the requirement of the command-of-the-sea doctrine that the single-type main force (of battleships) be opposed by the same type of ship but in greater numbers. As observed previously, when Aleksandrov first spoke of using types of forces other than battleships to circumvent the Law of Numbers, he clearly had submarines primarily in view.

Borrowing yet another principle from the Army, Aleksandrov advocated the conduct of combined-arms battle in sea warfare. This would require the participation of submarines and naval aviation as well as of the surface forces.

He specified that the foregoing contributions toward a new strategic theory for war at sea comprised the main directions to be taken by the positive, creative, theoretical and practical work in the naval forces and at the War College. He added, in closing, that the report Yakimychev had given before him had provided specific historical material which supported the correctness of his position in criticism of the theory of command of the sea.

Yakimychev, in a final word, commented inter alia that the problem posed by the battleship navies of the USSR's potential enemies was an extremely complicated one and that it was wrong to treat it as platitudinously as it just had been.[38] Although there had been a third War College speaker, the latter had said nothing about battleship navies (or otherwise of relevance) so Yakimychev's shaft clearly was aimed at Aleksandrov. The fact that Aleksandrov advocated submarines as the main force of the Navy while Yakimychev championed airplanes may well explain the animus that motivated Yakimychev's remark.

Old School TKO'd by Aleksandrov. In 1931 Stalin sent to the editors of the Party theoretical journal, *Proletarian Revolution*, a long letter criticizing them for having published Trotskyite trash which falsely represented Lenin's ideas on centrism in the Comintern and in the Soviet Communist Party and called on the editors to cease and desist forthwith. The Stalin letter was published along with an editorial promise not to publish any more lies in the guise of discussion articles.[39] Although Stalin's letter had no specific reference to military theory, let alone to naval matters, it was seized on by Aleksandrov and two other naval writers in early 1932 to attack Petrov and Gervais and bring about the complete discrediting of the latter. Before turning to the abject recantation by Gervais published in March 1932, the nature of which is significant for understanding the underlying Party line on naval warfare, it is relevant to examine the arguments that actually precipitated Gervais' downfall.

In February 1932 Aleksandrov published yet another long article attacking the command-of-the-sea theory in general and, in particular, Petrov's and Gervais' views on the subject.[40] He cited the Stalin letter, which in part is quoted here so the reader can appreciate the inimitable Stalinist style of ideological coercion that could fell two oaks such as Petrov and Gervais, first bending the former, and then breaking the latter:

In his speech to the Conference of Marxist Agrarians and in his historical letter to the editors of the journal *Proletarian Revolution*, Comrade Stalin spoke of the lag of theoretical work behind the practice of socialist construction and of the necessity for raising to a principled level the problems of working out our theories, and of strengthening our Bolshevik vigilance in the struggle against every deviation from the general line of the Party, and giving a knockout blow to the contraband theory which has been dragged into our literature from the inimical, counter-revolutionary Trotskyite and bourgeois reactionary theory. On the question of the lag in theory, Comrade Stalin said the following: "... our theory is not in step with our successes. We have some divergence between our practical successes and the development of our theoretical views. In this regard it is necessary that our theoretical work not only catch up with practice but outstrip it, arming our practitioners in their struggle for the victory of socialism." (pp. 2-99)

Aleksandrov interpreted Stalin's letter to constitute a direct order to strengthen Bolshevik vigilance along the entire military-theoretical front, including the naval sector of that front. "We are definitely lagging" in that sector, Aleksandrov asserted, and he laid the blame for this on "the infiltration of inimical theory" into Soviet naval scientific and educational literature by "bourgeois reactionary theorists" such as "Gervais, Petrov and others." (p. 29)

To reconstitute Soviet naval theory on the basis of the directives of the Party and Revolutionary Military Council, Aleksandrov outlined five necessary steps: (1) Brand the theory of Gervais and Petrov as inimical and as idealistic, due to having been derived directly from the mystical views of the tsarist navy captain and professor at the former Nikolayevsk Naval War College, Nikolai Klado; (2) "Expose the classical roots of, and denounce the thought content and political essence of, the doctrine of Gervais and Petrov—the theory of command of the sea—as a theory of the imperialist bourgeoisie, and show that this doctrine was basically the doctrine of the Naval General Staff of the Tsarist Navy"; (3) "Show the operational-tactical essence of the theory of command of the sea as a backward and therefore incorrect theory which does not take into account the influence on the methods of conduct of war at sea and on naval operations of the development of modern naval technology"; (4) "Show that the transfer of this theory of command of the sea to the circumstances of the Soviet Union is inimical to the basic aims of the Red Army—is a defeatist theory which sows doubt among our forces, feeds operational 'opportunism,' dooms our naval forces to passivity, and disarms us before our enemies"; and (5) "Draw appropriate conclusions from the criticism of this bourgeois reactionary theory for our future work." (pp. 29-30)

To discharge the first of the five tasks above, there followed a long polemic against Gervais and Petrov as idealists and disciples of Klado that attempted to make them look ridiculous on philosophical grounds having nothing substantive to do with their theoretical views.

On the second task, Aleksandrov began by saying that the command-of-the-sea-theory was the central concept of all the inimical books and speeches which Gervais and Petrov had continued to propagandize on Soviet soil. He argued that the theory had its classical roots in the efforts of the imperialist bourgeoisie to control the sea lanes of world shipping. To follow a similar policy served only to lend substance to the charges of Red imperialism that were being made throughout the world.

British Vice Admiral Philip Colomb was again identified by Aleksandrov as the author and founder of the theory of command of the sea in the early 1890s. His writings were cited to show the genesis of the view that the aim of naval warfare must be to establish command of the sea before the sea can be used, with acceptable risk, to carry out whatever naval missions and merchant shipping as might be indicated by the circumstances.

Mahan's work was said to have appeared almost simultaneously with that of Colomb and to have given support to the command-of-the-sea doctrine accepted by all of the capitalist powers right at the beginning of the era of the rapid growth of imperialism at the end of the last century. In its tsarist Russian form, Aleksandrov observed, the theory had led to the large pre-World War naval building program on the basis of the "active straits idea," that is, the strategic concept of seizing both the Turkish and Danish Straits whenever circumstances permitted.

Aleksandrov went on, in the next sentence, to condemn Gervais and Petrov as advocating "an independent naval strategy having warfare for command of the sea as its aim and as its main task the struggle on sea communications." Aleksandrov then proceeded to imply by several inconclusive quotations that Gervais and Petrov, too, had seizure of the Black Sea and Baltic straits in view as the ultimate aim for an independent Soviet naval strategy. Aleksandrov pointed out that advocacy of an independent naval strategy had "driven a wedge into the political and operational unity" of the Armed Forces and alienated the naval forces from the rest of the Army (of which it then was still a part).

Aleksandrov next alleged the impossibility of adapting the bourgeois content of the command-of-the-sea theory to the revolutionary form of the World Revolution he professed to consider imminent. He claimed that it was just such an effort in which Gervais and Petrov had been engaged and he once again impugned their sincerity. He concluded his comments on the second of his self-appointed tasks with an unmistakable reference to Gervais and Petrov, that "only slanderers and direct enemies of the Soviet Union would pass off this bourgeois-imperialist theory as the naval doctrine of our state." (p. 43)

To perform the third task of showing the backwardness of the command-of-the-sea theory by demonstrating that it had not taken account of modern technology (including new weapon systems), Aleksandrov began by summarizing in a single sentence what he considered to be the mistaken views of the two leading Old School exponents:

The operational essence of this theory of command of the sea is the preliminary destruction or blockading of the enemy navy, without the accomplishment of which not one operation may be carried out in a sea theater (Gervais) and the tactical aim is a close blockade and a general battle by a full-value squadron of line warships which will decide all problems of the conduct of war at sea (Petrov). (p. 43)

Aleksandrov noted that the operational essence of the theory had been criticized already in the Soviet literature by Ludri, Kozhanov, Dushenov, Yakimychev, and others, as well as by himself, but that the past few years had afforded rich, new practical experience that needed to be absorbed theoretically. The implication clearly was that the recent experience would contribute significantly to the earlier criticism of the Old School theory.

The rhetorical question was posed: "What are the basic aspects that make the theory of command of the sea bankrupt under contemporary conditions of war at sea?" Three such aspects were mentioned: The fact that naval forces could be built in substantial numbers during the course of a war, thanks to the significant development of industry; the appearance of wholly unblockadable or hard to blockade naval forces in the form of submarines, naval aircraft, and all classes of high-speed (i.e., light mosquito fleet) warships; and marked development of long-range coastal artillery, fixed and floating mines, and smoke screen laying capabilities.

Aleksandrov said that, despite all the criticism of the command-of-the-sea theory, Gervais and Petrov still continued their efforts at the Naval War College to modernize and touch up, cosmetically, the operational and tactical essence of the theory. These efforts, he went on, had been sympathetically received by "certain naive people, even at our Naval War College, who could not understand the essence of those basic changes made in tactics and operational art by new technology." Nevertheless, Aleksandrov saw the main task of theoretical work as elaborating the great theoretical significance of the practical decisions taken by the Revolutionary Military Council, decisions which were described as having historic significance for Soviet strategy in a war at sea. He again advocated the desirability of working out the problems of "successive combined-arms operations" which he noted were "common to us and to the Red Army." Such operations, he made it clear, were to replace the general engagement of battleships and cruisers and were to be conducted primarily by submarines, motor torpedo boats, heavy (bomber) aviation, and destroyers.[41]

Gervais and Petrov were then accused of "systematically attempting to divert our cadres from the necessary work and to disorient our naval practitioners, directing their thought and energy into a false course from which we cannot obtain the correct decisions for the problems facing us in the construction and combat training of our naval forces." Aleksandrov referred specifically to the work at hand, from which the Old School proponents allegedly were distracting attention, as that of elaborating the tactics for successive combined operations of all types of weapon systems of the naval forces and the ground force units of the Red Army.

Aleksandrov ended his long discussion of the third task of his article with a remark that probably helps to explain why it was Gervais alone who within a few weeks would be forced into a humiliating public *mea culpa*. Petrov's most important work was indicated to have been in naval tactics while that of Gervais was characterized as having been primarily concerned with "strategy and operational art" (i.e., grand strategy and theater or campaign strategy), the more politically sensitive and, hence, more politically dangerous areas.

Turning to his fourth task, that of showing that the command-of-the-sea theory was inimical to the Army's strategic aims and defeatist to boot, Aleksandrov first remarked that since gaining command of the sea was held to be an absolute prerequisite for conducting any Army flank support operations whatsoever, the USSR's inability to contest for command of the sea against the great naval powers condemned the Soviet Navy to passivity and defeat. He added, in a passage that implied that Gervais had already been removed from the Naval War College and his fate already sealed, that Professor Gervais, "in his time," had been the "propagandist and ideologue of this defeatist theory in his scientific works, especially his monograph *The Significance of Naval Forces for the State*, and in the lectures which he gave from the academic chairs of the Naval War College."

To illustrate the alleged damaging effect of Gervais' basic view on the Navy's mission capabilities, Aleksandrov quoted from a projected 1927 draft of Army Field Regulations for the Northern Caucasus Military District with its headquarters at Rostov (on the Sea of Azov with direct access to the Black Sea through the Kerch Straits). From a chapter on "Joint Operations of the Army and Navy," the following two passages were extracted:

> *Article 6.* Transfer by sea of a large-scale landing force (division or corps) is permissible only under conditions of full command of the sea. Under conditions of disputed command of the sea only small tactical landings are allowable which are supported [*i.e.*, whose chances of success are increased] by the conduct of rapid and surprise operations.
>
> *Article 7.* Under conditions of enemy command of the sea, all landings are impractical. (p. 50)

Aleksandrov cited, without quoting five additional articles from the 1927 draft of Army Field Regulations which he said reflected the work of naval persons who were under the influence of the command-of-the-sea theory. He added that naturally such draft field regulations would never be approved by the Army.

In Aleksandrov's indictment, Gervais' uncompromising views on the need for holding command of the sea in dispute, both for protecting maritime borders and for training adequately motivated officers, were next quoted at some length from his 1926 speeches. Then, in a further quote from Gervais, this time from the 1923 edition of *The Significance of Naval Forces for the State*, one is again apprised of the fact that holding command of the sea in dispute was held by Gervais to be the proper aim of a weaker big-ship navy. One notes, too, that Gervais considered the seaplane tender as a necessary ship type in the composition of a battle force.[42]

Both Gervais and Petrov were criticized for recommending large battleship fleets. The latter was quoted as considering that a proper navy should have several squadrons, each composed of 8 battleships, 6 heavy cruisers, 12 light cruisers, 32 destroyers, 64 destroyer escorts, plus unspecified numbers of other ship types including submarines.

The impossibility for the USSR to compete in a naval arms race with the rest of the world was cited as the reason the USSR must employ such means of naval warfare as would permit escape from the Law of Numbers. Aleksandrov quoted Gervais' opposition to his view in the form of the assertion that naval forces comprised only of submarines lack the means of holding command of the sea in dispute. The Young School proponent added that a characteristic of all the works of both Gervais and Petrov was their underestimation and ignorance of the new technology which was being introduced into the Soviet Navy and changing its strategy and tactics.

By ignoring the effects on naval warfare of submarines, aircraft, and improved coastal artillery, Gervais and Petrov were said to support views diametrically opposed to those of the Party and the Army. From superficially scientific positions, Aleksandrov alleged, the two Naval War College professors had "propagated defeatism and sowed distrust in the force and power of our Naval Forces of the Red Army." It was absolutely necessary, Aleksandrov said, "to remove from circulation in the worker-peasant Red Army these defeatist and at the same time reactionary 'theoreticians.'" Naval theory should be formulated so as to give Soviet practitioners "strength in orientation, clarity in perspective, confidence in work, and trust in the victory of our endeavors," said Aleksandrov, quoting from Stalin's observations on the qualities necessary for intellectual work in general.

With this quote from the all-powerful General Secretary of the Party, Aleksandrov moved on to his fifth and final task of drawing conclusions for the practical work of developing the Navy. First, he commented that both Gervais and Petrov had expounded their allegedly counterrevolution- ary ideology "until the very end of their scientific and pedagogical work," thus making it clear that Petrov too had been ousted from the Naval War College (although he was not to be subjected like Gervais to the public disgrace of having to publish an abject retraction of his views).

Next, it was asserted that documentary evidence could be produced to prove close contact between military and naval theorists of reactionary views. Reference was made to the public support given to Petrov's views on the small-war strategy by Svechin, a prominent but subsequently purged army theorist, and by two other army theoreticians, Verkhovskiy and Snesarev.[43] This support had been given in the face of opposition to Petrov's views that had been voiced by Deputy Navy Commissar Ivan Ludri, and must have seemed doubly subversive. The collusion between the military and naval theorists, Aleksandrov asserted, was too obvious to require further comment.

In a second conclusion, Aleksandrov answered in the negative the rhetorical question, "May we consider at the present time we are to some degree finished on our soil with bourgeois-reactionary theories?" He supported this pessimistic stand with a lengthy rehearsal of the voluminous writings of Gervais and Petrov that would continue to dominate Soviet naval literature for as long as it would take to bring each of them under the fire of Marxist-Leninist criticism.

In his penultimate conclusion, Aleksandrov commented that it still remained to "overcome the inertia of the alienation of theoretical work from the practice of construction." He added that such successes in naval construction as had been accomplished in practice were achieved despite all the inimical theories "precisely because they had been carried out under the direction of our Party by the Revolutionary Military Council under the direct control of the leaders of the Red Army, Comrades Frunze and Voroshilov."

Finally, Aleksandrov explicitly acknowledged a significant lag of naval theory behind practice. This should not be a cause for despondency, he asserted, but for mobilizing all the forces able to help correct the situation, particularly, the scientific workers and working-class people in the Naval War College and Leningrad filial of the Communist Academy along with those of the still valuable former tsarist naval officers who had proven to be honest. With the help of the Party, Aleksandrov vowed, there could be no doubt at all but that the lag of theory behind naval building policy would be overcome in short order.

Petrov Kicked While Down. A shorter companion piece to the lengthy Aleksandrov article just considered appeared in the same issue of *Morskoi sbornik* and obviously had been assigned the task of demolishing Professor Petrov's views. Entitled "Against Reactionary Theory in Problems of the Combat Employment of Submarines," the article concentrated its polemical fire solely on Petrov without even mentioning Gervais by name.[44]

Taking his clue, too, from Stalin's letter to the editors of *Proletarian Revolution*, the author claimed that the letter constituted an order to "decisively unmask bourgeois reactionary theory on the naval-science front and raise Bolshevik vigilance in the field of naval scientific thought." In particular, it was said to be necessary to subject the clearly inimical, defeatist theories of Petrov to Marxist-Leninist criticism since his books were still being used to train Soviet naval officers. These books, it was asserted, led readers to the conclusion that no naval warfare could be conducted whatsoever with the existing Soviet Navy.

Clearly referring to the existing Party policy of concentrating on submarine construction, the author wrote: "Stemming from the practical task facing us, it is absolutely necessary to dwell on the role and significance of the submarine weapon and how Petrov assessed it." Quoting a passage from Petrov that was admitted to acknowledge correctly that the main attack in a naval battle could be delivered by *any* given single type of naval weapon under particular circumstances, the author of the article asserted that Petrov's other writings showed that this acknowledgment had been mere window dressing to screen his secret views. The author went on at length to show what was already known— that Professor Petrov had been no submarine enthusiast.

Near the end of this article, which is of interest primarily for finally discrediting one of the two leading Old School advocates of big-ship surface navies, the author produced a quotation attributed to Petrov which read: "The attack is carried out simultaneously by all the means of the defending side: capital ships, light forces, aviation and coastal batteries." Ignoring the fact that submarines could be perfectly well subsumed under the "light forces" category, the author cried triumphantly: "But just where are the submarines? They don't even exist for Petrov . . . ." The author clearly believed he had made his point and the prosecution rested its case with the observation that "the Petrovian concept of 'the full-value squadron of the big navy' was tied in with the theory of the command of the sea." (p. 64) Obviously nothing more needed to be said. Petrov stood indicted.

Petrov Kicked Again While Down. In the same March 1932 issue of the Soviet Navy's professional journal that published Gervais' public recantation in the form of a letter to the editors (which we shall get to next), there appeared still a third article citing Stalin's letter to the editors of *Proletarian Revolution* as a directive to discredit "bourgeois-reactionary theory on the naval-science front."[45] Professor Petrov was criticized on a number of counts including his alleged support of "the active straits idea" (of seizing the Danish and Turkish straits whenever feasible). He was also accused of having been a leading exponent of an independent naval ministry and of having not only totally disregarded the need for joint cooperation with the Army for defense of the Soviet Union but of having set the Naval High Command against that of the Ground Forces. Finally, Petrov's idea of the general engagement as *the* method to gain command of the sea was denounced as a bourgeois-imperialist concept having nothing in common with Soviet policy for development of the Navy.

The Recantation of Gervais. Finally we come to the veritable verbal self-immolation of Professor Gervais in his "Letter to the Editorial Board."[46] It began by confessing that his works had contained incorrect views that were at variance with both Marxist-Leninist teachings on war and the general line of the Party.

It went on to concede that in the USSR no scientific work could be above class or outside the Party. Failure to employ the Marxist-Leninist method of dialectical materialism meant that a work could not be objective. Works based on mere outward appearance of dialectical materialism also meant that a work could not be objective. Works based on a superficial acceptance of dialectical materialism not only could not produce objective conclusions but gave harmful theoretical results. Then Gervais recanted:

> Reviewing and thinking over my naval scientific-literary works, I unreservedly acknowledge that the "theory of holding command of the sea in dispute" advanced in them constitutes in itself a "theory" which was born and developed in the process of struggle among the capitalist naval powers for division of colonies and that is imbued with the striving of the bourgeoisie for world rule over the sea lanes leading to the colonies—a theory for which the methods of implementation are outdated at the present time, even for struggle among the capitalist states, as a result of contemporary developments and the appearance of new means of struggle at sea." (p. 192)

In this final, tragic appearance in print—at least until his posthumous rehabilitation in the mid-1960s—Gervais continued his obviously forced self-denigration. After asserting that it was only the very nature of the bourgeoisie in the era of the decay of capitalism that prevented them from admitting the fallacy of such a reactionary theory as command of the sea, Gervais got to the heart of his confession of anti-Sovietism:

> I unconditionally admit that this theory which I tried to apply to the tasks of construction and to the combat training of the Naval Forces of the Red Army is a bourgeois-reactionary theory completely inapplicable to Soviet conditions and, consequently, unquestionably inimical to the requisite development of Soviet naval thought in the direction corresponding to the tasks and conditions of construction and training of the Naval Forces of the Red Army. (p. 192)

Gervais' humiliation was further prolonged; he admitted that his efforts to modernize the command-of-the-sea theory also had been harmful. Then, as the last bitter swallow, he acknowledged that, in accordance with Stalin's historic letter, he would devote all of his

> strength, knowledge, and experience [to the] implacable struggle on the theoretical front for the purity of Marxist-Leninist teaching on war and for the general line of the Party [and to] the current problems of construction, organization and combat training of the naval forces of the Red Army under the direction of the Party and the [Army High] Command. [There followed simply his signature, B. Gervais.] (p. 192)

Lack of Further Debate on Carrier Construction, 1928-1932. Before concluding the main text of this chapter, account needs to be taken of the paucity of further debate on the Navy's need for aircraft carriers. Despite the innumerable references to naval aviation in contexts in which additional discussion of the potential value of such ships for the Navy would have been highly relevant, such discussion was virtually lacking for the period from 1928 until 1932. This would seem to point to a rather strict ban on all such discussion—and one that was not eased until 1932. When the first of two volumes of the subsequently aborted *Soviet Military Encyclopedia* appeared in that year it contained an entry on "Aviation, naval" that both praised and damned the aircraft carrier.[47] On the one hand it was given full credit for being indispensable for operations of fighter aircraft at sea (beyond the effective operating radius of shore-based aircraft). It was also credited with being able to carry all types of aircraft and hence, capable of performing any mission which shore-based aviation could execute. On the other hand, the entry exaggerated the hazards of carrier flight operations:

> However, the work of wheeled aircraft at sea is constantly accompanied by great risk inasmuch as every necessary landing at sea may result in catastrophe due to the slightest trifle and not least a fire. Moreover, an aircraft carrier constitutes an exceptionally attractive target for the aviation of an enemy who will employ every measure for its destruction. Consequently, it is not to be excluded that, upon return to their forces after completing their missions, carrier-based aircraft will not find their carrier there or will find it so damaged that it would be impossible to land on it. (p. 148)

While there was an obvious element of truth in this, the use of the phrase "the slightest trifle" made it sound as if the author of this unsigned article were taking counsel of his fears although basically supporting the construction of aircraft carriers for the Soviet Navy. If the author were a naval person, it seems likely that he would have been someone of Young School persuasion and was contributing to that school's advocacy of fighting wars at sea largely with aviation, including with aircraft carriers, instead of with large battleship forces.

Whether or not the author of the entry was Army or Navy in his military service affiliation, the leading Young School advocate, A. P. Aleksandrov (and his brigade of instructors at the Naval War College), took exception to his description as constituting an unduly gloomy portrayal of the alleged great risk involved in operating aircraft from carriers and to the assertion that "the slightest trifles" might cause catastrophe. He did so in a review of the naval entries in the first volume of the *Soviet Military Encyclopedia* that appeared in the *Morskoi sbornik* in June 1932.[48]

A second entry on "Aircraft carriers" in the *Soviet Military Encyclopedia* was also criticized in the *Naval Digest* review as too general and for not mentioning the enormous cost of building and operating aircraft carriers. Nevertheless, Aleksandrov's review of this second entry betrayed his sympathy—and in all likelihood deliberately—for the procarrier advocates by making the convoluted criticism that the failure of the (unidentified) author of the entry on carriers to mention their "enormous cost" deprived the reader of any appreciation of the importance of aircraft carriers for modern imperialist navies and the consequent "frenzied construction of such ships that was said to be taking place."

Aleksandrov voiced a second criticism of the entry on aircraft carriers for failing to mention a trend, which he asserted existed, to construct light aircraft carriers of 10,000 to 15,000 tons. He alleged that this reputed trend was more significant than the one which the entry did mention—one of building heavy attack carriers by converting battle cruisers.

The most important development in this 1928-1932, period with regard to the future of aircraft carriers in the Navy came in late 1932 after the then Defense Minister, Marshal Tukhachevskiy, returned from witnessing the annual maneuvers of the Baltic Fleet. He stated publicly that the exercises demonstrated that the Navy required a new ship type that could "carry airplanes capable of climbing into the air at any moment for the defense of the capital ships against air attack."[49]

Further Analysis and Interpretation of the Evidence, 1928-1932

In this five-year period, we have seen the classical Mahanist command-of-the-sea views of the leading Old School proponents, Naval War College professors Gervais and Petrov, come under strong and concentrated polemical fire from 1928 on, by their recent students Aleksandrov, Dushenov, Ludri, and Yakimychev. These four constituted the most prominent early members of a self-styled Young School. Their unifying characteristic, despite acrimonious disagreement on the respective merits of submarines and aircraft, was the shared conviction that the command-of-the-sea doctrine that had dominated naval thinking since the turn of the century was overly ambitious (reactionary) and harmful to Soviet conditions of the time and should be replaced by a strategy more in keeping with the USSR's extremely weak naval situation, including its industrial incapacity to build large warships. The results of the Old School's views—the Young School maintained, and not without some justification—"would have disarmed us before our enemies, would have alienated the Naval Forces from the Army, and would have underestimated and ignored the effect on naval strategy of the advent of submarines and aircraft."

Being both Russians and Marxists-Leninists, Soviet leaders generally feel a compulsion to square theory with practice which more pragmatic non-Russians and non-Communists often find hard to comprehend. The Young School advocates were clearly acting under Party direction, supported by strong Army influence, and their goal was to force the Old School adherents to recant their views. Further, they wanted to provide the desired theoretical support for construction of defensive/deterrent naval forces comprised of relatively inexpensive and simple to construct submarines, aircraft, and light surface forces (such as PT boats and destroyers but including light aircraft carriers) and for retaining the old battleships and cruisers merely to provide combat support for the main force of submarines.

Professor Gervais stuck to his theoretical guns and was forced into a humiliating public confession. Professor Petrov succumbed to the pressure and so modified and suppressed his views on naval strategy, while helping elaborate the tactics for a small war by the weak Soviet Navy, that he escaped the public disgrace inflicted on Professor Gervais.[50]

The arguments for and against the command-of-the-sea doctrine have been presented in the preceding pages as fully as the available evidence allows. Some of these arguments will be recognized as having contemporary relevance despite the advent of nuclear and missile technology. It warrants mentioning that the neo-Young School rationale of the early Khrushchev years, that was to be used to justify the reversal of the Stalinist big-ship navy policy to the less expensive submarine-fleet policy favored by Khrushchev and Marshal Zhukov, exhibits a striking resemblance to the original Young School argumentation of 1928-1932.

The Decision Recounted. A number of points are particularly worth noting at this juncture. Most importantly, it is notable that despite the Young School advocates' strictures against the command-of-the-sea doctrine and big navies—as invalidated by the advent of the submarine and aircraft and supposedly, therefore, suffering an irreversible dialectical decline—they were ambiguous and contradictory in their quasi-assertions that the doctrine had lost its validity. This fact assumes particular contemporary relevance since Admiral Gorshkov in his *The Sea Power of the State*, espoused a limited command-of-the-sea doctrine of aiming at just gaining command in a sector or in a region of a theater while denying the validity of any general or full command.

It should be recalled that Professor Petrov, in 1928, as described above, denied that there could be such a phenomenon as a limited-area or regional command of the sea in just part of a naval theater of military action. This was grounded on the idea that it only preserved the form of command of the sea without accomplishing its basic aim of destroying or blockading the enemy so as to gain for one's own naval forces unfettered use of the sea while denying its use to the enemy. In other words, unless the classical Mahanist criteria were met, by which command of the sea was defined— the destruction or the neutralization by blockade of the enemy's main naval forces—any regional control that might be gained would be subject to enemy reversal at will by his bringing in more forces from other theaters and so could not properly be called command of the sea.

Also worthy of note is Aleksandrov's argument that building a primarily submarine navy has the merits of not only relieving a state of the necessity of playing the numbers game in big-ship naval construction but it also is exceptionally cost effective in comparison with the great numbers and expense of the naval forces that are required for any substantial degree of antisubmarine warfare. This argument may well be part of the present Soviet leaders' rationale for designating submarines as the basic force of their navy. Admiral Gorshkov has made the point, both in his 1972-1973 *Morskoi sbornik* series of articles and in the 1976 and 1979 editions of his book, that antisubmarine forces are disproportionately costly compared to submarines.

Yet another point of considerable current interest and relevance, because it comprises the basis for Gorshkov's long-standing justification for having big surface ships of various types in the Soviet Navy in addition to the basic striking force of submarines, is one mentioned by both Aleksandrov and Yakimychev: that big ships, including battleships, were required in the Soviet Navy to provide combat support to submarine operations at times when they are particularly vulnerable to antisubmarine warfare, i.e., leaving and reentering port. Of particular note is Aleksandrov's recommendation in May 1930 and again in April 1931, that command of the sea be considered to have been replaced by support for naval operations, usually for a main striking force of submarines by aircraft and surface combatant ships. There have been repeated articles in the *Morskoi sbornik* from 1928 up until now devoted solely to the often repeated requirement for combat support for Soviet submarines by the other types of naval forces. The context of these articles is such as to make clear that Aleksandrov's recommendations have found a strong echo in subsequent Soviet naval thought.

Another point worth noting was the apparent lifting, in 1932, of a ban existing since 1928 on discussion of aircraft carriers. Apparent were the differing views on the subject of their utility and desirable types that then emerged in two entries contained in volume 1 of the *Soviet Military Encyclopedia* and A.P. Aleksandrov's review of them. Both the unknown authors of the entries on "Aviation, naval" and "Aircraft carriers" and Aleksandrov were obviously of the Young School persuasion that favored the construction of aircraft carriers for the Soviet Navy as indispensable for fleet air support beyond the limited effective radius of shore-based fighter aircraft. However, Aleksandrov criticized the entries on three main grounds: for being unduly pessimistic regarding the hazards of carrier landing operations; for not conveying an appreciation of the importance of aircraft carriers; and for mentioning only heavy aircraft carriers to the exclusion of the data on light carriers which Aleksandrov obviously found more relevant for the USSR. After observing the 1932 maneuvers of the Baltic Fleet in his capacity as Defense Minister, Marshal Tukhachevsky reported that light carriers were required by the Navy (just) to provide air cover for the major surface combatant ships of the fleets.

An Army Retrospective. A particularly interesting Army view of what transpired in this 1928-1932 period between the Old School and the Young School in their debate over the force structure, missions, and strategies that should be adopted was published in 1968 by the well-established Army theorist, Major General Lomov.[51] He mentioned only the Young School's guerrilla-war version of the small-war strategy and passed over the Old School's small-war strategy of force equalization by gradual attrition until the day that a Mahanian-style general engagement might be undertaken to gain command of the sea—a theory that had always been anathema to the Army for reasons indicated earlier.

In this regard [to the subsequent construction of the Soviet Navy and the development of the theory of naval art], considerable interest was paid to the discussion over the issue of the doctrine of "command of the sea" and the theory of "small war." The old, classical understanding of the content of a war at sea, which was set out in the works of B. Gervais, was strongly influenced by the works of Mahan and Colomb and prescribed the mission of command of the sea, for which it was necessary to gain full command of the sea, that is, to effect the destruction of the enemy's navy or, at least, to blockade it reliably in its operating bases. The accomplishment of this mission required the creation of a corresponding navy of which the basis must be to build battleships, battle cruisers, destroyers, and auxiliary forces of submarines, mine-layers, minesweepers, etc.

These views on the character of the missions and the construction of the Soviet Navy met with the opposition of representatives of the "Young School"—I. Ludri, K. Dushenov, A. Aleksandrov, I. Isakov, A. Yakimychev and others. They held the following basic propositions. Firstly, the development of a submarine fleet and aviation fully discredits the doctrine of "command of the sea," the operational essence of which is comprised of the general engagement—the decisive part of a war at sea and the determinant of the outcome of a war. And secondly, "the construction of large, modern combatant ships requires enormous means which our country does not have at the present time. Proceeding from this, it is necessary to develop the construction of submarines, airplanes, and light surface forces in order to strengthen the coastal defense and to conduct a 'small war' at sea." The construction of capital ships, although not at all rejected by the "Young School," was made dependent on the development of a powerful heavy industry in our country.

The representatives of the "Young School" considered the missions of the Navy in the plan for a "small war," . . . to be "the defensive kind of warfare of a weaker side" against a stronger enemy who has a powerful surface fleet. They considered that "our state is not in a condition to build a powerful battleship fleet in the near future" while by constructing "a small [weak] capital-ship navy, we would play into the hands of our probable enemy. Based on this, it is expedient for us to develop naval armed forces with the means for a 'small war' and coastal defense, that is: aviation, submarines, torpedo boats and other fast, light forces of a surface fleet." It followed to place the conduct of minor operations at the basis of the action of the Navy.

Lomov's conclusions on this state of affairs is also worth noting:

The setting against each other of basic missions for the Navy and of one type of naval force against another by the proponents of these "schools" was a cardinal error. In this regard, it was necessary to bring the theory of naval art into correspondence with the actual missions of the Soviet Navy and establish a correct direction for its construction. A solution was found in a scientifically substantiated analysis and definition of missions. From it was determined the necessity for creating a modern navy which included in its structure the heterogenous forces of surface ships, submarines, and aviation. (p. 106)

Dushenov had been chosen in 1929 by the then Soviet Defense Minister, Marshal Voroshilov, to replace Professor Gervais as chief of the Naval War College. This was done with the express aim of suppressing the Old School views of Gervais and Petrov so as to bring about the correct direction mentioned above by Lomov for the subsequent construction of the navy. Admiral Kuznetsov, in his first book of memoirs, *On the Eve*, was to describe the means employed to this end as "inadmissible."[52]

The Fleet-in-Being Strategy. Upon returning to this analysis and interpretation of the evidence in Soviet naval and military writings from 1928 through 1932 after having completed draft chapters covering the developments in Soviet thinking on naval warfare during the postwar Stalinist and Khrushchev periods, the author was struck by previously unnoted evidence in this second chapter. Specifically it dealt with the two concepts of Soviet naval strategy of no little future relevance—the active fleet-in-being strategy and the Soviet School of naval warfare. Having revised the text of this chapter in a number of places to make the pertinent evidence more readily apparent, the author is able to adduce some additional but tentative findings with regard to these two key concepts.

First, as to the fleet-in-being strategy, it must be noted initially that as popularized by Sir Julian Corbett just prior to World War I, such a strategy essentially postulates a sort of "slingshot" method in dealing with the difficulty inherent to any David-Goliath confrontation for the weaker of two naval adversaries. That is, keeping the stronger fleet off balance and unable to make use of the sea for its own purposes by constant harassment, surprise raids, and efforts to successively divert and defeat smaller parts of the stronger fleet's forces in a small-war campaign of attrition until a force equalization has been achieved to the point that a general engagement of the main forces of the two sides can be sought or accepted with good prospects of victory.

Such a strategy has as its basic aim the relatively modest goal of merely holding command of the sea in dispute. This is a purely defensive aim of protecting one's own country against seaborne assault rather than the more ambitious one of gaining command of the USSR's peripheral seas for its own military use.[53] That this actually was the true state of affairs in the five-year period under consideration here is evidenced by the many references scattered throughout the main text of this second chapter which convey the Old School's advocacy of a strategy of merely "holding command of the sea in dispute." In particular, in this connection, one should note among the quotes from Professor Gervais' *mea culpa* in the March 1932 issue of *Morskoi sbornik* that the main substance of his coerced recantation was that he had mistakenly advocated the "theory of holding the command of the sea in dispute."

Confirmation that this actually had been the real substance of the naval strategy advocated by Gervais (rather than just some trumped-up pretext forced out of him by the obviously great pressure to which he was subjected by Aleksandrov and Dushenov to submit to the desired Young School party line on naval strategy) is to be found in a number of Gervais' earlier statements, but most explicitly in his definition of the offensive aspect of the kind of a small-war strategy which he espoused. In both his lectures at the Naval War College in 1919-1921 and in the 1923 edition of his three-edition book, *Significance of Sea Power for the State*, he called for operations against an enemy navy calculated to "weaken the main forces of an enemy in all [possible] ways" in order to "create for oneself a more favorable correlation of forces . . . and thereby to prepare favorable conditions for shifting to warfare for holding the command of the sea in dispute." That Gervais held steadfast to this basic view of the correct strategy for the weaker Soviet Navy up until at least through 1928 is reflected by its restatement in essentially the same form in his article in *Morskoi sbornik* in December of that year.

Moreover, evidence is to be found in the Old School writings of the 1928-1932 period that, although the small-war strategy advocated by the two leading proponents of that school, Professors Gervais and Petrov, was never overtly described as tantamount to an active fleet-in-being strategy, those two Old School theorists in fact must have been well aware of the remarkably close correspondence of the two strategies. There were even some hints at the great similarity in at least two of their articles.

Thus Professor Petrov actually used the term "fleet in being" in his May 1928 article in *Morskoi sbornik*. The reason he resorted to a particularly vague double foreign navy and historical surrogate may have been to protect himself from a likely accusation that he favored what—with virtual certainty under the existing circumstances of unbridled acrimony—would have been castigated by the Young School as a bourgeois strategy congenial only to capitalist imperialism. Rather, in defending himself against a Young School attack alleging that he had failed to appreciate the advantages of the defensive in naval strategy (as opposed to advocating only taking the offensive), Petrov responded that he had been tendentiously misinterpreted. The substance of his rejoinder was that, far from having advocated "invariably offensive operations," as had been charged, he fully appreciated that, while all of the great powers in the World War had grounded their war plans for land warfare on the strategic offensive, they had all based their plans for a war at sea on the defensive fleet-in-being strategy. The implication seemed to be that such a strategy was still the appropriate one for the weaker of two major navies and that if the USSR wanted to live up to its potential greatness, the Soviet Navy should also adopt a fleet-in-being strategy.

Similarly, in an article published in the same professional naval journal eight months later, Professor Gervais made essentially the same association between the small-war strategy that he openly advocated and the fleet-in-being strategy. Disdaining to take such deep double surrogate cover as had Petrov, Gervais resorted only to a single surrogate as was normal for all such discussions of strategic matters in the open press. Employing a foreign naval-theorist surrogate in his article on the small-war strategy in December 1928, Gervais observed that the Italian theorist Romeo Bernotti was advocating a strategy of "holding the command of the sea in dispute" as the correct one for the weaker of two belligerent navies. Such a strategy was defined by Bernotti, as Gervais explained it, as intended to "prevent a stronger enemy from using command of the sea for goals of important significance" by dint of depriving him of the advantage that normally accrues to the stronger navy as a direct consequence of its superiority of being enabled to "carry out the movement of his military and commercial ships in comparative security." Precisely to prevent such movements was the main aim of the small-war strategy, according to Gervais' further interpretation of Bernotti.

Gervais went on to define the small war in terms typical of the fleet-in-being strategy, stating that his views on the small war were similar to the views of Corbett (the foremost advocate of the fleet-in-being strategy for an "inferior" navy). Simply put, Corbett's was the correct strategy for a navy so much weaker than its adversary that it could entertain no realistic hope of being able to attrite that adversary's main forces a part at a time until cut down to manageable size so that a general engagement could be fought to victory. Inasmuch as Gervais had cited Bernotti with the consent that silence gives as having stipulated that a weaker navy could only hope to hold command of the sea in dispute if it had at least two-thirds as many battleships and battle cruisers as its opponent, it seems likely that Gervais deliberately was making it clear that the small-war strategy which he had so long advocated was quintessentially a fleet-in-being strategy intended to hold the command of Soviet coastal waters in dispute and that just to do this would require a force of capital ships two-thirds as strong as the enemy's.

In addition to the above intimations that Petrov and Gervais were conveying in 1928 to all of the readers of the Aesopian communications normal to Soviet naval and military writings, a definition of "fleet in being" published in the Great Soviet Encyclopedia in 1930 may be seen to have been tailored to the USSR's least unsatisfactory option for a naval strategy in view of its weakness: "retaining one's naval forces close to one's shores, constantly threatening the enemy with battle under unfavorable circumstances while making it impossible for him to make amphibious landings on one's own shores."

From all of the foregoing, it seems warranted to at least hypothesize that the top naval leadership, and hence probably the Army and Party leadership as well, were aware of the clone-like resemblance of the Soviet Old School's version of the small-war strategy to one of fleet-in-being, but preferred not to accord it recognition *per se*. For the Old School's part, they probably avoided making the connection of the two strategies explicitly, not only to avoid the Young School criticism it would invite but also to avoid advertising the lack of originality of the Old School theorists.

The Soviet School. On balance, it would seem that out of the Young School's hounding of the Old School in the 1928-1932 period came some real progress for the long run of ensuring that the combat capabilities of the submarine and aircraft would never again be underestimated in Soviet strategy for naval warfare. And to that extent, the disputes between the schools of naval strategy of this period were indeed to lead to a more objective appreciation of the capabilities and limitations of both the light, fast forces of the Young School and the capital ships of the Old School. This brings us directly to the second of the two subjects already identified as of key importance for the subsequent development of the Soviet Navy—the "Soviet School" of naval warfare.

What is markedly noticeable in the evidence for this period are the expressions of *need* for a new Soviet strategy to take into account the unique and rapidly increasing capabilities that submarines and aircraft (and aircraft carriers, although any explicit mention of them during the period was rare up until 1932) were bringing to the conduct of naval warfare. By 1930 Aleksandrov was asserting that a correct understanding of the lessons of the World War for Soviet naval strategy revealed that the theory of command of the sea was completely unsound and had led to a search being undertaken by the Young School for a new strategy that would enable the Soviet Navy to carry out the necessary missions in any future war. However, he insisted, the continued dominance of the command-of-the-sea concept was obstructing the search and would have to be discredited before that search could be successful.

Gervais, as the leading exponent of the Old School's small-war strategy of holding command of the sea of the USSR's peripheral seas in dispute by building up large surface fleets to be maintained in those seas, was excoriated for advocating, in effect, that the USSR enter a naval arms race with the other great powers that it lacked the industrial capacity to win. Rather, he was urged, by Aleksandrov particularly, to circumvent the Law of Numbers by placing the main emphasis on submarine construction rather than on capital ships.

Even more directly to the point is the implication in Aleksandrov's writings that the new strategy being sought would go beyond the Young School's emphasis on submarines, aviation, and light, fast surface forces—an indictment of Gervais and the other Old School advocates for their "underestimation and ignoring of the new technology which was being introduced into the Soviet Navy and changing its strategy and tactics." In a remark revealing the wellsprings of his vendetta against the Old School advocates, particularly Professor Gervais, Aleksandrov observed that by their alleged ignoring of the changes in naval warfare being wrought by submarines, aircraft, and improved coastal artillery, Gervais and Petrov had placed themselves in total opposition to the Party-Army line on the matter of naval shipbuilding policy. That line appeared to be largely based on economics, in general, and in particular on the industrial weakness of the USSR that ruled out as unfeasible any policy of undertaking a naval arms race in capital ships.

There is no evidence to be found in Soviet writings that Aleksandrov and the other young turks of the Young School had discerned the shape that the Soviet School would eventually take by combining the most utilitarian features of both the Old School and the Young School. Otherwise they almost certainly would have voiced their insight loudly and on every occasion, with the aim of eliciting more support for their campaign of polemical argumentation against the Old School. At any rate, while apparently not foreseeing the evolution of a Soviet School *per se*, Aleksandrov did advocate new methods for Soviet operational art which were to become the norm for that composite school of naval strategy: "successive combined operations," which were intended to replace the "general engagement," the primary operational manifestation of the command-of-the-sea theory and combat support for the designated main striking force (of submarines) by the other naval forces, as feasible—which was intended to compensate for inability to destroy or blockade an adversary's main naval forces.

The Old School neither predicted, at least not publicly, the form and content of the Soviet School of naval strategy nor the force structure of the Soviet fleets that would be required. One Young School adherent, Yakimychev, did foresee the basic changes that would be required. He observed in a September 1928 article in *Morskoi sbornik*, that the Young School did not reject in principle either command-of-the-sea theory or battleships. Their view was that the Soviet Union was forced to take expedient recourse to a small-war strategy until such future time as changed conditions enabled the USSR to develop the industrial capacity to build capital ships cheaply and rapidly enough to be prepared for the still feared amphibious invasion by the capitalist powers. Thus, it may be concluded that the 1928-1932 data did yield indications of the impending birth of a distinctively Soviet school of naval warfare.

In a prepublication serialization in 1965 of *On the Eve* in the literary journal *Oktabr*, Kuznetsov made the only explicit reference on the public record to a Soviet School of naval warfare, yet it was one definite enough to warrant its adoption to denote the synthesis of Young School partisanship for submarines,[54] aircraft, and light, fast surface ships with the Old School's fixation on capital ships. Kuznetsov stated (in a passage excised from his book):

> It was clear to us that the theory of the American historian Mahan and the Britisher Colomb of "command of the sea" in contemporary circumstances was reactionary. We were all of like mind that the Navy alone, without the Army, could not accomplish the basic missions of a war. The *Soviet School* [emphasis supplied] armed us, the young commanders, with advanced theory and this favorably affected all that followed.

And if Admiral Kuznetsov's above quoted description of the "advanced theory"—learned at the Naval War College—is taken literally to indicate that his rejection of part of both Old and Young Schools and acceptance of other parts of both constituted a Soviet School (Sovetskaya shkola) of naval strategy, then one is led to the conclusion that a new school known by that name had indeed been formed by the early thirties, while Kuznetsov was a graduate student at the Naval War College. Whether or not Kuznetsov can be taken literally, the name "Soviet School" admirably fills the bill to describe such a school's essentially Castexian[55] strategy of absorbing the less expensive, light, fast forces of the Young School into the costly capital ship fleets of the Old School along with that limited version of the latter's command-of-the-sea strategy which the Soviet School considered suitable for an inferior navy.

View from the Other Side of the Ring. In concluding this second chapter, the same Army account that was quoted in the first chapter will be continued here for the view from the "other side" which it provides for the 1928-1932 period. The source was a 1981 book by an Army colonel which bore the title *History of Soviet Thought*:[56]

> In the second half of the '20s and early '30s the Naval Department [of the Army] worked out a plan for military shipbuilding. A basic line was taken for the construction of submarines, PT boats, aviation, and a surface fleet without battleships and cruisers. It was precisely in these years that an agitated discussion took place in the press and at the Naval War College as to what navy was needed for the country.

> The [Young School] partisans of a so-called mosquito fleet advocated the energetic development of a submarine fleet and of naval aviation. Championing the feasibility of employing submarines and aviation in independent naval operations, they simultaneously emphasized the necessity for mutual cooperation with the Ground Forces. (p. 179)

> The views of the proponents of the second [Old School] course did not receive extensive development in the '20s because industry was not adequately developed, the wherewithal was lacking, and the Navy was limited to the restoration of old combatant ships. In discussions at the Naval War College at the outset of the '30s, they advocated the creation of a powerful surface fleet while according submarine construction its due. (p. 181)

Notes

1. Ivan Martynovich Ludri, who was only 22 at the time of the October Revolution, had good credentials as a Bolshevik sailor. He had served as Commandant of the Kronstadt Fortress in 1919 and then as political commissar of the Onega Flotilla. In 1921 he was appointed Chief of the Caspian Naval Forces. After completion of the Naval War College, he served successively as Commander of the Coastal Defenses

of the Black Sea and Chief of Staff of the Black Sea Fleet before his appointment in 1932 as Deputy Chief of the Naval Forces of the Red Army.

2. "Thus, we have at this time a small navy. With this we must be reconciled, whether we like it or not, but just how should we construct it? B. B. Gervais points out one way to us . . . that in creating the navy we must always foresee its further growth and *always* consider that the crown of its construction is the creation of a navy capable of holding the command of the sea in dispute. All other paths are, so to speak, 'naval deviations.' Thus, the creation of specific means of coastal defense are *unquestionably bad* deviations in the creation of naval forces designated for the active defense of our Great Union." I. Ludri, "O taktike malogo flota" ("Concerning the Tactics of a Small Navy"), *Morskoi sbornik*, March 1928, p. 21.

3. Konstantin Ivanovich Dushenov, who like Ludri was 22 at the time the Bolsheviks seized power in Russia in 1917, had impressive credentials as a revolutionary Bolshevik. He had served in 1916 and 1917 as a yeoman on the cruiser *Aurora* that had fired the opening gun of the coup and had taken an active part in the Civil War. Subsequent to his graduation from the Naval War College, he served briefly at sea and was sent back as both the "nachal'nik" (chief) and political "komissar" of the Naval War College where he allegedly was successful in carrying out Defense Minister Voroshilov's personal orders, in December 1929, to whip into line with Marxist views the professional staff of the Naval War College which supported "the theory of the general naval engagement" (i.e., command of the sea). See P. I. Mus'yakov, "Flagman K. I. Dushenov," *Morskoi sbornik*, October 1963, pp. 52, 76-80.

4. Konstantin Dushenov. "K istorii voprosa o 'maloi voine' na more" ["On the History of 'the Small War' at Sea"] , *Morskoi sbornik*, April 1928, pp. 29-44.

5. M. Petrov, "K postanovke voprosa o 'maloi voine'" ["Toward a Formulation of the Question of the 'Small War'"], *Morskoi sbornik*, February 1928, pp. 37-47; March 1928, pp. 3-18; May 1928, pp. 36-46; June 1928, pp. 3-20; and July to August 1928, pp. 8-21, (five articles by the same title).

6. "This addresses only the external appearance of 'command.' The aim of the theory—destruction or blockade—is here not considered; *all that remains of the theory is the form.*" (March, p. 6.)

7. "As long as the particular theory [of command of the sea] is propagated, as long as it pretends to the position of 'official doctrine' of the small navy will it contain within itself elements of alienation of naval strategy from ground force strategy." (March, p. 8.)

8. Aleksander Mikhaylovich Yakimychev had won his wings as a naval aviator in 1917, at the age of 20. From 1926 until 1931 he was a faculty member of the Naval War College. He mentioned in his article that he had interviewed Professor Petrov, which apparently led him to separate his from Gervais' views and place them in a school all unto themselves. Yakimychev's last known assignment was as an assistant Soviet naval attaché in Washington in 1934. This assignment abroad, as well as his views on naval strategy, probably led to his death in 1938 in Stalin's purge, which claimed many of the participants in the Young School-Old School debate on the best strategy for the naval side of a general war.

9. A. M. Yakimychev, "Voina 'malym (slabym) flotom' i malaya voina' v epokhu parovoga flota" ["War of a 'Small (Weak) Navy' and the 'Small War' in the Era of the Steam Navy"], *Morskoi sbornik*, September 1928, pp. 44-46. The reader should recall the first appearance of Yakimychev's name on a *Red Fleet* article in 1923 that called for aircraft carriers to enable the Navy to fight battles (rather than merely for providing air cover and reconnaissance for the fleets).

10. It seems that the Old School and Young School sobriquets were already in use at the Naval War College by the Young School adherents since Yakimychev states in a footnote that "we refer to the opposing views as 'schools' with the aims of convenience and simplicity." He commented (p. 48) that the Young School included some representatives from the Army who concerned themselves with naval problems for one reason or another. Marshal Tukhachevskiy was cited as having partly set forth Young School views in an article, "Strategiya organizatsii" ["Strategy of Organization"], in the Soviet military journal *Voyenniy vestnik*, No. 28, 1924. Tukhachevskiy's sole point in this short article was to argue that the USSR must not repeat the alleged error of prewar Russia, Germany, and Austria in spending so much on naval forces that the Army was neglected. The implication would seem to be that Tukhachevskiy favored building (only) Young School forces on the subjective grounds that the relatively less costly light forces required would not detract from the Army's share of the defense budget.

11. "As a result of rather heated discussions, the leaders of the Strategy Department acknowledged that, with the appearance on the scene of new means for war at sea (the submarine and air fleets), the theory of 'command of the sea' had suffered some breaches; as soon as the official doctrine was compromised in the eyes of the realistically inclined students, a 'search' began for a new theory for warfare at sea."

12. On 1 April 1966, 38 years later, the then Soviet Defense Minister, Marshal Rodion Malinovsky, was to state in his accountability report to the XXIII Party Congress that the Soviet Union had established a "Blue Belt of Defense," which was shown by analysis to impose on the Navy precisely the same limitation to a perimeter defense (although grown to oceanic proportions with the advance of technology) against which Yakimychev had railed in 1928. For details see the author's "The USSR's 'Blue Belt of Defense' Concept" in Paul J. Murphy, ed., *Naval Power in Soviet Policy*, v. 2 in the U.S. Air Force's "Studies in Communist Affairs," (Washington: U.S. Govt. Print. Off., 1978), pp. 169-178.

13. Under this point Yakimychev asserted that, "Large numbers of means is *the* basic condition for success, as shown by both the experience of the World War and by theoretical conclusions." He also justified the large numbers of weapons systems which he claimed would be necessary by the alleged requirement that the favored combined-arms strike tactic of all types of weapons systems must be sustained over "a protracted period of time" to insure success against the main forces of the enemy. (p. 65.)

14. Interestingly, this professed need to establish a unity of views in the Party and government to ensure the success of Soviet naval strategy is the identical expression used nearly a half century later in the editorial introduction to Admiral Gorshkov's unprecedentedly frank and detailed series of 11 articles on "Navies in War and Peace" published in *Morskoi sbornik* during 1972 and in early 1973. Such calls for "a unity of views" recur repeatedly in Soviet naval writings and usually are indictive of army opposition to naval ambitions that are seen as a threat either to diminish the army's share of the defense budget or the navy's support of the ground forces' coastal flanks in wartime, or both. (p. 66.)

15. B. Gervais, "Osnovnye voprosy (K diskusii o 'maloi voine')" [Fundamental Problems ("Toward a Discussion of 'Small War'")], *Morskoi sbornik*, December 1928, pp. 8-28.

16. "Also, I cannot but lament the ill-considered haste with which some comrades would bury the 'Old School' of our naval thought, setting up in its place a 'Young School.' Every conceptual work that has practical significance must follow the process of 'dialectical change' which characterizes revolutionary 'leaps' . . . . Premature burial of the 'Old School,' as history demonstrates, carries with it no little danger. In the history of the development of naval power of contemporary (bourgeois) France, a very unfortunate notoriety attaches to the very term 'Young School' [the *Jeune École* strategy of sea denial with a 'mosquito fleet' solely of light, fast forces that was dominant in France in the 1890s and is associated with the name of Admiral Theophile Aube]." (p. 9.)

17. Gervais quoted this passage from his book *Significance of Sea Power for the State [Znachenie morskoi sily dlya gosudarstva]*, which had appeared in three editions in 1921, 1923, and 1925. Although this book is unavailable in the West, the similarity in title to Admiral Gorshkov's two editions (1976 and 1979) of *Sea Power of the State [Morskaya moshch' gosudarstva]* raises the possibility that the former work served as a precedent and model for the latter.

18. Gervais also quoted the part giving this second definition of the small-war strategy from his book, *Significance of Sea Power for the State*, and went on to stress the importance for the blockaded fleet of maintaining a constant appearance of readiness to sortie to engage the blockading fleet. This should exhaust the opponent and degrade his readiness and so contribute to the attrition process of force-equalization, Gervais maintained. As Gervais expressed it:

> The main forces of the blockaded fleet should at all times in a small war give every sign of readiness for active forms of action in order not to permit the blockading fleet to weaken its forces standing watch on the blockade line. This apparent readiness for action on the part of the blockaded force—for example, to quickly sortie its main forces from their bases and undertake a firefight with the blockading forces—is the best means to keep the blockading fleet under constant pressure and to deny him the possibility of resting or making repairs in his maneuvering bases. The condition of the blockading forces can be exacerbated to the utmost by such measures, personnel will become exhausted, nerves will be overstrained, and the machinery of their ships will break down. All of these circumstances will steadily create more favorable conditions for the success of "small-war" operations. The main forces of the blockaded navy must closely observe the progress of this "small war" and choose the right moment when the weakening of the morale and material condition enables the blockaded force to shift to a prompt and most decisive offensive employing all of its forces for exploitation of the success achieved. (pp. 49-50)

19. A. P. Aleksandrov, "Kritika teorii vladeniya morem" ["A Critique of the Theory of Command of the Sea"], *Morskoi sbornik*, November 1929, pp. 3-27; February 1930, pp. 33-47; March 1930, pp. 1-16; and April 1930, pp. 27-45.

20. Aleksander Petrovich Aleksandrov was only 17 by 1917, took no part in the October Revolution that his biographers have found worth mentioning, but is credited with having been an active participant in the Civil War. Within a year after completing the Naval War College and the Leningrad filial of the Communist Academy in 1928, he was appointed a political commissar and Chief of the Department of Strategy and Operational Art at the Naval War College and held those posts until 1934. Aleksandrov was reported in V. A. Belli's July 1939 article "The Fundamentals of Operation at Sea" in *Morskoi sbornik* to have been unmasked as an enemy of the people for having one-sidedly favored submarines and airplanes at the expense of surface ships. Not surprisingly, this unpleasant reminder of Stalin's great purge and the mutual denunciations it had caused among colleagues—Belli had coauthored a book with Aleksandrov six years earlier—suffered ellipsis when Belli's article was reprinted in 1965 in *Questions of Strategy and Operational Art in Soviet Military Works 1917-1940* (p. 732). Aleksandrov survived the Stalinist purge and served as a flotilla commander and as Chief of Staff of the Baltic Fleet during World War II. He is reported to have died in a plane crash in 1945, by which time he had become a rear admiral.

21. Aleksandrov credited British Vice Admiral Phillip Colomb with having originated the command-of-the-sea theory in his 1890 work *Morskaya voina* [Naval Warfare], *Morskoi sbornik*, November 1929, p. 3.

22. Petrov's March 1928 article in *Morskoi sbornik*, already discussed, was quoted. (p. 4.)

23. Gervais had been the only writer to have publicly put forward the idea that the advent of the submarine and airplane had made breaches in the theory, but perhaps out of deference to his position as Chief of the Naval War College, his viewpoint was referred to only as "coming from a direction known to us."

24. Aleksandrov dramatized his assertions by alleging that the war had been a transition point that had thrown naval science into a great crisis by showing the bankruptcy of the command-of-the-sea doctrine that constituted the basis of naval science. (February 1930, p. 33.)

25. "To ignore the basic changes taking place in the conditions of warfare at sea and to insist on applying the theory of the struggle for command of the sea under contemporary circumstances of naval warfare would mean to lose all directing theoretical perspective and to lag far and hopelessly behind the changes taking place in the practice of war at sea." (February 1930, p. 33)

26. "However, in view of the fact that the theory of command of the sea is still dominant in modern naval scientific literature, without an exhaustive criticism of that theory which destroys it there cannot be a systematic approach to the correct working out of all the existing current problems of the Naval Forces—tactical, strategic, and constructional and especially the practical tasks of the material support of the construction of the Red Navy."

27. As examples of "world literature" which he claimed were also attempting to modernize the command-of-the-sea doctrine in one aspect or another, Aleksandrov cited two works published the year before. The first was the German historian Otto Groos' *Seekriegslehren im Lichte des Weltkrieges* (*Lessons of Naval Warfare in Light of the World War*). The second was French Admiral Raoul Castex' *Theories strategiques* (*Strategic Theories*).

28. In this connection, Aleksandrov argued that, due to imperialist hostility, the USSR would have to practice economic autarchy and that the possibility of forming an alliance with any of the capitalist states was closed to Moscow, (February 1930, p. 42.)

29. Aleksandrov noted in passing one aspect of the matter that Admiral Gorshkov was to raise again in the seventies—the disproportionately large numbers of ships and personnel required for antisubmarine warfare in comparison to the relatively small number needed for submarine warfare. He mentioned as an example that the British in the World War had found it necessary to build over 4,000 antisubmarine-warfare ships, a disparity in the order of perhaps 100 to 1.

30. Aleksandrov mentioned that, after the start of the unrestricted submarine-warfare campaign, the battleships and cruisers were relegated to the task of providing covering "support" for the German minesweepers that preceded each submarine as it transited the British-laid minefields both in leaving and returning to port. (April 1930, p. 35.) This is interesting both because Soviet writings in the seventies flatly denied that such support was given and because this tactical method is still in use and is known as the breakthrough (into the open oceans).

31. Aleksandrov stopped short of an explicit enunciation of such a radical policy prescription. He achieved the same result indirectly by recommending that the USSR should employ such forces as it could build in the near future. Since Soviet industry was still a decade away from any capability for constructing battleships or cruisers and, particularly, since he had just stated that submarines were uniquely capable of invalidating the Law of Numbers, his preference for submarines was unmistakable. (April 1930, pp., 38-39.)

32. The work cited was P.V. Gel'mersen's new book, *Operatsii na zapadnykh teatrakh* [*Operations in the Western Theatres*] (Leningrad: Naval War College Press, 1927). Since Professor Gervais reportedly wrote the preface to this book (no copy of which has found its way to Western libraries), Aleksandrov's attack on its author may have been generally viewed as another attack on Gervais and the Old School in general.

33. That command-of-the-sea doctrine was still dominant in the Soviet Union in 1930 was borne out by the inclusion of an entry on "Command of the Sea" in v. 18 of the 1st ed. of the *Great Soviet Encyclopedia* which was published that year. This lengthy entry (four full columns) was most notable for its classical definition of command of the sea ("such control as excludes enemy naval operations"), for its classical division of command of the sea into absolute, conditional, and disputed, and for defining fleet-in-being in a way particularly suited to Soviet conditions: "retaining one's naval forces close to one's shores, constantly threatening the enemy with battle in unfavorable circumstances while making it impossible for him to make amphibious landings on one's own shores." O. Solonnikov, "Gospodstvo na more" ("Command of the Sea"), *Bol'shaya Sovetskaya Entsiklopediya*, 1st ed., v. 18, 1930, pp. 270-274. (Of note is the fact that no entry for "command of the sea" was included in the 1953 (2nd) or 1973 (3rd) eds. of the *Great Soviet Encyclopedia*). Volume 21 of the same encyclopedia (which appeared in 1931) contained an unsigned article (later attributed to Admiral Ivan Isakov) on "Amphibious Landing Operations" which claimed (p. 542) that absolute command of the sea had been made impossible by the advent of the submarine and aircraft, due to the alleged fact that these two types of naval forces could not be blockaded. (April 1930, p. 45.)

34. A. Yakimychev, "Perelomnyi etap v razvitii metodov i sredstv vedeniya voiny na Baltiiskom more v voinu 1914-1917 gg" ["The Transition Stage in the Development of the Methods and Means of the Conduct of War in the Baltic Sea in the War of 1914-1917"], *Morskoi sbornik*, March 1931, p. 24.

35. A.P. Aleksandrov, "Iz diskussii po dokladu I. Yakimychev 'Perelomnyi etap v razvitii metodov i sredstv vedeniya voiny na Baltiiskom more v voinu 1914-1917 g.'" ["From the Discussion on the Report of Comrade Yakimychev 'Transitional State in the Development of the Methods and Means for the Conduct of War in the Baltic Sea in the War of 1914-1917'"], *Morskoi sbornik*, April 1931, p. 30.

36. Here Aleksandrov was quoting from a book which he had authored titled *Kritika teorii vladeniya morem* [*Criticism of the Theory of Command of the Sea*] which had been printed at the Naval War College in 1930 and may be assumed to have been quite similar to the four articles on the subject he had published in *Naval Digest* in late 1929 and the first five months of 1930. Like most of the other key Soviet naval books of the 1920s and 1930s, not a single copy seems to have found its way into any library of the Western World.

37. .The reader may recall that in his May 1930 *Morskoi sbornik* article Aleksandrov advocated that preliminary "support" for operations be considered the correct successor to command of the sea. Now he was revising his view to the extent that "direct [i.e., simultaneous, not preliminary] combat support" was to be one of four substitutes for command of the sea.

38. "From the discussion on the Report of Comrade Yakimychev . . . ," p. 35.

39. I. Stalin, "O nekotorykh voprosakh istorii Bol'shevizma" ["On Certain Questions about the History of Bolshevism"], *Proletarskaya revolyutsiya*, No. 6, 1931, pp. 3-13 and editorial apology, p. 14.

40. A. P. Aleksandrov, "Protiv reaktsionnykh teorii na voenno-morskom nauchnom fronte" ["Against Reactionary Theory on the Naval Science Front"], *Morskoi sbornik*, February 1932, pp. 28-58. This article was said to be a shortened version of a speech Aleksandrov had given to the Leningrad filial of the Communist Academy on 17 February 1932.

41. The column and line-of-bearing battle tactics of the battleship fleet were to be replaced by encirclement tactics that would permit simultaneous, continuing strikes from all directions.

42. "In order to be capable of holding command of the sea in dispute, contemporary naval forces, just the same for the weaker as for the stronger, must be composed of a combatant fleet made up of a brigade of battleships, cruisers, divisions of destroyers, submarines, seaplane tenders." (p. 52.)

43. Svechin had praised Petrov's view of the naval blockade as an exceptionally valuable and original contribution in that it had applied to naval strategy Svechin's then unpopular theory of "siege"—"the theory of the siege at sea" as Svechin put it.

44. B. Kotlovskiy, "Protiv reaktsionnykh teoriy v voprosakh boyevogo ispol'zovaniya podvodnykh lodok" ["Against Reactionary Theory in Problems of the Combat Employment of Submarines"], *Morskoi sbornik*, February 1932, pp. 59-65.

45. N. Basistiy, "Vrazhdebnaya ideologiya pod flagom neitral'nosti" ["Inimical Ideology Under the Flag of Neutrality"], *Morskoi sbornik*, March 1932, pp. 9-13.

46. B. Gervais, "Pis'mo v redaktsiy" ["Letter to the Editorial Board"], *Morskoi sbornik*, March, 1932, pp. 191-192.

47. "Aviatsiya, morskaya" ["Naval Aviation"], *Sovetskaya voennaya entsiklopediya*, v. 1, 1932, p. 148.

48. A. P. Aleksandrov, *Morskoi sbornik*, June 1932, p. 151.

49. M. N. Tukhachevskiy, *Izbrannye proizvedeniya* [*Selected Works*], v. 1, 1965, p. 15.

50. Ironically, as Soviet naval theory after Khrushchev shifted back to a composite Soviet School that adopted at least a limited version of Gervais' command-of-the-sea theory, it has been Gervais not Petrov who has been rehabilitated and whose biography appears in the *Soviet Military Encyclopedia* and who is cited with approval by Gorshkov in his *Sea Power of the State*.

51. N. Lomov, "Sbornik trudov o razvitii teorii Sovetskogo voennogo iskusstva v mezhvonnym periode," *Voenno-istoricheskiy zhurnal* [*Military-Historical Journal*], January 1968, p. 106. This was a review of a book *Questions of Strategy and Operational Art in Soviet Military Works, 1917-1940* [*Voprosy strategii i operativnogo iskusstva v Sovetskikh voyennykh trudakh, 1917-1940*], that had been published in 1965 by the Soviet Defense Ministry and contained selected excerpts from the works of both the Old and Young schools—and which already has been quoted from several times.

52. N.G. Kuznetsov, *Nakanune* (*On the Eve*), 1966, p. 51. With all of the evidence cited above that Gervais' *mea culpa* in 1932 was coerced out of him under great pressure, Kuznetsov's characterization of the methods used seems justified despite the unequivocal Old School leanings of the officer Stalin selected in 1938 and again in 1950 to build a "big sea and oceanic navy worthy of the great Soviet power." In *On the Eve* Kuznetsov recalls the "fiery debates" of the early thirties when he was a student at the Naval War College. He claims that the Young School's contention that the submarine could not be blockaded was disproved by wargaming charts and the majority of the staff and students took the "correct line" of supporting construction of [all] types of surface ships commensurate with the economy but "still according the necessary attention to submarines and PTs."

53. It was this distinction between merely holding the command in dispute and gaining a limited command that eluded the present author in his 1968 book, *Soviet Naval Strategy: Fifty Years of Theory and*

Practice, which resulted in making Stalin's long-range strategy for the naval side of a general war appear more ambitious in oceanic sea-control terms than it actually was.

54. N.G. Kuznetsov, *Oktyabr*, August 1965, p. 170.

55. "The works of French Admiral Raoul Castex," it was stated in the Soviet book *Blockade and Counterblockade*, "were directed primarily to naval warfare for command of the sea but nevertheless took into account the role of submarines in that warfare." (V. Belli and K.V. Penzin, *Blokada i kontrblokada*, 1967, p. 83).

56. I.A. Korotkov, *Istoriya Sovetskoi voennoi mysli* [*A History of Soviet Military Thought*], [Nauka Press, 1981].

III
All Spoils to the Young Victor
—Briefly—1933-1936

The Evidence and Some Partial Analysis

Command of the Sea Further Hit by Aleksandrov et. al.[1] In 1933 in the USSR, A. Aleksandrov, I. Isakov, and V. Belli[2] published *Submarine Operations*, a book that analyzed Germany's unrestricted submarine warfare in World War I and concluded *inter alia* that the war experience demonstrated that command of the sea had been discredited as an operational doctrine. Written by three Naval War College instructors in the Department of Strategy and Operational Art (Aleksandrov was head of the department), this last major Young School work in the interwar period holds a number of points of interest for the evolution of Soviet strategic thought on naval warfare.

The authors surmised that despite the very limited number of German submarines available relative to the size of the mission, they were dedicated to forcing Britain out of the war by interdiction of the latter's sea communications. This effort enjoyed some significant successes in the first years of the war, both against merchant ships and against the British warships employed in escorting convoys of those ships. The authors noted that the submarines were given invaluable support by the German High Seas Fleet surface and air forces in the form of escort in and out of port, reconnaissance, and mining designed to limit British antisubmarine operations. This support was said to have been so effective that it changed the whole character and tempo of the war at sea.

Submarines, they said, had proven to be a formidable weapon against major combatant ships—battleships and cruisers—and were successful both in restricting their employment at sea and in requiring a major diversion of other naval forces for their protection from submarine attack. Aleksandrov, Isakov and Belli asserted that the German submarines had been most effective in attacking British surface warships in joint operations with surface and air forces after preliminary attacks by the latter had reduced the British ships' freedom of maneuver. Such joint operations received only primitive development in World War I but enough for the Germans to recognize the need for their further development, even though they were unable to accomplish it themselves.

From the German experience, the authors concluded that submarines must not be assigned an anti-shipping mission without combat support by air and surface forces. Moreover, whenever submarines were to be assigned as the main striking force against major enemy surface warship formations, they would have to receive the full support of all other naval forces if their capabilities were to be fully realized.

A major conclusion to emerge from the book was that possession of a large number of submarines would permit an exceptional wealth of operational and tactical options. Appearing at a time when the USSR was still planning the big submarine-building program of the second 5-year plan, the book's emphasis on the importance of having large numbers of submarines available at the outbreak of war is likely to have had a definitive impact on Soviet shipbuilding policy and may well have provided the necessary theoretical justification for the program.

The book returned to Aleksandrov's earlier argument that the German submarines had breached the "law of numbers" by successfully running the British blockade and had remained invincible despite colossal antisubmarine-warfare developments. It was asserted that the possibility of achieving victory with single-type forces, a euphemism for battleships, had been discredited by the World War I experience. Also "finally discredited as the decisive element of a war at sea and as the determinant of the outcome of a war as a whole," the authors alleged, were "the operational essence of the doctrine of command of the sea and its tactical manifestation, the general engagement."

The Old School's Last Gasp: Ivanov and Smirnov. In mid-1933 the Soviet naval historian, Academician Lev Ivanov, and his collaborator P. Smirnov published a book, *Anglo-American Naval Rivalry*, that included a defense of the Old School and of command-of-the-sea doctrine.[3] It contained an illuminating chapter, "The Essence of War at Sea," which defined command of the sea in a classical manner: obtaining such control over sea communications as to "ensure the transit of one's own goods and to prevent that of any other's goods."

Professor Gervais was reported to have been responsible for introducing "possession of the sea" as an alternative for "command of the sea" in an unsuccessful effort to make the concept less objectionable.[4] But the new term failed to find acceptance. The problem was its literal meaning: Ivanov noted that in contrast with land operations, it is not possible to "possess" the sea beyond the limits of territorial waters and coastal defense artillery, although a naval presence can be maintained. But clearly Ivanov was much more concerned with refuting the argument of the Young School that the advent of the airplane and submarine had invalidated the concept of command of the sea. He expressed the term in English as well as in its two most used Russian wordings.

Command of the sea, Ivanov continued, could be either general or local, and either constant or temporary. It did *not* mean that an adversary could not do anything. It did mean that he could not frustrate the plans for a given naval operation of a belligerent who had gained command of the sea.

Furthermore, *Anglo-American Naval Rivalry* countered the Old School of Soviet military doctrine, as applied to the Navy, that destruction of the adversary's main military forces must always be the initial task in a war. This doctrine was said to have been derived from land fighting in which evasion of an adversary's forces was not possible as it normally is at sea. The book emphasized this point in an apparent effort to make the prospects for a war against a stronger navy seem less discouraging:

> The correlation of forces at sea is not determined just by numbers. That which seems possible for a big navy proves in the event to be unachievable. To the contrary, apparent numerical inferiority often conceals many surprises. (p. 206)

Citing Corbett's *Some Principles of Maritime Strategy*, Ivanov argued further that seeking a general engagement to gain command of the sea was not the established principle of British naval strategy it was commonly supposed to be and that the British naval leaders did not "break their heads" to seek out a general engagement but looked first to the security of shipping. Using this interpretation of recent British naval history, Ivanov concluded that those who said the Soviets could not gain command of the sea were guilty of jettisoning a command-of-the-sea theory that was alive and well, along with the general-engagement theory of battleship fleets that had been discredited by the Battle of Jutland.

Ivanov concluded with the inference that command-of-the-sea would remain the operative doctrine indefinitely by predicting that the "control" of the sea lines of communication which is conferred on a state by general or "full" command of the sea would remain a concern to every state that either depends on the sea for trade or that can be endangered by seaborne attack. While the traditional sea powers largely fall into the first category and so perhaps do not give enough thought to the naval force requirements of countries in the second category, the Soviet Union from its inception in 1917 has been a second-category state and has remained acutely mindful of the threat of seaborne attack.[5]

That Ivanov's comments were intended as criticism of the Young School in general, and its aircraft and submarine enthusiasts in particular, emerges with especial clarity from his concluding remarks on command of the sea. On the aircraft side, an unnamed enthusiast (probably Yakimychev) was said to have claimed, during a discussion at a 1930 conference on command of the sea, that aviation had changed even the very nature of war. This viewpoint, Ivanov asserted, stemmed from incorrectly evaluating that weapon system.

On both the submarine and aircraft sides Ivanov faulted Aleksandrov by name for having concluded in his book *A Critique of the Theory of Command of the Sea* that the theory of command of the sea was bankrupt for the twin reasons cited in the book: that neither aircraft nor submarines could be blockaded and that modern industry made it easy in wartime to replace losses in such light naval forces. Ivanov considered both reasons to be specious and command-of-the-sea theory still valid.

Ivanov's last riposte against the Young School (and hence implicitly in support of his beleaguered academic colleagues, professors Gervais and Petrov) was to mention that a well-known publicist of the Young School named Erukhimovich had made the same mistake as Aleksandrov in a foreword to the translation into Russian of Corbett's *Some Principles of Maritime Strategy*. With this, Ivanov ended his lengthy digression—and with it the only defense of the Old School and its practitioners to be found on the public record.

***Straddling the Ropes: Belli*.** The next piece of theoretical writing meriting notice was Belli's three-page review of V. P. Kalachev's book on naval combat which appeared in the fall of 1933.[6] In it Belli's early Young School partisanship for aircraft and particularly submarines[7] seemed evident. However, his ambiguously expressed view of command of the sea, battleships, and the general engagement made it uncertain whether he shared the view of his erstwhile collaborators, Aleksandrov and Isakov, that the command-of-the-sea doctrine had been invalidated by the advent of the submarine and the airplane. According to Belli the book he was reviewing asserted that the development of aircraft and submarines had brought an end to the battleship era and big-gun battles. Furthermore, submarines armed with torpedoes and mines had emerged from the shadows cast by the battleship fleets.

Additionally, he reported that in Kalachev's view the command-of-the-sea doctrine was bankrupt. The book argued, said Belli, that if the ship type (battleships) and the major tactic (general engagement) that had been so long associated with the command-of-the-sea doctrine were obsolete, the doctrine itself must of necessity be obsolete. He added that the old texts based on that doctrine were considered outmoded.

Most interesting, Belli reported without dissenting, was the book's assertion that several successive operations at sea had replaced the single general engagement of battleships, and that combined, concentrated strikes by all naval forces had replaced the artillery battle; this of course, was an expansion of Aleksandrov's views. Belli offered no argument in support of this thesis, but he did make it clear that Kalachev was thinking only of coastal naval operations in support of ground forces, rather than of offensive high seas warfare. (p. 144)[8] Professor Belli did not condemn the command-of-the-sea doctrine per se but merely stated that the old texts based on that doctrine were outmoded. It would seem that these criticisms could be accounted for by the changes in the "operational manifestations" of that doctrine, which he went on to relate (but with which he did not express any disagreement), without necessarily concluding that Belli shared Aleksandrov's view that the doctrine had been invalidated once and for all by the advent of the submarine and airplane.

Ludri Cites Jellicoe Against Command of the Sea. The best ammunition against the command-of-the-sea doctrine, which the Young School was to obtain during the interwar period, was gained from a 1917 memorandum by the First Sea Lord, Admiral John Jellicoe, saying that Germany's unrestricted submarine warfare had deprived England of its command of the sea. This was published in a volume of the official British history of the Royal Navy in the World War. It was exploited by Ludri in a book review in late 1933.[9]

Ludri began his review by observing that the World War had wrought an extremely significant change in the character and methods for the conduct of war at sea and, as a result of the development of technology, had caused revolutionary change in a number of areas. The official British operational theory of the command of the sea and the corresponding battleship tactics, he noted, were not put into practice. Volume 5 of the official history of the Royal Navy in the World War (Newbolt's *Operations of the British Navy in the World War*), Ludri asserted, "correctly may be termed a history of the abnegation of command of the seas by the British Navy."

Ludri further observed that the most remarkable document published in the British naval history was one written by Jellicoe on 27 April 1917. In light of Germany's unrestricted submarine warfare that was posing an "exceptionally serious" threat to the United Kingdom, Jellicoe concluded that the command-of-the-sea doctrine was to blame for England's endangered position.

Ludri quoted from the Jellicoe memorandum as follows:

> At the present time, we are conducting the war as though we had absolute command of the sea in our hands. Factually, however, we not only do not possess absolute command but not even anything approaching such command. True, to the extent that surface ships are concerned, we are in a controlling position, but it is necessary to quickly recognize the truth that the circumstance loses all significance as soon as enemy submarines paralyze—factually the paralysis has already started—our communications.

> History shows from time to time what fatal results obtain when strategy is based on such a changing factor as communications [to be read "command of the sea"]. In such cases catastrophe is inescapable. English military policy at the moment [read "contesting for command of the sea"—I.L.] is leading the country to catastrophe. It

would be unhelpful and in the highest degree dangerous to ignore this fact. Therefore, it is my duty to point out to the government the necessity of conducting military policy with the awareness that we do not possess either undisputed command of the sea or even partial command. If we don't want to take this into account, I'm firmly convinced that the war will be lost. (p. 164).

"From this quotation," Ludri maintained, "it is clear that the British not only recognized the indisputable fact of loss of command of the sea, they also gave up fighting for command of the sea, in view of its aimlessness, and turned to the immediate task of antisubmarine warfare and, especially, to the protection of convoys." (p. 164)

Ludri opined that giving up this fight led to England's decisive revision of policy, strategy, operational art, tactics, organization, and even shipbuilding. For Ludri the obvious conclusion was that the organization of convoys and their protection, the mining of the Helgoland Bight, and the laying of the Great North Sea Mine Barrage had nothing in common with the doctrine of command of the sea.

Ludri then cited the British history concerning an Admiralty conference in early 1918 which acknowledged that one year of Germany's unrestricted war at sea had changed British naval strategy significantly, including a costly dispersion of the surface ships of the Grand Fleet. Admiral Beatty was quoted as having observed at the conference that "under existing conditions it would not be desirable to bring about squadron battle [that is, a general engagement of the main battleship forces] even under favorable circumstances." Ludri interpreted this as England's reverting to a classical fleet-in-being strategy but in more open form (i.e., just holding the command in dispute so as to deny free use of the sea to Germany but without being able to gain command itself and thereby enjoy such free use for its own shipping and naval operations).

Ludri commented that the World War led to the appearance of "a new kind of operations—supporting (protecting) the sortie from bases of submarines and their return." The British history volume revealed that such support operations for submarines were very complicated and difficult and required meticulous preparation and skillful execution. Germany was credited with having coped with this task despite British efforts, through mining, to blockade the submarines in their bases.[10]

One of the main conclusions of Ludri's article was that submarines cannot be blockaded if they have adequate air and surface ship support:

The great minefields—Helgoland and the North Sea Mine Barrage—with support of all the might of the British Navy not only were unable to paralyze the operations of the German submarines [German war documents credit the North Sea Mine Barrage with having caused the confirmed loss of only two submarines and the possible loss of an additional two] but were not able even to have a serious effect on them. From this the important conclusion may be drawn that submarines constitute a warship type which possesses this characteristic [of being unblockadable] under the condition that the sortie and return to base is supported by other means (surface warships, aviation, and coastal defenses). (p. 168)

Nor was Ludri inclined to assign the British convoy system much credit for the failure of Germany's unrestricted submarine warfare campaign. Rather he ended his article with the observation:

> Even Newbolt in his work [on the British history of the Royal Navy in World War I] did not draw the conclusion that the submarines had been defeated; he asserted the opposite. He very carefully observed that convoying, in conjunction with other means and methods of combat, only reduced the tonnage loss in 1918. He explained restoration of the general tonnage balance as not due to having paralyzed German submarine operations but to the significant decrease in the period of repair of damaged merchant ships and the construction of new ones. (p. 169)

Defense Minister Voroshilov, in his accountability report to the 17th Party Congress in January 1934,[11] commented that the lack of aircraft carriers in the new Northern and Pacific fleets (with, compared to the old Baltic and Black Sea fleets, their great access to the open ocean) limited the offensive power of those two fleets; but then argued that this was an acceptable situation in that Soviet strategy did not involve taking the offensive at sea. Furthermore aircraft carriers were basically offensive and were not required for an adequate defense of the homeland, a defense in which the naval forces would so gravely cripple any attacking naval (amphibious) forces that implicitly the ground forces would be able to complete the destruction of such invasion forces as got ashore:

> It must be said that we cannot yet boast of the might of these young fleets. I have in mind the Northern and Far Eastern fleets. There we do not have battleships and aircraft carriers, those means for the naval offensive. But, after all, as is well known, we do not intend to attack anyone at sea. . . . We only want to defend our shores . . . and we are convinced that those light naval forces and coast defenses that we have there already, and above all our naval air forces and submarines, will gravely cripple an attacking enemy. (p. 166)

Aleksandrov Resumes the Fight. In February 1934 Aleksandrov published another in his long succession of articles[12] aimed at discrediting the command-of-the-sea concept among Soviet naval theoreticians and policy-makers so as to promote development of a largely submarine-aviation navy rather than one whose main forces would be battleships and heavy cruisers. In this article, Aleksandrov resorted to the most frequently used method of Soviet writers— he ostensibly concerned himself with other countries to make surrogate policy recommendations or announcements for the Soviet Union.

Aleksandrov argued that the doctrine of command of the sea had played the key role for the imperialist states in determining the means and methods of war at sea. This doctrine is "the operational expression of imperialist policy in the struggle of the imperialist states among themselves for raw materials, markets, spheres for capital investment and for redistribution of the already distributed [colonized] world."

Aleksandrov saw this doctrine as connected in the closest and most direct way with capitalist development of powerful battleship and cruiser fleets. These fleets, he believed, commanded the world's seas and oceans by the method of the general engagement of battleship squadrons or by close blockade of the enemy's fleet in its bases. Thus, Alexandrov held, this doctrine was the universal naval theory of contemporary capitalism, one that characterized its strategic aims, operational missions, technological means, and tactical methods of war at sea.

Again (as in 1930 and 1931) Aleksandrov credited British Vice Admiral Philip Colomb with having first formulated the command-of-the-sea doctrine, and Mahan with having developed the idea independently but only somewhat later on the other side of the Atlantic. Their command-of-the-sea theory was said to have been based on the Battle of Trafalgar and earlier wars but to have found its classical expression in the 1904-1905 Russo-Japanese War. The experience at Port Arthur typified the close blockade, and at Tsushima the general engagement of battleship fleets.

Battleship navies in World War I, according to Aleksandrov, were modern and the theory of their employment had been worked out in great operational detail. Nevertheless they remained in their bases during the first two years of the war until the Battle of Jutland. They seldom ventured outside their defensive system to make their presence obvious. When the two big fleets did meet, Aleksandrov further asserted, only the scouting forces of Beatty and Hipper engaged and the main fleets returned to their bases to resume their passive roles.

Aleksandrov concluded that during the course of World War I submarines were used against the fleets by making torpedo strikes at the battleships' weakest point, the unarmored underwater part. This weapon, according to Aleksandrov, made command of the sea an impossible goal and, together with air forces, completely discredited the command-of-the-sea doctrine.

Aleksandrov quoted Newbolt's fifth volume as having concluded that, since the Grand Fleet did not dare venture out of port without an antisubmarine screen of 100 destroyers, German submarine warfare had paralyzed the movement of British battleship squadrons to an extent that not even the most far-sighted and authoritative naval officer could have imagined.

Aleksandrov, like Ludri, made much of the Jellicoe memorandum of 27 April 1917. Jellicoe's statement was quoted at length but Aleksandrov included one sentence that Ludri had omitted after Jellicoe's professed conviction that Britain would lose the war if its policy continued to ignore the fact that it no longer could exercise command of the sea: "The British people will die of hunger and the allies will lose the possibility of obtaining coal and other things of prime necessity. . . .''

Aleksandrov observed that this passage was so clear that it required no comment but just the addition of the facts that, during the war, submarines had sunk about 200 warships of various types, including 12 battleships and 23 cruisers, as well as 13 million tons of merchant tonnage.

In addition to the submarines that made it so dangerous for capital ships to leave their bases during war, the subsequent development of bomber aircraft made even bases unsafe for warships. Accordingly, Aleksandrov argued, the prewar determination of the proportions and methods for employing the types of warships included in the Navy required review. This injunction appears to have been intended for the many Old School proponents of battleships and battle cruisers among the Navy's leadership.

Attack Aircraft Carriers Urged by Stolyarskiy. In the March and April 1934 issues of *Morskoi sbornik* two articles appeared on the uses of air power at sea, both written by a naval air brigade commander, S.E. Stolyarskiy. The first, "Air Forces in War at Sea," was notable for stressing aircraft carriers' ability to provide timely strikes at enemy naval forces at sea.[13] The second, "Missions and Methods of the Operations of Air Forces in a War at Sea,"[14] emphasized the importance to the Navy of cooperation by long-range Army aviation to supplement its own shore-based aviation and its few shipboard reconnaissance aircraft. Since several of the points in the second article expanded on points made in the first, the two will be considered together.

The great importance attributed to getting air power to sea in the form of "shipboard aviation," as Stolyarskiy described the aircraft on both capital ships and aircraft carriers, was made clear on the first page of his first article. It was obviously the most important of several requirements for naval aircraft and was prescribed as being "capable of staying at sea with the fleet to support it." Inasmuch as there were few battleships or cruisers and each could only carry one or two planes, it was apparent that advocacy of the construction of aircraft carriers for the Soviet Navy was Stolyarskiy's motivation. He made this unmistakable when he went on, after listing the unglamorous roles of battleship and cruiser-based aircraft such as reconnaissance and gunfire spotting, to note the real fighting roles that only aircraft-carrier planes could perform: timely and powerful strikes against an enemy's naval forces, including his carrier-launched bomber and torpedo planes; strikes at an enemy's coastal airfields, naval bases, fortifications, installations, and ground forces; and even deep strikes at the political and economic centers of the enemy homeland, like those by aircraft flown from Japanese carriers in their recent war against China. Judging from these offensive roles, Stolyarskiy's advocacy of aircraft carriers was not limited merely to the construction of light carriers to provide air cover for fleets.

Stolyarskiy noted that the roles of fleet air defense and torpedo and bombing strikes against an enemy were conducted mainly by two of the three types of aircraft that constituted the air park of aircraft carriers: fighters and torpedo bombers. The third type was described as a composite reconnaissance and light bomber plane. It was further noted that the aircraft complement of carriers varied from 25 to 120 and that the percentage of each type of aircraft could be altered according to the mission to be executed.

Stolyarskiy first dismissed command of the sea, portraying it as having been destroyed as a relevant doctrine for naval warfare by the advent of aircraft, with their production and mass use ashore and afloat. But he then used a previously identified euphemism ("preliminary support") for limited command of the sea in advance of operations to ensure "favorable conditions" for success. As is customary for such limited-command operations, the need for surprise was noted (so that the enemy would not have time to send reinforcements to the area before the operation could be completed).

In an enthusiastic paragraph on the value of aviation in naval theaters, Stolyarskiy barely managed to cloak his ardent advocacy of aircraft carriers by not naming them explicitly. But his context made his advocacy unmistakable:

> Air forces provide a powerful, devastating weapon that is effective against more powerful surface fleets. They constitute a long-range weapon covering the full extent of the Soviet Union's peripheral seas and their exits to the oceanic shipping lanes. Air forces may be concentrated quickly in designated directions of a theater, front, or region in a mighty massing of destructive power . . . and they cannot be blockaded. (Zadachi, p. 10)

Stolyarskiy denounced Douhet's theory of absolute command of the air as unsound, pointing out that not all of a large country's aviation and aircraft industry could be destroyed quickly. He added that in its search for a universal method for gaining victory in war the command-of-the-air theory reflected the same methodological error as the command-of-the-sea doctrine. Stolyarskiy thought Douhet's command-of-the-air theory was absurd and the command-of-the-sea doctrine notorious; both had "collapsed under the weight of evidence of the World War."

Aleksandrov Promotes the Young School.   In a 45-page article, in August 1934, entitled "Operations on the Sea Lines of Communication" Aleksandrov undertook to show that the submarine and air threat to both surface raiders against shipping and surface convoys of that same shipping had become so hazardous as to make the sea lanes unusable in wartime.[15] From this, he asserted that the epoch of command of the sea (understood both as protecting the passage of friendly shipping and denying that of hostile shipping, as well as the frustration of enemy naval operations) had vanished and could never return.

Aleksandrov based his argument on an analogy with contemporary armies. He noted their dependence on supply and their vulnerability to the interdiction of lines of communication to supply areas in the rear. He noted that the economies of the great capitalist powers (apparently meaning only the United Kingdom, the United States, and Japan) as well as the Soviet Union's small neighbors, depended heavily on overseas trade but that the Soviet Union and other continental powers did not.

Aleksandrov cited "the theory of independent naval warfare" for control of the sea lines of communication as purportedly considered by the strongest imperialist powers to be the primary strategic mission of their navies; cooperation with army ground forces was considered only an auxiliary mission. Aleksandrov commented on the belief of the greatest imperialist powers that their main naval mission was independent of ground operations.

The efforts of "the naval theoreticians of imperialism to refurbish and galvanize" the command-of-the-sea doctrine in the form of "local, temporary, or conditional command of the sea," Aleksandrov asserted, were "foredoomed to failure." (As will be seen, the Soviet School of naval warfare has in effect rejected Aleksandrov's view and has espoused precisely such a local and temporary conception of the "command-of-the-sea" doctrine.)

Joint operations of all kinds of naval forces were recommended for use against an enemy's sea communications, using combined, successive strikes. The presence of surface ships to support the strikes of submarines and aircraft against the enemy's sea communications would lend "combat stability" to Soviet naval operations, he noted.[16]

The Soviet Union's leading Young School advocate also remarked on the potential against an enemy's sea communications by groups of "maneuvering" submarines advised of the location of convoys by air reconnaissance. This combination of submarines and aircraft, he maintained, synthesized speed, invisibility, maneuverability, and surprise. The surface ships were desirable just to afford "combat stability" to the submarines and aircraft by preventing interference with their operations, whether by other surface ships, submarines, or aircraft. But "the basic nucleus of this combined-arms formation", Aleksandrov noted as a parting shot, "would be the submarines and air forces." Aleksandrov implied in this August 1934 article that aircraft carriers were radically changing war at sea, particularly in that merchant convoys and their escorting combatant ships were highly vulnerable to destruction by aircraft. This made it necessary to include light aircraft carriers in convoy-screening forces, Aleksandrov implied, in order to be able to provide air cover against enemy air attacks. Aleksandrov further implied that such light carriers for the air defense of convoys were the only feasible alternative to the highly impractical options of developing an extensive network of air bases or heavy naval aircraft with immense radii of action.

"Combat Support" Requirements Stressed by Novitskiy. In its May-June 1935 issue, the journal *War and Revolution* published an article by V. Novitskiy on a subject almost never treated in the Soviet open literature: "The Navy in the Initial Period of a War."[17] Novitskiy, a frequent writer on naval theory and strategy, discussed the requirement for—and the difficulty of providing—support for the initial deployment of submarines to their assigned operating areas.

Novitskiy said that "in our times, the initial period of a war [for the Navy] will be characterized primarily by the development of a struggle for the mobilization and deployment" of the forces of the Navy. The aim must be that of getting one's forces out on patrol station and prepared to strike before the enemy himself can ready his forces. This concept obviously was the forerunner of what today, in this age of permanent forward deployments and constant war readiness, the Soviets term "the contest for the first salvo."

In emphasizing the difficulty of providing adequate support for the forward deployment of naval forces during the initial period of a war and the need for more command attention to the matter, the article stated: "The task of supporting the deployment of one's own forces against the operations of the naval forces of an adversary must be recognized to be considerably more difficult, complicated, and responsible" than it is at present. (p. 52)

Belli Supports Submarines as the Navy's Main Force. In the July 1935 issue of *Morskoi sbornik*, V. A. Belli reviewed a British account of German submarine warfare in World War I which had just been translated into Russian.[18] It was his last appearance in print as a seeming Young School supporter. The review itself was largely unexceptional Young School fare in its praise of submarines. However, a few points are worthy of mention.

Belli claimed that, despite the limited development of submarines by the end of the World War, it had already become clear that they had shown themselves to be a "universal" means of combat because they could operate in distant theaters of naval warfare that were inaccessible to other warships. This attribution of universality to submarines as a ship type was to become a frequently used euphemism after Stalin's death in 1953, primarily due to the submarine's capability to operate in areas where Soviet surface forces dared not venture because they lacked shipborne air cover and so could not gain command of the sea or even attempt to hold the command in dispute.

While Belli acknowledged the obvious fact that the success of submarine operations could be affected by antisubmarine warfare, and hence the latter subject should be studied, he took exception to the credit given to British antisubmarine warfare by the authors of the book under review. Instead, he alleged, the failure of Germany's unrestricted submarine warfare against British shipping should be attributed to England's "vast" production of replacement ships and Germany's inability to produce enough submarines. While there undoubtedly was considerable merit to Belli's arguments, their one-sidedness in not giving antisubmarine warfare its due bespoke the Young School's unqualified enthusiasm for submarines as the main force for a navy faced with much stronger adversaries.

Stolyarskiy Amplifies His Advocacy of Attack Carriers. With a co-author, Stolyarskiy published another article in November 1935.[19] It nominally described the aviation of the capitalist states (the United Kingdom and the United States). Actually, they argued for some Soviet aircraft carriers. First, in describing the Royal Navy's air arm and subsequently U.S. naval aviation, the authors made it a point to mention that both air forces were comprised wholly (Royal Navy) or mainly (U.S. Navy) of shipboard aviation.

Most important for Stolyarskiy's cause was the portrayal of the potential threat to the Soviet Union from British and American possession of a sizable and growing number of aircraft carriers. Soviet leaders perceived both countries as likely enemies in the by-then inevitable Second World War. The Royal Navy was shown to have six operational aircraft carriers and a seventh, the *Ark Royal*, under construction. While the U.S. Navy then had only three carriers operational (and the *Ranger* nearly ready), they were all noted to be in the Pacific. Although the article did not explicitly state it, obviously in case of war against Britain and America, the Soviet Union would be encircled by the Royal Navy's aircraft carriers in the Atlantic and the U.S. Navy's in the Pacific.

Ludri Rebuts Old School Criticism of Submarines. Early in 1936, Young School exponent Ivan Ludri published a book review,[20] one patently intended to defend submarines against Old School charges that they were ineffective against battleships and not very effective against shipping. These charges had appeared in a 1926 British history of naval operations in World War I that just had been translated into Russian and published in Moscow. Appearing a full decade after its original publication, the translation seemed likely to have been accomplished at the inspiration of one of the Old School advocates of battleships in the navy high command, quite possibly Chief of Naval Forces, Admiral Orlov himself or perhaps Rear Admiral Lev Galler, an old battleship sailor.

The author of the book, Ludri commented, "believes in the effectiveness of the battleship fleet, single-mindedly asserting that submarines are powerless against contemporary classes of battleships and armored cruisers." Moreover, Ludri observed, the book's author also concluded from the experience of the World War that submarines are not a fully satisfactory means even for attacking maritime trade. Ludri rejected these charges as completely false, unsupported either by facts adduced in the book or by the evidence of the means mobilized against submarines. Certainly he had *bona fide* evidence on the latter point. The mere threat constituted by the submarines did cause the Allies to divert a far greater number and tonnage of surface ships to counter that threat.

Two Pro-Carrier Articles Appear in 1936. Two noteworthy articles on aircraft carriers appeared in 1936. The first, in the May issue of *Morskoi sbornik*,[21] was an abbreviated translation of a German article praising aircraft carriers. The second, in *Technology and Armaments* in August, was titled "Cruiser-Aircraft Carriers."[22]

The translation from German was outspoken in its enthusiasm for aircraft carriers. For example, the first page of the Russian translation said: "Carrier aircraft are the sole machines which, regardless of the time and place, can be employed for all of the mission that may be assigned a navy." On the same page, the article noted that the United States had exercised its right under the 1922 Washington Treaty to convert two incomplete 33,000-ton battle cruisers into aircraft carriers. Even Germany was reported (inaccurately) to be fitting out one or two aircraft carriers.

The high costs of building and operating carriers and their inherent vulnerability was canvassed as was the commensurate requirement that they be well protected. While the loss of a carrier plane would have little significance, the loss of an aircraft carrier would bring heavy penalties and would not be readily replaceable.

The *Technology and Armaments* article also appeared to be basically pro-carrier. After relating U.S. and Japanese construction of what were the first supercarriers, the article expressed the view that naval aviation had become necessary for every modern navy. The article went on to note that at that time almost every battleship and cruiser was being provided with air capability. Carrier vulnerability was characterized as a major shortcoming and one that necessitated its protection by cruisers and destroyers during each operation. The remainder of the article was devoted to discussion of the technical characteristics of light aircraft carriers of the early through-deck type.

Further Analysis and Interpretation of the Evidence, 1933-1936

The 1932 victory of the Young School in silencing the leading Old Schoolers, professors Gervais and Petrov, left the theoretical field open to the uncontested sway of the Young School advocates—by this time primarily Aleksandrov, Belli, Isakov, and Ludri. Through 1936, a great share of their effort was devoted to interpreting the First World War to show that the submarine, and secondarily the airplane, had superseded the battleship and that command of the sea was no longer a relevant doctrine.

One of the key aspects of the Young School's theoretical positions of the mid-1930s, whose relevance was destined to continue to the present, was its insistence that, to be fully effective, submarine operations require the support of surface ships and aircraft for virtually all major missions. This is particularly important in leaving and returning to port, in transitting geographical choke points, and in making the main strike against the major combatant ships of a strong opponent.

This view seems particularly valid for states like Germany and the Soviet Union that have restricted access to the open ocean. In fact it might tacitly be acknowledged that—regardless of whether a Young School doctrine of attempting at sea denial or an Old School doctrine of holding command of the sea in dispute were in official favor in the Soviet Union—another war could bring superior enemy naval forces that would rule out any hope the Soviets might have of maintaining command of even their own peripheral seas. This would require extensive surface-ship and air force support for any Soviet submarine operations outside Soviet coastal waters while naval aircraft and the bulk of the submarines and surface ships were trying not only to avoid being blockaded in port but also trying to hold command of the sea in dispute.

It would be important for the Soviet Union to have a large number of submarines in operation at the outbreak of war to increase the mission options and to force the enemy to the great expenditure of ships, planes, men, and effort on antisubmarine warfare. This was implicit in Soviet writings on war at sea during the mid-1930s and was explicitly stated in the 1933 book *Submarine Operations* by Aleksandrov, Isakov, and Belli and again in February 1936 by Ivan Ludri.

The consistent Young School argument was apparently made most explicitly by Aleksandrov in his book *Critique of the Theory of Command of the Sea*. That is, command of the sea was bankrupt (merely) because of the (alleged) uselessness of the main ship type (the battleship) and the major tactic for its use (the general engagement); the assumption is a logical fallacy. The battleship had, of course, been just the *means* of achieving command of the sea and the general engagement (or blockade) had been just the *method* of gaining and maintaining the supremacy that made the accomplishment of various naval missions possible. Consequently, the argument that the theory *per se* had been invalidated too just because the means and methods changed with the end of the battleship era provided the least implausible argument available to the Young School. Since changes in weapons and tactics do *not* necessarily invalidate a strategy, the Young School argument had to make up in denunciations and invective what it lacked in logic. Development of the aircraft carrier and the Battle of Midway in 1942 were to demonstrate the validity of the command-of-the-sea principle even though the traditional means for its achievement, the battleship, had been replaced by the aircraft carrier.

Belli's argument in the same October 1933 book review that a series of "successive operations at sea" had replaced the general engagement as "the contemporary form of operational activity," regardless of its plausibility, seemed primarily to have been a further effort to discredit command of the sea indirectly by discrediting its main operational manifestation.

The Young School's interpretation of the 1917 Jellicoe memorandum as further proof that command of the sea had been invalidated was equally fallacious. It was legitimate, of course, to argue that the Jellicoe memorandum provided telling support for the Young School argument that the submarine had greatly affected the viability of capital ships in contemporary war at sea. Also one was fully justified in taking the view that the submarine and airplane made battleships much more vulnerable— a conclusion that World War II was to substantiate further. Yet it does not seem to have been logically sound for Ludri and Aleksandrov to conclude that the principle of command of the sea had been invalidated merely on the basis of Admiral Jellicoe's view that further pursuit of command of the sea in the face of Germany's unrestricted submarine warfare would be disastrous for England under the particular set of circumstances then existing.

In the late 1920s Old School influence remained so strong that Aleksandrov professed not to be attacking the inherent validity of the command-of-the-sea doctrine but just to be denying its applicability to the Soviet Union at the time. By 1934, however, Aleksandrov and Stolyarskiy as well were arguing that command of the sea had been completely discredited. That Aleksandrov and Stolyarskiy felt free to go to this extreme constitutes significant evidence that a Young School strategy had come to enjoy official favor in the Soviet Union. Although neither explicitly identified aircraft carriers as critical to efforts to gain and maintain command of the sea, both Stolyarskiy and Aleksandrov discussed command of the sea and aircraft carriers in the same articles, so it seems likely that the synergism between the concept and main means was understood by both writers.

Marxists like to claim as a dialectical truth the obvious lesson of history, that the introduction of each radically new weapon system normally brings the eventual development of countermeasures that limit the effectiveness of the new system. The Young Schoolers, particularly Aleksandrov, overlooked or ignored this factor in their assessments of the effects on surface warships of the appearance of submarines and aircraft. For example, in his February 1934 article, Aleksandrov argued that not only had the advent of the submarine made the sea untenable for large warships but that the big ships' survival in port had been made unlikely by the development of bomber aircraft. If Aleksandrov thought that the further development of anti-submarine warfare and antiaircraft weapons might reverse this trend, his advocacy of Young School views was too unqualified to permit him to mention the possibility.

In his August 1934 article Aleksandrov observed what is probably even more relevant now than it was then. He noted that the major capitalist powers depended heavily on seaborne trade while continental powers such as the Soviet Union were not fatally vulnerable on this count.

Although the USSR had greatly expanded her overseas trade under the Five-Year Plan so that the Soviet economy was benefiting substantially from such trade, Aleksandrov's point, especially for wartime conditions, was valid. The asymmetry in naval missions created by this situation is important for understanding the Soviet Union's requirements in ship types and numbers to just hold command of the sea "in dispute" so as to deny the probable opponent use of the sea lanes in any future war. These requirements are quite different from those of the NATO naval coalition for gaining and maintaining command of the contested sea lines of communications in any but a brief nuclear war.

Nevertheless, apparently with the USSR's vital coastal military shipping in mind, Aleksandrov implicitly advocated construction of light aircraft carriers for protection of that shipping in wartime. But even to build light carriers was not a prospect at that time—a point made clear by Marshal Voroshilov in January 1934 when he stated that aircraft carriers were not required even in the more exposed Northern and Pacific fleets to execute the USSR's defensive strategy.

Perhaps the most important of all of Aleksandrov's formulations for its contemporary relevance was stated in his August 1934 article. The efforts of "the naval theoreticians of imperialism to refurbish and galvanize" the command-of-the-sea doctrine in the form of "local, temporary, or conditional command of the sea were foredoomed to failure." Since this is not only the argument of Naval Air Brigade Commander Stolyarskiy, but also exactly that which Admiral Gorshkov and his coterie of "official theoreticians" were to advance well before the publication of Gorshkov's 1976 book *Seapower of the State*, Aleksandrov's 1934 assertion merits keeping in mind.

The Old School's Professor Petrov (in his March 1928 article in *Morskoi sbornik*) had taken exception to the view that control of any region of a theater of naval operations could be considered to constitute "command of the sea" without the enemy's main naval forces having been destroyed (or at least neutralized by blockade). But Aleksandrov based his objection to the idea of any limited "command of the sea" on very different grounds. Technological advances (i.e., the advent of a "universal" weapon system, the airplane) had made even "permanent" control of a contested region of a naval theater of military action impractical inasmuch as the requirements for the combat support of surface ships in a hostile air environment would necessitate extensive preliminary and direct support measures and substantial naval forces, implicitly including aircraft carriers.

Belli's formulation given in his July 1935 book review has considerable present-day relevance, for as we have seen, it gives the only definition of the much-touted "universal" nature attributed to the submarine as a weapons system. The universality attributed to Soviet submarines has been cited frequently since World War II as a justification for designating submarines as the main striking force of the Soviet Navy. For Belli to have made this unprecedented admission—that submarines are advantageous primarily because they can operate in areas too dangerous for surface warships—is tantamount to admitting Soviet inability to provide the requisite continuous air cover in such areas necessary to even hold command of the sea in dispute against enemy carrier task forces. Not surprisingly, Belli's definition is one that, despite frequent present-day application of the term "universal" to submarines, neither he nor Admiral Gorshkov (nor any other Soviet writer in the postwar period) has ever found it politic to repeat.

Ludri's February 1936 defense of submarines, apparently against attacks by the Old School, proved to be the last expression of the Young School point of view that was to appear in print in the period between the world wars. In this connection, it should be noted that the appearance in 1936 of even the translation of a book asserting that submarines were powerless against post-World War I battleships and cruisers may have foreshadowed Stalin's decision to build a big navy emphasizing both those types of ship.

Soviet naval writings in 1937 were to reveal that the ascendancy since 1933 of the Young School supporters of a primarily submarine-airplane navy had ended. Such leading lights of the Young School as Ivan Ludri and Vladimir Belli were shortly to acknowledge the reascendance of the battleship and command-of-the-sea doctrine by reversing themselves to embrace these Old School tenets as ardently as they had the Young School and the alleged universality of the submarine. The Young School proponents, including Aleksandrov, Yakimychev, and Stolyarskiy, who had thought the airplane was the panacea for all naval problems simply fell silent.

This was a key development in the evolution of a distinctive Soviet School of naval strategy. The Soviet School would eventually combine the elements deemed most useful to the Soviet Union from the Old School and the Young School. The Old School advocated what was essentially the Corbettian concept of "fleet in being." Corbett had prescribed building capital ships, for even a few such ships could hold command of the sea "in dispute" in key maritime areas. The Young School advocated basically "mosquito-fleet" forces of submarines, land-based aircraft, fast and light surface forces, defensive minefields, and coastal artillery to actively harass any enemy naval strike or landing forces that might enter Soviet home waters. This composite naval strategy may expediently be termed the Soviet School even though it appears to owe its conceptualization to a French admiral, Raoul Castex.

Although Castex had been writing on naval strategy since 1920, his works had been largely ignored in the Soviet Union except for unfavorable Young School reviews in the January and June 1930 issues of *Morskoi sbornik*. Not until 1937 was Castex presented favorably. In the fall of that year the *Foreign Military Observer* published the translation of an article by Castex entitled "Sea, Land, Air" ["Mer, terre, air"][23] prefaced by an editorial comment that identified Castex as "the Chief Inspector of [French] Naval Forces" and as "among the most eminent leaders of the Naval Forces of France." The editorial remarks quoted Castex as holding that aircraft were "a universal and the most decisive type of weapon" and advised the readership that his article contained much of interest! Most notable was Castex's conclusion regarding the Soviet Union: "Soviet Russia, naturally, could have an incomparably greater . . . sphere of influence . . . if it were to add command of the sea to its land power." Also, the December 1940 issue of *Morskoi sbornik* published some 30 pages of volume 1 of *Theories strategiques* in Russian translation to acquaint the readership with the school of naval strategy represented by "the writer of greatest erudition in all aspects of naval study, as Castex appears to be." The editorial comment added that Castex's five-volume *Strategic Theories* was "one of the most important works to have appeared in the foreign literature in the past decade" and that it was being translated in full by the Naval Ministry because "its study and critical analysis will prove profitable for the development of an original Soviet concept of naval operations and strategy."

The Army point of view on the development of naval theory in the Soviet Union, as set out in the 1981 book *History of Soviet Military Thought*[24] and as quoted in relevant part at the end of the first two chapters, also proves illuminating on this 1933-1936 period. Repeating a sentence quoted in the last chapter as necessary context for what follows, the passages of the Army study appropriate here are as follows:

> The partisans of a so-called mosquito fleet advocated the energetic development of a submarine fleet and of naval aviation. Championing the feasibility of employing submarines and aviation in independent naval operations, they simultaneously emphasized the necessity for mutual cooperation with the ground forces. These views were first laid out at length in a work [*Submarine Operations*, Vol. 1, 1933] by staff members of the Naval War College's Department of Strategy and Operational Art, I.S. Isakov, A.P. Aleksandrov, and V.A. Belli. They explained the growing role of submarines and aviation for a war at sea. The young scholars advocated the employment of submarines in mutual cooperation with the air forces against the big surface ships of an adversary.

Subsequently other naval theoreticians also published works on the employment of submarines [including a 1936 book by A. Shtal, *Development of Methods for the Employment of Submarines in the 1914-1918 War in the Main Naval Theaters*]. Gradually the Navy came to approve the view that submarines and aviation, and especially PT boats among surface ships and craft, are strike forces [rather than just "auxiliary" forces limited to "support" tasks such as reconnaissance]. (pp. 179-180)

Notes

1. A. Aleksandrov, I. Isakov, and V. Belli, *Operatsii podvodnykh lodok*. Conclusions on strategy from this book were reprinted in the previously cited book *Questions of Strategy and Operational Art* (1965), pp. 710-717. The same three authors had published a long article, "Submarine Operations Against Combatant Ships," in the September 1932 issue of *Morskoi sbornik* that made clear that the authors were interested in emphasizing this aspect of submarine capabilities to offset the view that submarines were mainly good for sinking merchant ships. "Operatsii podvodnykh lodok protiv boyevykh korablei," *Morskoi sbornik* No. 9, September 1932, pp. 7-42.

2. Vladimir A. Belli was born in 1887, completed the Tsarist naval cadet school in 1906, and by 1916 commanded a destroyer. Accepting the Soviet regime, Belli became Chief of the Directorate of Naval Operations by 1924. From 1926 on he was an instructor at the Naval War College. From his seeming initial Young School leanings, as reflected by his joint authorship of *Submarine Operations*, his views seemed to change with the times so that by mid-1939 he had become the leading theorist of the new "Soviet School" of naval strategy which valued capital ships even more highly than submarines and aircraft.

3. L. Ivanov and P. Smirnov, *Anglo-Amerikanskoye morskoye sopernichestvo*, 1965, p. 205.

4. Since the traditional term was known to be objectionable to the Army because it connoted large naval expenditures for big ships and since Gervais's new term had particular reference to land warfare, it is a fair guess that he had been trying to placate the Army when he introduced the new term.

5. It was precisely this particular sensitivity to seaborne threats against the Homeland that prompted Admiral Gorshkov in his 1972-1973 series of 11 articles in *Morskoi sbornik* on "Navies in Wars and in Peacetime" to reveal that the Soviet Union had decided to develop its own "strategic counterforces of defense" (Polaris-like submarines) in order to find a way out of the dilemma by confronting the United States and other NATO naval powers "with the same problems with which they have confronted us." Prior to that the USSR had been greatly concerned over the imagined threat of a Normandy-type amphibious invasion of the Homeland and then of aircraft carrier-borne nuclear strikes against the Homeland.

6. V.A. Belli, review of V.P. Kalachev (ed.) *"Sovremennye boyevye sredstva morskogo flota"* [Contemporary Combat Means of a Navy], *Morskoi sbornik* No. 10, October 1933, pp. 144-147.

7. Belli's main criticisms were based on his view that the book did not mention naval aviation and did not do justice to the importance of submarines for a modern war as shown by their enormous effectiveness in World War I and the great improvements made in them since. (p. 145)

8. The relevant quote from this early (1933) statement is given here in view of Belli's subsequent prominence as a leading official theoretician for three decades: "The advent and development of new means, and of submarines and air forces in the first place, not only essentially changed the old methods of conducting operations but also refuted the old command-of-the-sea doctrine for conduct of war at sea which is not valid for the present."

9. I. Ludri, "Istoriya otritsaniya gospodstva angliiskogo flota na moryakh" [History of the Abnegation of Command of the Seas by the British Navy], *Morskoi sbornik* No. 11, November 1933, p. 162. Ludri criticized the authors of *Anglo-American Naval Rivalry* for disregarding the fact that the World War had discredited command of the sea and for asserting that the war had even affirmed the doctrine.

10. Ludri's view, like Aleksandrov's in 1930, that the Germans *did* provide support for their submarines with other forces in World War I merits particular note since Gorshkov and company will be seen to have flatly denied this throughout the 1970s. This same view contradictory to that later espoused by Gorshkov, cropped up in an article by a Captain First Rank M.E. Stepanov in the December 1961 issue of *Morskoi sbornik*.

11. *Stenographic Record, 27th Congress of the CPSU, January 1934*. Political Press, 1934, 600pp.

12. A.P. Aleksandrov, "Voenno-morskie sily kapitalisticheskikh gosudarstv" [Naval Forces of the Capitalist States], *Morskoi sbornik*, No. 2, February 1934, pp. 17-54.

13. S.E. Stolyarskiy, "Vozdushnye sily v bor'be na more", *Morskoi sbornik*, No. 3, March 1934, pp. 9-26.

14. S.E. Stolyarskiy, "Zadachi i metody operatsiyakh vozdushnykh sil v voine na more", *Morskoi sbornik*, No. 4, April 1934, pp. 9-19.

15. A.P. Aleksandrov, "Operatsii na morskikh soobshcheniyakh," *Morskoi sbornik*, No. 8, August 1934, pp. 18-63.

16. For a definition of "combat stability," see the Glossary. This argument, which was destined to become a tenet of the Soviet School of naval warfare, is particularly worth noting for its contemporary relevance; Admiral Gorshkov has made extensive use of it to justify larger surface forces.

17. V. Novitskiy, "Voyenno-morskiye sily nachal'nyi period voiny," *Voina i revolyutsiya*, No. 3, May-June 1935, pp. 46-55. This article, it should be noted in passing, mentioned the "fleet-against-the-shore" concept that Admiral Gorshkov has made a centerpiece of his analysis of how naval warfare has been changed by the advent of the nuclear-missile era. By way of considering the operations of naval forces against the shore, Novitskiy wrote that "the concept 'against the shore' is viewed in the most extensive meaning of the phrase including operations against the land lines of communications." (p. 50)

18. V.A. Belli review of "R. Gibson and M. Prendergast, *Germanskaya podvodnaya voina 1914-1918 gg*" [German Submarine Warfare 1914-1918], *Morskoi sbornik*, No. 7, July 1935, pp. 156-158.

19. S.E. Stolyarskiy and J.F. Kireyev, "Morskaya aviatsiya kapitalisticheskikh gosudarstv," *Morskoi sborkik*, No. 11, November 1935, pp. 108-122. In this article, aircraft carriers were still being categorized as auxiliaries (ships "of special purpose") rather than as capital ships.

20. I. Ludri, "Kh. Vil'son—*Morskie operatsii v mirovoi voine 1914-1918gg*" [H. Wilson—*Naval Operations in the World War 1914-1918*], *Morskoi sbornik*, No. 2, February 1936, pp. 157-159.

21. "Avianostsy v sovremennoi voine na more," *Morskoi sbornik*, No. 5, May 1936, pp. 117-123.

22. L. Gordon and N. Mal'tsev, "Kreisora—avianostsy," *Tekhnika i vooruzheniye*, No. 8, August 1936, pp. 50-61. These authors were to write again on the same subject in the April 1940 issue of *Morskoi sbornik*.

23. R. Castex, "More, susha, vozdukh." *Voennyi zarubezhnik*, No. 10-11, October-November 1937, pp. 22—23.

24. I.A. Korotkov, *Istoriya Sovetskoi voennoi mysli* [*A History of Soviet Military Thought*], (Moscow: Nauka Press, 1981).

IV
An Upstart Soviet School
Takes the Title, 1937-1941

The Evidence and Some Partial Analysis

Aircraft Carriers Advocated. From 1937 until mid-1940 Soviet writing about aircraft carriers became noticeably more frequent. In 1937 a "collective" of instructors at the Naval War College published a second edition of a 1933 handbook, *Modern Combat Means of a Navy.*[1] It set out a more balanced view than had Aleksandrov and Stolyarskiy in their articles from 1932 through 1935 of the place of naval aviation in the force structure of the Navy. But, like those two Young School advocates of aircraft carriers, the collective noted the value of aviation for naval operations beyond the range of land-based air. The handbook gave a capsulized version of what very likely was the prevailing military doctrinal view of the desired force structure of the Navy near the end of the brief period of the dominance of Young School theory in the mid-1930s which emphasized light forces rather than capital ships:

> Now the conduct of war at sea cannot be tied to a single general engagement; it requires the conduct of successive operations in the course of every war, with the augmentation of the individual weight of the light naval surface-ship forces of a fleet by submarines and aviation (p. 13).

Submarines were said to have become exceptionally important as a result of such improved speed and endurance that they could operate with the battle force. However, the development of antisubmarine warfare was said to have considerably complicated the utilization of submarines. Naval aviation was said simply to have grown, with heavy airplanes having replaced reconnaissance planes as the leading group. The presence of aircraft carriers in a fleet was noted to "enable aviation to operate together with the fleet on operations far from the coast and, moreover, to make flights against the coast of an adversary when shore-based aviation lacked sufficient range." (p. 14)

Large Combatant Ships Found Not Too Vulnerable to Air Attack. Also in January 1937 the *Naval Digest* published an abbreviated version of the report of a subcommittee of the British Imperial Defense Committee, "On the Vulnerability of Battleships to Air Attack."[2] The conclusions of this British report may be fairly assumed to have been of no little interest to the defense and naval ministries of all of the great powers, including those of the Soviet Union. Not only was the continued viability of the traditional main ship type for gaining and maintaining command of the sea at stake, but a negative finding that the battleship was highly vulnerable to air attack could have markedly influenced future policy decisions about carrier construction. On the one hand, if battleships had been found to be highly vulnerable, how much more vulnerable must relatively unarmored aircraft carriers be? On the other hand, how much more attractive must the construction of aircraft carriers be viewed? Only they could take the numerous aircraft far out to sea from whence they could be launched from relatively close range for mass air strikes on the enemy's battleships and aircraft carriers, while simultaneously maintaining a combat air patrol over their own battle force to ward off any enemy air strikes.

At any rate, the British report stated that "of course the modern battleship is not invulnerable to air attack but, as shown by the experience with the U.S. bombing tests against the battleship *Washington*, its (compartmented, water-tight) construction is a very effective protection." (p. 151) While the British defense subcommittee had endeavored to consider all of the relevant factors, including the future development and relative effectiveness of both antiaircraft defenses and of bomber aircraft (level and dive), they essentially concluded that more testing and a wait-and-see attitude were in order. The report dismissed the view that battleships simply were not vulnerable to air attacks: "Under favorable circumstances, numerous and powerful aviation may sink, or at least seriously damage, a battleship, even the most heavily armored one." (p. 148) The report recommended recognizing the vulnerability of battleships and taking all feasible measures to decrease that vulnerability. The British report cited the U.S. report of tests of the *Washington's* resistance to air attacks and concluded in its last sentence: "Therefore, the authors of the American report consider that it may not at all be asserted that, with the advent of air forces, the battleship has outlived its era." (p. 151)

Ludri Forsakes the Young School—Too Late. In his February 1937 article on "Naval Operations" First Deputy Naval Commissar Ivan Ludri found it expedient to forsake his Young School views and undertake the task of unifying the views of the top military leadership favorable to restoring the battleship to its former leading role. Writing in *Military Thought*, the restricted-distribution journal most read by his intended audience of senior Army officers, Ludri presented the argument—basically an Old School one—that submarines and aircraft could not replace capital ships.[3]

Submarines had been employed in the World War mainly against merchant ships and, consequently, Ludri said, had not proven themselves against warships, either independently or in cooperation with other naval forces. He argued that the warships that had been sunk by submarines (12 battleships and 23 cruisers) were at fault for not having taken the necessary defensive measures, such as high speed, zigzagging, and antisubmarine-warfare escort-ship screens. On the other hand, Ludri noted, antisubmarine warfare had gained a great deal of experience and accounted for at least 166 of the 178 submarines lost by the Germans. Moreover, not only were independent submarine capabilities for sinking warships unproven but efforts at providing surface-ship support for the submarines in joint submarine-surface-ship attacks had not been promising.

Ludri seemed outwardly to be endorsing the construction of light, fast carriers for use in the Soviet "limited sea theaters" until land-based air could be given enough range to replace them. This private communication seemed, in the face of it, in notable contrast to an openly published article 10 months later in the *Naval Digest* by Naval War College Professor, Captain Second Rank V. Chernyshev, which minimized the value of aircraft carriers in limited sea theaters as not an imperative necessity. Inasmuch as this seeming divergence of views on the need for light carriers may afford some insight into the actual Soviet naval views on small versus big carrier construction that apparently existed in the Navy at the time, it merits closer examination.

Ludri informed his largely senior military readership that the aircraft carrier had become enormously important—but that this importance, for limited sea theaters, at least, would decrease proportionately over time as the radii of action and speed of shore-based aircraft were increased. He seemed to be suggesting that light carriers would be of only short-term value in the Baltic and Black Seas because new, faster, longer-range planes operating from land bases would sooner or later obviate the need for aircraft carriers in the peripheral seas. This impression was strengthened by Ludri's subsequent observation that the aircraft carrier has the great weakness that, after one or two successful bomb or shell hits on the flight deck, it may be put out of action. It was this vulnerability to neutralization by just one or two hits that Ludri cited as the basis for a current trend to construction of smaller carriers.

The Deputy Navy Chief went on to deny that the suspension of battleship construction, agreed on at the 1922 Washington Conference and which lasted until 1936, had been due to the passive role of such ships in the World War. He flatly denied that the development of submarines and aviation capable of sinking battleships had ended the battleship era; the advent of the two had only necessitated radical revision of the tactics for battle forces operations. Ludri made his point clear with the emphatic statement: "Submarines and aviation have not and cannot replace the battleship." (p. 86) But his turnabout came too late to save him from being purged.

Ludri's argument to diversify was carried to its logical extreme by Naval War College professor of surface-ship tactics, V. Chernyshev in an article in the *Naval Digest* in December 1937.[4] Chernyshev argued that "in view of the great vulnerability of aircraft carriers . . . [in limited sea theaters], it is more feasible to base aircraft ashore." (p. 24) Chernyshev had described the aircraft carrier earlier in his article in generally favorable terms, as enabling the use of aircraft "far from one's own bases, far beyond the limits of shore-based aircraft." (p. 23) On balance, it would seem that both authors, despite their apparent differences, actually were promoting the construction of large carriers, if necessary at the expense of smaller ones.

Ludri's effort to rehabilitate the battleship in the minds of the military readers of *Military Thought* was complemented for naval readers by Chernyshev's article. Chernyshev, implicitly challenged the widespread assumption that the advent of the submarine and aircraft had made the battleship too vulnerable to warrant continued dependence on it as the main force of a navy. Chernyshev cited the fact that in mid-1937, 16 to 20 battleships were known to be under construction by the five major capitalist powers, as evidence that practice was disproving theory.

Moreover, Chernyshev asserted that the rapid postwar development of aviation had made air attack an even greater threat to surface ships than submarine attack and described the airplane as a universal weapon that could be used against any target. Particularly endangered were light surface-ships although even the most heavily armored capital ship could be sunk by a big enough bomb (of one or two tons).

Nevertheless, Chernyshev stated, tests made in the United States, the United Kingdom, and France had shown that the big ships were not as vulnerable to air attacks as had been thought. He added that the views of most authoritative foreign writers were rapidly tilting in favor of the use of battleships. Chernyshev cautioned, however, that since aviation was developing more rapidly than any other naval force, the definitive evaluation of this development as it affected surface ships would have to await the test of war at sea.

The Case for Large Carriers Made Again. Captain First Rank Shvede also published an article in the same December 1937 issue of *Naval Digest*.[5] The article, "The Development of the Navies of the Capitalist States Over the Past 20 Years," seemed to implicitly advocate that the Soviet carrier-construction program emphasize larger carriers. At least, the article cited the fact that Italy was doing nothing to develop aircraft carriers because it was feasible to employ land-based aircraft with the fleet in her "relatively restricted theaters."[6]

The evidence tabularized in the article showed graphically what great progress the Western powers and Japan had made in building aircraft carriers, both heavy and light; Britain led with eight while the United States and Japan each had six carriers operational, and all three powers had five more under construction. In percentage of the other naval powers' total tonnage in aircraft carriers built or under construction, Japan was shown to be in the lead with 14.4 percent, Great Britain second with 12.4 percent, the United States next with 10.9 percent, Germany fourth with 9.6 percent, France with 4.0 percent, and Italy trailing with only 0.9 percent. The reason for this very substantial emphasis on aircraft carrier construction by most of the other naval powers was indicated to be that aviation was "taking part in all combat actions at sea" and "multiplied the combat force" of the fleet.

Navy Announces Plans for Light Carrier Construction? January 1938 brought the publication, in the *Naval Digest*, of a condensed version of an address that then Captain-Lieutenant Pierre Barjot of the French Navy had given on aircraft carriers and which had been reprinted in a French aviation journal.[7] Barjot dealt at length with the merits of big carriers (such as the 33,000-ton U.S.S. *Enterprise*) versus light carriers (especially the 13,800-ton U.S.S. *Ranger*) and concluded unequivocally in favor of the latter. In particular he wanted France to copy the U.S.S. *Ranger*, scaled down slightly to 12,000-tons and with an increase in speed of 3 knots to 32, but still carrying 40 planes.

In view of the fact that the *Naval Digest* is an official naval journal and has a long history of selecting articles that support the Navy's policy line at the time, it seems unlikely that Barjot's address was published simply as an interesting contribution to an objective discussion of which type of aircraft carrier would be most suitable for construction for the Soviet Navy. More likely, publication of the Barjot thesis indicated that the Navy policy line had changed from favoring big carriers to esoterically announcing the planned construction of just light carriers.

Barjot's discussion of the merits of the two was sufficiently "scientifically substantiated" to meet even the criteria of Marxist-Leninst methodology. In order to determine the relative merits of the light versus the heavy carrier, Barjot designed a measure of effectiveness for what he termed "the dynamic coefficient of the operational efficiency of an aircraft carrier." This was simply the number of aircraft normally embarked multiplied by the maximum sustainable speed of the carrier in knots, divided by the carrier's standard displacement in tons. Using this measure of efficiency, Barjot found that the first three winners were all light carriers, and with only the first place U.S.S. *Ranger* even exceeding 10,000 tons. While the 30,000-ton U.S.S. *Saratoga* was in fourth place, it was still ahead of one light carrier that ranked sixth of eight entries. Nevertheless, *Saratoga's* dynamic coefficient of operational efficiency at ¼ was significantly less than that of the U.S.S. *Ranger* (1/6) and the new 10,000-ton Japanese carrier *Soryu* (⅛).

Perhaps appreciating that his measure of effectiveness for aircraft carriers might not by itself meet with total acceptance—among other reasons because it had not taken account of some important characteristics such as vulnerability, maneuverability, landing-deck length, and armaments—Barjot included discussion of these and other important characteristics. He concluded that the smaller carriers were less vulnerable and more maneuverable, and that the shorter landing decks of the smaller carriers and the great speeds of new fighters could be compensated for without going to bigger carriers by simply redesigning carrier fighters to have the aerodynamic features necessary for slower landing speeds.

Also reprinted from Barjot's address was the observation that the size of the naval theater in which a carrier was to be employed should be a prime consideration in determining its displacement tonnage. With the Soviet Union's restricted naval theaters of military action in the Baltic and Black Seas, it is understandable that small carriers might be advocated. But how about the less restricted theaters of the Northern and Pacific Fleets?

Barjot's speech to a French audience naturally did not directly address this point of Soviet concern, but it did provide one possible clue. Actually, in his conclusions Barjot recommended not only the one light carrier, a copy of the U.S.S. *Ranger* scaled down slightly to 12,000 tons, but also a second light carrier—one of even smaller tonnage and speed (8,500 tons, 28 knots). In light of Admiral Kuznetsov's postwar remark in his memoirs that Stalin first cancelled the small carriers and subsequently the big ones, the possibility arises that the "big" carrier in Stalin's prewar carrier-construction program was to have looked much like Barjot's 12,000-ton scaled-down U.S.S. *Ranger* and would have been intended for the Northern and Pacific Fleets while the "small" carrier would have been the 8,500 tonner which Barjot had said could be of "great utility" for providing air cover beyond range of land-based aircraft and probably would have been well-suited for the fleets in the Baltic and Black Seas. In view of both the Soviet Union's poor industrial preparedness for building even light carriers, and its inability to purchase aircraft carrier design drawings for large carriers,[8] both the big and small carriers, which Kuznetsov said were in Stalin's original carrier-construction program, may actually have been light carriers.

Be that as it may, Barjot's address reached the following additional conclusions of relevance here: the best tonnage for an aircraft carrier would be from 8,000 to 14,000 tons; large carriers, such as the 33,000-ton U.S.S. *Saratoga* are required only for an oceanic navy without bases; big-carrier advocates are recommending 20,000 tons as most suitable (but they err); and it would be expedient to build both types of light carriers. The context of Barjot's address suggests that he thought this would allow the most efficient employment of a given country's available carrier resources. That is, a navy that had both would not be forced to employ the larger 12,000-ton carrier with its 40 planes in theaters or for missions where the smaller 8,500-ton carrier with just half as many planes would meet the requirements. Operating costs would be much lower, as would the risk of incurring irreplaceable losses in carrier strength.

Barjot's views must have been read with great interest by those concerned with Stalin's projected carrier-construction program. Certainly Barjot's views were so apposite to Soviet concerns that they are likely to have served as a framework of reference to focus discussion among the advocates of carriers of varying tonnages and capabilities.

Soviet Carrier Construction Opposed by Army. In a speech to the Komsomol youth organization in early 1938, P.A. Smirnov, the Army commissar who had been assigned as naval minister at that stage of Stalin's Great Purge (and who very shortly thereafter was himself shot), portrayed Germany's recently undertaken construction of aircraft carriers as a definitive indication of aggressive intentions toward the Soviet Union.[9] Smirnov voiced his (and the Army's) views as follows:

> The German fascists are building four battleships, two aircraft carriers, two Washington Treaty-limited cruisers, more than 20 destroyers, and numerous submarines. The great number of aircraft carriers in comparison with the overall size of the fascist navy testifies that they are preparing an offensive navy (p. 15).

Smirnov's statement was notable for two reasons. First, it reflected the increasing Soviet concern over the growing German Navy that had been evident since the 1935 Anglo-German Naval Accord effectively released Germany from the severe limits on naval construction that had been imposed by the Versailles Treaty. Second, Smirnov's choice of the programmed aircraft carriers rather than the battleships as the telling indication of offensive aims constituted a further Soviet portrayal of the aircraft carrier as *the* offensive naval weapons system *par excellence*. As Marshal Zhukov was to do again while he was Khrushchev's defense minister, use of this appellation of "aggressive" to typify aircraft carriers was a standard Army method of countering Navy advocacy of carrier construction.

The fact that Smirnov presumed to term a weapons systems as inherently aggressive at a time when Soviet admirals hoped to obtain Stalin's consent for building just such weapons systems, suggests both that Stalin's consent had not yet been given (as of March 1938) and that Army Commissar Smirnov was representing his parent service's interest in voicing the Army's opposition to any construction of large surface ships. The fact that he had placed himself publicly on the losing side of such a major issue in itself might have served as sufficient reason for his purge before the end of the year—

certainly numerous highly placed persons throughout the military were being purged for far less substantial reasons.

Command of the Sea Rehabilitated for a New "Soviet School." In August 1938, an authoritatively phrased article unmistakably aimed at rehabilitating the battleship and the command-of-the-sea doctrine (in at least a limited form) made its appearance in the daily newspaper Red Fleet.[10] Bearing the attention-getting title "Eradicate Every Vestige of Inimical Theory in Naval Strategy," the title alone, with its inclusion of the word "inimical" (which carried overtones of Stalin's Great Purge), must have caught the immediate attention of every reader.

And well it might! It contained one of the few public reflections of Stalin's purge of anyone and everyone who might be suspected of opposing his policies or of even having reservations about them. Referring to both the Young School advocates (Ludri and others) who had criticized battleships and the command-of-the-sea doctrine and to the leading Old School advocates (Gervais and Petrov), the article stated with brutal directness: "The glorious NKVD [the secret police] has cut off the head of the snake." To make certain that the reader realized that this hydra-headed decapitation had not been confined to Naval Headquarters in Moscow, the article subsequently named the Naval War College in Leningrad:

> The Voroshilov Naval War College must become the forge of Marxist ideas of naval science. The enemies of the people have done no small amount of their work within the walls of the Naval War College. From within its confines, false leaders have been monopolizing the right to naval science. They have been shortchanging the young, developing cadres and trying to indoctrinate them with inimical theories of tactics and strategy.

Moreover, for allegedly "complying with the demands of foreign intelligence," these "enemies of the people" were accused of having "created various small schools among the expanding group of young officers that are inimical to the building of an unconquerable navy for the socialist great power. . . . While exposing the inimical theories of the agents of foreign intelligence, the Naval War College is required to work out Bolshevist strategy and tactics for a powerful socialist navy."

This implicit demand on the Naval War College theoreticians of both schools to revise their views as necessary to correspond with, and elaborate the tactics for, a "command-of-the-sea" strategy (at least for holding the command "in dispute") had been preceded by more of the unfounded kind of allegations of foreign intelligence involvement that had characterized Stalin's infamous show trials in which the defendants had pleaded guilty to all sorts of absurd allegations in the vain hope that their lives would be spared. In this case the charges were framed as follows:

> The enemies of the people and their voluntary and involuntary accomplices have done everything in order to weaken in every way the defense capabilities of our mighty homeland. These pernicious individuals have accomplished no small amount on the theoretical front. . . . For many years hostile and inimical views have been expressed in the press and on other occasions. The enemies of the people adopted as their goal the weakening of the combat power of the Red Navy.

Both the Old School and Young School were brought under criticism in this uncompromising article which asserted that they were "joined by their ideological nature" and together constituted an anti-Soviet group. Starting first with the Old School, the indictment read as follows:

> Especially harmful and hostile views were propounded on the fundamental strategic question of war at sea—command of the sea. Representatives of one of the small groups, one which calls itself the "Old School" (Gervais and Petrov), took a position that slightly altered and modernized the theoretical baggage of the theoreticians of the Tsarist Navy (especially Klado) and the works on strategy of foreign, bourgeois naval theorists.

Referring to the appellation of "high priests"[11] of naval science given to Professors Gervais and Petrov as Russian disciples of Mahan and Colomb, Evseyev went on to refer to and comment on the view of the Old School on command of the sea. The article's condemnation of the Old School included a criticism of Gervais that is worth noting for its gross distortion of his stalwart (but ultimately unsuccessful) defense of the validity of the command-of-the-sea principle despite the "breaches" in it which he acknowledged had been made by the advent of the submarine and aircraft:

> The last representative of the "Old School," Professor Gervais, propounded the "theory of the breach." He asserted that with the appearance of submarines and aircraft in a theater of war, the theory of command of the sea was struck a blow and that these new means of warfare consequently left little possibility for gaining command of the sea. Such a declaration, in substance, was nothing other than an assertion that war at sea was virtually impossible due to the existing new means of warfare. This "theory" was nothing other than an "inimical" theory for us, one aimed at distracting the attention of the Soviet Union from the danger which threatens the workers from the capitalist world's command of the seas which wash the shores of the Soviet Union.

The Old School was criticized on two points concerning the views on command of the sea ascribed to it. Its most heinous anti-Soviet crime was "above all else" to have "introduced confusion into the concept of command of the sea" by replacing that generally understood term with one meaning "sea control."[12] The unsubstantial nature of this charge was indicated in the article itself. It acknowledged, in effect, that the only result was the introduction of a superfluous term, "sea control," which would be discarded and thereby correct the assertedly egregious error of which the Old School was so trivially accused.

Finally, the Old School was charged with the methodological failure of having "perniciously" characterized command of the sea into the three categories of unconditional, conditional, and disputed. The first of these, unconditional command (gained only by the complete destruction of an enemy's naval forces), was said (e.g., by Aleksandrov) never to have been achieved in the history of war while disputed command was declared to be "a completely unnecessary" category since, "if command of the sea is in continuing dispute, then no degree of command exists." This latter point may well have been an oblique criticism of Corbett's recommendation for the weaker of two belligerent navies to adopt a fleet-in-being strategy of constantly harassing its stronger opponent in order to hold command of the sea in dispute.[13]

The portion of the *Red Fleet* article setting forth the newly approved views on command of the sea is quoted in full, since the passage is open to varied interpretations which in turn will be potentially critical as benchmarks by which to judge the significance of Admiral Gorshkov's lengthy postwar exposition of the subject in his book *Seapower of the State*, which has appeared in two editions, the first in 1976 and a revised one in 1979. The newly formulated (Soviet School) views of the regime were stated as follows:

> Strategic missions at sea stem from the general political aims that have been set. The condition for the carrying out of such missions is the destruction of an adversary's naval power with the help of our military means.

> To the Navy in wartime may be assigned the following basic and major strategic missions: to cut the sea communications of the enemy; conduct assaults on the coasts of the enemy by landing ground forces from seaward and from the air; protect our own coast from strikes from seaward and make impossible landings by the enemy; threaten the flank and rear of the coastal land front of the enemy from seaward; and protect the coastal flank and rear of our own ground forces from attack by the enemy's naval forces.

> Assignments of one or more of these several missions would be determined by the military objectives of the war at sea, at the basis of which lie politico-economic factors, the condition of the naval forces, the conditions of the naval theaters and naval positions, bases, the foci of merchant shipping, the terminal points for shipping, and geographic factors. One of the most decisive aspects of the fulfillment of naval missions is the establishment of command of the sea.

> Command of the sea, as a strategic theory for the conduct of naval warfare, has as its aim the establishment of such conditions at sea by which the naval forces of an enemy are nearly or fully denied the possibility of conducting their own planned naval operations while one's own naval forces retain such possibility in full measure.

> In such circumstances, however, it by no means follows that, by establishment of command of the sea, the enemy naval forces cannot conduct counter-operations. The naval forces of the enemy will conduct such operations but they no longer can alter fundamentally the situation existing in a theatre.

Basically, command of the sea has the goal of gaining for one's own maritime forces (naval and merchant shipping) free communications and denying them to an enemy. For this it is essential to support the conduct of all naval operations carried out jointly with the ground forces and to put an end to comparable operations by the enemy.

The gaining of command of the sea is accomplished mainly by the way of (a) direct support to operations; (b) blockade of the naval forces of the enemy; and (c) destruction in battle of all or most of the enemy's naval forces. Command of the sea may be full or conditional, depending on the correlation of forces, either general or local, and by time—permanent or temporary.[14] However, full and general command can never be absolute.

Only so may be understood the fundamental question of naval strategy—"command of the sea"—which is confirmed by Marxist analysis of the study of naval warfare from ancient time (p. 2).

The Mahanian notion of the statement in the first paragraph of the above quotation that destruction of an adversary's naval power was a condition for the carrying out of the strategic missions at sea, was seemingly confused by the listing of missions in the penultimate paragraph in which the first listed mission was for direct support, i.e., for Army coastal flank missions; the second for blockade of the enemy's naval forces, and only in third and last place was mention made of destroying the enemy's naval forces. However, the list of missions in this case appears to have been in the order in which capabilities would be developed for carrying them out: (1) support for Army coastal operations; (2) a submarine blockade of enemies' key naval bases; and (3) fighting attack aircraft-carrier fleets.

The last sentence of the third paragraph characterized gaining command of the sea as one of the most decisive aspects of the fulfillment of naval missions. This, taken together with the first paragraph's specification of destruction of the enemy's naval power as a "condition" for the carrying out of the requisite naval missions make it apparent that the theory of the new "Soviet School" was basically Old School in its long-term aim of gaining command of the sea by destroying an enemy's main naval forces.

Yet it is noteworthy in the fourth through the penultimate paragraphs of the quotation above that while the version of a command-of-the-sea strategy prescribed (for the new Soviet School strategy) accorded full credit to the Old School's long-term aim of gaining an essentially full command of the sea, nothing more was proffered by way of an implementing method than the first-listed alternative for fighting a superior adversary—that of providing direct support of operations (i.e., the Soviet School's basic tenet of achieving a limited command of the sea by gaining superiority in the main direction of an operation for only as long as required to carry it out).

It was made clear that just temporary superiority in the main direction (or "sector"), gained by providing adequate support for operations just long enough to bring them to a successful conclusion, was considered enough.

This limited command-of-the-sea concept formed the basis for Soviet School theory. And although the missions that could be conducted with only such minimal support were dilated on at length, they were restricted to those for attacking an enemy's sea lines of communication and providing Army-flank support.

The article next took aim at the Young School for its "defeatist" denial of the validity of the command-of-the-sea theory. Targeted by the polemical fire was the heart of Aleksandrov's criticism of the Old School's key tenet of full or general command of the sea. Aleksandrov had argued that unblockadable weapons platforms (the submarine and airplane) had appeared at sea and spelled the end of command of the sea as an operative doctrine. With vitriolic scorn that equalled Aleksandrov's at his peak form, the article denounced this view as not only militarily unsound but as politically inexpedient:

> Another inimical group is that called the "Young School" (Ludri and others).[15] Masking themselves with "revolutionary" phraseology and employing every means at its disposal, it covertly introduced into the Soviet Union a defeatist theory for the conduct of war at sea. This was basically in the form of criticism of the theory of command of the sea. Instead of a "critique" this inimical group proposed and propagated in the ranks of the Workers-Peasants Red Navy nothing other than a strategic mental vacuum and fault-finding.

> The leitmotif of the defeatist theory of the "Young School" is full denial of the theory of command of the sea in the next war with such applesauce as that this theory, so to speak, is a bourgeois theory and therefore unacceptable to our state.

> The enemy agents of the "Young School" assert that blockade is impossible under the conditions of modern means of war at sea (submarines and airplanes). They teach that the presence of unblockadable means in the composition of navies excludes the possibility of achieving command of the sea. This assertion is false from both the political and the military point of view.

> Defeat of a blockade is improbable. . . . In the opinion of the Young School an opponent would not conduct blockade operations in naval theaters under the conditions of the new means of combat [i.e., airplanes and submarines]. Moreover, according to Young School views, we should not conduct blockade operations, that is defeat [the enemy] in detail on occasion [by] the feasible [i.e., blockade] activity of our submarines and airplanes on sea and ocean communications and off the coasts of an enemy.

> In such fashion the [Young School] enemies attempted to divert us from the dangers of blockade operation on the one hand and on the other diverted us from the tactics of active operations by our light forces at a great distance from the bases of our country. Current developments in Spain support all that we have said about blockade operations. The navies of the interventionists have succeeded to a considerable degree in blockading the Spanish coast. . . . In view of the threat of blockade in our restricted sea regions, we must take it into account and conduct work for countering a possible blockade (p. 2).

The article went into some detail to support this argument, that submarines and aircraft were not the unblockadable or other-wise unstoppable weapons system that the Young School had made them out to be:

> It is apparent to us that in narrow and restricted regions, submarines can be blockaded completely. . . . We realize by the same token that submarines cannot be everywhere and always blockaded. . . . As concerns aviation in a maritime mode, it is difficult to blockade. But this does not mean that there are no military means to counter aviation. Aircraft can be scouted and located. Aircraft can be destroyed on the airfield. Aircraft can be met in the air and destroyed. Naval and air bases, we maintain, are more accessible to air attacks than is a fleet. . . .

> As for aircraft and submarines, it is completely clear to us that with some means it is possible to provide preliminary support to one or another operation at sea, especially to landing operations. But the positive result of this preliminary support is nothing other than command of the sea in the exact sense of its meaning (p. 3).

Here we may note an important innovation of the Soviet School: while, in effect, gaining command of the sea in an intended area of operations was no longer a preliminary prerequisite to the conduct of any other missions in the area (as the Old School maintained and as indicated above by specifying "direct" support of operations as the first-listed way of gaining command of the sea), nevertheless, preliminary control might be sought in the circumstances that adequate forces were available. And when such preliminary support were provided and succeeded in eliminating all serious opposition to the impending operation, Evseyev further implied, nothing less would have been achieved than "command of the sea" (limited in space and in time though it would be). By this innovation, the Evseyev article preserved for the Soviet School, although in seriously qualified form, the substance of the Old School's key tenet that command of the sea should be gained before undertaking other naval missions.

Far from aircraft and submarines constituting a net threat to command of the sea, the article alleged that their operational characteristics would "help the surface fleet to a greater degree even than before the war in gaining command of the sea." Based on the foregoing argument, and ignoring the major aspect of the capabilities of enemy submarines and aircraft to hinder Soviet operations, the article asserted: "Thus, we may conclude that the appearance of new means of combat—aircraft and submarines—does not in any way discredit the theory of command of the sea but, to the contrary, strengthens it" (p. 3).

Finally it should be noted that the Evseyev article, in effect, also made the following points:

> • Command-of-the-sea strategy trumpeted in the article so propagandistically as offensive in nature, actually had a defensive aim—to protect the Soviet Union from seaborne attack. Creation of the People's Commissariat of the Navy of the Soviet

Union shows with all clarity that the Soviet people, in order to ward off attack by the enemy, are strengthening their command of the seas and oceans (p. 3).

- All types of warships including the most powerful were to be built;[16] and

- It was demanded of the ship-building industry to overcome the formidable obstacles that lay in the way of construction of capital ships.[17]

Gorshkov Describes the Denouement of the Debate. Writing in 1972, Admiral Gorshkov gave an illuminating if brief description of the nature of the Young School-Old School clashes that took place in the process of working out a new Soviet School strategy for employing the big navy Stalin had directed.[18]

> In correspondence with the new missions of the Navy, the theoretical problems of naval art were worked out in the (naval and military war) colleges and scientific research institutes. This creative process took place in a milieu of a sharp struggle of opinions between supporters of defensive and offensive views on the role and employment of the forces of the navy in a future war. The former were still under the influence of the theory of "the small war" which had been correct for its time. The latter, who considered that our navy already had become capable of conducting combat operations outside the limits of its coastal waters, adhered to the theory of command of the sea (p. 21).

Gorshkov, in order to explicate the view of command of the sea that he claimed was then dominant went on to quote from a 1938 academic dissertation that the then Captain Second Rank Belli had completed while instructing at the Naval War College:

> However, the interpretation of the term "command of the sea" was somewhat different from that accepted in the West. Thus, in the course of lectures at the Naval War College at that time it was stated: "To gain superiority in forces over the enemy in the main directions and to pin him down in secondary directions during an operation means to gain command of the sea in the theater of operations or part of a theater, that is, to create a situation in which the enemy will be paralyzed or pinned down in his operations, or weakened and thereby hampered from interfering with our execution of a given operation or with our carrying out of our own operational missions[19] (p. 21).

From all of the foregoing, it would appear that Belli was a leading architect of the new Soviet School (along with Evseyev) in that he had contrived an expedient revision of the Old School and Young School theories which preserved the long-term aim of the Mahanist command-of-the-sea theory of the former school and the major role which that school accorded to large surface combatant ships while giving full weight to the combat capabilities of submarines and airplanes as favored by the latter school.

Italian Naval Expert Cited on Need for Carriers. In September 1938, an Army journal on foreign military developments carried a translation of an article from *Marine Rundschau,* "Naval Art and the Lessons of Naval Warfare." The article included an editorial introduction which cited an Italian naval theoretician, Oscar Giamberardino, as favoring the construction of (large) aircraft carriers for the Italian Navy.[20] In December 1937 Captain First Rank Shvede had cited as a surrogate for the policy preference of the Soviet Navy advocates of large attack carriers the Italian decision not to build any aircraft carriers because the restricted waters of the Mediterranean allegedly could be controlled by land-based aircraft. However, by citing an influential Italian naval theoretician who was implying that his country's decision had been wrong, proponents of larger carriers may be seen to have been trying to negate a foreign precedent that had obvious application to the Soviet situation in the Baltic and Black Seas.

In so doing, it is interesting to note, the big-carrier proponents had removed aircraft carriers from the light-forces category less unacceptable to the Army and Party leadership and reclassified them as capital ships, an intrinsically pejorative classification. The big-carrier proponents may have been trying to eradicate any distinction Stalin might have had in mind that made big carriers look less acceptable than small ones. While that is mere speculation, the context of the editorial preface that cited Giamberardino lends itself to such an interpretation:

> Concerning the structure of a modern navy, Giamberardino calls for the construction of a powerful capital-ship navy, speaking out against an increase in the light forces. . . . He also is calling for the construction of aircraft carriers which will be necessary for oceanic warfare. In a word, Italy must build such a navy as will make her a great naval power (p. 73).

As may be seen from the above quotation, Giamberardino is said both to have opposed building more light forces and to have favored construction of carriers large enough for oceanic operations. Obviously, Frunze's 1925 categorization of aircraft carriers as light forces was here being either challenged or nominally changed to the capital-ship category, apparently mainly in the hope of influencing Stalin to approve a construction program of heavy rather than light carriers. Describing the carriers being advocated as oceanic ones that would make Italy into a great naval power was similar to then-current Soviet calls for building "a sea and oceanic navy worthy of the Soviet great power." It was not that the Soviet Navy leadership was entertaining illusions about operating any of their projected carriers in the mid-Atlantic or Pacific, but just that the Northern and Pacific theaters of military action were considered to be "oceanic" by virtue by their much less restricted access to the Atlantic and Pacific than that of the Baltic Sea and Black Sea Fleets in their "sea" theaters of combat actions (TVDs).

The Carrier Construction Conundrum. Some evidence indicates that Admiral Kuznetsov, the architect of Stalin's navy and the Soviet Navy's leader

throughout World War II, at least intended to construct light carriers just
for fleet air defense, whatever his position may have been with regard to
the construction of attack carriers. In the 1969 expanded second edition of
his 1966 memoirs, *One the Eve*, Admiral Kuznetsov added a new sentence
which read:

> Where we felt a sharp inadequacy in the Great Patriotic War was in small aircraft
> carriers, without which even then destroyers and cruisers could not operate with the
> greatest success.[21]

At the 18th Party Congress (10-21 March 1939) Admiral Kuznetsov, then
commander in chief of the Pacific Fleet, was introduced as such by the
speaker just "to say a few words." In actuality, however, it was quite clear
from the content of his remarks that he was presenting the accountability
report on the Navy since the last party congress, five years earlier.
Obviously, he was doing so in place of the recently purged naval minister,
P.A. Smirnov. The circumstance doubtless was taken as a sign of his
impending appointment to head the Navy—which did take place within the
year.[22]

In listing the naval force types that should be in the composition of a
modern navy, Kuznetsov placed aircraft carriers with the light forces toward
the end of the listing. Despite Shvede's having promoted aircraft carriers
to capital-ship standing by listing them immediately after battleships and
ahead of cruisers, they still were officially considered light forces, as ships
"of special purpose," as they had been ever since Defense Minister Frunze
had so categorized them in 1925. The passage in question runs as follows:

> A modern navy has in its force structure, in addition to battleships and heavy cruisers—
> those floating fortresses—light cruisers and destroyers, a great number of various types
> of submarines, aircraft carriers, minelayers, minesweepers, and a number of other types
> of ships (p. 477).

Kuznetsov dilated on the naval threat to the Soviet Union posed by the
world naval arms race, which he characterized as proceeding at full tilt.
He stressed the need for additional protection for the Soviet Union's 48,000
kilometers of maritime borders, and averred that Soviet industry was already
in shape to give the country combatant ships of every type, large as well
as small. And, he noted, "We already have ships of large tonnage and are
mastering the construction of the remaining [types of] ships, too." (p. 478)

All of this was a reflection of what Kuznetsov referred to as Stalin's
decision to shift from the construction of small ships to "the organization,
development, and creation of a mighty sea and oceanic Soviet Navy with
big ships not inferior in their power to the best military ships." (pp. 478-
479) In retrospect Kuznetsov's reference to the "remaining" types of ships
must have been to aircraft carriers. As *the* instrument for contesting for
command of the sea as a "mighty" navy would have to do to be worthy

of the name, carrier construction must have been seen by Kuznetsov as *the* missing element. He continued:

> Creation of a powerful navy requires also a corresponding theory . . . for employment of the programmed big-ship naval forces. It requires having correct . . . tenets on war at sea. Enemies, masking their actions with irrelevant twaddle about the possibilities or impossibilities of command of the sea and under the guise of studying the experience of the last war and its deep "theoretization," have deliberately delayed the development of individual types of ships (p. 478).

In an obvious effort to forestall any more such bureaucratic delay, Kuznetsov added that Stalin's orders were clear: "We must have a powerful navy . . . and if an enemy undertakes to attack us, the Navy . . . must become an offensive fleet which not only prevents the enemy from reaching our shores, but which will destroy him in his own waters." (p. 478)

Then continuing directly, Kuznetsov again implicitly suggested that "the Government" (i.e., Stalin alone) had approved a carrier-construction program by stating that, as part of building its proclaimed "mighty sea and oceanic navy," the Soviet Union would have to build "the types of combatant ships comparable to those of the possible enemy,"[23] whether it was Germany, Japan, France, Great Britain, or the United States. All but the first already had a number of attack carriers in operation and Germany, as noted earlier, had started construction on several.

Finally, Kuznetsov also specified that the Soviet Union must build the types of combatant ships "suitable for our sea theaters." From what we have already learned on this subject, Kuznetsov was probably thinking about, and perhaps esoterically announcing to those "in the know," that not only were smaller carriers to be built (to provide air cover for the Baltic Sea and Black Sea Fleets), but that also programmed were somewhat larger light carriers (i.e., ones with substantial strike capabilities in addition to being able to provide air cover for the Pacific and Northern Fleets).

Whatever he was esoterically conveying to the *cognoscenti* at the 18th Party Congress in March 1939, it was probably less confused and less confusing than the numerous variations on the prewar aircraft-carrier construction program which Kuznetsov has presented to us in his writings. Before publication, his first book of memoirs, *On the Eve*, was serialized in Russian in the literary journal *Oktyabr'*. After publication, the book was serialized in English in *International Affairs*, the English version of the monthly Soviet foreign policy journal *Mezhdunarodnaya zhizn*.

To help evaluate Kuznetsov's varying versions and comments from two other sources the following conflicting points should be noted with regard to the ten-year big-ship construction program adopted in late 1937:

(1) ". . . the program did not accord any significance at all to aircraft carriers";[24]

(2) ". . . the construction of aircraft carriers was not deleted but only delayed until the last year of the Five-year Plan";[25]

(3) "the program made no provision at all for aircraft carriers";[26]

(4) "the program . . . provided for . . . battleships, heavy cruisers, and aircraft carriers";[27]

(5) "the program did not receive official approval."[28]

As is readily apparent from the above juxtaposition of the relevant statements about aircraft-carrier construction in the ten-year shipbuilding program begun in the winter of 1937-1938,[29] points (1), (3), and (5) emphatically claim that *no* aircraft-carrier construction was included in the 1937-1938 program as (presumably) officially approved before the keels of three battleships and several heavy cruisers were laid down pursuant to the program. However, points (2) and (4) seemingly flatly contradict the other three points by asserting unequivocally that the 1937 program did indeed include the construction of aircraft carriers, even though delayed until almost the mid-point of the ten-year program.

Can these seemingly contradictory statements be reconciled? Yes, although only with some tortuosity. Before this can be done, however, it is necessary to note the context of each of these five points plus two significant changes with regard to aircraft-carrier construction made in the second (1969) edition of *On the Eve*, the first book of Kuznetsov's memoirs.

The prepublication serialization of *On the Eve*, in the November 1965 issue of *Oktyabr'*, has the first of the five conflicting statements on the ten-year program of shipbuilding. Kuznetsov's first version was that the 1937 program attributed no importance whatsoever to carrier construction. He made this claim in the context of arguing that, while there was some justification for having placed too much emphasis on battleships and heavy cruisers, "what was inexcusable was that the program did not accord any significance at all to aircraft carriers." (p 142) He went on directly to adduce a vivid illustration of the potentially disastrous wartime consequences:

> Just imagine for a moment that the program had been successfully completed in the second half of the 1940s. We should have had large battle forces of capital ships but . . . without aircraft carriers. Then how far out to sea could the capital ships have gone? (p. 142)

Kuznetsov further asserted that it was obvious by 1937 that "it was necessary to have aircraft carriers if only to protect the capital ships" but that Stalin, "who usually took the views of the specialists into account, for some reason underestimated the role of aircraft carriers" and "somewhat later during the review of the proposal plan for another program"[30] which did include aircraft carriers, deleted "first the big and subsequently also the small carriers from it." (p. 1)

All well and good—had Kuznetsov stuck with this story in the two editions of his book and the serialization of the book in English, there would have been no substantial evidence available in the non-Communist world to contradict him. However, in the interval between publication of the *Oktyabr'* version in November 1965 and the appearance of the first edition of *On the Eve* about 9 months later, the Party line on aircraft-carrier construction apparently was perceived by Kuznetsov and the military censors to have shifted to such an extent as to make it acceptable to finally acknowledge publicly that the Soviet Union had planned to build aircraft carriers more than two decades earlier At any rate, *On the Eve* included the assertion that construction of aircraft carriers actually had been included in the 1937 program. This *volte face* seems to have been a hasty change made to take advantage of an apparent softening of the Party line's long ban on saying anything favorable about aircraft carriers.

However, the additional editorial changes to *On the Eve* required removal of several rather glaring inconsistencies that were not made, even partially, until the second edition appeared 3 years later. Thus, the first edition of *On the Eve* continued to state, as had the *Oktyabr'* version, that the 1937 program "did not accord any significance at all to aircraft carriers," a flat contradiction to the affirmation that the 1937 program *had* provided for the construction of aircraft carriers, even if delayed long enough to make the necessary preparations. The second edition of *On the Eve* changed a word so that it then read that the program failed to accord the "necessary" significance to aircraft carriers rather than "not any at all."[31]

Despite this correction of one of the inconsistencies resulting from Kuznetsov's reversal in the first edition of *On the Eve*, the second edition, like the first, included the equally inconsistent scenario for a future war in which, despite the assumed completion of the ten-year program launched in 1937, Soviet surface forces still would have no aircraft carriers to provide air cover beyond the 100-mile coastal strip in which land-based naval fighter airplanes could give such cover.[32]

When the English-language serialization of the part relevant to this subject of Kuznetsov's first book of memoirs appeared in *International Affairs* in December 1966, although only 4 months had passed, Kuznetsov's story on aircraft-carrier construction in the 1937 program had completely reversed itself again and had essentially reasserted its original position.[33] Had there not been a second edition of *On the Eve* that returned to the version of the first edition, one might have concluded that the Party line on aircraft carriers had itself been reversed to the *status quo ante*—that nothing favorable should be published about aircraft carriers in general and, in particular, the Soviet Union had never wanted to build such an essentially offensive, "aggressive" type of ship. However, with the reappearance, 3 years later of Kuznetsov's acknowledgment that construction of aircraft carriers actually had been included in the 1937 program, the only plausible conclusion seems to be that the Soviet military censors had determined that it would be unacceptable to acknowledge in an English-language journal intended mainly for a Western audience even what was already in print in Russian for the domestic readership.

This English-language serialized version of Kuznetsov's *On the Eve* contained the same future-war scenario that envisioned large surface forces without any aircraft carriers to provide them air cover in the open sea that had been in both the serialized Russian version and in the book itself. Now again that scenario was consistent with the assertion that the 1937 program had not included any aircraft carriers. Also consistent with this claim was the similar passage from both earlier versions that Stalin "for some unexplained reason" had not understood the importance of aircraft carriers and that he had cut out both "big and small" carriers from a proposed shipbuilding program "somewhat later."

When the second edition of *On the Eve* appeared in 1969, it carried one additional passage on aircraft carriers. While not contradictory to Kuznetsov's reassertion that carriers had in fact been included in the 1937 program, the passage is notable for the emphasis it places in hindsight on just how badly the Soviet Union erred in not building aircraft carriers in the interwar period:

> Thus, the enthusiasm for battleships and heavy cruisers was unwarranted considering the facts of our limited sea theaters—and in this I see the basic error in the big-ship construction program of 1937. Where we felt a sharp inadequacy was in small aircraft carriers. Without them, even at that time, destroyers and cruisers could not operate with the fullest success.[34]

Since Admiral Kuznetsov's remarkable reversals in the second half of the 1960s as to whether or not aircraft-carrier construction was included in the 1937 big-ship building program, there have been two notable further comments on the subject. One appeared in a 1982 article by Gorshkov's Deputy Commander-in-Chief of the Navy for Shipbuilding and Armament, Engineering Admiral Kotov. The complete passage reads as follows:

> A new stage in Soviet military shipbuilding was related to the course of the Party for the organization and construction of a big sea and oceanic navy for the Soviet Union. In 1937 a ten-year shipbuilding program was worked out which provided for the building of combatant ships of all types, including battleships, heavy cruisers, and aircraft carriers.[35]

Here we have it on the authority of the Navy's top shipbuilder (and a no-nonsense and relatively apolitical "naval specialist" who has been consistently straightforward over the two decades he has been appearing in print) that the 1937 program did indeed include aircraft carriers. While Kotov's article does not go beyond providing particularly authoritative confirmation of Kuznetsov's version in the two editions of *On the Eve*, it does refute the serialized versions of that book in Russian and English which implied that no aircraft carriers were included. The source of the fifth and final conflicting point on prewar carrier construction was a book by a well-known and reputable Soviet naval writer, Captain First Rank Basov,[36] that appeared in 1979 under the title *The Navy in the Great Patriotic War 1941-1945*. Its claim that the 1937 program never received official ratification comes in a very informative context, as quoted at length below:

> At that time [when the Navy had been established as a separate ministry on 30 December 1937 and a Main Military Council of the Navy officially decreed on 31 March 1938], a Shipbuilding Program was worked out on the basis of the Party's policy to develop the Army and the Navy. It was directed at the construction of big surface combatant ships suitable for the protection of our state interests on the open seas and in the oceans. A policy for the construction of battleships, cruisers, and aircraft carriers seemed correct inasmuch as the capabilities of submarines and shore-based aviation for war at sea . . . were considered limited. However, it would have required two decades of intensive construction before our fleets could equal those of the strongest naval powers in numbers of big surface combatant ships.

> Consequently, the program did not receive official approval but was revised to be commensurate with the existing capabilities of industry. Simultaneously, the Party and government took measures for the modernization and strengthening of the shipbuilding industry. . . . (p. 31)

> In the course of 1940 and the beginning of 1941, the Shipbuilding Program continued to be revised: the number of battleships was decreased but the number of cruisers was increased. In the program appeared two aircraft carriers (for the Northern and Pacific Fleets). . . . (p. 32)

> In October 1940, in view of the growing threat of attack on the Soviet Union by fascist Germany, the government reviewed the program for military shipbuilding: it was decreed that there would be no further keel-layings of battleships and heavy cruisers; work would be continued only on nearly completed ships; and construction work would be stopped on ships with lengthy construction periods. (p. 33)

These foregoing comments by Captain First Rank Basov seem to go far to clarify what most likely transpired with regard to the construction of aircraft carriers in the 1937 program. It appears likely that four light aircraft carriers were included in that program initially and that two larger light carriers were substituted for two of the four smaller ones prior to the program's suspension in October 1940 and formal cancellation at the beginning of 1941. The Defense Ministry was likely to have given tacit advance approval in 1937 provided that the necessary shipyard facilities could be developed in time and suitable blueprints for aircraft carriers and the necessary propulsion machinery obtained abroad. Any such plan was overtaken by the outbreak of World War II in September 1939.

It is particularly worth noting that, of all five of the available Soviet accounts of the 1938 program, the only explicit information we are given as to the number of aircraft carriers involved is Basov's statement that two were added to the program in 1940 or early 1941 and that they were being built for the Northern and Pacific Fleets, presumably one for each. A former Soviet naval officer and commanding officer of a Baltic Fleet destroyer has supported Kuznetsov's statement that the 1937 program included aircraft carriers.[37] Kuznetsov's comment that "somewhat later" (than "the approval of the projected combatant ships for 1939" and probably in the revision of early 1940 that Basov described) Stalin had deleted from the revised shipbuilding plan "first the large, then also the small carriers," clearly indicates that the 1940 proposed program included at least two of each for a total of a minimum of four carriers. In light of all of the relevant evidence, it seems most likely that the two presumably light carriers mentioned by Basov as intended for the Northern and Pacific Fleets were added to the program in lieu of two of the four light carriers in the initial 1937 shipbuilding program.

No later than the spring of 1940, Kuznetsov relates, "construction of the big ships began to be cut back" in favor of production of tanks and artillery for the Army.[38] The statement in the Basov book that the 1937 program was never approved officially suggests that lack of approval may account for some of the confusion; that is, it may have served as a basis for some of the conflicting statements. This speculation is given some support by the fact that Admiral Kuznetsov, in his version published in the November 1965 issue of *Oktyabr'*, stated that the first draft of the 1937 program had been revised (in unspecified ways) by Stalin and verbal approval given and "work begun without waiting for the details to be completed."[39]

One strongly suspects that one of the unattended details was obtaining official ratification from the appropriate Party and state bodies. In those days, the expression "the Government" was used commonly to refer to Stalin alone; he *was* the Party and state. Moreover, Stalin was known to prefer to withhold his final written approval of major projects until they had been "proven by life itself." This practice facilitated scapegoating, of course, and presumably applied to all projects as uncertain of success as this 11th-hour crash program of constructing ships far larger and more complex than anything yet undertaken in Soviet shipyards.

While there is unlikely to have been any practical difference in execution of the 1937 Shipbuilding Program just because it had not been formally ratified, that fact may have served to help produce some of the conflicting statements we have seen about that program. At least the conclusion seems well supported by the evidence that Stalin, at least tacitly approved for a time of the construction of four light aircraft carriers.

Of equal interest is to determine, to the extent the evidence allows, what types of carriers were programmed and for which of the four Soviet fleet areas. The available evidence suggests (as hypothesized above) that even the "big" carriers that Kuznetsov said Stalin had cancelled ahead of the "small" ones were light carriers too, even though probably several thousand tons larger than the "small" ones. This tentative conclusion is based mainly on the fact that the three statements found in Kuznetsov's writings on the roles that any Soviet-built aircraft carriers would be expected to play were all devoid of any indication of an offensive strike role such as can only be played by heavy carriers. Rather, all were limited to the primary role of light carriers—that of merely providing air cover to the battle forces of the fleets, that is, to the "capital ships," the battleships and heavy cruisers.

The first of these three Kuznetsov statements was (with regard to 1937-1938 when the program was formulated) that "it was obvious already that aircraft carriers were essential, if only to protect the capital ships."[40] In the English serialization this was changed in a way that made it explicit that the main role intended for the aircraft carrier was that of providing air cover: "It was obvious already that aircraft carriers had to be there to give protection to the battleships."[41] The second of these three statements was in Kuznetsov's future-war scenario without aircraft carriers and with the capital ships consequently limited in their operations for lack of air cover to a narrow coastal strip.[42] The third of Kuznetsov's three statements relevant to the largely defensive role he envisioned for Soviet aircraft carriers of providing air cover to the battle forces of the fleets came in the previously quoted paragraph from the 1969 (second) edition of his first book of memoirs, On the Eve. This stated in effect that the worst mistake of the big-shipbuilding program was not to have realized that battleships and heavy cruisers were not suitable for warfare in the Soviet Union's "limited sea theaters" and, by implication, that a comparably bad mistake had been, as the reader will recall, in not building the "small" carriers "without which even the destroyers and cruisers could not operate with the fullest success."[43]

As for the intended fleet areas for the aircraft carriers planned for construction under the 1937 program, the evidence is conflicting with only the Pacific emerging as a certain choice as either first or second preference. Admiral Kotov indicated that the next priority was the Baltic theater,[44] while Captain First Rank Basov implied that it was the Northern Fleet area. Basov claimed that the two carriers added to the 1937 program in 1940 were for the Northern and Pacific Fleets.[45] While Kuznetsov was uninformative about the explicit fleet areas for which the carriers had been planned, he did make the revealing comment that "probably we tended to underestimate the Northern Theater and attached too much attention to the Baltic."[46] In light of this Admiral Kotov's very credible argument that it required "powerful fleets" to "withstand the naval forces of the probable adversaries" (obviously Germany and Japan, respectively, with perhaps also the United Kingdom in the Baltic), the Baltic seems likely to have been considered a priority. Kotov made it clear that it was not held necessary to develop such a powerful fleet in the Northern Fleet area—just to "strengthen" the existing (weak) forces there. In the Black Sea, Kotov made clear, it was apparently believed that little or nothing more needed to be done to ensure that the Black Sea Fleet would be able to maintain its virtually uncontested sway over that area. Quite likely they also believed that the relatively good flying weather in the region would make it possible to provide adequate air support by the Black Sea Fleet's shore-based aviation without benefit of aircraft carriers.

Accordingly, it appears reasonably certain that providing carriers to the Baltic and Pacific fleets were the first and second priorities, respectively. Hence it may well be, that the two smaller tonnage light carriers were intended for the Baltic, the two larger light carriers for the Pacific and none at all for the Northern and Black Sea Fleets.

Finally, with regard to the 1937 big-ship construction program, two of Kuznetsov's comments appear to afford a glimpse into the nature of the strategy that Stalin envisioned for his "big sea and oceanic navy worthy of the great Soviet power." This insight in turn supports the tentative conclusion that the projected aircraft carriers were primarily intended just for fleet air support in the two most threatened of the Soviet Union's peripheral seas—the Baltic and the Sea of Japan, —rather than for oceanic operations that would require general engagements of the main battle and carrier forces with the major naval powers for command of the sea.

The first of Kuznetsov's revealing comments in this regard was his reported conversation with Stalin in which the latter observed that the Soviet Navy would not be expected "to fight off America's shores."[47] This may have been intended by Stalin to contradict Kuznetsov's previously quoted statement at the 18th Party Congress on March 1939 that the Soviet Navy if attacked, must take the offensive and destroy the enemy's navy in its own home waters.

This point takes on particular significance because Soviet military doctrine for all services then required (and still requires) attacking an adversary to "the full depth of his dispositions." This would only have become practical for the Soviet Navy when and if a strong force of attack aircraft carriers were in operation in the Soviet Navy. Accordingly, Stalin's observation may well have been intended to relieve the Navy of the otherwise binding obligation to follow the tenets of military doctrine. From the Navy's viewpoint, this probably was taken as Stalin's way of saying that the Soviet Navy did not need and would not get big attack carriers that eventually could enable it to fight the Western navies with their own favored weapons system—the attack carrier.

The second of Kuznetsov's revealing remarks was that the probable reason for Stalin's obvious underrating of aircraft carriers was his underestimation of the air threat to surface ships. While this is true as far as it goes, it appears to be a deliberate half-truth on Kuznetsov's part. The other half was that Stalin had no intention of operating his "big sea and oceanic navy" (if the Nazis should allow the Soviet Union time to complete it) outside the Soviet coastal seas where it was to provide prestige and deterrence in peacetime and an "active" fleet-in-being deterrent and defense should the Nazi-Soviet Pact of 1939 prove insufficient to avoid war with Germany.

The feeling that Kuznetsov was dissembling on this subject becomes even stronger when he remarked with what seems obvious disingenuousness (concerning Stalin's insistence on continuing to build battleships): "I thought that he had his own plans which he did not consider necessary to share with us. That may well have been so."[48] Quite possibly it was not that Kuznetsov did not understand Stalin's very limited aspirations at sea but that he could not bring himself to admit publicly that he had failed to inspire Stalin with his own Mahanian vision of the Soviet Union as one of the world's leading naval powers. To avoid that, it would seem, Kuznetsov played out a charade of professing Stalin's allegedly "curious passion" for heavy cruisers, his strong attachment to battleships, and his allegedly unfathomable failure to appreciate the true value of aircraft carriers.

The "Soviet School" of Warfare Spelled Out. In April 1939 the *Naval Digest* included an article by the same Captain Second Rank V. A. Belli, whose 1938 dissertation Gorshkov quoted to such significant effect. Quite likely a summary of his dissertation, Belli's article was entitled "Fundamentals of the Conduct of Operations at Sea."[49] It amplified and restated the Soviet School tenets expounded by Evseyev 10 months earlier, which were patently designed to reorient Soviet naval strategy to the big-ship navy that had been undertaken. In a striking metamorphosis, since he had appeared to be an ardent Young School supporter in his advocacy of aircraft and particularly of submarines, Belli emerged in this article as the leading Soviet School proponent.

Belli's radical shift may have been not unrelated to a demand that had been aired publicly in early 1938 by the naval minister, P.A. Smirnov[50] (the former Army political commissar). Smirnov insisted that the work of the Naval War College must fully satisfy the changed requirements for a strategic theory corresponding to the big navy under construction. Smirnov had prefaced his demand with the criticism that "it could not be said that the Naval War College was fully satisfying those requirements laid on it by the Navy" in the area of "military-scientific ideas." Smirnov had added that "new situations require new answers." He went on to make it abundantly clear that only a theory that would have practical application to the strategy for a war at sea would suffice.

In his article, Belli notably indicated no less than three times that the favored Soviet strategy for (eventual) adoption was the Old School's prescription for a navy not too greatly inferior to those of the likely adversaries. The strategy was force-equalization by first destroying enough of a stronger adversary's forces piecemeal ("in detail") until a general engagement could be sought with good prospects of victory.

In the first instance of the threefold prescription of a force-equalization strategy, Belli listed as most important of the missions for the Navy, destruction of the enemy fleet "in detail." In the second passage stipulating a force-equalization strategy, Belli, in essence, disclaimed the Mahanian view that an enemy's main naval forces must first be destroyed (and command of the sea thereby gained) before any other missions (to achieve "ulterior objectives") could be undertaken:

> The essence of contemporary war at sea is not that it is obligatory to effect the destruction of all of the enemy's combatant ships and aircraft but to be capable, at each stage of a war, of fulfilling those missions assigned the navy and hinder the adversary in executing his missions.[51]

Belli's formulation reaffirmed, as the central tenet of the Soviet School, that which Evseyev had posited in his August 1938 *Red Fleet* article for a limited command of the sea. However, Belli's formulation amplified Evseyev's by specifying that the extent of the command of the sea required could be limited in area and in time to the minimum required "at each stage of a war" to enable the Navy to fulfill "those missions assigned" to it. In effect, Belli's formulation appeared to have grafted the campaign or theater "operational art" of a limited command of the sea that had been implicit in Evseyev's article onto the composite fleet-in-being strategy of force-equalization by attrition that Sir Julian Corbett had prescribed for the weaker of two strong navies. To carry out this strategy, Belli specified "the destruction of the enemy in detail by concentrating a great superiority of forces in the decisive place at the decisive moment." (p. 16)

In what was a classical description of the tactics for an active fleet-in-being strategy that could have been taken from Corbett's writings, which had greatly popularized that concept, Belli's article went on directly after the above to spell out the tactics for the Soviet School to employ in implementing the force-equalization strategy:

> By surprise and swift action must an adversary be caught unawares. Small but steady successes must be achieved to retain psychological ascendancy over the adversary. He must be deprived of his freedom of maneuver by actions on communications and by mine warfare, paralyzing his combat activity, snatching the operational initiative out of his hands, spoiling his plans, and delaying and paralyzing the movements of his ships. It is necessary to hit the adversary in his own bases (p. 17).

Belli reiterated his earlier point that, in substance, the general engagement no longer constituted the "essence of contemporary war at sea" and that at least some of the normal missions of a navy could be carried out prior to having destroyed the enemy's main naval forces (present in a Soviet coastal area) and so gain a limited command of the sea in that area:

> The complete destruction of an enemy in a given theater . . . seldom is possible by a single strike. [Rather] missions are carried out and the final aims in a theater achieved mainly by way of execution of a number of successive and simultaneous operations coordinated by a unity of strategic aims (pp. 16-17).

> It would be incorrect to assume, therefore [based on the experience of the first World War and the Russian Civil War] that the final aims are achieved by an obligatory single general engagement of fleets to which all other combat activity at sea is subordinated. Such an assertion would lead to a denial of the possibility of carrying out a number of missions which may be assigned a fleet before the question of a general engagement is resolved by a battle between the main forces of the fleets (p. 17).

Returning to the subject of the "general engagement" later in his article, Belli drew out an important implication from his theory as quoted above. He pointed out the uncomfortable truth that systematic evasion of battle was not always possible and that even a premature general engagement of the main forces of a fleet quite possibly might prove unavoidable:

> The Navy cannot avoid battle while carrying out its assigned missions. As a rule, the aim of each operation is achieved through battle.

> In dependence on the assigned missions and the existing circumstances, it may come even to a clash of the main forces of the two sides, that is, a general engagement may occur, one which can be favorable only in the case that we have succeeded in organizing a decisive superiority in forces in the main direction, in paralyzing the adversary in secondary directions, in effecting cooperation of the heterogeneous forces operating in the one (main) direction to the full depth (of the enemy's disposition), and in coordinating the operations of forces and units acting in the other directions. And if success is achieved in creating such a situation, it might even be desirable to seek out a general engagement.

> Therefore, it would be wrong to completely deny the possibility and expediency of a general engagement and not prepare for one (p. 20).

In his third and final discussion of the force-equalization strategy, Belli continued his line of thinking above and went on to elaborate both on the necessity of not making the general engagement the centerpiece of naval warfare and on the need to employ all kinds of naval forces in any such general engagement rather than just the large surface combatant ships formerly employed for such decisive battles:

> In this regard, it would be incorrect to place the general engagement at the basis of all combat activity of the Navy and, as already observed, to accept it as the sole and obligatory method for achieving the final aims in a theater.

> The modern general engagement differs from those of earlier eras not only in its aims but also in the means and methods for its conduct. It is won by the cooperation

of the various branches of the naval forces rather than just by surface ships as it was up to and including the Battle of Jutland.

> In all cases of combat clashes with an adversary, it is necessary to strike to defeat him in detail, attempting to destroy all of his forces. However . . . in individual cases it may be more advantageous to limit the destruction of those units of the adversary's forces which prevent the completion of our operations. And if the preconditions for the successful conduct of a battle have not been met, then the operational goal may even be the evasion of battle (p. 21).

Mission Capabilities Limited Basically to Coastal Defense and Army Support. Belli mentioned that "missions are carried out . . . by a number of successive and simultaneous operations" for "the complete destruction of an enemy in a given theater." Belli eschewed including explicit discussion in this article of the important caveat that the missions that could be executed in the face of a stronger enemy were quite restricted. He did allude to this fact indirectly in his mention of the "possibility of carrying out a number of missions" without having first destroyed the opposition.

Belli further implied the limited nature of the missions which were considered at the time to be feasible of accomplishment, in the face of a much superior naval adversary, by specifying the "general basic mission of the Navy of the Soviet Union" as nothing more ambitious than "the active defense of the sea borders of the Soviet Union."

The article went on to make an important point regarding Soviet naval missions in general—a point that has been reiterated on occasion ever since— that the missions assigned to a given fleet are highly dependent on the military-political situation that obtains in a given theater:

> The fleet in each theater has its specific missions which are determined in dependence on the military-political situation in the theater, on the correlation of forces in the theater, and particularly on the disposition [of forces] relative to the adversary (p. 16).

Belli followed this by listing the possible kinds of naval missions that might be assigned in wartime to the naval forces in any given theater:

> To summarize the possible missions of the Navy in the various theaters, understanding that they become definite only in particular situations, the following may be established as the most important missions of the Navy:
>
> • Destruction of the enemy navy in detail:
>
> • Warfare on sea communications, that is, the protection of one's own military communications and (commercial) shipping;
>
> • Interrupting the enemy's sea communications;
>
> • The struggle for the shore, that is, protecting one's own shores against invasion and shifting the war to enemy territory by sea;

- Support of the coastal flanks of the Army by way of cooperating with its offensives; and

- Protection against an adversary's strikes from the sea (p. 16).

Two points are notable in Belli's prescribed mission structure, in effect, for the new Soviet School. First, despite his substantial discussion of the possibility of fighting a general engagement under certain circumstances, when it came to listing the actual missions that might be assigned in whole or in various combinations to a given fleet, nothing more was said about the general engagement. Only the force-equalization strategy of gradually defeating the enemy's naval forces "in detail" was included in the overall mission structure.

Second, with the one exception of engaging in fights with smaller, inferior enemy forces, all of the other missions—with the possible exception of the antishipping one—had to do in general with protecting the homeland from seaborne assault and, in particular, with providing cover and support for the Army's coastal flanks. In the case of the antishipping mission, that too is most often associated in Soviet military and naval thought with preventing military supplies and troop reinforcements from reaching the Eurasian Continent to the detriment of the Soviet ground forces. This is the case even though antishipping warfare is a traditional method resorted to by weaker naval powers in an attempt to sap the economic strength of the adversary by hindering or cutting off his seaborne trade.

Belli testified to the primacy of the ground forces' operations in determining naval missions when he applied the "mutual-cooperation" tenet of Soviet military doctrine to the Navy's case:

> The missions of the Navy derive from the general plan of action of all of the Armed Forces and the combat activity of the Navy develops on the basis of strategic, operational, and tactical cooperation with the ground forces (p. 16).

He made two noteworthy comments about this doctrinal formulation. First he entered the caveat that, while usually "the outcome of a war is decided mainly in the ground theaters and the Navy supports accomplishment of the missions in them," cases may arise "at some stage of a war in one theater or another" in which "the naval direction may be in the main one." In such cases, Belli concluded, "the Navy may be charged with execution of the main missions and the other services of the Armed Forces will support the Navy." (p. 15) This point was one that top naval officers and official theoreticians were to repeat, on occasion, from the late 1950s to the present.

The other comment suggests that it was an early example of the Aesopian adjurations by the Navy that have continued to the present day. It was that more extensive joint planning should take place so that the Navy can be informed as to what missions it is most likely to be assigned to carry out in any future war:

> The experience of a number of wars demonstrates what negative consequences ensue from lack of a unified strategic leadership and a unified strategic plan of action for all of the Armed Forces (p. 15).

Belli gave two examples to illustrate this point. Both read as though they were chosen to appeal to the Army leadership and so soften the understandable, if parochial, Army opposition to providing the Navy with a specific listing of its wartime missions in advance of war and so giving the Navy the requisite formal requirements that would justify the different, more costly force structure to enable it to execute those missions, particularly the antishipping mission:

> The lack of a unified strategic plan found vivid illustration in the Dardanelles operation, the strategic results of which on the course and outcome of the war were underestimated by the Allied command. . . .

> The lack of a unified strategic plan also influenced the passive nature of the action of the German Navy, the command of which sought resolution of the missions of the war at sea mainly just in battle with the enemy's navy, insufficiently relating the activity of the navy to operations on the ground front (p. 15).

In what seemed like a further effort to overcome Army opposition both to formulating the Navy's wartime missions in advance and to granting the Navy any objectively warranted missions independent of the Army, Belli produced a list of wartime naval missions, even heading the list with antishipping. All were formulated so as to be subsumable under the general rubric of strategic cooperation with the Army:

- "Blockade of an enemy state with the aim of smashing its economic power, and also its military might;"

- "Protecting one's own shores against deep strikes by the adversary;"

- "Protecting against his attempts to make strategic landings;" and

- "Systematic destruction of enemy troop shipments or transport of war materiel by sea" (p. 16).

As an example of "operational cooperation of a fleet with a front," Belli cited the operations of the Batum detachment of the Russian Black Sea Fleet in the World War. This detachment was noted to have provided "systematic support to the flank of the army at sea and against the shore."

By this carefully formulated statement Belli brought in not only the fleet-against-the-shore operations that involved direct support to the Army coastal flank (which is more immediately obvious and understandable to Army officers not trained in naval matters) but also the indirect fleet-against-fleet Army-flank "cover" operations that usually take place out of sight of land (and hence are less readily comprehensible to Army officers without joint training or experience).

Required Naval Force Structure. In this longest and most comprehensive of all of Belli's prewar articles, he devoted careful attention to elaborating the force structure of the Navy required, in effect, to implement a Soviet School strategy. He began by justifying the inclusion of battleships and heavy cruisers (and implicitly aircraft carriers) in the force structure of the Soviet Navy:

> Capital ships, as the platforms with the greatest offensive and defensive power which are capable of all missions in cooperation with other types of ships and with other kinds of naval forces and of sustained combat action against an adversary, play the major role in the order of battle of a big sea and ocean navy (p. 21).

In what seems reasonable to interpret as a rejoinder to certain detractors of capital ships, who remained nameless but many of whom are likely to have been senior Army officers, Belli appeared to be trying to counter specific objections:

> The temporary weakening of the rate of construction of battleships by the capitalist states after the war was caused by political, economic, and technical reasons and did not at all signify a renunciation of that type of ship. (p. 22)

As the reasons for "the vacillation of ideas" in "the role and place of the battleship in a future war (only by bourgeois theorists, of course) Belli cited both the 1922 Washington Conference and the 1930 London Conference on naval limitations, and the alleged slowness with which the lessons for naval strategy of the experience of the World War were analyzed.

The leading theoretician of the new Soviet School went on to conclude: "Consequently, the question is not one of the obsolescence of the battleship as a type but of their technical modernization . . . and of the new methods for their employment in close cooperation with the other types of combatant ships and the other kinds of naval forces." (p. 22)

Having provided this rationale for the big surface combatant ships that had been so greatly favored by the Old School, Belli proceeded next to briefly consider the submarines and aircraft that he and the young Soviet officers of the Young School had so ardently advocated in the late 1920s and up through the mid 1930s:

> Recognition of the major role of battleships in contemporary operations does not deprecate the significance of submarines and aviation, whose technology and tactics have grown considerably since the World War. The experience of the war in Spain shows that major successes can be achieved with aviation in operations against combatant ships and especially against bases (p. 22).

Earlier in the article, in a discussion of the antishipping mission, Belli had given submarines their rather limited due under the Soviet School of naval warfare by stating that "submarines remain the main means for operations on sea communications but the development of these operations is trending to . . . aviation and surface ships in tactical cooperation with submarines." (p. 19)

Also earlier in this article of April 1939, Belli had expatiated (at a length betokening that substantial importance was accorded to the subject) on the importance, in effect, of fleet-against-the-shore strikes against the enemy's naval bases (as well as at the ships that might be caught by surprise in them):

> The experience of the first imperialist war shows that operations against enemy bases and the ships in them have great importance in the general system of the combat activity of a navy. Operations against bases may have the following aims:
>
> (1)   To weaken the adversary by way of the destruction of his ships at base;
>
> (2)   To paralyze the deployment and combat activity of an adversary by way of deranging his system of basing, by depriving him of a given base, or by making its use difficult; and
>
> (3)   To limit his freedom of maneuver, weaken the forces of the enemy in his bases, and paralyze his deployment to new bases.
>
> The prerequisites for the conduct of operations against bases are: (1) the potent development of aviation technology and tactics; and (2) an increasing potential for employing motor torpedo boats, submarines, and mines for these aims (p. 18).

The only thinly disguised preference of the Soviet School for capital ships rather than submarines showed itself in the description Belli gave of the employment of surface combatants for raiding operations against enemy bases:

> The speed of modern surface combatants facilitates the conduct of raiding operations against an enemy coast with the aim of the destruction of selected coastal objectives, and also of an enemy's antisubmarine warfare barriers, of his convoys, etc. The raid becomes one of the most advantageous forms of action. . . . The basic methods for raiding operations must be swiftness and covertness of action (p. 19).

Quite possibly with the aim of persuading the Army leadership that the shipping-protection mission, which normally had been considered independent of the Army, really was for Army support, Belli introduced a new term, "strategic support" for ground forces, to characterize the shipping-protection mission. He illustrated his point to show the intrinsic value of shipping protection for the weaker of two naval powers who did not enjoy command of the sea by citing as an example the Spanish Civil War in which the Franco forces had control of the sea lanes involved:

> The superiority at sea of the forces of the Spanish insurrectionists and the interventionists (Germany and Italy) hindered the Republican Navy in the carrying out of its main mission—the strategic support of the rear of the Spanish Army by way of the defense of the sea communications by which the front was supplied (p. 19).

Belli went on to note the increasing importance in the Navy's mission structure of blockade and counterblockade (of maritime shipping):

> With regard to the improvements in the technology and tactics of submarines, aviation, and mines, and along with the improvements in the means of countering them, the importance . . . is increasing . . . of blockade and of counterblockade operations (p. 19).

"Combat Support" as a Substitute for Limited "Command of the Sea." Due probably to Army dislike of the term, Belli never once employed "command of the sea" in the article's more than two dozen pages of small print. Nevertheless, the centrality of the limited-command concept for the Soviet School was given implicit recognition by the exceptional amount of space devoted to the by-then-readily-recognized surrogate for that concept— calling for "combat support" of the main force assigned to conduct a given operation by the other naval forces suitable for the task. Thus, immediately after the foregoing quote, Belli made note of the most important case of combat support of concern to the Soviet School—that of (surface ship and air) support for submarines. In so doing he reiterated the major reason given by Evseyev as to why submarines alone could not be sufficient for a successful antishipping campaign—that contrary to the Young School tenet, submarines *could* be blockaded:

> The feasibility of a blockade of submarines has increased and (therefore) so has the necessity for providing operational support for their sortie for operations and their return to base (p. 19).[52]

Belli had earlier noted the importance of battleships and heavy cruisers (and implicitly aircraft carriers) for providing support to mine-warfare operations by supplying covering forces:

> In the conduct of mine warfare . . . in a number of cases, the participation of the combat nucleus of a fleet is required for the cover and protection of mine-laying and mine-sweeping operations (p. 18).

Subsequently, in discussing the importance of amphibious landings, he was to also note the value of large surface-combatants (and submarines) for cover and protection of such operations:

> Sea landing operations continue to play a major role. . . . Surface combatants and submarines not only cover and protect the merchant ships during a landing but can themselves transport the landing forces under special circumstances (p. 20).

Another support role for large surface-combatants was also noted by Belli—that of providing support for the smaller ships and craft engaged in antisubmarine warfare operations. He gave as an example the successful Allied effort in the World War to counter the Germans' unrestricted submarine warfare campaign against the Allies:

... [T]he struggle against the submarine threat and the blockade of Germany by the Entente were made possible by the support given by the surface ships to the many small antisubmarine warfare ships and craft and to those on daily blockade service (p. 22).

Belli's discussion of the importance of support operations was not limited to support by other naval forces for the type of naval force assigned as the main force for a given operation but also gave Army-flank support operations their due. Counterlanding operations were said not only to constitute "one of the most important operations of the Navy" but also to be "especially difficult" when the enemy was employing "heterogeneous forces (read as to include aircraft carriers) in operational and tactical cooperation." Fire support by surface naval combatants for the Army coastal flank was said to be "no less important in modern war" than the counterlanding operations. To dramatize the importance of the Navy's role in providing cover for Army-flank operations, Belli claimed that as a rule such covering operations would not necessarily serve to deter enemy strikes at Army coastal operations—with the result that "now and then a clash of major forces" would occur.

In the last main part of his lengthy article of April 1939, Belli considered combat support operations in Soviet-School theory. He began by observing that to operate successfully under contemporary conditions, it would be necessary to "take such measures of combat support as would hinder the countermeasures of an enemy to our actions." In a notable understatement phrased in the opaque language of Soviet military writings, Belli went on to note that with adequate combat support gaining a "superiority of forces in the main direction" and pinning down the enemy in secondary directions "could be more easily achieved."

There is, of course, a strong element of double talk involved in all such Soviet formulations. What they often mean in practice is simply that submarine operations cannot be successful unless accompanied by surface and air forces in adequate strength to drive off or defeat the adversary's naval forces. And that, as we have already noted, is exactly what the Soviet School still considers to be a limited command of the sea.

Most indicative of the limited command-of-the-sea strategy is Belli's inclusion of a requirement for preliminary support as well as direct support—inasmuch as the former, in essence, requires that enough of the enemy naval forces be destroyed prior to the start of the main operation planned so that the residual opposition can be safely taken care of by the direct support to the forces conducting the main operation. This, of course, was a point that had been stated in the Evseyev article in the 28 August 1938 issue of *Red Fleet*.

Belli described in detail the specific measures for both preliminary and direct combat support after first stating that "combat support of operations consists of measures for preliminary support and for direct simultaneous support." As measures for preliminary support, Belli listed:

- The weakening of the surface forces and the submarines of an adversary in his bases and at their exits with aviation, submarines, and surface ships, by mine warfare, and by blockade;

- Suppression of enemy aviation on his airfields and in the air to gain command of the air at the outset of an operation;

- Search and destruction of enemy submarines in the theater and especially in those regions in which the execution of an operation is planned;

- Misleading the enemy as to the main operational direction selected for the fleet by employing operational deception; and

- Shifting bases for a part of one's own forces specifically to ensure achieving the aims of a given operation (pp. 22-23).

Similarly, the "measures for the direct (simultaneous) support of operations" were listed by Belli as follows:

- Concentrating the nucleus of the naval forces in the main operational direction and covering the secondary directions;

- Striking in depth at the enemy's dispositions, movements, and operations;

- Supporting the sortie of one's own forces from base and during their deployment for operations;

- Maintaining the suppression of enemy aviation on airfields and in the air; and

- Persisting in the search for and destruction of the enemy's submarines (p. 23).

Belli concluded his discussion of combat support by giving consideration to the particular situation in which preliminary combat support should not be given:

. . . In individual circumstances support may be limited to just direct support. In particular such a situation may arise when there is danger that the measures for preliminary support may disclose our intentions, but [only] when the correlation of forces in a given circumstance categorically does not require preliminary weakening of the enemy. Yet in all other situations it is necessary to employ both kinds of support (which applies mainly to the execution of the most difficult operations—for those to which considerable forces have been assigned or when strong opposition from the enemy is to be anticipated).

Finally, in particular circumstances when the Soviet forces available to overcome the expected enemy opposition are not available, the best method for support will be the stealth and surprise of operations. . . . (p. 23)

At the end of his article, Belli noted the difficulty of exercising command and control of the heterogeneous forces that the Soviet Navy would be expected to employ in a future war (under the Soviet School of warfare) and concluded with what was tantamount to a warning not to make offensive operations for the destruction of the enemy's naval forces to gain even a limited command of the sea an end in itself:

> In these [contemporary] conditions of difficult and constantly changing situations (of a war at sea), the defensive missions of the Navy must never be forgotten. The offensive breakthrough [prescribed by Soviet military doctrine] must not be taken to rule out a well organized defense (p. 24).

Belli published another article, 11 months later, analyzing the naval strategies and missions of the British and Germans for the first six months of the war.[53] Like his earlier article, it is particularly interesting for what it reveals of the views of the Soviet School on the most significant theoretical issues of naval warfare by the only Soviet naval theoretician whose writings were appearing frequently and who dealt with the main issues.[54]

Belli began as a good Marxist-Leninist should, by portraying the war as primarily economic in character. The military expression of this economic warfare, he observed, was the struggle over the sea lines of communications, with Germany trying to interdict British shipping and Britain employing the convoy system, mining, and antisubmarine warfare patrols in its efforts to keep the sea lanes open. There had been no decisive operations on the land fronts. As a result of this situation, the war in the naval theaters had assumed primary importance, Belli asserted, and the contesting navies were determining the main strategic issue.

Noting Britain's overwhelming naval superiority (15 battleships and battle cruisers to Germany's 2 battleships, plus 3 "pocket" battleships; 7 aircraft carriers to none yet operational for Germany; 15 heavy cruisers to 2 for Germany), Belli concluded that the disparity in naval forces was so great as to make unsuitable for Germany the *Krafteausgleich* (force-equalization) strategy of attrition (by defeating successive parts of the enemy's forces) that Germany first had employed in World War I and that Belli had posited explicitly as the basic Soviet School strategy in his April 1939 article. Since Belli did not point out that the strategy had been unsuccessful for Germany, he again, if only tacitly this time endorsed this Mahanian strategy for an inferior navy, provided only that the disparity in forces not be hopelessly great (probably not greater than a third less, as per Professor Gervais and his Italian mentor, Bernotti).

Belli's analysis of Germany's alternative naval strategy is worthy of particular note because it is a matter discussed further by Soviet naval leaders and theoreticians in the 1970s. Germany's naval inferiority was so great, Belli continued, that it was unable to concentrate enough forces in a given place at the right time to gain superiority and hence to accept battle with *any* British naval force. Rather, Germany could only "destroy enemy warships to the extent necessary for the conduct of each assigned mission."

Belli again, as in his April 1939 article, did not find it necessary to explicitly point out the very limited nature of naval missions that could be undertaken by German surface naval forces in face of such an unfavorable naval balance but he did enumerate the kinds of operations that were still feasible for the German Navy. He listed these as "operations on communications, operations against enemy bases, mine warfare, and raids." He probably did not think it necessary to point out the obvious facts that the antishipping operations would have to continue to be largely carried out by submarines and those against enemy naval bases largely by aircraft since the German Navy's surface forces could not risk any general engagement with the far superior British naval forces.

British naval strategy, as it appeared to Belli after six months of hostilities, was interpreted as a continuation of a traditional British one of a passive "fleet-in-being," which term Belli translated as "a fleet in existence, a threat without strikes." This strategy was incorrect; Belli argued: Britain's correct naval aim should be to take advantage of its strategic superiority by actively seeking a naval engagement in order to destroy the enemy's surface warships and submarines; neutralize the enemy's aviation; destroy production facilities for warships and aircraft; and paralyze the enemy's freedom of maneuver for his warships, particularly for his submarines.

Belli made much of Germany's occupation of Denmark and part of Norway by sea in May 1940, which he saw as completion of an "exceptionally important mission for improvement of her strategic position." It released the German Navy from the dead end of the "maritime triangle" in which it had been contained, and facilitated both attacking British shipping and efforts to counter Britain's distant blockade of shipping to Germany, Belli explained.

Heterogeneous naval forces were being used in joint operations to carry out German naval strategy, according to Belli. At the tactical level, he assumed for lack of information, joint air-submarine operations were being employed in which the aircraft not only searched for and reported the location of convoys to the submarines but provided support for the latter's attacks.

Britain's distant blockade of German shipping and surface warships was described by Belli as extending only between the Shetland Islands and Ireland and so leaving unattended the sea passage from the Shetlands to Norway. He considered that Britain's distant blockade had been successful in that it had "unquestionably paralyzed German shipping." He indirectly implied that the British blockade also had been effective against surface warships by faulting it for not having employed "positional means" to more effectively blockade German submarines.

A similar implicit criticism was made of Britain's antisubmarine warfare effort. Belli reported it as consisting of an antisubmarine warfare barrier across the Straits of Dover and an "element of a close blockade" in the form of offshore mining positioned to block the exit and return to base of the German submarines. Although the British mine-layers were said to have been provided support by submarines during the mine-laying, it appeared to Belli that Britain was not giving continuing support for its minefields against German mine-sweeping. Belli concluded that Britain should have undertaken "a more active struggle against the sortieing of German submarines from their bases out to sea."

From his reconstruction of the strategies and missions of the German and British Navies in the first six months of World War II, Belli drew eight additional conclusions relevant to the new Soviet School of naval warfare which he was elaborating:

(1)   As in the 1914-1918 war, German submarines have shown themselves as the main means for the struggle on [the sea lines of] communications; . . .

(2)   In comparison with the 1914-1918 war, the significance of aviation has grown, both for reconnaissance of the sea lines and for strikes at merchant ships and especially at [merchant ship] convoys. Aviation has shifted the struggle on communications from the sea to the ports and land lines of communications. This type of force becomes of special significance when (maritime) theaters are frozen so that submarines are unable to operate;

(3)   Use of fast, armored cruisers on the sea lines is not only completely feasible but also necessary. In the first place, armored cruisers can destroy an entire convoy and, secondly, their operations at sea force the enemy to strengthen his covering forces . . . [thereby dispersing his main forces—instead of keeping them concentrated and so in readiness for a general engagement—and, consequently, vulnerable to piecemeal attrition by force-equalization tactics of the weaker navy];

(4)   Joint operations of submarines, aviation, and cruisers on communications give greater results (than by submarines alone);

(5)   For conduct of war in general, and particularly for the struggle on communications, the matter of a favorable strategic position at sea assumes primary importance. The struggle for the improvement of one's own strategic position may be one of the most important tasks of policy and strategy. [This was written just at the time when the Soviet Government had taken over the Baltic Republics of Estonia, Latvia, and Lithuania in order to improve the Soviet Union's "strategic position at sea" by affording bases for the Baltic Fleet outside the confines of the Finnish Gulf.];

(6)   For the defense of communications, in addition to the struggle for strategic position, there may be employed combined surface-ship-submarine-aircraft-mine blockades, convoys, operations against the enemy bases and the warships present there, and mobile means of antisubmarine defense. Like every other operation, defense of communications requires well-organized intelligence;

(7)   The system of convoying, just as in the 1914-1918 war, continues to comprise an effective means in the struggle against submarines. To combat the attacks of enemy aviation, convoys must have a powerful antiaircraft defense. Otherwise convoys are not only helpless but, even worse, in comparison with merchant ships proceeding

singly, convoys facilitate attacks by enemy aviation. If armored cruisers are operating on the sea lines, convoys must have powerful escorts; and

(8) The present war has introduced the use of aircraft carriers for the defense of communications. This can be of particular importance for distant regions of a theater which cannot be reached by shore-based aviation. . . . (p. 20)

In conclusion, Belli predicted that the further course of the war would see "a wider operational employment of surface warships in joint operations with submarines and aviation."

Both Heavy and Light Carriers Justified. Two months before this Belli article, the *Naval Digest* had carried a long article, "On the Question of Aircraft Carriers" by two well-informed authors, Gordon and Mal'tsev.[55] Their previous article on the same subject (in the August 1936 issue of *Technology and Armaments*) was noted earlier. The authors first showed, in detail, the requirement for mobile air power at sea, noting that it was "particularly important in the conditions of broad, open theaters." Then they resourcefully produced "a special class of combatant ship"—the aircraft carrier—to meet that requirement. Although the treatment was well-balanced in general, the authors seemed to take great care to demonstrate an equally important role for land-based air: "Thus the aircraft carrier, being a means for increasing the endurance of shore-based aviation, does not exclude the importance of . . . the missions carried out by shore-based air; to the contrary the aircraft carrier merely supplements it." (pp. 65-65) Considering that the Soviet Naval Air Force at that time was basically a land-based establishment, this sort of deference probably was considered to be in order, whether or not the resultant views accurately reflected those of the authors. The tenor of the remainder of the article suggested that the deference to land-based air was only *pro forma.*

Since the strike aircraft of the attack carriers of the time could not carry bombs of sufficient weight to penetrate the armor of battleships and heavy cruisers, their task was defined as paralyzing an enemy battle force by damaging his gun batteries, command and control, and propulsion machinery and by sinking the adversary's lighter combatant ships. Such damage to the heavy ships and destruction of the light forces was calculated to prevent an enemy from accomplishing his naval missions and so exert "a considerable influence on the outcome of battle."

The article was notable for its unambiguous presentation of the requirement for aircraft carriers to provide air cover for naval forces beyond a narrow coastal sector:

A fleet which is separated from its bases by even the comparatively short distance of 200 miles or even less is already deprived of the protection of fighter aviation. But a fleet having aircraft carriers can put up a very effective air cover of several flights of fighter planes at any distance from its bases (p. 65).

Also stressed was the value of carrier-based aircraft for reconnaissance and for attacking an enemy's merchant shipping. The great advantage of ship-based aircraft being placed in near proximity to the area of intended reconnaissance or strike operations against an enemy's convoys and their naval escorts was duly noted along with the benefit of requiring "a smaller number of aircraft flights." Moreover, this article pointed out the disastrous outcome that could be expected from bombing raids against an enemy's naval bases and airfields if beyond the short range of land-based fighter aircraft and attempted without fighter escort. Carrier aircraft could provide such escort against an enemy's fighter aircraft for the critical final approach and time-over-target period for the otherwise slow-flying and vulnerable bomber aircraft.

Of equal interest to this study is the defense of employing small carriers in the Soviet Union's peripheral seas that was included in the Gordon and Mal'tsev article. As they expressed it, such employment should be viewed as "wholly expedient":

> In the broad but limited theaters, aircraft carrier operations in cooperation with the light forces and shore-based aviation may be seen to be wholly expedient. Moreover, in these peripheral-sea theaters, the coordinated action of aircraft carriers, the light surface forces, submarines, and shore-based aviation can for some period of time supplant the operations of heavy ships and pin down the heavy ships of the enemy in their bases (p. 67).

The above is particularly interesting as an updated version (to include aircraft carriers) of the Young School strategy of fighting a powerful capital-ship navy with the lighter (cheaper) naval forces of a second-rate naval power. The aim would be to at least hold command of the sea "in dispute" so that even though one could not conduct his own missions, the enemy would not be able to carry out his missions either.

The expedient value for the Soviet Union of building small carriers just to carry fighters for fleet-air support was said to find convincing proof in the fact that Japan not only had big carriers that could carry light bomber planes as well as fighters for air cover but had built small aircraft carriers of the *Soryu*-class to carry fighter planes exclusively. Included in the article were two tables showing the characteristics of small and big aircraft carriers. The tonnage of the *Soryu*-class was given as 10,050 tons and the year of launch as 1936. Two earlier Japanese classes were included as was the 1933 U.S.S. *Ranger* class (14,500 tons) and the newest U.S. class, the 1938, U.S.S. *Wasp* of 14,700 tons.

The big attack carriers were described as intended for operations in unlimited (i.e., oceanic) theaters and as having completely different operational-tactical uses in that joint action with land-based aviation was not practical. But in mutual cooperation with a fleet, carrier aviation was said to be able to discharge all of the most important missions, both against ships and against the bases of an adversary.

In a particularly revealing paragraph, the *Naval Digest* article stated first that "a fleet not having aircraft carriers cannot fully exploit the advantages and capabilities of aviation in war at sea, even in the condition of closed theaters." This was followed by a listing of the five countries that were then building 15 aircraft carriers among them and then the conclusion: "As this shows, the agitated arguments over whether or not aircraft carriers are required have ended by themselves (i.e., without official intervention, apparently) and are not starting up again." (p. 68)

The last half dozen pages of the article were devoted to a lengthy description, first of small aircraft carriers (10,000 to 14,000 tons) and their missions; then of big carriers (17,000 to 20,000 tons but with the impending need foreseen to increase tonnage to 23,000 to 25,000 tons to permit adequate defense). The final page was given over to the authors' conclusions—of which the following are of enough relevance to quote here:

(4) Beyond the range of shore-based aviation, a fleet must be assisted by carrier aviation. This is particularly the case for fighter aviation, which has short endurance.

(5) The aircraft carrier is the only solution to the problem of increasing the endurance of aviation beyond the limits of the range of shore-based aviation.

(6) A modern navy, which conducts an active maritime policy, must have aircraft carriers.

(7) Two types of aircraft carriers are tactically and operationally justifiable—the reconnaissance-convoy carrier (of small displacement) and the aircraft carrier of the main forces of a fleet (of large displacement).

(8) The small aircraft carrier is a ship of 10,000 to 14,000 tons that is armed with 30-40 airplanes, basically fighter aircraft, with guns of universal calibre (8 to 12 weapons of 114 to 127 mm), and with the hull and deck armored only around the engine and boiler rooms, and having the same speed and cruising range as light cruisers (32 to 34 knots, 4,000 to 6,000 miles).

(9) The big aircraft carrier is a ship of tonnage of 23,000 to 25,000, armed with 60 to 70 airplanes (without reserves), primarily bombers, and with guns of universal calibre (16 and more weapons of 114 to 127 mm calibre), protected by armor for the great part of the hull's length, having anti-torpedo defense and with a speed of 30 to 34 knots (p. 73).

No Preliminary Command of the Sea Required to Conduct Naval Missions, Just "Preliminary" and "Direct" Support. In the last of his available writings until late in World War II, Professor Belli analyzed the naval operations of the Germans and British incident to the former's invasion and occupation of Denmark and part of Norway. Having treated the general aspects of the naval strategy of the opponents in his article published the month before, Belli turned, in July 1940, to a more detailed study, "Scandinavian Naval Operations and Their Lessons."[56]

Concerning, as it does, joint forces and other naval operations in peripheral northern European waters of the nature the Soviet Union would be most likely to conduct with its Northern Fleet, or supplemented by the Baltic Fleet, if it succeeded at the outbreak of a war in taking the Danish Straits, Belli's study of these operations retains much of contemporary interest. As he expressed it, there was much to be learned of "significant theoretical and practical interest."

The article was prefaced with the comment that the Germans had benefited from "deep research" on their mistakes in World War I and were correcting them in their current operations. Belli took as his point of departure a main conclusion from his previous article, that Germany's aim in occupying Denmark and part of Norway had been the "exceptionally important" one of "improving her strategic position." In this article his thinking had progressed to the point that he had come to view "the struggle for Scandinavia" as "above all" a German campaign to gain "a favorable strategic position" and a British effort to deny success to that campaign.

Germany's strategic offensive into Scandinavia was said to have "radically altered the situation in the North Sea theater." Britain's task of blockading German naval and merchant shipping as well as neutral shipping had thereby been made more difficult. Corridors had been gained through the Norwegian fjords by which ships, and especially submarines, could reach the open Atlantic and return to German ports and naval bases. Moreover, Germany had both secured its right flank and denied England a springboard for attacking Germany. In particular, the full control gained over the Danish Straits prevented any Royal Navy incursions into the Baltic. German sea communications in the Baltic were thus secure (as were Germany's vital imports of Swedish ore). The last, but by no means the least, of the advantages gained for Germany by seizing such a favorable strategic position were said to be improved striking ranges and operating bases. German planes operating from Danish and Norwegian airfields were within strike range of any point in England and Scotland and, consequently, of all of the United Kingdom's naval bases. Moreover, the Norwegian fjords provided excellent advanced operating (maneuvering) bases for German submarines and cruisers for operations on England's sea lines of communications in the Norwegian Sea and the Atlantic.

German failure in World War I to appreciate Scandinavia's great potential advantages as outlined above had adversely affected overall German chances of winning and had doomed the "formidable German Navy" to passivity in the "strategic vacuum" of German harbors. This conclusion had been reached by many naval writers, Belli noted, including a number of German ones.[57]

One of Belli's conclusions was clearly addressed to any and all who still championed single types of naval forces (whether submarines, aircraft, or battleships) either to the exclusion of the others or to their reduction to supporting roles:

> In contemporary war at sea there cannot be talk of separately conducted type operations. The question is considerably more complicated. Every major naval operation is comprised of a combination of particular operations among which, along given segments of operational time, a given type of force is assigned the leading role (p. 43).

Since Belli cited most of the major developments in naval technology of the 20th century, including those in submarines and aircraft, he may have been directing his remarks largely to any unreconstructed battleship proponents who still considered the proper role for submarines and aircraft to be that of mere auxiliaries to a main force of battleships.

Another conclusion was that "the Germans were successful because they operated under a single strategic plan that required a strict coordination of operations of the three branches of the armed forces: Army, Navy, and Air Force." (pp. 45-46) This suggests, as had an analogous sentence in Belli's April 1939 article quoted earlier, that the Soviet naval command considered that preparation of such a joint plan, and especially an explicit assignment of the Navy's missions, would enable the Navy to justify larger forces and to structure them more rationally for a general war. As noted earlier, such calls for increased joint planning recur in Soviet naval writings every now and again in the post-World War II period and suggest a long but unsuccessful Navy effort to obtain an explicit list of its wartime mission assignments under the Soviet Union's "unified military strategy" and its general staff war plans.

In his article a month earlier, it will be recalled, Belli had noted that, due to Britain's vast superiority in forces, Germany could not adopt the *Krafteausgleich* (force-equalization) strategy of gradual attrition of the British forces that it had used in World War I until the time of the Battle of Jutland in 1916. Since it was probable that any naval force the Royal Navy might send out of port against the German Navy would be so superior that Germany could not expect to defeat it with her whole fleet, a force-equalization strategy would be unfeasible. Accordingly, Germany was reduced to the very limited operations that could be carried out only when the German forces concentrated for a given operation, could count on being superior to all of the British forces that could reach the scene-of-action within the time limit set for the operation.

Belli next developed an aspect of the general situation thus created that would appear to be most relevant to contemporary Soviet strategy for naval warfare. He claimed that the widely held view that no naval operation could be risked until after command of the sea had been gained in the intended area of operations was false and that, instead of there being such a requirement for *preliminary* establishment of command, the German experience in Norway had shown that it was quite sufficient to gain the control requisite for success of any given operation *simultaneously* with conduct of the operation.

The German success in Norway, Belli asserted, finally had disproved Colomb's 80-year-old dictum in *Naval Warfare* and Mahan's in *The Influence of Sea Power on History* that, in Belli's words, "without preliminary command of the sea, no major naval operation can be carried out." He added that "according to the theory of Colomb and Mahan, in order to gain command of the sea the enemy navy either must be defeated in battle or blockaded in its base." In the Scandinavian operations, however, the "German Navy did not command the sea in any measure (in the Colomb-Mahan sense) and in the Norwegian operations it neither destroyed the enemy in battle nor blockaded it in its bases." The weaker German Navy, Belli noted, would have been unable to do either. "Nevertheless, the complicated Norwegian operation had been carried out by it with full success." Belli concluded that "this means that preliminary destruction or blockade of the enemy navy is completely unnecessary for the support of operations." What *is* essential, Belli concluded, is to "always attempt to create a superiority of forces over the enemy in the area of operations." (p. 46)

Belli further asserted that the necessary scene-of-action superiority should be achieved by a "combination of preliminary and direct support." That is, the enemy's surface, submarine, and air forces should be weakened by preliminary operations as necessary so that the forces concentrated for the main operation (using the element of surprise) would be superior to those the enemy could bring to bear at the decisive moment, in the decisive place.[58] In another article nine months earlier Belli had similarly called for "preliminary support in the main directions" of major naval operations to create "the favorable conditions" of scene-of-action superiority that would be most conducive to success.[59]

The preliminary support for the Norwegian operation had included three tasks for the German Navy: reconnaissance; a strike on the British Fleet (at Scapa Flow on 9 April by 20 German bombers); and deployment of German submarines to stations off British naval bases.

The direct support in the Norwegian operation had been given by the "nucleus of the German fleet," i.e., by the battleships and heavy cruisers that put to sea and screened the amphibious landing forces. The latter were transported in fast warships in view of the critical time element. British warships at sea were attacked by German bombers while fighter aircraft were employed to protect the landing forces from any air strikes.

Belli concluded, in obvious reference to the dictum he had just attributed to Colomb and Mahan, that preliminary command of the sea was not essential before undertaking major operations, and that had the German command held to "theoretical classicism," the Norwegian operation would never have been attempted. Belli asked, rhetorically, if the German operations should be considered as "adventurism." Apparently the German operations in Norway had already been condemned as such in high places in Soviet councils. The issue apparently was considered an important one since as late as February 1943, the Chief of the Main Naval Staff, Fleet Admiral Isakov, found it important enough to raise in the middle of the war by an article entitled "The Adventurism of German Naval Strategy."[60] Also, after the war, Admiral Alafuzov, who had been chief of main staff of the Soviet Navy at the time of the German operation against Norway in 1940, questioned the decision on the basis of the heavy ship losses to the German Navy.[61] At any rate, Belli answered, with unaccustomed tact in approving the German operation without explicitly denying the charge of adventurism:

> The operations off the southern and southwestern coasts of Norway, that is, in the main directions, were supported successfully. The circumstances of a night transit [of the landing forces], together with surprise and the deployment of covering forces and the favorable geographic situation thus afforded chances of success under all conditions (p. 47).

In generalizing the experience of "the ongoing war in Europe and the Norwegian operation in particular," Belli made it obvious that his conclusion, that preliminary command of the sea was unnecessary, was based solely on a consideration of Army-Navy operations under a joint plan which, consequently, must be coastal, not open-ocean, operations. Belli stated that these operations supported the postulate that "the essence of contemporary war at sea is not that it is obligatory to destroy all of the enemy's naval forces first, and only then to carry out the assigned operations, but that a navy be able, at every stage of a war, to carry out the missions assigned under a single strategic plan by destroying the enemy (only) in that measure required to prevent interference from his side." (pp. 48–49)

From Belli's lengthy discussion of Germany's Scandinavian operations, two additional points deserve mention. He commended the Germans for having opted to expose their whole navy to the risk of losses by using it to cover its amphibious forces. This, he said, had been "completely right." He added that major operations could not be carried out without losses. Rational risk should be accepted as the unavoidable price for success, particularly for the weaker side. Here Belli would seem to have been replying indirectly to those who had condemned the German operation as adventurism.

The other point was that the battleship retained its leading role. This was apparent from the Norwegian operation, Belli asserted, despite the extremely difficult situation that German dive bombers had created for Britain's capital ships. Hence the battleship was still a necessary component of the heterogeneous forces that must be combined in the proportions appropriate for the given mission to gain success in battle.

In concluding his article, Belli returned to the matter of command of the sea as he interpreted it on the basis of Germany's Scandinavian naval operations. He observed that there were four interrelated factors involved in any navy's potential superiority in war at sea. These he formulated as: superiority in forces; superiority in strategic position, in laying out the network of bases; combat training; and the political indoctrination and morale of personnel. (p. 53)

After discussing to what degree each side benefited or was handicapped by these factors, Belli concluded that it was not enough to possess a superior navy if it were used just for a "passive" fleet-in-being strategy. A potentially superior navy had to be put into action "to maintain one's superior position at sea." Specifically, the stronger navy must fight to maintain its strategic position if favorable or to improve it if not; it must operate systematically against the enemy's naval forces at sea, attack his bases, and conduct mine warfare. Fighting to ensure "a favorable strategic position" was implied to be an essential "element of command of the sea." On this note Belli ended his article.

More on "Direct Support" as a Substitute for Command of the Sea. One final article significant for the prewar development of Soviet naval theory appeared before the Nazi invasion of the Soviet Union in June 1941. Written by an instructor, later a professor, at the Naval War College who was to become a leading light among Soviet naval theoreticians in the first two postwar decades, Captain First Rank Pavlovich, the article appeared in the *Naval Digest* in November 1940.[62] Entitled simply "Combat Support," it made implicitly evident that the real aim of providing such support was to temporarily redress an unfavorable correlation of forces in a region and, in effect, to gain a local tactical control (i.e., a limited command of the sea in Soviet School thought) just long enough to carry out a naval operation.

Pavlovich defined combat support at the outset as "the sum of the measures that facilitate the carrying out of combat missions and that ensure the freedom of action necessary for strikes or for an attack." (p. 43) Since "freedom of action" comes only to the side exercising sea control, it is apparent that the concept of combat support is one devised to enable the weaker navy to avoid being condemned to passivity in the face of superior naval forces by dint of gaining control of the area of intended operations just long enough to at least carry out raiding operations. This was consistent with the Soviet School views expressed by Evseyev in August 1938 and Belli in April 1939.

In addition to the actual physical protection of the main striking forces by the other naval forces that is implied by the term "combat support," Pavlovich listed a number of other measures of support, such as reconnaissance and patrolling which included one of particular relevance then and now—developing an adequate infrastructure of bases and other facilities in (coastal) regions over which the Soviet Union would plan to maintain control in wartime. As Pavlovich expressed it in a masterful bit of understatement: "The use by one's own forces of bases set up in an infrastructured region substantially aids developing combat superiority over an adversary." (p. 36)

Near the end of his article, Pavlovich again made use of the "freedom of action" phrase as well as of another term descriptive of the advantage uniquely enjoyed in naval warfare by the side controlling the sea in any theater of war—"the initiative":

> Support for the movements of one's own forces not only within an infrastructured region but outside of it—out at sea—must always be a matter of special concern for a command because otherwise freedom of action will be lost and the initiative will pass into the hands of the adversary (p. 43).

From the foregoing it seems probable that Pavlovich was warning other Soviet naval officers that command of the sea should not be taken for granted in any Soviet operating area, even in well-protected coastal regions. Fleet and force commanders had always to ensure that forces at sea were given supporting forces superior to any force an adversary might be able to concentrate against them for the period of time that they would be out of port.

A Retrospective on the 1937-1941 Period. To conclude the main text of this chapter, as with the preceding three chapters, the pertinent extract is given below from the 1980 Army account by Colonel Korotkov.[63]

> Later on (after publication in 1933 of *Submarine Operations* by Isakov, Belli, and Aleksandrov) an advocate of the first (Young School) course (Professor I. S. Isakov) took the initiative in working out a theory of naval operations. The viewpoint of the first persuasion found expression in an official document—*Combat Regulations of the Naval Forces 1937 (BUMS-37)*—in which consideration was given to the factual condition of the order of battle of the Navy at the end of the Second Five-year Plan. The special significance of submarines for independent operations on the maritime communications was emphasized in the *Regulations.* Much attention also was paid to the methods for employment of PT boats in various kinds of combat actions. A separate chapter in the *Regulations* concerned the defense of naval bases. It was stated that they were under constant threat of a surprise strike by the adversary, from the air

particularly. The necessity was emphasized of being constantly in readiness to repel an unexpected attack, even in peacetime (p. 180).

As the experience of the Great Patriotic War showed, the proponents of joint actions by the Navy with the Ground Forces proved to be the more realistic. These actions held first place at a time when there was not a single big naval engagement with the participation of capital ships during four years of war. Instead the latter were requisitioned as transports and for escorting convoys of merchant ships which brought necessary materiel for the armament of the Soviet Army. In subsequent years . . . especially in the period of the construction of the Navy in 1938-1941 . . . powerful submarine forces were created and a radical revision was made in the basic types of surface forces. . . . (p. 181)

In naval theory, views favoring the use of a big surface fleet naturally were revitalized. Such views found expression in official documents, most importantly the 1940 *Temporary Instructions for the Conduct of Naval Operations* (*NMO-40*). The conduct of independent operations was planned for fleet-against-fleet operations against the adversary at sea, on his maritime communications, against enemy bases and coastal objectives, and for seizing skerry and island regions. By way of operations to be conducted jointly with the Ground Forces there were operations for support of the Army flank, for [amphibious] landings, counterlandings, and operations against coastal objectives.

Submarines were seen as a type of naval force assigned basically for action on maritime communications. Naval aviation was assigned the role of one of the main means for supporting the combat actions of the Navy. However, the role of a big surface fleet was somewhat exaggerated. In operational training a dominant importance was accorded to the naval engagement of surface forces of capital ships— which did not correspond to the actual prospects for the employment of the Naval Forces in a continental war (pp. 181-182).

Further Analysis and Interpretation of the Evidence, 1937-1941

From the sharp clash during 1937 and 1938 of Young School defensive views with Old School offensive views (as mentioned by Gorshkov in 1972) there resulted a distinctive Soviet School of naval warfare. This school of thought integrated the Young School's submarines and airplanes with the Old School's battleships and heavy cruisers (much as the French Admiral Raoul Castex had been recommending). The distinguishing feature of this composite strategy was its professed belief in a limited command-of-the-sea strategy for Soviet coastal waters. Limited command was to be gained by the force-equalization strategy open to a not greatly inferior navy.

It seems probable that it is precisely this composite strategy which Admiral Kuznetsov has referred to as the Soviet School of naval warfare. Before such a strategy could be realized at least another decade would be required to complete the Soviet Union's 1937 capital-ship building program, which included four aircraft carriers for sea-control employment. In the interval the Soviet Union could merely aspire to attempting to deny command of its coastal waters.

Prior to the final decisions in late 1937 on the numbers, types, and tonnages of the aircraft carriers to be included in the big-ship construction program announced in early 1938, both *Military Thought* and *Naval Digest* published articles in 1937 implicitly advocating the construction of heavy carriers for use in the open oceans. Early in 1937 the general staff journal carried the view of Deputy Naval Minister Ivan Ludri, that aircraft carriers had become enormously important—implicitly for oceanic warfare (since he indicated that the increasing range of shore-based planes would before long obviate the need for carrier-based air in the Baltic and Black seas).

Professor Chernyshev of the Naval War College, writing late in 1937, asserted the desirability of employing shore-based air in the peripheral seas due to the allegedly great vulnerability of carriers operating in confined waters. The proper use of aircraft carriers, he maintained, was far from bases and beyond the range of shore-based aviation.

Once the Party/government decision had been taken at the end of 1937 to build only light carriers, advocacy of heavy carriers such as that voiced by Ludri and Chernyshev earlier in the year was stilled for a time. Instead, the January 1938 issue of *Naval Digest* carried a condensed version of a speech by a French advocate of aircraft carriers that made a persuasive case for the light carrier. By April 1940, when Stalin agreed to replace two of the four smaller carriers (apparently intended for the Baltic and Pacific) with two larger-tonnage light carriers (probably for the Pacific), another article on aircraft carriers appeared in *Naval Digest* that reflected this change. Use of carriers to provided fleet air cover was declared to be merely expedient in the peripheral seas but essential beyond 200 miles offshore.

From 1938 through 1940 Professor, Rear Admiral Belli incorporated much of the potentially most useful results of the Young School's decade of theorizing and the most feasible Old School tenets into the composite Soviet School of naval warfare. Thus, submarines and aircraft were accorded recognition as important sea-line-of-communications warfare forces not just for auxiliary uses, as per the Old School. At the same time, however, they were deprived of their Young School status as the "main forces." Capital ships once again were to constitute (nominally just) the combat nucleus (rather than the "main forces" as under the Old School) of the big sea and oceanic navy. Obviously, all of this was significant progress away from the extremes of favoring one type of naval force to the virtual exclusion of the others and toward more balanced, flexible naval forces that were planned to include aircraft carriers.

Particular note should be taken of the point Belli made in his June 1940 account of the first six months of the war at sea: Germany was so inferior to England in naval strength that it could not use its force-equalization-by-attrition strategy of World War I but could only "destroy enemy warships to the extent necessary for the conduct of each mission." Soviet concern at finding itself in just such a situation in a future war seems to underlie a continuing dispute as to whether it would be necessary in a war at sea to establish temporary superiority in a given maritime area as a preliminary prerequisite to undertaking a major operation of any kind or whether the necessary superiority could be gained simultaneously with the conduct of a given operation.

This latter method of depending solely on direct support without any preliminary support was implicitly recognized as enabling the naval forces providing such support to avoid battle with a stronger enemy's naval forces, especially when surprise could be achieved. If, on the other hand, superiority were first to be gained over the enemy's naval forces in an intended area of naval operations, evasion of battle could no longer be practiced. It would be necessary to engage the enemy's forces and so incur the risk of losing irreplaceable big ships. Moreover, although one finds only implicit recognition of this in Soviet writings, such efforts to gain preliminary control of areas of intended operations would soon be recognized for what they were: a capable adversary would immediately send reinforcements to any area where Soviet naval forces had been committed to combat.

Additionally worth noting is the nature of Belli's criticism of Great Britain's passive fleet-in-being strategy early in World War II. Rather than such an inactive strategy of "a threat without strikes," Belli argued that Britain should have exploited its naval superiority to force the German High Seas Fleet to fight a general engagement so that the latter would be destroyed. This was a pure Mahanian prescription for a stronger navy, of course, and in agreement with Soviet military strategy's emphasis on the offensive and the need to destroy an enemy's main forces. While this observation may have accurately expressed the long-range aspirations of the senior naval officers, it was not indicative of the fleet-in-being strategy of "active defense" based on naval mine-artillery positions that Stalin's much advertised big sea and oceanic navy actually was intended to implement— at least until enough capital ships could be built to adopt a force-equalization strategy.

It seems well warranted to conclude that Belli had transformed the original German concept of an essentially offensive force-equalization (*Krafteausgleich*) strategy of *seeking out* and defeating smaller parts of an enemy's main forces wherever they could be found at sea. In its place he had substituted an inherently defensive strategy (although with offensive tactics) of *merely accepting* combat against the weaker enemy naval forces estimated to be able to reach the area of an intended Soviet naval operation in the Soviet Union's coastal waters before completion of the operation. However, it is important to note in this regard that, while Belli maintained that the German naval operation against Norway in 1940 had disproved the Mahan-Colomb dictum that it was necessary to destroy or blockade an enemy's main naval forces and so gain full command of the sea before other naval operations could be undertaken, he nevertheless held it necessary to provide such strong preliminary support prior to an operation so as to ensure that a limited command could be gained by the additional direct-support forces assigned to provide cover for the operation itself.

Also, Belli's statement that submarines would (at least) remain the main force in conduct of antishipping warfare and so be entitled to the support of surface ships and aircraft was so heavily qualified subsequently as to make it appear virtually meaningless. In addition to submarines for an antishipping campaign, Belli announced that cruiser-raiders would be necessary in order to divert substantial parts of the enemy's main forces to provide escorts and covering forces for merchant ship convoys. Moreover, aircraft also would be required for the stated reason that they could operate against merchant ships during winter when submarines would be frozen into the ice of (most) Soviet ports. Belli concluded, in what must have been the final disillusionment of the submariners' hopes of retaining the leading role for at least one important mission, that a successful antishipping campaign would require the mutual cooperation of the heterogeneous naval forces having antishipping capabilities. Accordingly, any further pretense to submarines remaining *primus inter pares* with capital ships would have been fatuous.

Belli also made some significant observations on the shipping-protection mission. He asserted the continuing worth of convoying merchant ships with combatant escorts and covering forces. In the role of covering forces, he endorsed the utility of aircraft carriers by noting that they could be of particular value in the far regions of a TVD that was beyond the operating radii of land-based aircraft.

It merits note here that in 1937 Ivan Ludri, the deputy naval commissar, and Professor Chernyshev of the Naval War College staff were potential candidates along with Belli as theorists and spokesmen for the new Soviet School of naval warfare. However, only Chernyshev made the transition safely with Belli—by giving all due credit to capital ships and aircraft but without unduly diminishing the role of submarines. Ludri carried his newly discovered enthusiasm for capital ships so far as to decry the value of submarines in any and all combat roles, even against merchant ships in an antishipping campaign. Ludri, it will be recalled, was the only (former) Young School advocate who was named in Evseyev's August 1938 denunciation of both the Old and Young Schools and had probably already been shot in Stalin's Great Purge by the time the article appeared. For his careful discrimination of what was permissible and what was not under the aegis of the new Soviet School, Chernyshev survived the extensive purge of military and naval officers and lived to complete an important book on the role of surface ships in modern warfare which was published in 1945, the year of his death.

In view of the foregoing, it seems warranted to conclude that by the time the Nazis invaded the Soviet Union in mid-1941, Professor, Rear Admiral Vladimir Belli had established himself as the leading official theoretician and spokesman of the new Soviet School. He had achieved this by a judicious melding of the most serviceable tenets of the Old and Young Schools to fit the practical needs of the big-ship navy whose construction Stalin had undertaken by 1938 (but too late to complete any of the battleships or lay down even one of the four aircraft carriers which Stalin had authorized before the Soviet Union was caught up in World War II). In a full-page testimonial to Vladimir Aleksandrovich Belli to wish him continued good health on his 90th birthday in 1977, the *Naval Digest* noted that Belli had taught many future admirals, including Gorshkov, in his years at the Naval War College from 1926 until after World War II.[64] Belli's prewar writings, "in particular the research monograph he coauthored with Isakov and Aleksandrov on the activity of submarines in the first World War," were said to still be of "marked value even today."

Notes

Unless otherwise indicated, the publisher of books listed is the Military Press of the USSR Ministry of Defense in Moscow.

1 I. Kalachev ed., *Sovremennye boyevyye sredstva morskogo flota*, 2nd ed., Signed to press 23 January 1937.

2. "Ob uyazvimosti lineinykh korablei pri vozdushnykh atakakh," *Morskoi sbornik* No. 1, January 1937, p. 142. These excerpts were footnoted to have been taken from the November 1936 issue of the Swedish naval journal *Tidskrift i Sjoevaesendet*.

3. I. Ludri, "Morskiye operatsii" [Naval Operations], *Voennaya mysl'* No. 2, February 1937, pp. 75-86.

4. V. Chernyshev, "Morskaya taktika za dva desyatiletiya," [Naval Tactics Over Two Decades], *Morskoi sbornik* No. 12, December 1937, pp. 17-29. Like several earlier articles noted above, this one continued to categorize aircraft carriers as ships "of special purpose" rather than as "capital" ships, as in the major navies of the non-Communist world. Vsevelod Chernyshev had been a battleship navigator and PT squadron commander before assignment to the Naval War College teaching staff. He was serving in the rank of rear admiral at the time of his death in 1945 at the age of 47.

5. E. Shvede, "Razvitiye flotov kapitalisticheskikh gosudarstv za 20 let," *Morskoi sbornik* No. 12, 1937, pp. 113-126. The author, a naval captain, is known to have been an instructor at the Naval War College and the editor of several editions of a Soviet-style Janes *Fighting Ships* reference work on the world's navies. Perhaps only for comparison, he listed aircraft carriers immediately after battleships and ahead of heavy cruisers, thereby effectively categorizing them as "capital" ships rather than as auxiliary ships "of special purpose." The Soviet Navy quite likely was continuing to use the latter designation, since doing so placed carriers among the "light forces" that were generally more acceptable to the Army.

6. In another article in the *Naval Digest* in September 1938 Shvede made the same point and expanded on it to claim that the shore-based air of the Italian Navy was capable of "covering any sector of the Mediterranean from coastal and island air bases," *Morskoi sbornik* No. 9, 1938, p. 92.

7. P. Barjot, "Samoleti i avianosets" [Airplanes and the Aircraft Carrier], *Morskoi sbornik* No. 1, 1938, pp. 99-110. Barjot's report was said to have appeared in *Bulletin Association Technique Maritime et Aeronautique* No. 40 for 1937 and apparently it was to that association that he had made the address. In the mid-1950s, Barjot (by then a successful carrier admiral), wrote a book on navies in the nuclear era that dealt extensively with the merits of aircraft carriers. Translated into Russian by the Defense Ministry, the book appeared to be of marked relevance to the carrier debate of that period.

8. Soviet efforts to obtain design drawings of the 33,000-ton U.S.S. *Lexington* in 1937 are documented in *Foreign Relations of the United States, Diplomatic Papers and the Soviet Union, 1933-39*, (Washington: U.S. Department of State, 1952), p. 460. Subsequent efforts were made in 1939 to obtain plans for a large aircraft carrier from Germany. There are unconfirmed reports that the United Kingdom was also approached in the late 1930s for blueprints for an aircraft carrier.

9. Speech of P.A. Smirnov, 19 March 1938, *Morskoi sbornik*, April 1938, p. 15. Although just two carriers might seem like too small a number to lend substance to Smirnov's charge, he may have known from intelligence sources that the then-current German "Plan-Z" naval construction program actually provided for the construction of four aircraft carriers within the decade. And, of course, even two aircraft carriers could have been perceived in the Kremlin as potentially making a critical difference in the limited confines of the Baltic.

10. A. Evseyev, "Do kontsa razgromit vrazheskiye teorii v morskoi strategii," *Krasnyi Flot*, 28 August 1938, pp. 2-3.

11. "High priestism" is the name given to the naval science that "teaches" that command of the sea is a concept typified by the correlation of forces between contending fleets and that the stronger one of them always can concentrate superior power at the decisive moment in any region of the open sea. Furthermore the "high priests" hold that command of the sea is the creation of such complete control of the sea that the possibility is excluded of the enemy's conducting maritime operations.

12. "Above all else, the representative of the 'Old School' introduced confusion into the understanding of 'command of the sea' [*gospodstvo na more*] and 'sea control' [*vladeniye morem*]. The terminology 'command of the sea' is not analogous to 'sea control.' The term 'sea control' was used in the literature of the 'Old School' when they modernized and adapted the principles of maritime strategy of the English theoretician Corbett. Leaving this behind, we shall in the future speak only of 'command of the sea' and avoid bringing in superfluous terms which explain nothing." The Russian expression *vladeniye morem* connotes the mastery of a sea area by "possession," i.e., by actual physical "presence." The translation of this expression as "sea control" corresponds to the interpretation of that term's current usage in English as applying to limited sea areas where naval forces are maintaining a "presence" to actively oppose any efforts by the enemy to gain supremacy in the area. Command of the sea, by contrast, is a concept of unlimited geographic scope and connotes such "full" or "general" control that it may be exercised effectively even in areas without the "presence" of any of one's own forces by the mere *potential* for sending superior forces into those areas whenever needed.

13. The Evseyev article already had cited Corbett's influence on the Old School by characterizing that school's principles of naval warfare as merely an update and adaptation of Corbett's principles.

14. This key elaboration of the limited command-of-the-sea concept was elucidated on further along in Evseyev's article: "It is known that in the entire course of the history of war only full or conditional command of the sea has been gained. . . . As concerns the degree of achievement of conditional command of the sea, it has existed and will continue to exist and such a degree may still be termed a relative degree of the gaining of command of the sea. It would however be completely inadequate to say that there exist (only) two aspects of the gaining of command of the sea, full and conditional (or, relative). Such a formulation ignores time and space. From a study of the experience of naval warfare it is concluded with regard to naval power that command of the sea may be full or conditional (for the extent of a naval theater), general or local (for [just] part of a naval theater of military actions), and with regard to time, permanent or temporary." (p. 3)

15. First Deputy Naval Commissar Ivan Ludri was purged in 1937. Surprisingly, however, considering Aleksandrov's preeminent position in the Young School, the fact that his former colleague, Professor Belli, had denounced Aleksandrov as an enemy of the people in an April 1939, *Naval Digest* article (p. 21), and Stalin's extensive purge of both schools, Aleksandrov's life reportedly was spared, or at least his death is reported not to have occurred until 1945 ,and then in a plane crash. Nevertheless, he was replaced as deputy editor of the *Naval Digest* and nothing more was heard from him on naval strategy.

16. "The task will be fulfilled that has been set before the Soviet Government to create a mighty sea and ocean navy comprised of all types of warships up to the most powerful" (which logically included aircraft carriers—and as postwar evidence confirmed to have been planned between 1937 and 1941) (p. 3).

17. "In the Soviet Union the most powerful industry in the world has been created. In the Soviet Union is to be found all that is required for the construction of warships of all classes, modern battleships included." (p. 3)

18. S.G. Gorskov, "Voenno-morskiye flotov v voinakh i v mirnoye vremya" [Navies in Wars and in Peacetime], *Morskoi sbornik* No. 8, August 1972, p. 21.

19. In his book *Sea Power of the State*, Gorshkov essentially repeats Evseyev's thesis that command in a theater of military actions or in part of one may be gained either preceding or accompanying execution

of its basic missions by a fleet, *i.e.*, by either "preliminary" or "direct" support. S.G. Gorskov, *Morskaya moshch' gosudarstva*, 1st edition, 1976, p. 379; 2nd edition, 1979, p. 345.

20. Mohr (pseudonym), "Voenno-morskoye iskusstvo i uroki morskoi voiny," *Voennyi zarubezhnik* No. 9, September 1938, p. 73.

21. N.G. Kuznetsov, *Nakanune* [On the Eve] 2nd revised and expanded edition, signed to press 8 February 1969, p. 330.

22. "Rech' tov. Kuznetsova" ("Speech of Comrade Kuznetsov'), *Stenographic Record of the 18th Party Congress (10-21 March 1939)*, Political Press, 1939 pp. 477-480.

23. Kuznetsov, ibid. ". . . we must build the various types of ships suitable for our sea theaters and comparable to those of the possible enemy."

24. N.G. Kuznetsov, "Pered voinoi" [Before the War], *Oktyabr'* No. 11, November 1965, p. 142.

25. N. G. Kuznetsov, *Nakanune*, signed to press 15 August 1966, p. 258.

26. N.G. Kuznetsov, "Before the War" (in English), *International Affairs* No. 12, December 1966, p. 95.

27. P. Kotov, "Etapy razvitiya Sovetskogo voennogo korablestroeniya" [The Stages of Development of Soviet Military Shipbuilding'], *Military-Historical Journal* No. 7, July 1982, p. 55.

28. A.V. Basov, *Flot v velikoi otechestvennoi voine* [The Navy in the Great Patriotic War], signed to press 20 November 1979, p. 31.

29. Kuznetsov, "Pered voinoi," p. 143.

30. That is, the one described by Basov, which had two (presumably larger) light aircraft carriers for the Northern and Pacific Fleets. See footnote 28 and the text associated with footnote 36.

31. N.G. Kuznetsov, *Nakanune*, 2nd revised ed. p. 283.

32. *Ibid.*, p. 283. This passage also appeared on p. 258 of the 1st edition.

33. Kuznetsov, "Before the War" p. 95.

34. Kuznetsov, *Nakanune*, 2nd revised ed., p. 330.

35. Kotov, p. 55.

36. Basov, p. 31ff.

37. "Soviet Naval Strategy," Address to the U.S. Naval War College, Newport, Rhode Island on 31 October 1964 by Nicholas Artamonov, who used the name Nicholas Shadrin after his arrival in the U.S. in 1959.

38. Kuznetsov, *Nakanune*, 1st ed., 1966, p. 260. The Finnish War of 1940 has revealed a pressing need to reequip the Army with modern tanks and artillery.

39. Kuznetsov, "Pered voinoi," p. 142.

40. Kuznetsov, *Nakanune*, 1st ed. p. 258.

41. Kuznetsov, "Before the War" 1st ed., p. 95.

42. Kuznetsov, *Nakanune*, p. 258.

43. Kuznetsov, *Nakanune*, 2nd ed., p. 350.

44. Kotov, p. 55.

45. Basov, p. 32. And on p. 46 it is stated that "in the mid-1930s. . . the construction of aircraft carriers for the open seas was planned."

46. Kuznetsov, "Before the War," p. 93.

47. Kuznetsov, *Nakanune*, 1st ed., p. 259.

48. Kuznetsov, "Before the War," p. 96.

49. V. Belli, "Osnovy vedeniya operatsii na more," *Morskoi sbornik* No. 7, April 1939, pp. 13-24.

50. P.A. Smirnov "Sozdadim moguchiy voenno-morskoi flot SSR" [We are Creating a Mighty Navy of the U.S.S.R."], *Morskoi sbornik* No. 3, March 1938, pp. 7-18.

51. Belli, "Osnovy vedeniya operatsii na more," p. 16.

52. Two pages later Belli claimed that "the well-known successes of German submarines on the sea lines of communications could occur only because the submarine operations (sorties from base and return, mine sweeping, etc.) were supported by the surface forces."

53. V.A. Belli, "Pervyye operativno-strategicheskiye itogi voiny na more" [Initial Operational-Strategic Aims of a War at Sea], *Morskoi sbornik* No. 6, June 1940, pp. 8-21.

54. Since Belli was identified as a captain second rank in his April 1939 article, a captain first rank by a September 1939 article, and as a rear admiral in this June 1940 article, it is apparent that he was promoted to captain first rank and then to rear admiral in the intervening 14-month period. Since his already long tenure of 14 years at the Naval War College was continued throughout the war (and until at least 1965, when he was identified as Chief of the Command [officer] Faculty), it may be assumed the rapid promotion signified great satisfaction with his contributions as the leading Soviet School theoretician.

55. L. Gordon and N. Mal'tsev, "K voprosy ob avianostsakh," *Morskoi sbornik* No. 4, April 1940, p. 64.

56. V.A. Belli, "Skandinavskaya morskaya operatsiya i ee uroki," *Morskoi sbornik* No. 7, July 1940, pp. 39-53.

57. *Ibid.*, "Among them was Admiral Otto Groos (in the book *Studies of Naval War in the Light of the Experience of the World War*) and especially Wegener (in his book *Sea Strategy of the World War*)." (p. 82) The Groos book, *Seekriegslehren in Lichte des Weltkrieges*, appeared in the original German in 1928 and in Russian translation in 1930 as *Ucheniye morskoi voine v svete opyta mirovoi voine*. Vice Admiral Wegener's book and also 20 pages of Groos's *Fundamentals of Naval Strategy* were translated and published in 1941 by the Naval War College in Leningrad under the title *Operational-Tactical Views of the German Navy; A Collection of Articles* (*Operativno-takticheskiy vzglyady Germanskogo flota; Sbornik statei*).

58. By first maintaining that the Germans' 1940 Norwegian operations had disproved the Colomb-Mahan dictum that gaining command of the sea by the destruction or blockade of an enemy's (main) naval forces was a preliminary prerequisite to the conduct of any "major naval operation" and by then going on to assert that a "combination of preliminary and direct (i.e., simultaneous) support was necessary for the successful conduct of (major) naval operations," Belli followed the lead of the 28 August 1938 Evseyev article in preserving for the Soviet School of naval warfare the very same Old School principle (that no "ulterior objectives" could safely be pursued by major naval operations unless command of the sea had been gained) which he had just so polemically denounced. By dividing the gaining of command of the sea into two stages, a preliminary one that would cut the anticipated opposition down to a manageable size and a direct-support one that would take out the remaining opposition, he presumably forestalled criticism by all but the more perceptive of the Army opponents of the limited command-of-the-sea concept he was advocating.

59. V. Belli, "Sovmestnye operatsii armii i flota" (Joint Operations of the Army and Navy), *Morskoi sbornik* No. 17-18, September 1939, pp. 17 and 19.

60. I.S. Isakov, "Avantyurizm germanskogo morskoi strategii," *Morskoi sbornik* No. 6, June 1943, p. 7.

61. Professor, Admiral Alafuzov, in an objective study of *German Naval Doctrines*, acknowledged "the unquestionable improvement in the strategic position of Germany" but nevertheless questioned the "dear price" of losing three cruisers and nine destroyers (almost half of those in the German Navy at the time). V.A. Alafuzov, *Doktriny Germanskogo flota*, 1956, p. 164.

62. N.B. Pavlovich, "Boyevoye obespecheniye," *Morskoi sbornik* No. 11, November 1940.

63. I.A. Korotkov, *Istoriya Sovetskoi voennoi mysli* [A History of Soviet Military Thought] (Moscow: Nauka Press, 1981).

64. M. Stepanov, "Sluzhba na flote . . . s 1900g" ["Service in the Navy . . . Since 1900"], *Morskoi sbornik* No. 7, July 1977, p. 72.

V
The Soviet School Rests Unchallenged On Its Laurels, 1941-1945

The Evidence and Some Partial Analysis

Soviet naval theory, including that of the dominant Soviet School of naval warfare, gained relatively little from the Navy's own participation in World War II but substantially more from analyzing the naval operations and underlying concepts of the Soviets' allies in that war. A deep and lasting imprint on Soviet naval theory in general and Soviet School theory in particular was made by the aircraft-carrier task-force strike operations of the U.S., Japanese, and British Navies, by their large-scale amphibious landings, and by their antisubmarine warfare. While the war years brought some evolution in the Soviet School's views on naval warfare, no opposing school of strategy arose within the Soviet Union to challenge and thereby modify those views.

To substantiate the initial assertion that Soviet naval theory profited relatively little from the experience of the Soviet Union's own naval forces in the Great Patriotic War, it is of central importance to appreciate that Soviet naval operations from 1941 through 1945 were restricted almost entirely to supporting the Army ground forces in what was essentially a continental war for the Soviet Union. This fact was stated in basic detail in a 1982 book published by the Soviet Ministry of Defense under the title *Military-Technological Progress and the Armed Forces of the USSR*.[1] It noted that "the Navy gained great experience with the ground forces in the defense of important coastal bases and regions" and "beginning in 1943 the Navy successfully participated in front operations with the ground forces." Even these joint operations were described as (only) ones in which "shipboard and shore-based artillery and aviation devastated the enemy with preparatory artillery fire and support of attacks [by the ground forces] to penetrate his defense." (p. 213)

The 1969 textbook for Soviet naval cadets, *A History of Naval Art*,[2] claimed that Soviet military and naval art was "greatly developed in the Second World War." This statement, which came in a final summary chapter (p. 516), was credited to one of the leading "official theoreticians" of the Navy,

Professor Stalbo. The context reveals that it applied only to providing support for coastal Army operations as far as the experience of the Soviet Navy was concerned. When Stalbo came to spell out nine alleged "changes in naval art," they proved to be only nine "results of the war" that should eventually affect naval theory—such as "the ascendance of the aircraft carrier over the battleship" and "the increased importance of the submarine." However, he failed to mention a single change that actually had taken place in Soviet naval theory.

In the 1973 study *Soviet Naval Art in the Great Patriotic War*,[3] two other naval theoreticians, Professors Achkasov and Pavlovich, made it implicitly evident that all of the advances claimed for Soviet naval theory were directly or indirectly in support of Army ground forces' operations. They did this by stating the two most important missions of the Navy from 1941 through 1945:

> Soviet naval art . . . was improved continuously during the Great Patriotic War and by its end had achieved a high level of development. . . . The character of the actions of the Navy of the USSR determined the main mission—cooperation with the ground forces in their operations in coastal sectors. . . . As a no less important mission, the Soviet Navy was assigned to the defense of their own naval bases *from landward* and from the air [emphasis supplied] (pp. 515-525).

Similarly, the third edition of the standard popular Soviet history of the Navy, *The Combat Course of the Soviet Navy*,[4] summarizes the missions performed by the Navy in the war as either directly or indirectly related to supporting the coastal flanks of the ground forces. Neither in the main text nor in a forward attributed to Admiral Gorshkov is anything said or implied about Soviet naval theory having benefited during World War II from the experiences of the Soviet Navy. Despite the fact that seven of the book's 12 chapters are devoted to that war, none of them repeat the usual claim that Soviet naval art had been advanced by the lessons learned from the Navy's participation.

Finally, as regards the understandable lack of development of Soviet naval thought toward independent naval operations by a navy whose own wartime activities had been limited to those of a "faithful handmaiden" to the ground forces, the 1980 book *The Navy in the Great Patriotic War*[5] states flatly:

> Cooperation with the ground forces was the main assignment of the Navy. All of the remaining missions—those for destruction of the naval forces of the enemy, for interdiction of his sea lines of communications, and for the protection of our sea communications— were carried out primarily in the interests of the ground forces (p. 253).

In addition to the foregoing statements stressing the basically Army-coastal-flank-support missions performed by the Navy in World War II, there is a companion statement in a military textbook which implicitly affirms that the independent-operations aspects of Soviet naval theory were not developed. In *History of Military Art*,[6] the following revealing assertion was made with respect to the lack of any theoretical developments regarding independent "operations" as contrasted with the defensively defined "daily combat activities . . . Just as for the ground forces, the theory of the conduct of naval operations was not developed during the War." (p. 364)

Despite this limitation of the Navy's experience in the Great Patriotic War to mainly an Army-coastal-flank-support role, strong impressions were made on Soviet naval theory by the carrier task-force, amphibious-landing, and antisubmarine operations of the U.S. and Japanese Navies in the Pacific during World War II. In particular, many examples were drawn from these operations to support the Soviet school's limited command-of-the-sea theory by Professor Belli in three articles published in the *Naval Digest* in late 1944 and 1945.[7]

Limited Command of the Sea - Basic Tenet of the Soviet School. In the article in late 1944 on "The War in the Pacific"[8] Professor Belli found a wealth of examples in the naval operations of the United States and Japan in World War II that supported a central tenet of the Soviet School of naval warfare which he had been developing since 1938. It was that of the possibility that the weaker of two strong navies could gain and hold a limited command of the sea (or "sea control" in Western usage) in a given region of a sea theater of military action (TVD) or even in the whole of such a TVD for just long enough to carry out a particular operation before the stronger navy could send in superior forces.

He acknowledged that fleet-against-fleet operations basically aim at gaining command of the sea by destruction (or blockade) of an enemy's main naval forces (in order to be free to conduct one's own naval theater campaigns without serious hindrance while preventing the adversary from doing likewise). The implication of this acknowledgement seemed to be that it would be unrealistic and counterproductive for the weaker Soviet Navy to be assigned the mission of destroying (or blockading) the main naval forces of the stronger U.S. Navy and its allies. Moreover, Professor Belli asserted that gaining command of the sea in an intended area of operations would be a prerequisite to fleet-against-the-shore operations (other than surprise raids followed by rapid withdrawal before the enemy could react), including those for large-scale amphibious landing operations and antisubmarine operations.

The foregoing elaborates the limited command-of-the-sea context of the Soviet School of naval warfare as amplified by Professor Belli from samples taken from U.S. and Japanese naval operations in the Pacific War. From this we gain an appreciation of the force-equalization-by-attrition campaign (theater) strategy by which the Soviet School held that the requisite extent of sea control could be gained to permit carrying out one's own operations while preventing the adversary from carrying out his. Belli attributed to the systematic weakening of the air, sea, and economic strength of Japan by the U.S. carrier-based air offensive against Japan proper, the fact that the necessary preconditions had been created for the final operation that would bring victory—an amphibious invasion and occupation of the enemy's homeland (p. 113).

In other words, a process of gradual attrition had not merely equalized the U.S. naval forces with those of Japan but had created such an enormous superiority of forces at sea and in the air to the U.S. advantage that Japan could no longer contest command of the sea in the western Pacific and, therefore, the outcome of the war had been "predetermined." It was "not by accident," to use a favorite Russian expression, that in his final summary Belli failed to include the land-based air, especially the B-29's to which he had earlier given credit. He credited only *naval* aviation, that is the aircraft carriers and their planes, as responsible for having created the necessary "preconditions" (i.e., command of the sea in the western Pacific) to make possible an amphibious invasion of Japan. Belli seemed to be making the implicit point that aircraft carriers had indeed proven themselves to be *the* essential ship type for gaining strategic command of the sea in oceanic warfare.

Belli Again Discusses Operational "Support" as the Soviet-School Method for Gaining Limited Command of the Sea. As he had done in his April 1939 article, Professor Belli again made the implicit distinction between preliminary and direct support. Preliminary support for each major operation must be sufficient to establish "a favorable operational regime" (that is, local sea control) while direct (simultaneous) support must be adequate to overcome the maximum opposition the enemy could mount in the operations area during the period of time required for completion of the operation.

Belli described the U.S. amphibious invasion of Mindoro in the Philippines in January 1945 as owing its success to having involved both types of support:

● "Preliminary support for the operation" to create "a favorable regime" by preparatory air strikes from the carrier planes of the U.S. Third Fleet against the Japanese air bases and ships at Formosa and the Ryukyu Islands from whence the Japanese troops on Mindoro could be reinforced, supplied, and provided with naval gunfire support and cover against seaborne attack.

● "Direct support for the operation" comprised of the following three measures:

(1) "Continued mass flights of planes from carriers and from shore . . . against airfields, combatant ships, and other enemy targets;

(2) Provision of "operational cover" for the amphibious invasion force during its sea passage and during the landings by the U.S. Third Fleet deployed in the direction from which Japanese naval forces were expected to try to interfere with the operation; and

(3) Close support for the landing itself provided by the U.S. Seventh Fleet operating as a "support detachment." (p. 101)

Belli described how the U.S. provision of preliminary support had eventuated in naval battles—but without again pointing out explicitly (as he had done in his prewar articles) that by so doing, the advantage of surprise was forfeited and with it the hope of evading battle and the consequent loss of ships. From the general tone of his remarks it was apparent that Professor Belli, as the leading architect of the Soviet School of naval warfare, favored constructing sufficient surface naval forces, including aircraft carriers, to ensure that the Navy would be able to provide adequate preliminary support to initially gain temporary command of the sea in any likely areas of operations.

Belli had the Soviet School's central tenet of limited command of the sea in mind when he described the Mindoro landing as having consisted of preliminary support to gain sea control in the landing area and direct support to ensure retaining that control during the landings. This assumption became apparent in Belli's 1945 summation of the reason for the U.S. Navy's successful recapture of the Philippines as having been due to "concentration of superior forces in the decisive sector at the decisive moment."[9] (p. 104)

It merits noting that Belli repeatedly mentioned the limited-area nature of the command of the sea he perceived had been gained by the U.S. Navy at various times and places. Thus, he referred variously to command in a region of a theater, as having taken on "a local character—not having widened to the broader expanse of a theater," and as only having involved a part of Philippine waters.

The "Second Aspect of Command of the Sea." Also, Belli made several references to what in classical sea power theory has been termed the "second aspect of command of the sea": the need to control the sea lines of communication that extend back to one's supply ports and ship repair bases from the scene of action of any given operation. This much overlooked second requirement, Belli indicated, was as essential as the first one for gaining command of the sea in the operations area itself. Thus, in his 1944 article, Belli mentioned the Japanese Navy's successful protection of its sea lines of communication back to Japan from the area of operations to capture New Guinea (p. 44). Further on in the same article Belli spoke of Japanese selection of air bases to be seized to further their advance into the Indian Ocean as including consideration of the defensibility of the sea lines of communication to the home country. Belli also observed, with respect to the Japanese seizure of the Aleutian islands of Kiska and Attu, that the protection of the sea routes, over which reinforcements and supplies were transported to the troops on those islands, had involved the Japanese Navy in combat clashes. Apparently Belli intended to remind his readers that gaining command of the sea was incompatible with a (Young School) strategy of hit-and-run to evade any combat with a stronger enemy.

Also on the subject of the second aspect of command of the sea, Belli alleged in his 1945 *Naval Digest* article, ending his series of four on the war in the Pacific, that the Japanese had counted on the U.S. Navy's inability to protect its extended sea lines of communication across the Pacific to the Philippines but had erred fatally in overlooking the general "superiority at sea" that enabled the United States to adequately protect its transpacific communications. Finally Belli analyzed the Allies' gaining of control over the sea routes between the home islands of Japan and its ground forces in Indochina, Burma, the Dutch East Indies, and the Malacca Straits as the development that "tightened the noose" around the collective necks of those troops.

Limited Command of the Sea for "Strategic" Amphibious Landing Operations. The lasting effects on Soviet School theory of the major amphibious landings made in World War II were reflected nicely in an article titled "Strategic Amphibious Landing Operations" that appeared in early 1945 in the Armed Forces General Staff journal, *Military Thought*, under the signature of Professor Belli.[10] He began the article by defining landing operations as "strategic" "in those cases in which it is necessary to create an active front on enemy territory or on a territory occupied by an enemy with which there is no common ground frontier." (p. 30)

Lacking either tactical or operational connections with other ground fronts, Belli asserted, such landings had "independent significance," apparently meaning that they were conducted as independent naval operations. Belli pointed out that they could be so important that they could influence the further course of a war and even its outcome. Belli stressed the importance of such landings for the "second aspect of command of the sea." As he phrased the matter: "A characteristic of such a landing is its dependence on sea communications, which must be protected by a fleet systematically and for a protracted period inasmuch as not only the landing of the troops but their supply, troop replacements, and weapons and equipment as a rule come over sea routes." (p. 30) The Egyptian expedition of Napoleon met with defeat despite a succession of tactical successes due to the inability of the French to protect their sea communications back to metropolitan France.

Belli attributed the fact that his tabulations showed nearly twice as many strategic landings in World War II alone as for all earlier wars to the fact that World War II had been global in extent. Inasmuch as Soviet military doctrine holds that any nuclear war will become worldwide in scope, it may be that Belli was implying that in any future general war the Soviet Navy would require naval forces capable of such "strategic" amphibious operations. And, if so, this would posit having strong enough carrier task-forces not only to provide cover for the landing forces while in transit and during debarkation but also for protracted protection of the sea lines of communication back to home ports in order to resupply the landing forces as long as necessary.

Belli defined the tasks of strategic amphibious landings as conducted in the Second World War in the following terms:

- The occupation of key isolated territories or islands, primarily with the direct aim of their seizure and elimination of the enemy troops on them; and also

- Establishment of a jumping-off place for a further strategic offensive; and

- Establishment of a more favorable operating regime over the adjacent sea routes (p. 31).

Belli interpreted the aims of the Allied landing in North Africa as seizing the coast of North Africa; clearing it of Axis troops by cooperating with Allied troops advancing from Egypt; at the same time creating a more favorable strategic position in the Mediterranean Sea; and improving the protection of the vitally important sea communications between Gibraltar and Port Said, that is, the protection of Great Britain's communications with India and Australia. The Japanese landings at the Malacca Straits, in the Philippine Islands, and in the Dutch East Indies, Belli continued, were conducted to give Japan a commanding position in the southwest Pacific and were made pursuant to political and economic aims as well as strategic ones.

Belli concluded that the Allied landings in Normandy and in the south of France had more ambitious strategic aims than most landings: to jointly create a new strategic front and with it the necessary conditions for smashing the enemy army by coordinating the operations of the two fronts in Europe (i.e., of the Western Allies in the west and the Russians in the east). As a result, Belli said, the landings in France exerted an influence on not only the course of the war but also on its outcome.

Moreover, the Allied landings "narrowed the system of naval bases" of the German Navy by liberating the coasts of France, Belgium, and the Netherlands. This loss of bases on the Atlantic coast was noted to have deprived the German U-boats of "their previous freedom of operational deployment" for attacking Allied convoys at a great distance from the coast. In effect, Belli added, this loss of Atlantic bases amounted to Germany's loss of its "former strategic position on the Atlantic Ocean." Belli summarized:

Thus, while strategic amphibious landings had the accomplishment of strategic missions in the ground theaters as their main aim, they also ensured the improvement of the regime at sea by way of the seizure of significant parts of the coasts or of isolated territories of an enemy (pp. 31-32).

Professor Belli applied the Soviet School's tenet of limited command of the sea to strategic amphibious landings, employing the then-current euphemism for "command of the sea:" the establishment of "favorable conditions" in the landing areas:

> One of the conditions for success of [such] operations is the choice of favorable conditions for its accomplishment, that is, of such conditions under which the organizer of such an operation disposes of sufficient forces for execution of the mission and the enemy cannot mount a serious opposition at sea, in the air, or on land (p. 32).

The overall U.S. and British naval forces potentially available in 1944 for the landings in France were listed in Belli's article, "Strategic Amphibious Landings." Those forces included 15 escort aircraft carriers of the British Navy and 100 of the U.S. Navy. Belli added: "Of course, only a part of the American naval forces were employed in European waters." He could as easily and far more relevantly have listed only the U.S. forces actually employed for the landings in France. Therefore it seems warranted to conclude that Belli selected his facts to exaggerate the impression of the total number of naval forces involved in the landings, especially the number of escort aircraft carriers.

Belli was almost as noticeably chary of speaking of attack aircraft carriers in this January-February 1945 article in the *Naval Digest* as he had been of mentioning "command of the sea" in its usual translation (gospodstvo na more). Eventually, however, on the penultimate page of his ten-page article, he did once mention the "covering detachments" for landing forces as consisting "of aircraft carriers."

On the last page, Rear Admiral Belli returned to the Soviet School's tenet of limited command of the sea to define the two kinds of operational support involved implicitly in ensuring a sufficiently extensive sea control to be able to carry out such landings successfully:

> Preliminary support of a landing operation in general found its fullest expression in the Japanese landing at the Straits of Malacca. It was preceded by the air attack on the American combatant ships at Pearl Harbor and on the airfields on Oahu. In the Sicilian landing on the night of 5 June [1944] the light naval forces and aviation attacked the enemy's bases on the island of Crete with the aim of putting the German planes and PT boats out of commission.
>
> Direct support is an essential element of every landing operation and especially those of a large scale. It consists of operational intelligence, of the delivery of strikes at bases and airfields, of searches for submarines, of the mining of channels and maneuvering areas, and of deployment of a covering detachment (p. 38).

By specifying that direct support was necessary for *every* landing and by not saying the same about preliminary support, Belli was obliquely referring to a Soviet School position. While the latter kind of support is desirable whenever surprise is not essential (to compensate for not being able to concentrate sufficient forces to overwhelm the maximum enemy force that might otherwise be assembled in opposition), it is not essential on occasions when the forces in direct support are superior enough to any and all forces than an adversary either already has present or could move into the projected operational area during the planned duration of a given operation.

As noted, the implicit aim of providing preliminary support was precisely that of gaining a limited command of the sea before undertaking other missions. However, the Soviet School, by making preliminary support optional depending on circumstances, had found an expedient way out of a theoretical dilemma that otherwise would have required an inferior navy such as that of the Soviet Union to remain passive when confronted by a greatly superior naval opponent. With the preliminary and direct support alternatives, the Navy could at least justify making hit-and-run raids on enemy shore installations in order to meet the requirement of military doctrine to continuously exhibit "activeness" while on the defensive. This possibility had applicability most of the time since opportunities to engage enemy task forces small enough to attack with good prospects of success under the theater campaign strategy of force-equalization-by-attrition were not expected to occur frequently.

Limited Command of the Sea For "Tactical-Operational" Amphibious Landings. A *Naval Digest* article in early 1944 by then Rear Admiral S. G. Gorshkov described and analyzed his experiences in planning and executing four successive "tactical-operational" amphibious operations within less than one month.[11] The future commander in chief of the Navy for nearly three decades noted that the compressed time frame for planning and conducting amphibious operations had allowed only a week between landings for planning the next one. Moreover, it was necessary while planning and conducting such operations, to continue to provide forces and command direction of the "daily combat activity" for providing support to the coastal flanks of the ground forces.

A number of points relating to the evolution of Soviet naval theory during the Second World War emerged in this first published article by Gorshkov. They are summarized in the following three paragraphs:

- "Favorable conditions" (the euphemism at the time for limited command of the sea) were created for the landing operations by "active" routine "daily combat activities" and by "operations" such as raids on the ports and [coastal sea] communications of the adversary; laying minefields; combined strikes by surface combatant ships, aviation, and coastal artillery to interdict the sea communications of the enemy; destruction of his combatant ships; blockade of his ports; hindering the adversary's maritime shipping to the front; and evacuating own troops encircled and pinned down in coastal areas. Of particular note is the close correspondence of these "daily combat activities" and "operations" with both the tenets of the Soviet School of naval warfare, which require that a limited command of the sea be gained prior to undertaking the mission at hand, and with those of the "active fleet in being" strategy endorsed by Sir Julian Corbett for a strong but inferior navy and which the Soviet School had adopted and adapted for its own use.

• The flexible command and control that Gorshkov noted was the basis of success in any operation and especially in an amphibious landing operation, was claimed to have been established for the joint actions of sea and land forces to effect cooperation of the Azov flotilla which Gorshkov commanded with units of the Red Army in the occupation of bases and ports on the Sea of Azov. The one "positive fact" that Gorshkov found worthy of mention as contributing to the success of the amphibious landings executed under his command was that "the staffs of the flotilla and the Army commander exchanged representatives."

• Stressed was the requirement for "comprehensive combat support" of the landing forces by the other naval forces.[12] As already suggested by the analysis of Professor Belli's article, "Strategic Amphibious Landings," the concept of providing "support" for the type of naval forces assigned the main role in an operation by other naval force types had become a tenet of Soviet School theory as the approved method for gaining and maintaining the necessary limited command of the sea in an intended area of operations for (just) the period of time allotted for execution of an operation. Gorshkov claimed that "combat support" for an operation was provided in proportion to the strength of the enemy forces expected to be encountered. He noted particularly that effective combat support always had involved the covering forces and prevented the German forces from interfering with the landing forces. Gorshkov cited the Taganrog landing as notable for good combat support in that the covering force had blockaded the enemy naval forces in port and thus had pinned down the enemy forces, thereby excluding any interference by them. This Soviet School tenet of pinning down (or "paralyzing") an enemy in secondary directions to prevent his interference in the main direction is a Soviet military doctrinal principle (pp. 73-74).

Value of Aircraft Carriers Stressed, Particularly for Oceanic Operations. The circumspection shown by Professor Belli in only once mentioning carriers in his article had a precedent in an article by an apparent naval aviator that had appeared in the *Naval Digest* a month earlier under the title "Action of Aviation on Sea Communications."[13] On six occasions in the 17-page article (pp. 54-68) the value of air cover for both naval and merchant ships operating on the high seas was indicated implicitly. Obviously the author felt it would be impolitic to praise aircraft carriers explicitly. However, he made his high professional esteem for them abundantly clear by demonstrating their importance in a number of World War II battles and by repeating in his conclusions one of a half dozen passages in the main text that unmistakably referred to aircraft carriers: "The mobility of aviation is one of the most important advantages in actions against combatant ships." (p. 69) Moreover, the great value of aircraft carriers for providing air cover to merchant ship convoys was broadly hinted at by the statement: "Only a shortage of aircraft carriers prevented their inclusion in the composition of each Allied convoy." (p. 53)[14] The article also made it apparent that shore-based fighter planes were incapable of providing fleet air cover beyond the confines of coastal waters.

The Navy's requirements for aircraft carriers was more openly expressed in a book entitled *Surface Combatant Ships in Modern War* that appeared in May 1945.[15] Written by Professor V. F. Chernyshev, a colleague of Professor Belli's at the Naval War College, the book clearly implied Navy requirements for both light aircraft carriers with mainly fighter aircraft (for employment in limited-sea theaters) and attack (heavy) aircraft carriers with bomber and torpedo planes in addition to fighters (for oceanic operations).

As late as the end of 1937 Professor Chernyshev had not been convinced that construction of aircraft carriers was "an imperative necessity" for the Navy (as seen from his *Naval Digest* article in December of that year). Yet, by the last year of the war, he had concluded that the range of shore-based aviation had been shown to be too limited to provide air cover for the fleets, even in the Soviet Union's peripheral sea theaters. "Consequently," Chernyshev wrote with respect to World War II, "aviation could manifest its combat power only on the condition that its airplanes were based on surface combatant ships—on attack aircraft carriers." (p. 155)

The requirement for aircraft carriers to provide air cover for surface naval forces while at sea, even in home waters in all but exceptional cases, was clearly stated in *Surface Combatant Ships.* Shore-based fighter planes could only provide reliable support for surface combatant forces in coastal waters close to coastal airfields (pp. 32-33). Chernyshev cited the case of the Italian Navy in World War II and contrasted its failure to provide timely and adequate air cover for its surface naval forces in the Mediterranean with the success of the British carrier squadrons there. The Italian Navy's dependence on shore-based aviation was identified as the reason for its failure. For oceanic operations, aircraft carriers must function not only to provide air cover for naval forces at sea but also to serve as "platforms for bomber, torpedo, and reconnaissance aviation." (p. 33)

In the 1937 *Naval Digest* article referred to above, Chernyshev had observed that only the next war would show whether the aircraft carrier was destined to replace the battleship as the nucleus of the main battle forces of navies. In his 1945 book *Surface Combatant Ships* he concluded that the aircraft carrier's role had increased in importance to the point that it had become equal with the battleship—"a second backbone" of a fleet.

> It may be said that the aircraft carriers of large navies become a second type of surface combatant which is included along with battleships in the basic nucleus of the main task forces (p. 88).

Without explicitly stating as a main lesson of World War II that naval warfare had become a contest between aircraft carriers, and deprived the

battleship of its former leading role, Chernyshev tactfully noted with regard
to the battles of the Coral Sea and Midway:

> These two battles are interesting in that the battleship fleets in neither case came within
> gunnery range of each other. Rather, the attacks on the combatant ships were made
> by the shipborne aviation of aircraft carriers (p. 41).

However, Chernyshev also noted that battleships had found "extensive
and varied employment" in oceanic theaters—although he observed that
they had been virtually unemployed in closed or intersecting theaters in
which no enemy battleships were present. Of most relevance was
Chernyshev's indication that World War II had made it clear that aircraft
carriers were an essential component of battle forces in the Soviet Union's
peripheral seas as well as in oceanic theaters. The only proviso was that
the forces operate beyond the narrow coastal band of 100 miles or so in
which shore-based aircraft might hope to provide continuous air cover and
reconnaissance for them:

> Battleships, as a rule, operate in the composition of a task force. Two or three of them
> constitute the nucleus of the force which also includes cruisers, destroyers, and ships
> of other classes. For operations in the open sea, aircraft carriers are included in the
> composition of such a task force (p. 53).

Chernyshev had followed up his second-backbone metaphor regarding
aircraft carriers with the caveat that aircraft carriers could only operate
successfully when they were provided the support of other naval types
ranging from small escorts to battleships. He attributed this need for the
support of other types of surface ships to the aircraft carrier's inherent
vulnerability:

> The weakest side of contemporary aircraft carriers remains their low survivabil-
> ity. . . . They constitute large, very visible, and highly vulnerable targets for bombs
> and torpedoes as well as for artillery shells [of capital ships]. Moreover, even a slight
> list puts a carrier out of action while the presence of large volumes of aviation fuel
> (gasoline) creates conditions especially conducive to fires. . . .

> What was said above must not be taken as a derogation of the role of aircraft carriers
> in modern war. Rather, it was said just to call particular attention to the need to support
> their operations with other forces. . . . Aircraft carriers require for their operations
> an extensive and developed support by surface combatant ships of other types, starting
> with battleships and extending to destroyers (p. 88).

Chernyshev had remarked earlier that World War II had provided
examples of cases in which aircraft carriers had been accorded the support
of other types of major surface ships in order to make strikes against enemy
ships in port. Taranto and Pearl Harbor were cited as examples.

With an apparent eye on future fleet force levels of aircraft carriers,
Chernyshev resourcefully parlayed the liability of carrier vulnerability into

the asset of a justification for building between 8 and 12 carriers for the Soviet Navy (i.e., "two or three" for each of the four fleet areas);

> In view of their low survivability, it is risky to have just a single aircraft carrier in a given task force assigned to carry out an important mission. Accordingly, two or three carriers are normally employed in each operational direction (p. 88).

Aircraft carriers, Chernyshev asserted, "are capable of carrying out all of the basic strike tasks against ships at sea and against bases, and also of carrying out a number of tasks of a support nature." (p. 88) An earlier listing of five tasks which Chernyshev had credited aircraft carriers with having performed successfully in World War II enables determination of which tasks were the basic strike ones and which were of a support nature. In the former category, as the basic tasks, would come "torpedo and bomb strikes against ships at sea" and "strikes at bases and the ships in them." In the support category would fall the remaining three tasks of "reconnaissance," "anti-air defense of naval forces at sea," and "protection of convoys." (pp. 82-83)

With regard to the "strikes-at-bases" task, Chernyshev commented: "The presence of aircraft carriers made it possible to shift the air battle onto the [overseas] territory of the adversary, onto territory that would have been unreachable by shore-based aviation." Inasmuch as shifting the battle to the enemy's territory is a major tenet of Soviet military doctrine (and hence obligatory for all of the armed services), this comment may be read as a justification for providing the Soviet Navy with aircraft carriers that had been calculated to have special appeal to the Army-dominated Defense Ministry and Armed Forces' General Staff.

In an *ex post facto* interpretation of the lessons learned from the World War II naval operations of the major naval powers, Professor Stalbo was to write in 1978 that carrier strike forces had brought into being "a new field of naval art" while carrier-based antisubmarine planes had "opened up a completely new page in the history of naval art."[16] The relevant comment reads:

> A new field of naval art came into being: the operational-tactical employment of aircraft carrier striking forces. Naval art incorporated questions of the operational employment of such task forces in [theater] campaigns and of the tactics for the conduct of battle under various conditions (p. 95).

> The employment of antisubmarine aviation from aircraft carriers in warfare against submarines opened up a completely new page in the history of naval art. Escort carriers . . . operated in the broad expanses of the Atlantic together with destroyers and frigates on moving antisubmarine barriers. . . . The depth of such barriers was extended out to 80-1000 miles and their front to 150 miles (p. 97).

Stalbo went on to make explicit that sea-based aviation was the *sine qua non* for naval forces to be able to contest successfully for command of the sea. Speaking of World War II, he wrote: "The gaining of command of the sea was determined in full measure by carrier aviation." (p. 98)

Other Key Points of Chernyshev's book. *Surface Combatant Ships* contained much more of interest than just the views on aircraft carriers discussed above. Most notably, the Soviet School concept of limited command of the sea clearly underlayed the book's discussion of surface combatant ships and their employment, and the narrow range of missions submarines were held capable of carrying out. Like his colleague, Professor Belli, Chernyshev held that the time had passed when a general or full command of the sea could be gained by show-down battles between opposing main forces of capital ships. Rather Chernyshev adhered to Belli's limited command-of-the-sea concept that the extent of "command" required could feasibly be limited to just control of an intended area of operations and only for as long as required to carry out the mission in that area. The forces assigned to carry out a given mission need only be provided combat support by sufficient additional naval forces to fight off any enemy forces already in the intended mission area or that could reach it during the period of time planned for the operation. No longer was it considered necessary, as previously under classical sea power theory, to limit naval operations to just surprise raids until or unless a full command of the sea could be gained by decisively defeating or blockading the enemy's main naval forces.

Professor Chernyshev quoted approvingly from Admiral Isakov's 1944 book, *The Navy of the USSR*, to the effect that the one or two decisive general engagements of battleship squadrons had been replaced by thousands of small combat episodes of daily clashes and battles that occasionally grew into such major operations as ones for defense of naval bases, large-scale amphibious landings, the escort of convoys of merchant ships, the ship bombardment of naval bases, and systematic warfare on the sea lines of communication. The aim of all of this, according to Chernyshev still quoting from Isakov, was to attack and eventually destroy the adversary's main naval forces in a war of annihilation such as conducted on land but extended to sea. The considerable intervals that previously had transpired between combat clashes had given way to unceasing actions, Chernyshev noted. Moreover, war at sea had expanded from primarily surface actions to include the subsurface and the air space above surface operations.

The submarine was credited by Chernyshev as constituting a threat to an adversary's surface combatant ships and as "a powerful means for warfare on sea communications." Nevertheless, he concluded, "an organized antisubmarine defense can deal with this threat effectively."

Furthermore, Chernyshev concluded as had Professor Belli in his April 1939 *Naval Digest* article, that the utility of submarines lay mainly in their capabilities for conducting a *guerre de course* against merchant shipping. Even for the antishipping mission, the operational cooperation of submarines, aviation, and surface combatant ships was noted to be required to accomplish the most successful results. Chernyshev further cut the submarine down to what he deemed suitable size for Soviet School acceptance by concluding that "submarines never can take on themselves the full spectrum of missions that are accomplished by surface combatant ships." He added that submarines were "wholly unsuitable for some of these missions and have no advantages over surface ships for accomplishing the other missions." These unusually outspoken views on the limited value of submarines seemed to be an accurate reflection of the Soviet School's underlying preference for large surface combatants.

In addition to reducing submarines to their real missions-performance size, Chernyshev also gave critical treatment to the fast, light surface-forces that always had been the Young School preference along with aircraft and submarines. While giving fulsome credit to the "mosquito fleets" of small ships and craft that serve either alone or together with land-based aircraft to conduct the routine daily combat activity in the Soviet Union's coastal waters, Chernyshev warned in effect against the characteristic Young School belief that light, fast surface-forces can defeat major surface combat ships:

> It would be dangerous, however, to draw from this a hasty conclusion that would attempt to put small ships up against large ones. The successful and greatly varied activity of the "mosquitoes" still does not mean that they alone or with the help of aviation are capable of carrying out all of the missions that are assigned to modern navies without the participation of large combatant ships and under any conditions. It is relevant to recall that the exceptionally significant role of small combatants . . . could and can take place only under certain specific conditions . . . in the absence or inaction of the large surface ships of the enemy. The experience of war shows with sufficient clarity that when an adversary has even a small number of large combatant ships in the expanses of the large naval theaters, one's fulfillment of a whole range of operations becomes impossible without the participation in them of large surface combatant ships [of one's own] (p. 8).[17]

The importance at the outset of a war of improving strategic positions for oceanic antishipping operations by submarines and surface raiders was noted to have been demonstrated in World War II by Germany's seizure of the Norwegian and French coasts. As compared with the German situation in World War I, in which the German Navy's bases were confined to the narrow limits of the "wet triangle," the Norwegian bases afforded Germany "exceptionally favorable conditions" for the operation of submarines, surface raiders, and aircraft against the entire length of the Allies' sea lines of communication in the Atlantic and Mediterranean.

Further Analysis and Interpretation of the Evidence, 1941-1945

Nothing beyond Army flank-support theory was added to Soviet naval theory directly from Soviet experience during the Great Patriotic War. This was due to the fact that the Navy served almost exclusively as "the faithful handmaiden" of the Army ground forces. Nevertheless the wartime experience of the major navies against each others' aircraft carrier task forces (to win local-area or theater-wide command of the sea), in employing those forces to support strategic amphibious landings, and to conduct antisubmarine warfare made an indelible imprint on Soviet naval thought.

The thorough subordination of the naval forces to the ground forces during the war worked to deprive the Navy of an opportunity to put its Soviet School theory to the test. Consequently, although it survived the war unscathed, that theory remained only theory—but with the experience of the major navies to draw on for its further development. The main conclusions for Soviet naval thought drawn from the operations of the U.S., Japanese and British Navies are summarized below:

- The Soviet School tenet that even the weaker of two strong navies could realistically expect to gain and maintain a limited command of the sea just in the region of a theater or even in an entire theater for at least long enough to carry out a given operation before a stronger adversary could send in superior reinforcements was bolstered and seemingly validated in Soviet naval thought by numerous examples drawn from the aircraft carrier battles and operations by the U.S. and Japanese navies in the Pacific during World War II.

- To gain such limited command of the sea was seen to require aircraft carriers to provide two kinds of "combat support" for fleet-against-shore operations, particularly major amphibious landings such as conducted so many times by the U.S. and Japanese navies: (1) preliminary support given prior to the landing forces even putting to sea—with the aim of gaining command of the sea in the region of intended operations; and (2) direct (or simultaneous) support to fight off the enemy forces in that region or that could reach it during the time planned for the operation. The latter required repeated large-scale air attacks by carrier planes (augmented by any land-based planes whose airfields were nearby) as well as "operational cover" by carrier planes for the amphibious forces during transit and debarkation.

- The Soviet School's basic strategy for theater war—force equalization to gain sea control in the intended area of operations—also was considered validated by the Pacific War. Professor Belli noted that it would not always be possible to hit-and-run so as to avoid combat with a stronger adversary. Rather, the requirement of his limited command-of-the-sea concept not only involved gaining temporary "command" in the region of an intended combat operation but also of the sea lines of communication running from the scene of action back to home ports—and that defending these sea lines of communication for any protracted period in the case of amphibious landings would require at least "combat clashes" with the stronger adversary.

- The conduct of "strategic amphibious landings" was noted by Professor Belli to require at least sufficient "direct support," if not "preliminary support" as well, to make possible the seizure of key isolated territories or islands and the elimination of enemy forces thereon. This, in turn, truncated an enemy's basing system and also made it possible to use the new conquests both as jumping off places for further offensive operations and to gain control over the sea lines of communication that passed through the area. The Allied amphibious invasions of Normandy and of the south of France were termed "strategic" in that they opened new ground fronts that forced the enemy to divide his forces for a two-front war.

- The conduct of "tactical-operational amphibious landings" was said in early 1944 by the then Rear Admiral S. G. Gorshkov, who had commanded a number of them, to involve preliminary creation of "favorable conditions," a euphemism for limited command of the sea (much in use at the time, as acknowledged later by Gorshkov).

- That Gorshkov had already embraced the Soviet School of his former Naval War College mentor, Professor Belli, was suggested by several other Soviet School tenets stated in this first published article by Gorshkov in addition to his reference to limited command of the sea. Notable among these were his acceptance of the need of "combat support" for the main striking force by other naval forces and of the concept of pinning down an enemy in secondary directions to prevent his interfering with the key operation in the main direction. Gorshkov's first published article also made it appear that he had accepted the underlying strategy of the Soviet School of an "active" fleet in being designed to deter an enemy's seaborne attack or, if that failed, to defeat the enemy in Soviet home waters or so weaken his attack, in the case of amphibious invasions, that the Ground Forces could repulse any such attempt.

- An important addition to Soviet School theory appears to have been made by Professor (Rear Admiral) Chernyshev's 1945 book *Surface Combatant Ships in Modern War*. This addition was in the form of a postulate that, despite the threat to surface combatants and merchant ships posed by submarines, that threat could be dealt with effectively by an organized antisubmarine defense. Chernyshev made it unmistakably clear that submarines were wholly unsuitable for many naval missions and that their value lay largely in antishipping operations. And even for that mission the cooperation of surface combatants and aircraft was essential to achieve really good results. This critical portrayal of the limited range of mission capabilities of submarines accurately reflected the preference that had been exhibited by the Soviet School for surface combatant ships over submarines. This preference quite likely was deliberately exaggerated in that school's efforts to overcome the predisposition of the Army officers dominant in the Defense Ministry and Armed Forces' General Staff to limit the allocation of funds to the much less expensive submarines and delete the far more costly major surface ships from the Navy's proposed shipbuilding programs.

- In the same 1945 book on surface combatant ships, Professor Chernyshev quoted from Admiral Isakov's 1944 book, *The Navy of the USSR*, to the effect that the decisive engagement of capital ships by which a general command of the sea could be won had been replaced in World War II by a continuing series of minor clashes. This was consistent with the Soviet School principle that engaging in major battles with superior enemy naval forces was to be avoided unless enemy forces could be whittled down by gradual attrition to a manageable size before accepting battle.

● A requirement for aircraft carriers to provide air cover for combatant ships operating at sea, even in home waters where there were no adjacent airfields, was quite unambiguously implied in Chernyshev's 1945 book. Even in the Soviet Union's peripheral seas, Chernyshev further implied by making surrogate use of the Italian Navy in World War II, land-based air cover could never be counted on to be available when needed. The proper solution, just as earlier prescribed by Professor Belli and by an apparent naval aviator writing in the *Naval Digest* in March 1944, was indicated to be a program of aircraft carrier construction.

● The evidence shows that the leadership of the Navy would have liked to have both light and heavy (attack) carriers built for its use after the end of World War II. (Apparently only in the mid-'70s did the Soviet Union reach the point of actually starting to build the first aircraft carrier with even the potential for carrying conventional takeoff-and-landing planes. Clearly several decades of sustained building of heavy nuclear-powered attack carriers, such as the first one begun in the mid-'70s, would be required to construct, shakedown, and train the carrier forces that would be needed in terms of size and commensurate capabilities to contest successfully for a general command of the sea against the strong carrier forces of the United States and its NATO allies. Possession of such carrier forces to gain and maintain command of the sea would be a prerequisite for permitting oceanic antisubmarine operations against U.S. strategic submarines and for conducting fleet-against-shore operations, particularly any transoceanic amphibious operations.) Rather than any economically unfeasible planning for a large force of heavy carriers and for developing a transatlantic amphibious capability, the Navy had no alternative but to follow the dictates of military doctrine and the Army's and Party's decided preference for constructing the coastal defenses, land-based naval aircraft and fast, light surface ships and craft that could help protect the Homeland from an amphibious invasion of the Normandy-landing type made by the Soviet Union's Western Allies in 1944. Any thoughts in the collective mind of the naval leadership of developing transatlantic amphibious forces would have been put out of mind rather quickly in view of the lack of any prospects for building the large force of heavy carriers that would be required to contest for oceanic command of the sea. And, in fact, a great deal of evidence in the naval and military literature of the Soviet Union supports a conclusion to that effect. This evidence includes the initially very limited command-of-the-sea theory that Professor Belli had first formulated in the late '30s and then dilated on during the Great Patriotic War and that Admiral Alafuzov was to further elaborate in 1946. According to this elaboration even what he called "strategic" command of the sea did not extend beyond control of a given peripheral sea.

● With regard to the lessons learned by the Soviet School of naval warfare from the operations of the major navies in World War II, two *ex post facto* judgments of Professor (Rear Admiral) Stalbo in 1978 are notable. Firstly, carrier forces were explicitly stated to be the *sine qua non* for a state aiming at command of the sea. Secondly, Stalbo asserted that carrier strike forces had brought into being "a new field of naval art" while carrier planes were said to have "opened up a completely new page in the history of naval art."

Notes

1. M. M. Kiryan, ed., *Voenno-teknicheskiy progress i vooruzhennye sily SSSR*, 1982, pp. 336.
2. S. E. Zakharov, ed., *Istoriya voenno-morskogo iskusstva*, 1969, pp. 576.
3. V. I. Achkasov and N. B. Pavlovich, *Sovetskoe voenno-morskoe iskusstvo v velikoi otechestvennoi voine*, 1973, pp. 398. On pages 399–400 were given six allegedly new "aspects of naval art" but all predated World War II, including ones for "combat support" and "mutual cooperation" of all types of naval forces.
4. V. I. Achkasov, A. V. Basov, *et. al.*, *Boyevoi put' Sovetskogo Voenno-Morskogo Flota*, 1974, 3rd ed., signed to press 13 February 1974, pp. 239.
5. A. V. Basov, *Flot v velikoi otechestvennoi voine 1941-1945* (Moscow: Nauka Press, 1980), pp. 432. By this point, Basov was a well-established historian of the Soviet Navy.
6. O. A. Rotmistrov, ed., *Istoriya voennogo iskusstva*, 1963, V. 1, pp. 528.
7. V. A. Belli, "Voina na Tikhom okeane. Obzor voennykh deystvii za vtoruyu polovinu 1942g, 1943 i 1944gg" ("The War in the Pacific Ocean. A Survey of Military Actions in the Second Half of 1942, 1943, and 1944), *Morskoi sbornik*, No. 11-12, November-December 1944, pp. 41-54. According to a footnote in this article, there had been an initial article of 31 pages in the March-April 1942 issue and another of 11 pages in the July 1942 issue. Neither of these two issues has found its way to the free world. A fourth article in this series was V. A. Belli, "Voina na Tikhom okeane. Konets 1944g— Sentyabr' 1945gg" ("The War in the Pacific Ocean. The End of 1944g-September 1945), *Morskoi sbornik*, No. 10, October 1945, pp. 98-114.
8. Belli, "War in the Pacific," November-December 1944.
9. Actually, this term boils down to the "superiority-in-the-main-direction" favored by the Army but held by the Navy to only connote a tactical command of the sea. It would rarely be adequate for operations of any size and duration because the enemy by definition would have at least operational command in the given region of the theater (if not "strategic command" of the entire theater) and so would be able to promptly send in superior forces to defeat the operation. This was to be spelled out in detail a decade later in a July 1955 *Military Thought* article by a Captain First Rank Shavtsov. Apparently Belli's choice of the most limited form of command of the sea was prompted by his understanding of the situation that the Japanese Navy might have intervened decisively if it had been properly employed to that end.
10. V. A. Belli, "Strategicheskiye desantnye operatsii" (Strategic Amphibious Landing Operations), *Voennaya mysl'*, Nos. 1-2, January-February 1945, pp. 30-38.
11. S. G. Gorshkov, "Desantnye operatsii Azovskoi voennoi flotilii" (Amphibious Landing Operations of the Azov Military Flotilla), *Morskoi sbornik*, No. 4, April 1944, pp. 61-76.
12. "The [Azov Flotilla] staff was successful in secretly shifting [to new forward] bases and concentrating the necessary forces, in preparing them, in taking into account the requisite support (combat and materiel), in conducting reconnaissance, and in simultaneously directing the daily combat activity for accompanying and providing cover for the coastal flanks of our troops. . . . As evident from [this] experience, landing operations proceed more successfully and with minimal losses under conditions of comprehensive support."
13. P. I. Voronov, "Deystviya aviatsii na morskikh kommunikatsiyakh" (Action of Aviation on Sea Communications), *Morskoi sbornik*, No. 3, March 1944, pp. 52-69.
14. Right after this "shortage" of aircraft carriers is alleged, the article mentioned that the United States had 40 aircraft carriers by the beginning of 1943—thereby giving the impression that in any future war the Soviet Navy too would hope to have a large number of such ships completed and ready for combat operations.
15. V. F. Chernyshev, *Nadvodnye korabli v sovremennoi voine*. Officers' Library of the Navy, Directorate of the Naval Press of the Peoples' Commissariat of the Navy of the Soviet Union, Moscow and Leningrad, signed to press 15 May 1945, pp. 158.
16. K. Stalbo, "Avianostsy vo vtoroi mirovoi voine" (Aircraft Carriers in the Second World War), *Morskoi sbornik*, No. 1, January 1978, pp. 91-100.
17. Chernyshev qualified his implicit refutation of the basic tenet of the Young School by subsequently noting both that the invention of the torpedo had put an end to "the unlimited command by the battleship fleet" and that the new weapon had conferred "special advantages on the weak in naval relations among countries."

VI
The Soviet School Matures
to Championship Calibre,
1945-1953

The Evidence and Some Partial Analysis

Attack Carriers Essential, Light Ones just Useful. In October 1945 the *Naval Digest* carried an exceptionally lengthy review of V.F. Chernyshev's *Surface Combatant Ships in Modern War.*[1] Written by Professor N.B. Pavlovich,[2] the review made several important emendations to the Soviet School views on aircraft carriers. The most relevant of them for this study were three additional tasks that aircraft carriers could perform successfully in a modern, nuclear-missile war at sea. Also, there was a policy preference implied for the construction of heavy (attack) carriers over light carriers—apparently made on the assumption that under the existing circumstances the Navy would be fortunate to get even a few heavy carriers. As the matter was presented, the reader can deduce that Pavlovich was adding three specific tasks that the Navy considered could be carried out against the Soviet Union by Western aircraft carriers (and against which, accordingly, adequate defensive capabilities must be developed):

> V.F. Chernyshev lists in his book the tasks carried out by aircraft carriers in World War II. This list can be expanded substantially by adding to it the tasks that are involved in landing operations, blockade duty, and offensives into the fortified regions of an adversary (p. 124).[3]

In general, Professor Pavlovich was even more candid than had been Professor Chernyshev in his appraisal of the leading role of aircraft carriers in naval warfare, as shown by World War II. For example, at one point Pavlovich remarked in his long review:

> The experience of the combat employment of aviation in the Second World War showed with all clarity the immense importance of aircraft carriers for the accomplishment of both offensive and defensive tasks in regions at a considerable distance from the most forward airfields (p. 119).

The practical significance of Pavlovich's endorsement of aircraft carriers for defensive tasks (as well as for offensive ones) was to argue that the Soviet Union required at least light carriers for reconnaissance and fleet air defense in the Soviet Union's peripheral seas (in addition to heavy attack carriers for the Northern and Pacific fleet areas which afforded relatively unrestricted egress to the oceans). Moreover, Pavlovich spelled out in unequivocal terms the inadequacy of shore-based aircraft for support of fleet operations, even in the Baltic and Black Seas, beyond the narrow coastal strip which land-based fighter aviation could cover for at least some sustained period:

> In resolving questions related to the planning of tactical cooperation with shore-based aviation, it should not be forgotten that even when the main forces of a task force are just 100 miles from the closest airfield, there is a "dead time" of from 40 to 60 minutes between the alerting of one's air groups and their arrival on the scene of action (p. 124).

Despite Pavlovich's above-mentioned endorsement of aircraft carriers for defensive tasks, as well as for offensive ones, with its likely connotation of endorsing light carriers as well as heavy attack carriers—he went on to make a further observation which suggests that he was stating a Navy preference for attack carriers over light carriers if the Navy could not be provided with both:

> One cannot but agree with the author when he says that ships can cooperate with shore-based aviation in theaters of limited extent or in one's coastal waters but that the cooperation of combatant ships with aviation for operations in the open sea far from one's shores, and especially for actions in the operational zone of an enemy, can only be ensured by having aircraft carriers (p. 124).[4]

The fact that Chernyshev and Pavlovich both stressed the value of aircraft carriers for power projection into an enemy's operational zone, as indicated in the above quotation, would seem to indicate that the Navy was lobbying for attack carriers as its priority preference. In this regard, it is notable that Chernyshev, after describing attack carriers, went on to praise them implicitly by indicating that they could carry out all of the five possible tasks of aircraft carriers whereas a light carrier was limited basically to reconnaissance and providing air cover for a fleet or convoy. Moreover, although he clearly implied a need for light carriers too, he spoke only of the "expediency" of building light carriers from an overall cost-effectiveness standpoint and refrained from explicitly stating that light carriers were essential supplements to the heavy attack carriers that were being much more strongly advocated.

From this it may be seen that Chernyshev's thinking about aircraft carriers had remained basically unchanged since his 1937 *Naval Digest* article. While he no longer dismissed light carriers as "not an imperative necessity," he still gave no indication that he considered them anything more than expedient. The more important change in Chernyshev's view was that he acknowledged that attack carriers had come to be essential. By agreeing with Chernyshev on the particular value of carriers for offensive operations in an enemy navy's operational zone, Pavlovich seemed to be reflecting a

Navy policy position that favored the construction of attack carriers at the expense, if necessary, of building any light carriers.

Speaking in early 1945 of "the enormous experience acquired by navies during the present war in protecting combatant ships and supporting the transits of convoys," Professor Chernyshev had cited new circumstances as having necessitated both the development of new types of combatant ships and the modernization of existing types to provide such protection. Of these new circumstances, Chernyshev cited in particular the outstanding role aviation plays in modern war. Prior to that statement, he had noted the enormous role aviation played in a war at sea as especially confirming the importance of aircraft carriers which he said constituted a ship type that had not been subjected to the actual test of combat until the Second World War.

Two relevant points emerge from this pair of statements. Firstly, the light escort aircraft carrier as a type of ship was developed in World War II. Attack carriers had existed before World War II but had undergone considerable modernization during that war. Given these two facts, it may be seen that Chernyshev actually was saying that both light escort aircraft carriers and heavy attack carriers had been "necessitated" by the new developments of World War II. The most notable development was the great importance for naval warfare assumed in that war by sea-based air power.

Secondly, it is apparent from the two statements quoted above that Chernyshev had adopted a lobbying tactic: he was finding justification for the Soviet Navy to be provided in the postwar period with the aircraft carriers it had been denied in the late prewar period. He argued that not until World War II had the aircraft carrier been subjected to and withstood the acid test of actual war. Moreover, aviation in general had become of such cardinal importance in naval warfare that any ship type that could take air power to sea should, *ipso facto*, be considered of great intrinsic value.

Finally, with regard to Professor Chernyshev's 1945 book, *Surface Combatant Ships*, and Professor Pavlovich's review of it in the October 1945 *Naval Digest*, it should be noted that the latter seriously misrepresented his deceased colleague's views on the antiaircraft warfare requirements for naval forces at sea. Furthermore, his manner was calculated to imply that any need for light aircraft carriers to perform their primary task of providing fleet air-cover could be obviated by simply increasing the number or effectiveness of shipboard antiaircraft guns. The passage in Pavlovich's review that appears to misrepresent Chernyshev rather egregiously—and that quite likely was written to imply a Navy preference for heavy over light carriers—reads as follows:

> On the basis of the study of the experience of the [Second World] War, the author proposes several new requirements for the tactical-technical characteristics of surface

combatant ships, in particular he speaks of the necessity for increasing the antiaircraft guns. . . .[5]

The only passage in the chapter to which Pavlovich had referred (chapter III) that could have served as the basis for his remark was one that merely listed first among the "influences" aircraft had been shown by World War II to exert on surface ships, that of "high effectiveness of aviation weaponry against combatant ships and the corresponding necessity of strengthening the antiair defense of those ships."[6] Since, by Soviet definition, fighter aircraft flying combat air patrols over fleet formations are contributing to antiair defense, Pavlovich's claim was false on the face of it. Moreover, Chernyshev explicitly stated at the end of the same chapter that "the problems of antiair defense of ships naturally are not exhausted by the strengthening of the antiaircraft guns. . . . Rather," he added, a "whole system of measures" had been required which, as he enumerated them, embraced "antiair protection by other ships and airplanes including cover from the air." (p. 32) And if this were not clear enough, Chernyshev later in a chapter on escort ships, stated flatly: "The task of antiair defense of combatant ships and convoys is fully discharged only by the cooperation of antiaircraft guns and fighter aviation." (p. 132)

While Pavlovich's statement, as quoted above, does not *explicitly* assert that Chernyshev advocated full reliance on more and better antiaircraft guns to the exclusion of fighter air cover, that seemed to be the intended implication when read in context. At a minimum one may conclude that Pavlovich's failure to give the subject of antiaircraft defense a balanced treatment comparable with that accorded it by Chernyshev at least raises the possibility that Pavlovich, on the Navy's behalf, was unduly minimizing the value of small carriers for providing fleet air cover in order to enhance the Navy's chances of being provided with a few heavy attack carriers.

Large Attack Carriers Preferred. The June 1946 issue of *Military Thought* carried an article on "Aircraft Carriers and Their Role in the Operations of a Navy," signed by a colonel who likely was a naval aviator.[7] The article had a number of points in common with Chernyshev's book and Pavlovich's review the year before. Most notably it mentioned, but minimized, the role and existence of light carriers as a carrier sub-type in an apparent effort to maximize the Navy's chances of obtaining some heavy attack carriers. The article gave scant mention to the existence of the light aircraft carrier as a carrier sub-type and its role. Stating that while the future of aircraft carriers would be hard to predict, clearly there would continue to be two sub-types: "light carriers for the antiair defense of a fleet underway at sea" and "the major fleet carriers" for "carrying out operational—tactical tasks against an enemy fleet at sea and against his bases."[8]

Before he got around to noting the existence and role of light carriers at the end of the article, the author stressed the importance and the roles and tasks of heavy attack carriers no less than five times:

- "As early as the first period of World War II, the necessity of having more powerful aircraft carriers made itself manifest" (p. 79).

- A listing of the "basic tasks" carried out by "aircraft carriers" in World War II made it apparent that attack carriers were being discussed—inasmuch as the listing included strike roles against enemy ships and bases not performable by light carriers and their largely fighter aircraft (p. 79).

- Aircraft carriers must be of such large tonnage that they can launch and recover "all types of aircraft" and thereby be capable of carrying out all of the listed tasks of aircraft carriers (p. 79).

- "The possibility of basing torpedo and bomber planes in significant numbers aboard aircraft carriers had expanded the operational capabilities of aircraft carriers. They have become an inseparable part of naval forces . . . without which . . . major operations at sea are unthinkable." (p. 80)

- Citing the decimation by carrier aircraft of the Italian Fleet at Taranto and of the U.S. Pacific Fleet at Pearl Harbor (as Chernyshev had done) and adding the sinking in the Atlantic of Germany's newest and largest battleship, the *Bismarck*, the article substantiated the claim: "The experience of naval warfare shows that aircraft carrier aviation has delivered exceptionally effective strikes against enemy fleets." (p. 80)

Like Chernyshev, the author of this article, Colonel Schner, made no claim that the aircraft carrier had superceded the battleship as queen of the seas but took the line that aircraft carriers were becoming "part of the combat nucleus of a fleet along with battleships."[9] However, Schner at least hinted at that possibility when he provided an account of what he indicated had been an interwar debate over aircraft carriers. He identified one group as having held that aircraft carriers were the single necessary type of large surface combatants. The brief account is of no little interest for its probably intended relevance to the postwar period and is quoted in full:

In the period between the First and Second World Wars, along with the growth of aviation, there grew too a recognition of the necessity for a wider employment of aviation in naval operations. The view, was asserted that powerful aircraft carriers capable of insuring the success of all of the Navy's operations were essential. However, there was a great deal of discussion on this subject. Some considered that it would suffice to have a strong carrier fleet . . . but others saw in aviation only an auxiliary means capable of insuring the Navy's protection against air attack and for carrying out a number of tactical tasks. There were even those who considered aircraft carriers to be a great [presumably financial] burden (p. 78).

A necessarily tentative interpretation of this account—that powerful aircraft carriers were required—was the view of the Navy leadership under Admiral Kuznetsov from 1938 to 1941. The "some" who thought the Navy needed only "a strong carrier fleet" would have been the Young School advocates, most notably Yakimychev, Dushenov, and Kozhanov. The "others" who saw in aviation "only an auxiliary means" primarily for fleet air-defense would probably have included the Old Schoolers, Professors Gervais and Petrov, who (until they disappeared from public view in the early 1930s) apparently favored building mainly light carriers for fear that attack carriers might challenge the primacy of their beloved battleships. Quite likely, the "even-those-who-considered-aircraft-carriers-to-be-a-great-burden" description was a reference to the Army marshals in the Defense Ministry and General Staff who viewed aircraft-carrier construction programs essentially as bottomless ruble ratholes for funds better spent on Army needs.

Almost certainly as part of a Navy effort to lobby those same Army marshals to support the authorization of at least a few heavy attack carriers for the Navy, Colonel Schner was as lavish in his praise of aircraft carriers in general as had been Professor Pavlovich. (It will be recalled that the latter had considerably outdone Professor Chernyshev on this score.) On the first page of his article, Schner wrote: "Aircraft carriers have become of exceptionally great importance for contemporary naval warfare; this is the case despite the fact that they appeared in the system of naval forces only relatively recently." (p. 77) The article also asserted the indispensability of aircraft carriers for naval operations in "the broad oceanic theaters" and even just in "regions of sea theaters far from coastal bases."[10]

A particularly noteworthy feature of Schner's article was the telling example it adduced to show the unsuitability of land-based aircraft for fleet air support. Many Soviet naval writers argued that airplanes operating from shore bases could provide adequate air cover against enemy air attacks. However, it will be recalled that Professor Pavlovich had noted the 40 to 60 minutes "time late" for land-based airplanes to reach the scene-of-action even 100 miles from a coastal airfield. Now Schner gave the example of the 10 December 1941 sinking by Japanese carrier aircraft of the British battleship *Prince of Wales* and heavy cruiser *Repulse* just 60 miles from the fighter airfield from whence air cover for the two ships was supposed to have been provided.

Fleet Against the Shore. Less than a month after publication of Chernyshev's *Surface Combatant Ships in Contemporary War*, there reappeared in Soviet military writings, in an article by L. Eremeyev, the rudiments of the fleet-against-the-shore concept.[11] The concept was not originated by Eremeyev[12] but was one that Admiral Gorshkov was to make his own nearly 18 years later. The latter was to claim that such projection of naval power against the land had displaced traditional naval battles at sea of fleet-against-fleet—and was a "fundamental change in the nature of naval warfare." In the June-

July issue of the Armed Forces' General Staff restricted-distribution journal *Military Thought*, Eremeyev, then a very junior naval captain third rank, laid out the fleet-against-the-shore thesis in all of its essential details. It was only left for Gorshkov (in the 19 May 1963 issue of *Izvestiya*) to spell out the details of the claim that the change was so basic as to alter naval warfare itself.

In a nominal review of recent British literature on naval warfare, Eremeyev addressed the fleet-against-the-shore topic at length. He started with the nicely ambiguous statement early in the review that what formerly had been "pure" naval strategy had been shown by World War II to have become mainly strategy for ground warfare. The author returned to the subject two pages later to assert that the weight of naval operations in World War II had shifted from the sea battle and blockade (for protecting the lines of communication at sea and so furthering a country's defensive stability) to "a completely different kind of naval operation—the [amphibious] invasion operation, which consisted of actions overseas against the ground forces of an adversary." (p. 172) This, of course, was the most typical pre-nuclear-era form of fleet-against-the-shore power projection.

Two pages further on, the author began to generalize his findings, stating the conclusion: "Fleet-against-the-shore operations occupied a considerably larger place [in World War II] than in former wars." This was supported by a comparison of the mere handful of amphibious operations listed as having comprised the sum total for World War I with the "massive" number of such operations that were carried out in the Second World War (p. 174).

Eventually, the review got around to its single most complete statement even, though not as clearly formulated as the preceding one:

> Finally a few words on naval engagements. The . . . evidence adduced above gives adequate support to the fact that naval operations with the basic aim of destroying the enemy at sea, although they do occur, are however being accorded ever decreasing importance in their individual standing in the general system of operations. . . .
>
> From the foregoing, it is quite apparent that naval engagements, regardless of whether they take the form of a general battle . . . or the form of individual combat clashes, are becoming increasingly associated with the operations of the ground armies and are subordinated to them. In this connection, even command of the sea and sea blockade . . . have emerged [from World War II] completely changed (p. 174).

Although the author of the review did not quite yet spell out just how he believed the nature of command of the sea had changed in theory, he did mention a number of advantages that accrue to the side having that command. He asserted that by gaining command a belligerent:

- secures his own sea lines of communication, (p. 169)

- permits choice of a limited war rather than a general one, (p. 170)

- deprives an opponent of the use of his surface ships in warfare at sea beyond coastal waters and forces him to depend solely on submarines, (p. 179) and,

- permits cutting off an opponent's sea communications or, at least, interfering with them (p. 171).

Without naming it, the *Military Thought* article referred unmistakably to the Germans' very successful amphibious invasion of Norway in May 1940. It asserted that German use of the tactic of "successively concentrating superior forces in individual directions" had enabled the seizure of "exceptionally advantageous naval strategic positions," including the bases essential to offensive naval operations.[13] However, Eremeyev did not draw the same lesson from this key success that Belli had in a July 1940 *Naval Digest* article. In it, Belli had concluded that the German landings in Norway demonstrated that major naval operations could be conducted without first gaining superiority in the main "direction" or "sector" of a theater involved. Eremeyev, to the contrary, attributed the notable German success to the fact that the British had (unaccountably) not opposed the landings and so made possible the German seizure of such a strategically priceless "naval position" as the west coast of northern Norway.

In this respect, whether intentionally or not, he was taking the same position that Pavlovich had taken in his *Naval Digest* article of November 1940. In effect, superiority of forces must be achieved in the main direction before other naval operations can be safely undertaken. In his July 1940 *Naval Digest* article, Belli had defended against charges of "adventurism" the German seizure of Norway without first having established a superiority of forces in the area of operations. Pavlovich's and Eremeyev's articles seem to have implicitly carried precisely that charge (of attempting more than the available forces can accomplish). Apparently this was an effort to discredit Belli's view that such major successes normally could be had without encountering strong opposition from the enemy and without the necessity of defeating that opposition and thereby gaining command of the sea as a preliminary to the conduct of other operations. Gorshkov was to affirm Belli's view in the 1970s as approved Soviet naval theory. Its restatement in 1945 testifies to the longevity of what the present author has elected to describe as a *limited* command-of-the-sea concept; that is, one of gaining local, temporary control of a sea theater, or part of one, by successively concentrating superior forces in individual sectors just long enough to carry out a particular naval operation before the stronger naval adversary can concentrate stronger forces to intervene.

Although this July 1945 *Military Thought* article indicated that the emphasis in naval warfare had shifted in World War II from fleet-against-fleet (or, per Eremeyev, from "warfare on sea communications") to fleet-against-the-shore, nevertheless, the former was seen as of continuing importance but changed in nature. *Defensive* operations on the sea lines of communication were perceived as having changed from protection of shipping at sea to protection against amphibious invasion of one's own territory. So too the nature of *offensive* operations against enemy shipping was seen as having undergone a change—from emphasis on sinking enough of the ships carrying raw materials for the enemy's economy to force him out of the war, to primary attention to cutting off the shipping of military supplies for the enemy's ground forces.

The article further asserted that the majority of naval operations in all naval sectors of World War II had been combined navy-ground force operations for support of the latter rather than operations for destruction of the adversary at sea (i.e., fleet-against-fleet). The nature of the change to command-of-the-sea theory, which Eremeyev had asserted earlier but had not explained, now may be inferred from the immediately preceding remarks. It was tantamount to a claim that gaining command of the sea had changed from being an end in itself to constituting only a means to the end of conducting fleet-against-the-shore operations in support of the Army's coastal flank. This, in effect, rationalized systematic evasion of the battle almost invariably necessary in a successful fleet-against-fleet operation.

The article next stated a point that appears to be a corollary to its earlier insistence on the necessity of concentrating superior forces in an area of an intended operation for just long enough to complete the operation: "the necessity for major concentration of [one's own] forces and means both at the sortie points for deployments [i.e., mainly in the approaches to Soviet naval bases] and also in the regions of [Soviet naval] operations" was asserted to be one of the new aspects of naval operations to have emerged during World War II. The real message behind this oblique formulation seems to have been: "We are now faced with a very strong coalition of naval powers and so can only expect to be able to carry out operations at sea, or even in our own coastal waters, if we are able to concentrate major forces to deter or defeat the Western allies who have a preponderance of naval forces capable of gaining a general command of the sea and exercising it whenever and wherever desired."

Apparently as a means to the end of being able to concentrate sufficiently large forces to offset the West's great naval superiority long enough to carry out other (largely Army-flank support) operations, the article opined that "frequent and substantial regrouping of fleets, their transfer from one theater to another" was another one of the new aspects of naval operations to have emerged from World War II. This "swing strategy" of interfleet transfer was presented as normal and desirable to permit the maximum concentration of naval forces for support of the coastal flank of the ground forces.[14]

A 1946 Naval Conference Reviews Command-of-the-Sea Theory. In March 1946 the Navy held a four-day scientific conference at the Naval War College in Leningrad on the subject of "The Development and Modernization of the Theory of War at Sea from Mahan and Colomb to Our Day."[15] The first speaker, a Major Vetchinkin, asserted that although the "basic propositions of the theory of Mahan and Colomb" had been correct for the sailing-ship era, they were not of universal validity, as they had been represented, because "the conduct of war at sea is completely dependent on productive capacity." This was an elaborately esoteric way of saying that command of the sea is not of universal applicability since only the major industrial powers are capable of building navies that can contest for command of the sea. This same theme was sounded at the end of the conference by Rear Admiral Belli who gave as the only substantial reason for "the fallaciousness of [transplanting] the old theories onto our Soviet soil" that they did not correspond to the (small) size of the Navy nor to the (low) "level of development of the productive capacity of the times." He seemed to be implying that, once the Soviet Union had built up a big capital-ship fleet, command-of-the-sea theory would be seen—even by the Army—to have relevance for the Soviet Union.

Further on in his paper, Major Vetchinkin noted that the followers of Mahan and Colomb had continued to "reduce the ultimate aim of war at sea to the gaining of command of the sea by way of the general engagement and sea blockade." The one-sided analysis of subsequent wars to fit them into the command-of-the-sea mold was said to have led to still greater errors. Nevertheless, the speaker continued, what was needed was both "a deep analysis of the mistakes of these authors [Mahan and Colomb]" and "utilization of the correct propositions of their theories." The nature of these "correct propositions" the Soviet Union should adopt was not spelled out. However, the context made it likely that this alluded in part to the idea that command of the sea did not have to be general and permanent but rather could be just local and temporary. It is not at all unlikely that the speaker also had in mind the advocacy of Colomb and Corbett, that a fleet-in-being strategy of constant activity to harass a stronger naval opponent and thereby hold command of the sea "in dispute" was the correct mode for the "inferior" navy.

The second speaker, a Captain Third Rank Kholodov, dealt with the Sino-Japanese and Russo-Japanese Wars. The only point that the rapporteur of the conference found worth reporting was the charge that "the wholly superficial" analysis of those wars had "aided bourgeois theoreticians to raise the propositions of Mahan and Colomb to the level of immutable laws of war."

The third report was entitled "The Influence of the First World War on the Theory of War at Sea and the Theory of Foreign States in the Postwar

Period." It was given by Senior Lieutenant Penzin.[16] Citing [Sir Julian] Corbett's book, *Some Principles of Maritime Strategy*, as having most fully formulated the views on war at sea dominant in Great Britain, Penzin noted that Corbett had continued (in the footsteps of Colomb and Mahan) to proclaim that the aim of war at sea is "command of the sea established by the methods of the general engagement or blockade." After a remark about the naval blockade (that Corbett had divided it into two forms: the tight blockade and the open blockade), Penzin implied that the First World War had refuted the validity of command of the sea gained by a general engagement because routine "daily combat activities" had replaced the general engagement as the normal form of war at sea.[17] In his remarks near the end of the conference, Rear Admiral Belli touched on the same subject with the claim that one of the two reasons for the erroneous conclusions drawn about the Russo-Japanese War by "the majority of authors ([A.] Stenzel, [Romeo] Bernotti, and [Nikolai] Klado)" was that "they had not noted the appearance in rudimentary form already at that time of daily operational activity. . . ."[18]

Penzin concluded the rapporteuring of his own report to the conference on command-of-the-sea theory by adducing the following rather misleading account of the shifting fortunes of what was basically the French Jeune Ecole (Young School) and the Mahanian Old School in the period between the two World Wars:

> In the majority of states up to the '30s the idea of a main force of light combatant ships dominated. However, as the result of deeper research into the details of the First World War, views changed and by World War II the leading sea powers had come around to powerful battleship fleets (p. 111).

Since this misrepresented the development of "the leading sea powers" between the wars, it seems likely that it referred to the evolution of *Soviet* shipbuilding policy. Penzin had perpetrated a rewriting of history which obscured the three facts that in the Soviet Union: (1) the Old School had not even been seriously challenged until 1928; (2) a Young School policy of emphasizing the construction of submarines, airplanes, and light surface craft was not adopted until 1933; and (3) it was not until the end of 1937 that Stalin belatedly acted on a realization that he would have to follow Germany and the other naval powers in building a battleship navy.

The apparent aim of Penzin's violation of Clio was to make it appear that the Soviet Union's notably erratic evolution in the matter of its shipbuilding policy had been the same as that of the leading naval powers of the time and, in effect, been more devoted to battleships and a command-of-the-sea doctrine than actually had been the case. Just why such a gross misrepresentation of the historical facts was deemed expedient is moot. Quite possibly it could have been calculated to staunch a flow of Army criticism by arguing that the Navy could scarcely be blamed since it had been in the mainstream of international naval thought wherein the "majority of states" had mistakenly found themselves too.

The fourth and final report at the naval scientific conference in March 1946 was entitled "The Development of Naval Theory in the U.S.S.R. and Contemporary Views on the Character of War and Operations at Sea." It was delivered by a Captain Third Rank Sviderskiy. In describing the discussions on Soviet naval theory in the years 1927 and 1928 (when the Young School had unleashed its vicious attack on Professors Gervais and Petrov for their Old School views on the primacy of command of the sea and battleship fleets), the speaker noted that it was decided at the time "to build small ships first, above all submarines and motor torpedo boats, and also to develop aviation." However, Sviderskiy claimed: "The requirement for the subsequent construction of major combatant ships was not denied."[19] (p. 112)

It was further claimed that as a result of these discussions new methods for war at sea were developed, notably "the combined strike" and "the mutual cooperation of heterogeneous [naval] forces."[20] The latter method, according to Sviderskiy, was essential for the Navy to carry out any missions to be performed independently of others of the Armed Forces (mainly the ground forces for support of the Army coastal flank, of course).

In an interesting departure from the standard procedure of not indicating any priority ranking between operations and a navy's routine daily combat activities, Sviderskiy placed the latter in an "also-ran" second priority. This would seem to have reflected a new interest in holding command of the sea "in dispute" in areas outside coastal waters where the specially laid-on operations would be in order, by definition to hamper an enemy's use of the sea to the extent that he cannot carry out his planned naval operations against the Soviet Union.[21]

First, Sviderskiy (apparently) announced a compromise between the Old School's longstanding fascination with a single "general engagement" or two (which professedly would determine the outcome of at least the war at sea and sometimes of the land war too) and the Young School's insistent denial that such a form of naval warfare could occur again in the modern era. He then asserted that "large sea engagements could occur as in the past" but that they would only determine the outcome of "individual operations and not of a war as a whole."

Near the end of the conference Rear Admiral Belli also implicitly signified his belief that the Young School (himself included) had been justified in its rejection of command-of-the-sea theory. He excused its adherents for having discarded that theory, citing the pressing need to more quickly develop the forces required for the (minimum) protection of Soviet coasts.[22] As in the case above, in which Sviderskiy gave priority to operations (on the high seas) over daily combat operations (largely in coastal areas), a preference for getting away from the Navy's coastal confines of World War II was detectable.

At the conclusion of the conference the chief of the Naval War College, Admiral Alafuzov, reportedly summed up the views that had been presented. No details of his summation were given, perhaps because they were considered too sensitive from a standpoint of military security. However, the *Naval Digest's* account of the conference did say that he added an analysis of the views of Clausewitz, Corbett, Castex, and Groos. He opined that naval theoreticians should not concern themselves with an objective search for truth but for theories that would best serve the interests of the state. Alafuzov was reported to have shown that this had been done by the four aforementioned foreign military and naval theorists whose views he had discussed.[23] This was a clear injunction to the proponents of all schools of naval warfare to avoid theoretically nice but impractical proposals.

In his closing remarks, the Naval War College head seemed to have been counseling patience on the part of the Navy's leaders. He said that, although it was necessary for the time being to accept the continentally oriented "Stalinist strategy—that great source of naval science—as the basis for the further development of the theory of naval warfare," nevertheless "our teaching on naval warfare is developing and changing parallel with the development of our Navy." Although Alafuzov probably had no choice but to voice the Stalinist injunction that the experience of the Great Patriotic War "must occupy the leading place in our research," he did enter the significant caveat: "But it is necessary to foresee other forms of warfare" including ones to be employed when the day should come that the Navy would be assigned "broader missions."

He ended his remarks, commenting that "only taking this into account may we have a navy worthy of our country." This seemingly implied that the Soviet Navy of the time, tied as it was to coastal defensive missions in support of the Army, was not worthy of a great power like the Soviet Union as it had emerged from World War II.

Postwar Perceptions of Carriers and Command of the Sea. An article, "Aircraft Carrier Forces of the U.S. in the War in the Pacific," appeared in the *Naval Digest* in July 1946.[24] It provided an illuminating account of the subject that went far to afford its readers a thorough appreciation of both how important postwar Soviet naval officers regarded carrier aviation and of their roles, missions, strengths, and limitations in oceanic warfare. That this experience was to remain relevant in the postwar era was indicated by a number of statements in the article, including one at the end: "Aircraft carriers were weapons of decisive importance in the Pacific war and have remained the cornerstone of the postwar U.S. Navy." (p. 81)

This lengthy article reflected many early postwar Soviet naval perceptions of the proper (and improper) employment of aircraft carriers (both of the heavy attack and light types). Among them were the aircraft carrier's roles, missions, and accomplishments. The latter were judged according to the extent and degree of the command of the sea they had gained. Further discussion centered on the residual importance of the "fast battleship" as a component of the "fast carrier task force." Since these topics are intertwined, the relevant parts for both will be quoted before discussing them separately. The importance of enhancing understanding of Soviet views on aircraft carriers well warrants the extensive quotations:

> In the British Navy before the war, [merely] the secondary role was accorded to aircraft carriers of providing support to the combatant ships of other types (basically to the battleships). . . . The British made little use of their aircraft carriers. . . . The Japanese, however, having planned on making extensive use of ships of this type . . . accorded them a leading role in naval operations. (p. 61) . . . The result of this planning was the air attack on Pearl Harbor . . . the first example of the resolution of problems by employing aircraft carrier forces. The aircraft carriers of the U.S. Pacific Fleet escaped the strike by Japanese aviation in the attack on Pearl Harbor only by chance inasmuch as they were delayed at sea by weather and only reached Pearl Harbor 24 hours after the crushing defeat. As a result, only aircraft carriers and cruisers were left to the Americans as the basic means for the delivery of effective strikes at sea against the adversary (p. 62).

> The first operation of such a [fast carrier task] force was the raid on the Gilbert and Marshall Islands on 31 January 1942. . . . For raiding operations against Wake Island on 24 February 1942, a force was formed comprised of the aircraft carrier *Enterprise*, two cruisers and seven destroyers (p. 63).

> The basic mission of these [fast carrier task] forces was the gaining and maintaining of command [of the sea] in the sizable sectors of the Pacific naval theater designated with the aim of creating favorable conditions for the conduct of operations of the amphibious forces, which were the basic operations in the war with Japan against the islands which dotted the oceanic expanses (p. 61).

> The Battle of the Coral Sea was the first naval engagement in history in which the ships of the adversaries were far beyond the range of visibility and not in direct contact and in which not a single shot was exchanged. The engagement was decided by the actions of aircraft carrier aviation which even on this [first] occasion confirmed their capability to independently carry out difficult and responsible missions. The result of the Battle of the Coral Sea was that the Japanese gave up the operation they had undertaken. It may be concluded in this regard that this battle was a real victory for the American aircraft carrier force (p. 64).

> All in all, the important role of aircraft carriers in decisive naval operations had become definitively delineated as early as the middle of 1942. In this connection, the Battle of Midway Island of 3-6 June 1942 was a typical example of the employment of aircraft carrier forces in their primary role (p. 64).

The Americans succeeded in bringing up to the region of Midway Island naval forces from the southwestern part of the Pacific and Army aviation from the Hawaiian Islands. The aircraft carrier task force of the American Navy, which was composed of three aircraft carriers . . . eight cruisers, 14 destroyers, and 20-25 submarines and which operated together with Army aviation from Midway Island, was numerically inferior to the enemy (with the probable exception of submarines). Nevertheless, it intercepted and cut off the Japanese forces which were bent on seizing Midway and then making a landing in the Hawaiian Islands. As a result of the battle, four aircraft carriers [out of the eight operational in the Japanese Navy at the time] were sunk—which constituted a severe weakening of the Japanese aircraft carrier fleet (p. 64).

Thus, this battle changed the strategic situation in the Pacific Ocean. This battle made it possible for the U.S. to shift from purely defensive operations in this theater to offensive-defensive ones and for the aircraft carrier fleet to gradually shift from the delivery of strikes against the aircraft aviation of the adversary to the delivery of strikes against land-based aviation and its bases (p. 65).

However, this success [at Midway] could have been of still more decisive import if there had been fast battleships in the composition of the aircraft carrier task forces in June 1942. Later such battleships became an integral part of these forces. Due to the lack of battleships in the composition of these forces at the Battle of Midway, the American forces could not fully develop the success achieved . . . because the Japanese force still included four battleships (p. 65).

The battles [in the waters off the Solomon Islands] ended with the exclusion of the Japanese from these island launching pads which they had designated for subsequent operations for the invasion of Australia (p. 65).

The lesson was learned in these very first battles with the aircraft carriers of the adversary that success goes to him whose [air reconnaissance] scouts first detect the enemy and who first launches his strike and fighter aviation. The slightest delay in launching aircraft proved fatal for aircraft carriers. And in this respect, there was developed an effective system of close-in and distant reconnaissance and of constant antisubmarine and fighter cover. . . (p. 66).

The high mobility [of the fast carrier task] forces, which were supplied with good intelligence, enabled the aircraft carrier task forces to deliver surprise strikes. This was of particular value for the U.S. Navy which was obliged after Pearl Harbor to compensate with mobility for its lack of ships with powerful gun armaments (p. 66).

Execution of the basic missions in the subsequent battles with the Japanese surface fleet was assigned to torpedo planes and dive bombers. However, when the combat action shifted to the west of the Philippines to Formosa and subsequently to Japan proper and Japanese land-based aviation became the main adversary, the main offensive weapon of the forces became the fighter aircraft. . . . Subsequently, when the main mission became the conduct of strategic bombing against Japan itself, another type of aircraft carrier plane became of primary importance—one able to carry heavy bomb loads. This of course did not change the basic assumption that the delivery of the main strategic bombing strike was the basic task of land-based heavy bomber aviation (p. 67).

Japan lost the initiative [at sea] . . . and there took place between the adversaries an unceasing competition in the fields of technology and tactics. The lead in this competition was gained by the Americans. . . . The reason the lead shifted to them was the vast materiel superiority of the Americans who, in the short interval of a year and a half or two years, not only produced a sizable fleet of aircraft carriers, which the Japanese were not strong enough to match, but also succeeded in bringing it into action with great skill and proficiency (p. 67).

Incorporated into the organization of the fleet was a basic operational thrust according to which the armed forces of the Allies conducted a concentric offensive against the positions the Japanese had seized in the first period of the Pacific war (p. 67).

With the U.S. shift in the Pacific from the defensive to the offensive, the escort carriers, which initially had been assigned for the protection of convoys against the submarines and aircraft of the adversary, were successfully adapted to meet the urgent need of the amphibious forces for constant, close air support in the landing areas (pp. 69-70).

Simultaneously with the expansion of the U.S. Navy in general, the force structure of the aircraft carrier task forces began to acquire a qualitatively different character. . . . The fast carrier task forces . . . retained all of the combat features of speed, mobility, and the capability to deliver surprise strikes and at the same time acquired the power of gunnery fire and armor required in order to accept battle with any substantial part of the navy of the adversary. Yet, the Japanese themselves for a long time did not decide to risk their entire fleet by committing it all to battle at one time. Rather, they ventured to do this only when (in the fall of 1944) they had already irrevocably lost superiority at sea. On the other hand, it may be asserted that had the fast carrier task forces not had new battleships in its composition, they nevertheless would have remained, despite the increase in the number of aircraft carriers (p. 69), just the same as the carrier task forces of the initial period of the war—which were capable of delivering a powerful strike but lacked the capability to prosecute their success to the full destruction of the adversary (p. 70).

For battle with the main forces of the adversary, it was planned by the U.S. to have in the composition of the fast carrier task force ships with a superiority in gun armaments. The fast battleships were to be the combat nucleus. This [fast] battleship force, which also included [heavy] cruisers, light cruisers, and destroyers, could be withdrawn from the aircraft carrier task force to meet a top priority requirement for delivering gunnery strikes against an adversary. Formation by the Americans of such a "force within a force" was brought about by the necessity of stopping any attempt by the Japanese to use the battleship force of their navy against the vulnerable aircraft carriers or against the amphibious forces of the U.S. Pacific Fleet (p. 71).

In actuality, no occasion arose for such a force of [fast] battleships to engage the adversary in a general naval battle inasmuch as even the engagement in Leyte Gulf, which is known as the "Second Battle of the Philippine Sea," had the character of individual engagements— and in the majority of which aviation played the main role. However, the importance and influence of this force on the course of the war cannot be judged by this circumstance alone. The mere fact of the existence of the battleship forces included in the fast carrier task force (like the four-year watch of the British Grand Fleet in Scapa Flow in the First World War), exerted a strong influence on the thinking and operations of the adversary. The "force within a force" which accompanied the aircraft carriers constituted a highly significant example of sea power in action. That force fulfilled its missions without employment of its powerful guns in battle but by merely being ready for such employment (p. 73).

The support forces consisted of 10 to 12 old battleships which had been put back into commission after major overhauls and modernization. . . . Besides the battleships, the support forces included about 12 aircraft carriers and a number of cruisers and destroyers (p. 69).

The successful employment of the slower combatant ships [in the support forces] made it possible to free the fast carrier task forces from constant participation in carrying out tasks in direct support of the amphibious forces. It then became possible to assign the carrier task forces to bolder and more demanding tasks for the delivery of long-range strikes—strikes associated with the amphibious landings, which were more of an operational than tactical nature. In carrying out these tasks, the fast carrier task forces operated at great distances from the other forces of the fleet, providing distant cover for the ungainly amphibious forces, neutralizing Japanese airfields, and preventing the Japanese surface fleet from opposing the debarkation on the Pacific islands of strategic and operational-scale landings by the Allies (p. 71).

In the successive operations for landings on Leyte Island (October 1944), on Luzon (January 1945), and on Okinawa (March 1945), the fast carrier task force . . . played the decisive role in ensuring the successful conduct of these operations. In the engagement off Leyte 23-26 October 1944 the fast carrier task force and the support force in joint operations destroyed the basic part of the main forces of the Japanese Navy (p. 76).

But the main characteristic of the war did not change [during the remaining course of the war]: it was an oceanic war and military operations continued to be operations of military fleets. Until the end of the war the basic mission of the fast carrier task forces was to provide operational cover for the more vulnerable forces—troop ships, cargo ships, supply ships, and for the escort carriers that together comprised the amphibious forces. . . . Aircraft carrier task forces ensured overall cover for the army forces and their munitions during the course of landing operations—a traditional function of any navy (p. 77).

In those cases in which the circumstances of a landing operation entailed danger for the amphibious force and the other forces, the fast carrier task force was assigned the mission of delivering preliminary strikes on the islands designated for seizure (p. 78).

The most important and basic role played by aircraft carrier task forces in the Pacific war becomes still clearer from a comparison of the earlier landing operations of the Americans in the region of the Solomon Islands with the later landings carried out after the shift in the superiority of forces in the Pacific to the Allied naval forces. . . . In August 1942 units of the U.S. Marine Corps landed on Guadalcanal without the adequate and thorough preparation characteristic of later operations. . . . In view of the fact that the Japanese had superiority at sea in the first period of the campaign in the

Solomons, they could reinforce and supply their garrison and their surface combatant ships could deliver accurate gunnery salvos on the coastal flanks and rear of the American landing. Even two years later, despite the enormous expansion of the U.S. Pacific Fleet, the American divisions landing on Leyte in October 1944 had first to overcome a strong Japanese garrison and then still larger forces transferred from islands to the west of Leyte. And even then [that is, as late as October 1944] the Americans could not fully exert command over all of the approaches to the island selected for seizure: they could not establish an effective close blockade of the designated point or sector of the coast. The situation changed completely after the devastating defeat of the Japanese Navy in the Leyte Gulf engagement on 23-26 October by the delivery of joint strikes by the fast carrier task force and the support force for the amphibious forces. As a consequence of this engagement, the balance of forces of the Allies and Japan in the Pacific was changed completely and for the entire subsequent period of the war. Consequently, when the troops under the command of General MacArthur landed on Luzon on the shore of Lingayen Gulf in January 1945, they only had to deal with the island garrison. This time there was no sending of reinforcements . . . because of the American fleet's control of the waters around Luzon. The command of these waters by the U.S. Navy was so indisputably obvious by then that the fast carrier task force could be sent away to the South China Sea. . . (p. 78).

From all that has been recounted above, the conclusion may be reached that the mission assigned to the fast carrier task forces and successfully executed by them was nothing new in principle. They carried out what has traditionally been one of the basic missions of a navy: the establishment and maintenance of command of a limited sector of . . . a theater of military action so that invasion forces could carry out their assigned mission without interference, or with the minimum of interference, from the naval forces and aviation of the adversary (p. 79).

However, the means . . . for executing this mission by aircraft carrier task forces were fundamentally new; . . . their offensive weapons were not . . . [big] guns but aircraft machine guns . . . and air-launched torpedoes. In short, their offensive weapon was the carrier airplane. For defense, which normally meant defense against the planes of the enemy, aircraft carrier task forces relied upon fighter plane cover . . . and anti-aircraft weapons. The method by which carrier task forces executed this mission in the second half of the Pacific war was by the destruction of the air power of the enemy— of his carrier aviation and of his shore-based airplanes, or at least by the neutralization of those of his airfields from which his planes could oppose an invasion force at the point of debarkation. This type of activity may be classified as modern, multifaceted, simultaneous naval and air operational cover for forces penetrating into an enemy zone. It is a new form of naval operations for executing the task of providing cover against the surface forces of an adversary—a form which came into being with the appearance at sea of the airplane (p. 79).

Carrier task forces executed broader missions than just those for gaining command in a designated sector of a naval theater. This mission became one of conducting an air-sea offensive with the aim of establishing command of the air over the territory of an enemy. In this case, we unquestionably are witness to a new function for naval forces. With the lodgement of the American armed forces on Okinawa . . . the role of the fast carrier task force had been played out. . . . The U.S. was the complete master of Japanese skies— which was the basic prerequisite for the invasion of the territory of Japan itself that had been planned for the fall of 1945. . . (p. 80).

> The fast carrier task force constituted a mobile "air base" which, by war's end, carried more than 1,500 planes. With the great mobility and endurance of such a force, the American fleet could effect a concentration of powerful forces of fighter and bomber aviation at the requisite moment and at any point, thereby creating a superiority of forces over the adversary [that is, over his main naval forces (as well as over one's own)] and over his airfields (p. 81).

From the foregoing quotations from Captain-Lieutenant Razumnyi's July 1946 article in the *Naval Digest* on aircraft carriers in the Pacific war, a number of conclusions may be drawn. The following points compare his views with related opinions expressed in the early postwar period by Chernyshev, Pavlovich, and Schner:

• Attack aircraft carriers were perceived as being indispensable for modern warfare, at least for oceanic naval operations. On this key point, Razumnyi was in full accord with the three writers named above and with Colonel Schner, in particular.

• Fast battleships still had an indispensable role to play as, in effect, an active fleet-in-being "force within a force" of fast carrier task forces. If the occasion arose, they could be detached to fight a major battle against an enemy's surface-strike force should he employ his battleships to attack one's aircraft carriers or amphibious invasion forces. Fast battleships would accompany each fast carrier task force. The mere existence of such a force would deter him from attempting any such attack. Thus, this article was less conservative in its evaluation of the relative importance of the aircraft carrier vis-a-vis the battleship than Chernyshev and Schner had been. They had concluded that aircraft carriers were only in the process of becoming a part of the basic nucleus of main naval task forces along with battleships. Razumnyi, however, had interpreted the lessons of the Pacific war to mean that fast battleships already were just a necessary element of fast carrier task forces. The battleships were required to deter an enemy from employing his battleships against one's own aircraft carriers or amphibious forces, or to engage him in a classical general engagement if he tried. However, Razumnyi probably would not have taken strong exception to Chernyshev's final conclusion that aircraft carriers had become "a second backbone" of naval forces along with the battleship. Chernyshev merely hinted (in his description of the battles of the Coral Sea and Midway) at the fact that naval warfare, at least in oceanic theaters, had become a contest between aircraft carriers. But Razumnyi asserted (from his analysis of the same two battles) "the important role of aircraft carriers" for "decisive naval operations."

• Razumnyi limited his topic to the war in the Pacific Ocean, and did not have occasion to state his views on the value of light aircraft carriers for use in peripheral seas. (Chernyshev said that their construction was expedient from a cost-effectiveness standpoint for naval operations in peripheral seas.) Razumnyi did mention, twice in passing, the value of escort carriers for providing constant, close air cover for amphibious landing forces. In this regard, Razumnyi somewhat minimized the role of light carriers just as had Chernyshev, Pavlovich, and Schner. His aim was quite likely the same— lobbying for the construction of attack carriers as first priority even if at the expense of any light carrier construction. Razumnyi's whole treatment of heavy and light carriers made it readily apparent that he agreed with Chernyshev. Carriers had been shown by World War II to "be necessary for more than just employment in the capacity of floating airfields for fighter aviation" (which is the main role of light carriers, of course). They were also required, at least in oceanic operations, to permit the employment of torpedo and bomber planes.

• Razumnyi resisted any impulse to derogate the role of land-based aviation in naval operations. Pavlovich had done just that by noting the overlong "time-late" for shore-based aircraft to even appear on a scene-of-action 100 miles at sea. Chernyshev had only credited the existing Soviet shore-based naval aviation with having any value in the Soviet Union's narrow coastal waters. Schner had cited the failure of nearby land-based aircraft to prevent the sinking of the *Prince of Wales* and *Repulse*. But Razumnyi passed up the opportunity to note the severe limitations of land-based aircraft in his reference to the role of U.S. Army fighter aviation operating from Midway Island in the Battle of Midway.

• Although he did not develop the zonal-defense and limited command-of-the-sea concept as Alafuzov was to do the following month, Razumnyi did give several indications that his conceptual framework for naval warfare was basically the same as that to be shortly set out by Alafuzov. Most notably Razumnyi twice mentioned Japanese defense zones and referred eleven times to one or another aspect of the command-of-the-sea concept. Most of these references reflected an assumption of the validity of the limited command-of-the-sea concept.

• Moreover, Razumnyi's eleven references to command of the sea, when taken together with his elaborations on the role of battleships, constitute convincing evidence that he viewed naval warfare through an Old School lens. That is, he held to the validity of an essential role for battleships (although no longer *the* basic role) for fighting a Mahanian general engagement, if circumstances dictated, between the big-gunned surface combatant-ships of belligerent sides. The aim of such a battle, again in accordance with the dictum of classical sea-power theory, would be the destruction of the main forces of the enemy. This would gain a general command of the sea as the prerequisite to gain freedom to use the sea for one's own naval and shipping operations while denying such use to the defeated opponent.

• Of most importance for this study, three of the eleven statements expressed the total synergism between attack carriers and the command-of-the-sea construct: they imputed to the former the role of the key ship type for gaining and maintaining the latter. The Razumnyi article also referred to the other form of naval warfare for gaining command of the sea (besides that of the "destruction of an enemy's main naval forces"), that of blockade. Furthermore, the article used two terms with strong command-of-the-sea connotations—"initiative" and "preliminary" strikes. Razumnyi did so by mentioning that the Japanese had lost the "initiative" in the Pacific war as the consequence of having lost "superiority at sea." Furthermore he cited a requirement for "preliminary strikes" before the Leyte, Luzon, and Okinawa invasions could be undertaken.

• The necessity for gaining command of the air as an essential element of command of the sea was noted by Razumnyi—at a juncture in time when the thought had not yet become the commonplace it is today.

• Finally, of note for our purposes is the article's conclusion that naval forces (rather than ground or air forces) had played the leading role in the Pacific war. While this seems unremarkable except perhaps as a masterly statement of the obvious, it is actually a rather significant statement when taken in the overall historical context (both before and since) of the subordinate relationship of the Soviet Navy to the Army as "faithful assistant" (or, occasionally, as "faithful handmaiden" when intended in a demeaning way). Razumnyi was the first Soviet naval writer known to have publicly expressed the slightest reservation to this orthodoxy subsequent to the Navy's having been forced to play this subordinate role in World War II. Even though he did so only in a specific case where the evidence afforded ample support, his view is most unlikely to have found favor with the Army marshals who had always dominated the Soviet defense establishment. Admiral Gorshkov tactfully ventured to state on a number of subsequent occasions, including in his 1972-73 "Gorshkov Papers" and in the two editions of his book *Sea Power of the State* (1976 and 1979), that history shows examples, that must be expected to recur, of navies having played the leading role in one or another theater for one or another period of a war. He cited numerous historical examples to support his assertion. Despite the heavy weight of the historical evidence that Gorshkov and his "official theoreticians" have been able to exhume from the archives, the Army appears loathe to concede even such a well-supported claim. Likely the Army fears that the Navy would do the predictable thing and use any such concession to justify more ships for the Pacific and Northern Fleets—attack carriers in particular.

The Zonal Defense Concept of Military Doctrine is Misapplied to the Sea.
Admiral Alafuzov published a long article in the August 1946 issue of *Military Thought* entitled "Concerning the Nature of Naval Operations."[25] *Military Thought* is the theoretical journal of the Armed Forces' General Staff, intended only for the eyes of senior officers of the Soviet armed services. This article was particularly significant for revealing the Soviet military doctrinal war-at-sea concepts of naval zones of defense and of command of the sea.

The Soviets consider such concepts to be military secrets. Perhaps they are understandably chary of publicly discussing any defensive concepts that might dissuade Western writers from gratuitously enhancing the image of the Soviet military strength by portraying the Soviet Navy as primarily an offensive "blue water" navy on the model of the U.S., British, and French navies. At any rate, Soviet writings published for unlimited circulation almost never mention, let alone discuss, their strategically *defensive* concepts except on the rare occasion that to do so serves larger political or propaganda purposes.[26] It is particularly noteworthy that two-thirds of Alafuzov's article had been published three months earlier, and with the same title, in the unrestricted *Naval Digest*,[27] but, significantly, without the revealing parts on naval defense zones.

Alafuzov began his article by noting that, due to technological developments—such as the advent of mines, submarines, and naval aircraft—surface warships had become largely task-specific in their primary capabilities. As a result, he observed, "the sea may be divided into a number of zones in which the possibilities of using a fleet as an integrated whole to employ all of its elements will not be identical." Consequently, the overall power of a fleet will vary depending on the particular zone in which it is operating, and the suitability of the various types of naval forces available for sustained and effective operations in that zone. Alafuzov explained this in part by remarking that "a fleet has the most power close to its base, close to its coasts; the farther way from them it gets, the less power it has."

Three different zones in which a fleet's power would vary were described by Alafuzov as follows:

• the zone in which "large surface ships and submarines can be employed far from their base without diminution of their capabilities." (In the case of larger surface ships, it was made clear that their operations should be conducted with combat air cover provided in the open ocean by aircraft carriers);

• the zone in which "medium and small craft become effective as the scene of action comes closer to the base area, and so do bombers and torpedo-carrying aircraft;" and,

- the zone in which land-based "fighter aircraft and light surface-torpedo craft can be used as one comes closer yet."[28]

Alafuzov's article goes on to remark that "the appearance in present-day fleets of aircraft carriers has enormously increased the possibilities for the use of aviation." He also noted, with obvious reference to the first zone of those described above, that "in the wide theaters that embrace large expanses of ocean, the role of surface forces and submarines is increasing, especially that of major surface ships and aircraft carriers."[29]

In this article Alafuzov characterized the most frequently heard criticism of command of the sea as invalid. He argued that the mere fact that the particular forms of combat used in Mahan's time for contesting for command of the sea (the general engagement and the blockade) were no longer in use did not provide logical grounds that would invalidate the command-of-the-sea theory itself. He added that "the theory of command of the sea" that "command of an entire theater would be gained by one strike (general engagement) or by a single deployment of one's forces (blockade)" had been disproved by the two World Wars. Such command was said to still be achievable although "not right away but gradually." However, after seeming to have declared himself in favor of the Soviet Union's building a navy that eventually would be capable of contesting for general command of the sea, Alafuzov implied two pages further—perhaps only in deference to Army views—that "command of the sea" was not to be sought as an end in itself but just as a means to carry out the Navy's assigned missions.

Alafuzov presented a lengthy rationale in support of the two assertions that: a weaker fleet still may enjoy and exercise command of the sea over an extended coastal zone; and that "the essence of war at sea in the final analysis consists of warfare for expanding one's own zone of permanent command so that it eventually embraces the entire theater."

Since these two assertions seem to underlie the defensive aspects of the Soviet postwar strategy for any general war at sea, the relevant parts of Admiral Alafuzov's supporting arguments are translated in full in the following paragraphs.

   . . . [E]ven a very strong fleet, operating close to the enemy's coast, may lose its advantage and not have the relative strength to carry out its mission. If one's coast is favorably configured and if there are islands extending out from the coast on which naval and air bases may be set up, then the zone over which even quite a weak fleet may still remain "master of the situation" can be quite extensive. In a concrete situation then, one must consider not an abstract comparison of the capabilities of the opposing fleets but their capabilities for the use of the forces from the point of view of the missions they are assigned. If the missions assigned to a fleet are such that in a given zone they can be carried out by the forces capable of operating in that zone and if the enemy cannot prevent these missions from being accomplished and is only able to interfere with their accomplishment by occasional harassment (for example, he is capable only of causing losses which have no substantial effect on the overall outcome), then that zone is known as "the zone of command" of the fleet (pp. 16-17).

Present tendencies in the development of naval armaments point to a continuation of the trend toward further specialization. Therefore, there is every basis to suggest that in the very near future the zonality of action of the various components of the fleet will take on even more significance than it has at present. In particular, this means that to an ever greater extent we shall have to set aside the proposition that the fleet which is initially the stronger will be able at the outbreak of war to establish command over a whole theater of operations. It will become more and more a matter for the stronger fleet of actually having to fight to gain this command and this may take years of war to win.

On the other hand, the weaker fleet will not be obliged right away from the first days of the war to take cover in its bases and beguile itself with the impractical procedure of trying to achieve an "equalization of forces" by hit-and-run actions against the stronger enemy. At present, from the beginning of a war, the weaker fleet is master of its own zone of command in which it is able to carry out its missions and having in view, through adroit utilization of its resources, the expansion of its zone of command and, consequently, the improvement of its capabilities for accomplishing its missions. Finally, if this weaker fleet is reinforced with strong land-based air power, then its zone of command is increased for the period during which the fleet and the land-based air power operate together. The accomplishment of missions assigned a fleet may be considered as virtually assured if they lie within the fleet's zone of command. The zone of command is determined by the relative strength of the two opponents and by their strategic dispositions in the theater of war.

If the factors which determine the boundaries of a fleet's zone of command are permanently operating, then the zone of command will be permanent. But in the course of a war, changes occur in the relative strength of two opponents; old bases are lost; new ones are established. All these factors cause changes in the extent of the naval zone of command. So, in practical terms, one may call a zone of command permanent if it serves the day-to-day needs and corresponds with the normal disposition of a fleet. But, if in place of this, the fleet is temporarily redeployed in such a way as to widen its zone of command without its being able for the long term to maintain this new disposition of forces, then the additional area in which the fleet has command is called the zone of temporary command. . . .

The essence of naval operations consists in achieving one's objectives through gaining command in the decisive region for the time needed for the accomplishment of the mission. If the decision takes place in the zone of established command of a fleet, then the essence of an operation will be to achieve the objective by reinforcing this command by special measures. The character of the special measures will be determined by the detailed requirements of the mission and by the possible opposition which the enemy can mount. The basic nature of these measures should be such as to prevent the enemy to the fullest extent possible from developing his secondary and incidental opposition— normally the only practicable kind of opposition he can bring to bear in our zone of command—into a decisive opposition capable of seizing from us our command in the area where the issue will be decided. Gaining command in the area where the decision will occur often means gaining command through causing losses to the enemy. This, in turn, brings about a change in the balance of power and leads to a further expansion of our zone of established command. A number of operations, such as the seizure of coastal areas, islands, and the destruction of enemy bases and positions, leads directly to the widening of our zone of command.

> The essence of naval warfare in the final analysis lies in striving to widen one's own zone of established command so that it eventually embraces the whole theater. Therefore, each operation should be considered not as a separate affair isolated from the others but as a logical step in the process of gaining the final objective. The course of the Second World War fully confirms these statements. Operations in our Baltic and Black sea theaters are examples of the struggle to widen one's zone of established command. . . (p. 17).

On the subject of the place of air power at sea and aircraft carriers in the new zones-of-defense concept, Alafuzov's *Military Thought* article stated:

> Air forces are the most universal type of force of a navy. On a par with surface ships and along with the latter, air forces play a decisive role in warfare for maintaining and expanding a [fleet's] zone of command. . . .
>
> The allocation of individual tasks among the various kinds of naval forces . . . depends on the conditions of the theater. In small sea theaters the role of coastal artillery and especially of shore-based aviation increases. In . . . oceanic theaters, the roles increase of the surface-ship and submarine forces and, in particular, of the major heavy surface-combatant ships and of aircraft carriers (p. 18).

What Alafuzov seemed to be implying here was that, although shore-based aviation obviated any need for light aircraft carriers in the Baltic and Black Seas, the Northern and Pacific Fleets should be provided with heavy attack carriers. In renouncing the need for light carriers to provide reconnaissance and air cover for naval forces in the two "small sea theaters," Alafuzov raised the possibility of the naval forces' receiving additional air support from the Army air forces: "If a modern army which has a powerful aviation component allocates a part of it for joint action, the might of a fleet in the zone in which those allocated air forces can operate is increased considerably, perhaps decisively." (p. 16) Alafuzov's phrasing "zone in which those allocated air forces *can* operate" (emphasis supplied) is likely to have been carefully formulated to remind the reader that even the Army air forces were incapable of providing the continuous air cover for naval forces far out at sea for which the Navy was urging the construction of attack aircraft carriers. Moreover, as already quoted above, Alafuzov commented that if a weaker fleet were "reinforced with strong land-based air power, then its zone of command is increased for the period during which the fleet and the land-based air power operate together." (p. 17) With the memory still fresh of the Navy's having been almost totally deprived of the use of its naval air arm for the first two years of the Great Patriotic War, Alafuzov may reasonably be interpreted as considering such "periods" of land-based air support as largely theoretical. Certainly he did not think they offered any realistic substitute for the Navy's having its own carrier-based aviation.

The Essence of War At Sea: Increasing One's Zone of Permanent Command by Daily Operational Activity Supplemented by Special Operations. In yet another appearance in print in 1946, Admiral Alafuzov wound up his busy year of publishing with another major article in the December issue of *Naval Digest*.[30] This one was entitled, "The Development of the Daily Operational Activity of a Navy." Using the same term, "daily operational activity," that Rear Admiral Belli had employed at the naval scientific conference eight months earlier, Admiral Alafuzov defined the term. He made it seem synonymous with daily combat activity: the routine activity within a fleet's zone of permanent command. In so doing he reiterated the point made in his articles in the April-May 1946 issue of *Naval Digest* and the August 1946 issue of *Military Thought*; that the main thrust of naval strategy (for an inferior navy) should be to expand its "zone of permanent command:"

> If the essence of war at sea in the final analysis consists of warfare for expanding one's own zone of permanent command and if every operation consists of the accomplishment of aims by gaining command in the region for carrying out a mission [reference made to the author's earlier article in the April-May 1946 issue of *Naval Digest*]; then the essence of the daily operational activity that fills the intervals between operations and does not cease during operations, consists of warfare against the occasional harassments of the adversary in order to complete our own missions in the zone of our permanent command (p. 14).

Alafuzov explained the reason daily operational activity is "expressly limited to the tasks of extinguishing a flare-up of activity of an adversary and of [just] maintaining command in our zone of permanent command," rather than gaining command of an area initially or for expanding it subsequently. It is because no additional forces can be provided for "daily operational activity" beyond those "permanently assigned for it."

However, should an enemy change from mere harassment to an effort to regain command in the "zone of permanent command" of a Soviet fleet, an "operation" would be initiated to defend against the attempt (employing as large a buildup of forces as necessary and available).[31] Alafuzov distinguished between daily operational activity and "operations conducted systematically and daily against some [external] objective—for example, systematic bombardment of air bases or systematic actions of submarines on communications." The major difference is to be found in the fact that the operation takes place outside any Soviet zone of permanent command (rather than being just routine maintenance of a command already gained) and "amounts to a systematic undermining of the command of the enemy and of causing him losses." This latter reference to sinking enemy ships and destroying his aircraft is of particular interest in connoting an unprecedented willingness to fight enemy forces if necessary to maintain control in a "zone of temporary command" or even to expand a zone of permanent command rather than to evade battle against a superior force (as both Young School and Old School strategy had prescribed).

The Naval War College head listed the three categories of measures considered to constitute daily operational activity:

- conduct in a theater of all kinds of defense (antiair, antimine, antisubmarine, antisurface torpedo forces, and counterlanding);

- infrastructuring naval positions and supporting them in an appropriate condition of readiness; and,

- organizing a system [of convoy escort or other protection] for the transit of one's forces in a theater (p. 14).

Alafuzov further noted that the role of protecting against a surprise attack from seaward was assigned to the forces designated in peacetime to conduct daily operational activity. To them fell the responsibility for protecting the other forces of the Navy (e.g., today especially ballistic missile submarines), the Soviet coasts (including ports and naval bases, of course), and the Soviet Union's (coastal) sea lines of communication.[32]

A likely rationale for the potentially confusing substitution by Alafuzov and Belli of "operational" for "combat" in the customary daily combat activity was provided by the former in his article at the end of 1946. Probably having in mind that the Russian word for "combat" had a tactical connotation in its naval usage, Alafuzov observed:

> Thus, the daily operational activity of the Navy . . . in general is of an operational character since it is directed at the support of a favorable operational regime in the region of a theater comprising a zone of permanent command of the Navy (pp. 15-16).

One of the most important parts of Alafuzov's *Naval Digest* article was what it had to say about "naval positions." The second of the three categories (above) of daily operational activity was one for providing such positions with the infrastructure and support needed to maintain them in full readiness. Imagine that Gorshkov had decided during his nearly three decades as navy commander in chief that the Norwegian Sea from the Greenland-Iceland-United Kingdom Gap northward (or the entire Sea of Japan or Sea of Okhotsk) was one big "naval position." Then Alafuzov's description of the Soviet conception of a naval position takes on no little interest:

> Infrastructure and support of naval positions . . . has in view the creation of such conditions that relatively small forces of the Navy operating on these positions bar a strong adversary from the approaches to naval bases, to the [coastal] flank of the ground forces and, if there are favorable geographic conditions (narrows and straits), could bar him from the whole region of a theater [i.e., bar NATO from the Norwegian Sea].

At the same time, these positions and the forces and means guarding them include the forces and means of PLO [antisubmarine warfare] and PKO [anti-PT boat] assigned to prevent penetration of given regions by submarines and light surface-torpedo forces of the adversary. The forces and means of naval positions also include the means of PMO [antimine defense] that are provided for preventing the enemy from laying mines in the approaches to naval positions (p. 20).

In a further paragraph on naval positions, Alafuzov asserted that a comparative study of naval positions in the two World Wars showed the "close connection of their roles and fortunes with the fortunes of the ground fronts to which they are adjacent." This may have been an allusion to what the Soviet Navy learned, to its great misfortune, in World War II. When the Soviet Army was forced to retreat and Soviet naval bases were overrun from landward, the naval positions were lost along with the naval bases that anchored or supported them. Nominally, however, Alafuzov was only explaining that the naval positions were a seaward extension of the land defenses and an integral part of the coastal defenses of any given region. The naval positions should provide cover against seaborne attack or invasion and protect coastal shipping of troop replacements and materiel for Soviet ground forces operating in coastal sectors.

By far the most interesting and significant new implication to emerge from this article was that Soviet strategy for a war at sea should be a modernized, tactically offensive version of the fleet-in-being strategy as interpreted by Corbett: by active defensive operations that avoided any general engagement but counterattacked whenever possible to keep command of the sea "in dispute."[33] (This would prevent a stronger navy from gaining command and exploiting it to land amphibious invasion forces, conduct naval bombardments of coastal areas, interfere with shipping, or to make whatever use of the sea might be called for in the campaign plans of the enemy.) Alafuzov's article seemed to imply that, until the day it might prove feasible at least to gain and retain a "general" or "full" command of the sea in Soviet home waters, the command should at least be held "in dispute" in zones of command on naval positions in those waters. The naval positions would embrace whole regions of a theater whenever geography permitted. They would enable a weaker Soviet fleet to bar enemy naval forces from approaching Soviet naval bases or the ground forces in coastal sectors. Every enemy operation to reduce the zone of permanent command was to be met with a defensive operation that would repulse the attack.[34] Then a counterattack was to be made with the aim of further weakening the enemy and with the eventual result of expanding the particular zone of permanent command that the enemy had planned to reduce.

From the foregoing, it seems well warranted to formulate the working hypothesis for testing subsequent evidence that Soviet naval strategy from 1946 to 1953 was one of a modernized, tactically offensive fleet-in-being in the sense that Corbett attributed to Nelson: "an inferior fleet kept actively in being" in order to exploit its "general power of holding such command [of the sea] in dispute."[35] As expressed by Corbett in a more formal manner, the "doctrine of the 'Fleet in being' . . . goes no further than this, that where the enemy regards the command of the sea area as necessary to his offensive purposes, you may be able to prevent his gaining such command by using your fleet defensively, refusing what Nelson called a regular battle [general engagement] and seizing every opportunity for a counterstroke." (p. 226) Corbett stressed that, "rightly understood", fleet-in-being strategy extended far beyond its initial conception as "essentially a method of defense against invasion" to embrace "defense against any kind of maritime attack, whether against territory or sea communications." (p. 215)

Limited Command of the Sea and Forward Bases are the Best Forms of Support for Operations. The same November-December issue of the *Naval Digest* contained another article of marked interest.[36] It was signed by a Captain First Rank A.K. Evseyev.[37] It argued that the first priority mission for providing proper support for a newly deployed naval force was to gain command of the sea in the region of deployment. The relevant quotation merits setting down in full:

> The main measure on which the successful conduct of a deployment depends is its support. The best form of support for a deployment is gaining command of the sea and air in the region of deployment if command of the sea has not already been gained (in the entire theater) as a result of previous operations.

> In the circumstances of lack of command of the sea and air in the presence of strong opposition, the first priority mission is the gaining of temporary command of the sea in the zone of deployment, with the next mission being the accomplishment of permanent command in the given zone.

> A fleet deployment may be considered finished, successful, and secured [only] when it is founded on command in the zone of deployment, in other words, when in the zone of deployment such circumstances have been created in which the enemy can mount only an occasional harassment or is completely deprived of the capability for conducting naval operations at the same time our forces retain the capability in full measure.

This same Evseyev article dealt at length with the requirements for advanced bases to support forward-deployed forces so that Soviet naval forces could be sufficiently dispersed (against air strikes), yet when required they could be quickly concentrated "in a designated place at the requisite moment and in the required number and types." (p. 26) They must be prepared to "occupy a designated region of new forward basing," thereby permitting "the timely concentration" of the required number of "heterogeneous forces" in the sector where they would be needed. Evseyev noted that the proper selection of forward bases was a "most responsible part" of Soviet war planning (p. 35).

On 16 January 1947 there appeared in *Red Star* an article entitled "Warfare for Command of the Sea" by Vice Admiral Yuriy Panteleyev.[38] Panteleyev commanded the Pacific Fleet and subsequently was "chief" of the Krylov Shipbuilding Academy. Among his key points was that, in order for the Soviet Navy to conduct "the successive, systematic operations" necessary to gain command of the sea in a given sea area, "it is essential to . . . seize enemy bases and airfields in order to position the Navy closer to the area of operations." Moreover, he asserted that it had become absolutely necessary to destroy an adversary's naval and air bases in addition to his naval forces.

Limited Command of the Sea Reaffirmed. Panteleyev reaffirmed Alafuzov's view that command of the sea could be gained just in limited areas for only as long as required to carry out any given operation. Panteleyev spelled it out in the conclusion of his article, quoted below. He left theoretical scope for an eventual gaining of full command of the sea in the peripheral Soviet seas of key importance. (In effect this is the same force-equalization strategy Alafuzov described.) But Panteleyev took into account the Soviet Navy's marked inferiority to the U.S. and other Western navies by noting that command of the sea was required above all (just) in limited regions and only for as long as necessary to carry out any given mission that had been assigned:

> In modern warfare, command of the sea is no longer gained by destruction of the entire navy of an enemy or by blockading it in port but by achieving command of the sea in a given region of a theater for the time which is required by a fleet (or force) to accomplish the assigned mission. . . . Command of the sea is now gained by conducting successive, systematic operations. . . . Thus the experience of the Second World War teaches that the discharge of the missions of naval warfare require gaining command of the sea. But the way to gain this command no longer lies through the general engagement between fleets or through a blockade of the enemy navy. Command of the sea now is gained by way of conducting a number of successive operations whose successful completion results in the destruction of the sea power of the enemy. Command of the sea is necessary above all in a given region of a theater just for the time required by a fleet to carry out an assigned mission. The methods for doing this include both destruction of the enemy navy at sea and the seizure of his bases and airfields, and in some cases of the entire coast in a limited sea theater.

Apparently this Mahanian strategy of force equalization by an inferior navy before accepting a general engagement had been subjected to significant criticism.[39] Or at least Panteleyev was protesting that such a strategy was *not* impractical and would *not* disorganize the Navy. To the contrary, he maintained, the command-of-the-sea principle would serve as "an organizing and directing factor."

The Command-of-the-Sea Debate. Apparent confirmation appeared two decades later that significant criticism of the classical command-of-the-sea strategy in the first postwar decade had not only occurred but that a very substantial debate actually had taken place. Three senior Army officers in a 1967 issue of *Military Thought* summarized Soviet writings on military strategy over the preceding half century.[40] Only a few paragraphs were devoted to the naval side of the Soviet Union's unified military strategy for the first postwar decade. However, about half of the discussion allotted to the Navy was given over to a debate on command of the sea—giving the impression, certainly, that the subject was considered to be of no little significance.

Although not specifically cited, it seems clear that the articles by Eremeyev, Belli and Penzin, Alafuzov, Evseyev, and Panteleyev were part of at least the beginning of this debate. The 1967 article, however, did refer to one specific 1947 article in *Military Thought* and an unspecified number of unidentified articles in *Naval Digest* in 1947 and 1948, none of which is as yet available in the West.[41] The 1967 *Military Thought* article went on to indicate that the debate (although apparently dormant from 1950-1954) was not concluded until 1955.

According to this article, the outcome of the all-Navy theoretical debate on command of the sea when it ended in 1955 was an agreed definition of command of the sea—one implied to have been acceptable to the Army. The three Army officers claimed that command of the sea (gospodstvo na more) had been defined by the five naval authors of the four articles as follows: "favorable conditions created for a specified time in a theater of military actions during which the naval forces of the given side [which had established the favorable conditions] are able to carry out their missions in the naval theater of military actions successfully while the adversary is unable to prevent the carrying out of these missions and is limited to only local interference." (p. 93)

Note that this definition of Soviet-style limited command of the sea, supposedly agreed upon by 1955, and specifically the extent to which that command of the sea is to be gained and maintained—i.e., throughout (entire) key theaters of military action—is tantamount to "strategic command" as defined by Captain First Rank Shavtsov in a *Military Thought* article of July 1955.[42] Any suggestion of the possibility of eventually gaining "full" or "general" command of the sea (in the Mahanian sense) beyond the confines of the key theaters of military actions however is noticeably missing.

The April 1967 article in *Military Thought* by the senior Army officers went on to note that the definition allegedly agreed upon had "emphasized especially that command of the sea is not an end in itself but only a condition for carrying out active missions." This, while logically applicable to any navy was an Aesopian formula that had been used both by the Young School and the Army since the late 1920s. It indicated opposition to both the Old School's recommended full command-of-the-sea strategy for the superior navy and the fleet-in-being strategy for the inferior navy of attempting to hold the command "in dispute."[43] Thus, the fact that this formulation was cited by the three Army authors emphasized especially the Army's opposition to canonizing as military doctrine even the limited command-of-the-sea theory that the Navy favored. Perhaps the strategy was too inherently expandable to a general or full command. The Army may well have anticipated that once established, even such a limited command-of-the-sea doctrine would be used to justify a large battleship and aircraft carrier building program at the likely expense of the Army's share of the military budget. Then the Navy would no longer be confined to its customary subordinate role as just the "faithful assistant" to the Army, providing cover and support for the coastal operations of the ground forces.

As indicated above, one implication of the 1967 article is that a consensus on a limited command-of-the-sea doctrine was not reached until 1955 (that is, not until two years after Stalin's death). The article states further that in reaching final agreement "the methods of warfare for gaining command of the sea and especially the changes wrought by the advent of nuclear weapons were thoroughly examined." A recurring theme of Soviet writing is that such original thinking was considerably inhibited during Stalin's rule and that the "revolution in military affairs" consequently did not hit the Army and Navy in full force until the mid-fifties, after Stalin's passing. Here the Army authors were implying that adoption of a new strategy for the nuclear era had to await Stalin's replacement by a less conservative successor. (Khrushchev certainly was open to innovation, particularly with regard to developing nuclear missiles that could replace large, costly conventional forces.)

An important part of the essence of the above statement, in addition to the reference to the changes brought about by nuclear weapons, is that "methods of warfare for gaining command of the sea . . . were thoroughly examined." This sentence was followed immediately by: "It became firmly established that an integral part of the contest for command of the sea under modern conditions is the contest for command of the air in a naval theater." (p. 93) Seemingly the Army authors found it expedient to profess that the most significant result of the reconsideration in the early post-Stalinist period of the methods of warfare for gaining command of the sea had been recognition of the concomitant need for command of the air.

Four additional pieces (by Andreyev, Piterskiy, Kulakov, and Mil'gram) of somewhat esoteric evidence appeared in *Military Thought* and *Red Star* during 1948 and 1949. They help to fill the 1946-1960 void on command of the sea created by the unavailability of the *Naval Digest*, for that period.[44]

Colomb's Command-of-the-Sea Views Criticized. The first of these four articles was by Captain First Rank (later admiral) Andreyev, and bore the title "The Pseudo-scientific Theory of Admiral Colomb."[45] It discussed at unprecedented length the command-of-the-sea concept (as enunciated by Colomb and as affected by the advent of new weapons). It defended in more detail than any other article in the Soviet literature, the possibilities for a weaker navy to gain temporary command of the sea despite the opposition of a stronger naval adversary. Andreyev did not condemn the command-of-the-sea principle *per se*. However, he did deny that global command of the sea was an attainable goal. The reasons he gave for this may well have been framed to mollify the Army. He reasoned that the advent of new weapons and the global scale of naval operations had changed the nature of naval warfare so radically that gaining an overall command of the sea around the globe in wartime would be impossible for any country.

At the outset, Andreyev indicated that his article had been prompted by "the number of articles published recently in our military press concerning the question of 'command of the sea'."[46] He complained that none of them had "revealed the historical essence of this concept." British Vice Admiral Philip Colomb's views had been selected for analysis because they had gained renewed currency in Soviet military writings but without having been accorded the "necessary critical clarification and analysis" (a standard signal to Soviet readers that the views to be expressed would differ significantly from those expressed by previous writers). Andreyev added that "it seems to us" that such an analysis as in his article was particularly needed inasmuch as a correct understanding of the command-of-the-sea concept has "important practical significance." (p. 49)

Colomb's principal work, *Naval Warfare, Its Basic Principles and Experience*, first appeared in 1891. It was first translated into Russian in 1894, but had not been brought out in a Soviet edition until 1940. Andreyev, citing Colomb throughout, gave a generally fair presentation of Colomb's basic views. Nevertheless, the latter's motives and historical objectivity were denounced as calculated primarily to advance Great Britain's supremacy at sea by theoretically grounding the fallacious idea that unless an adversary had a battle fleet strong enough to at least hold command of the sea "in dispute", there was no possibility of making temporary use of the sea anywhere to carry out one's assigned naval missions.[47]

The main thrust of Andreyev's article was to argue, on the basis of the experience of the Anglo-Dutch wars and World Wars I and II, that it is indeed feasible under post-World War II conditions—Colomb, Klado, Petrov, and more recent (but unnamed) Soviet theoreticians notwithstanding—to gain and exploit a "temporary" command of the sea that would allow the Soviet Navy to carry out at least some of the normal missions of a Navy. He particularly decried Colomb's "allegedly scientific" thesis that "the results to be achieved by just a temporary command of the sea are worthless" and that "consequently it is essential to gain permanent and full command of the sea." (p. 53) Andreyev belabored this point, asserting subsequently that Colomb's "thesis of the impossibility of achieving success in partial operations without gaining a general command of the sea was . . . pseudo-scientific." (p. 55)

The article went on at considerable length to assert the feasibility of gaining temporary command of the sea under the (nonnuclear) conditions that then existed for the Soviet Navy (and that continued until Stalin's death in 1953). The "numerous successful actions of the Dutch, Spanish, and French navies in the English Channel and North Sea," during the three centuries until the time Colomb wrote, were merely mentioned. England was at this time mistress of the seas and considered to have held unbroken command of the sea since the end of the Anglo-Dutch wars. Andreyev claimed that "even the experience of the Anglo-Dutch wars showed that operations at sea were feasible in a number of cases without gaining command of the sea." (p. 56) However, he gave no names or dates of such operations to substantiate his claim.

Skipping over the Napoleonic Wars and the many others of the 19th century, as well as the Russo-Japanese War of 1904-1905, Andreyev commented on World War I as follows: "The appearance and development of aviation enhanced the feasibility of gaining temporary command of the sea." (p. 57) Again, however, Andreyev failed to mention any examples of such operations.

The article stated that the Second World War had been "especially instructive" in this regard. In this last case, Andreyev did give three examples to support his claim:

> Such major operations as the landing of German troops in Norway, the penetration of a German squadron through the English Channel, and a number of Japanese amphibious landing operations in the Pacific, etc., proved feasible under conditions of temporary command of the sea. The experience of this war shows that temporary command of the sea in individual regions of a theater or even in individual operational sectors unquestionably leads to the successful accomplishment of the missions assigned a navy provided that they are skillfully conducted (p. 57).

Several times in his long article, Captain First Rank Andreyev brought up the subject of the naval missions for cover and support of the coastal flanks of ground forces. These uses of the Navy have always loomed large in the thinking of continental powers and they characterized Soviet naval operations in World War II. Andreyev's tact in discussing this topic suggested that he wished to be understood by the senior military readership of *Military Thought* as fully appreciating the Navy's responsibility to provide such cover and support to coastal Army operations. Nonetheless he did not offend his Navy superiors for whom the fact that the Navy was still largely tied to coastal operations by this mission may have made the Army-flank support mission something of a *bête noire*.

Andreyev first raised the subject by means of a formula he attributed to Colomb. It had been at issue in Soviet discourse since the 1920s. Namely, gaining command of the sea was not an end in itself that justified the Navy's having missions independent of the Army; it was correctly seen only as a means to an end. And the end was gaining such limited superiority at sea as might be required to carry out its assigned missions, usually, if not invariably, ones for assisting the Army in carrying out ground operations in coastal areas.[48] In his initial mention of this matter, Andreyev signalled the subject he intended to discuss by use of the word "independent." He wrote that one of Colomb's major theses had been (in the British naval historian's words) that "command of the sea as an independent field of activity must be assigned as the necessary aim of those nations who count on being victorious in a war." Moreover, he added, that "nothing substantial may be done in naval warfare without ensuring . . . control or command of the water surface." (p. 51) Andreyev denied the validity of Colomb's thesis, asserting that it had "no scientific basis." The article went on to remark that Colomb had only selected as historical examples to support his conclusions the wars in which navies had played significant roles. Even in those, Andreyev maintained, "in the majority of cases the fate of the war depended on the outcome of the warfare in ground theaters." (p. 54)

When Andreyev later returned to this subject, it was again in the implicit context that gaining command of the sea was not an end in itself but just the means to an end. Andreyev wrote:

> The experience of the Second War War demonstrated that warfare for command of the sea within an entire theater or in individual regions of a theater was conducted only in those cases when a necessity for such warfare was dictated by the general strategic or operational missions of a fleet and when warfare for command was directed to provide support for daily or mission-oriented operations conducted in correspondence with the overall plan for the war or for a [theater] campaign. (p. 58)

In other words, warfare in a theater or in a region of a theater was never conducted to gain command of the sea as an end in itself. Rather, command of the sea would only be sought as a means to the end of providing essential support for fleet operations required to implement the general war plans. Despite the elaborate circumlocution with which Andreyev had expressed himself, few Army critics would have failed to note that the Andreyev formula left the Navy free to determine the occasions on which preliminary command of the sea would be deemed necessary. But, as noted previously, such missions normally took the form of Army ground operations in coastal sectors with the Navy tied to offshore areas to provide cover and support. Hence, such theoretical gyrations held little promise of winning the Navy increased maneuvering room.

The third time Andreyev discussed the Army-flank cover-and-support mission he asserted that—Colomb to the contrary notwithstanding—the experience of contemporary wars had shown that "it is feasible for a numerically weaker navy to conduct numerous operations." The article listed those missions that were deemed within the realm of the possible for an inferior navy. Not surprisingly, none of them involved direct combat operations against the main forces of an adversary. Such operations would have to be undertaken if destruction of an enemy's naval forces to gain command of the sea were considered an end in itself. Rather, all of the listed missions were more or less closely associated with providing cover and support to the Army's coastal flank: antishipping, army-flank support, mine-laying and minesweeping, amphibious landing operations of operational or tactical scale (i.e., no strategic-scale operations to conduct transoceanic invasions), and protection of coastal (military) shipping.

Colomb's basic flaw was said to have been his failure to give his studies of naval warfare a broader context: the development of the states involved; the bitter economic and political struggle between the belligerent powers; the underlying causes of the war; the general course and outcome of the wars he considered; and, lastly, "the general course of military operations on land" as well as at sea. In so doing, Colomb was said to have "followed in the footsteps of the reactionary ideologist of German militarism, Clausewitz." Clausewitz was said to have based his teachings on war solely "on . . . land campaigns without any of their ties with events at sea." (p. 60) Since this was precisely what the dominant Soviet military historians and theorists were doing at the time with regard to World War II, there is little reason to doubt that the Navy, through Andreyev, was esoterically voicing a strongly felt complaint.

Andreyev continued to castigate Colomb by claiming that he had made the same major error with regard to sea warfare that Clausewitz had committed concerning land warfare. That is, Colomb concluded that all of the main forces had to be concentrated for one general engagement (or per Clausewitz, one simultaneous strike) rather than a number of successive operations. On the naval side, Colomb was correctly cited as also having mentioned blockade as the one approved alternative to a single great general engagement. These two forms of naval warfare also were duly noted as having been prescribed by Colomb as the sole methods of gaining command of the sea—and hence, the only methods for achieving the aims of a war at sea.

In what seemed to be the most unconvincing of Andreyev's arguments, he asserted that no general engagement could have taken place in World War II[49] (or since then) because the contemporary situation of naval forces and the ground and air forces that cooperate with them does not allow concentrating all of the naval forces of a state in one place. (p. 60) Of course, neither Mahan nor Colomb held that no more than a single general engagement could be required for one side to destroy enough of an enemy's naval forces to gain command of the sea. However, of most interest here is Andreyev's argument that the requirement, in effect, for a navy to provide army-flank cover and support constitutes a reason that no general engagement could take place. This fallacious argument could only have been calculated to please the Army readers of *Military Thought*, since it was tantamount to reassuring them that the Navy recognized its duty to support the Army and not go off on independent missions to fight for command of the sea.

Among his several points with regard to a navy's missions for cover and support of army ground forces operating in coastal sectors was one that credited ground forces with sometimes being able to gain command of the sea merely by occupying the littoral of a theater of operations.[50] Andreyev, in all likelihood, had foremost in mind the bitter memories of the Wehrmacht's rapid advance along the Baltic coast in 1941 that deprived the Baltic Fleet of all its bases outside the Gulf of Finland and hence of any chance to at least hold command of the Baltic "in dispute." At any rate, this remarkable claim is unprecedented in the Soviet naval literature, either before or since Andreyev's article in July 1948. The purpose of the claim can only be speculated:[51] Was it a dig at the Soviet Army for having allowed the Nazis to overrun the Soviet naval bases in the former Baltic States with so little resistance? Was it an effort to show that the Army could have an important role in gaining new bases for the Soviet Navy in any world war III effort to push across Western Europe to the Atlantic? Was it both reasons or neither?

On the penultimate page of his long article, Andreyev, through yet a further condemnation of Colomb,—this time for allegedly trying to set the Navy against the Army—seemed again to be esoterically assuring the Army of the Navy's fidelity, of its virtually total dedication to the Army-flank cover-and-support missions under the Soviet Union's unified military strategy:

> Colomb was a stranger to the concept of a unified strategy, to the assignment of missions to all services of the armed forces, the navy among them, for the accomplishment of unified strategic aims. In his book [*Naval Warfare*], he tried to set the navy against the army (p. 63).

Andreyev, near the end of his article, referred to the Navy's relations with the Army. This time he said he wanted "to expose reactionary contemporary theory of military art (including naval art) which bourgeois researchers are trying to create on the basis of nonexistent or improbable types of weapons and technology." (p. 64) Although Andreyev attributed this "reactionary theory" to "bourgeois researchers", Soviet writers habitually have employed such foreign surrogates to discuss their own problems. So he may fairly be taken to have been speaking of Soviet military theoreticians. That this indeed was the case is suggested by the next sentence, placed at the end presumably for emphasis: "The further development of Soviet military science requires resolute exposure of the attempts of imperialist agents on the ideological front, including in the field of military theory." Since this sentence specified *Soviet* military science, it is clear that it was the Soviet Union's own problems that were under discussion. Hence, the "imperialist agents" were to be understood as "Soviet agents of imperialism," as had become so familiar a term during Stalin's Great Purge of the late 1930s (and his not so well-known, continued, smaller-scale purges in the postwar 1940s).

These final sentences imply that Andreyev was contributing to a postwar debate, known to have taken place, as to what the Navy's missions should be—and even whether (as in the early 1920s) any navy was needed at all. Andreyev's mention of "nonexistent or improbable types of weapons" sounds very much like the substance of a Soviet Navy rebuttal to Army missile enthusiasts who dreamed of sinking all ships (even submarines) at sea, as well as in port, with land-based missiles.

That Andreyev was venting some Navy spleen against the Army had been suggested four pages earlier when the following, otherwise irrelevant, pair of sentences seemed at first reading to be out of context:

> Nor can one remain silent about the judgment of Colomb that superiority of forces right in the initial period of a war's development has decisive significance for the outcome of the war. The experience of war in the Pacific demonstrated that the surprise attack of the Japanese Navy at Pearl Harbor, while changing the correlation of forces at sea in favor of Japan, did not, however, determine the general outcome of the war in that theater (p. 60).

The "modernizers" in the Soviet Army are known to have urged the likelihood of a short war (conducted mainly with land-based missiles). Acceptance of such a military doctrine would have put the Navy as well as the ground forces largely out of business, so it is not surprising that a Navy-authored article in the Armed Forces' General Staff journal would in some way, no matter how veiled it might have to be to survive the military censorship, take issue with this doctrinal view and offer a historic example as evidence to counter the views of all who believed that a general war, which they anticipated would become nuclear sooner rather than later, would determine the outcome of any future conflict in a relatively short time.

Andreyev's main interest appeared rather clearly to be to persuade his readers that, despite the existence and opposition of a stronger naval adversary, gaining a temporary command of the sea in a limited area for just long enough to carry out some important naval missions was a feasible campaign (theater) strategy for the Soviet fleets. As noted earlier, he nevertheless did not denounce general command of the sea *per se*, as so many Young School enthusiasts had done in the 1920s and first half of the 1930s. Rather, he acknowledged that a permanent command of the sea was of course preferable but that it went against the facts of the matter to maintain— as not only Colomb had done but also as the detractors of a limited command of the sea were agreeing—that gaining such limited command was worthless.[52] Andreyev argued in support of his position on the value of a limited command of the sea that "even in the time of Colomb permanent (or constant) command of the sea began in many cases with temporary command."

To further demonstrate the necessity of relying on a limited command of the sea (and in an effort seeming to obscure the importance of having a navy so strong that it could contest for gaining oceanic command), Andreyev went on directly to assert:

> Particularly in contemporary conditions of warfare, permanent command in oceanic theaters (for the entire period of a war) is simply impossible, even in the case of opposing an adversary who has a weaker fleet, inasmuch as the weakness of a fleet can be compensated for to a considerable degree by aviation and by other means for the conduct of war [at sea] (p. 57).

Having delivered himself of this optimistically encouraging dictum, Andreyev went on to claim that the experience of the World Wars showed that not once had either side been able to gain and maintain permanent command. Moreover, Andreyev asserted, even Colomb himself had admitted that only a single case of "permanent" command was to be found in history: during the period of the Crimean War after the Russians had sunk their own fleet at Sevastopol. Andreyev scarcely could have helped but realize that limiting his discussion to the extreme situation of the one war in history in which command had been held for the entire course of a war begged the question of the innumerable times when one belligerent had exercised command for prolonged and decisive periods. This specious argumentation warrants the conclusion that Andreyev's interest did not tend to a full and objective discussion of command of the sea. He wanted to persuade his readers by any argument at hand that the limited command-of-the-sea campaign strategy (which was the Soviet Navy's best option until and unless it could be built up to be superior to its probable naval opponents) constituted a viable strategy for its weaker navy. This subjective approach was fully in accord with Admiral Alafuzov's earlier injunction to Soviet naval theoreticians at the Naval Scientific Conference at the Naval War College in March 1946. Alafuzov, it will be recalled, had recommended following in the footsteps of Clausewitz, Corbett, Castex, and Groos in that they (allegedly) eschewed theoretically appealing but impractical theories and elaborated only theories that would best further the interests of their respective countries.

In this regard, Andreyev found it expedient to denounce the anti-"limited" command views of some of the Young School adherents as he previously had done regarding the Old School views of Professors Klado and Petrov. The Young School, claimed Andreyev (although without naming that school beyond labeling adherents as "the other group of theoreticians" opposed to Colomb, Klado, and Petrov), went "to the opposite extreme." The Old School insisted on all or nothing as concerned command of the sea and "completely denied the possibility and necessity of fighting for command of the sea under certain conditions and had limited the missions of the Navy to just ones of a tactical scale."[53] (p. 57)

Seemingly to add weight, or at least length, to an otherwise not very persuasive argument, Andreyev gave long critiques of the two methods for gaining command of the sea which Colomb (and Mahan) had found relevant in their day—the general naval engagement and the sea blockade. It suffices for our purposes to record that Andreyev concluded his remarks on the big battle and the blockade by observing: "It may be concluded from what has been said that the methods prescribed by the British admiral for gaining command of the sea also were obsolete." (p. 60)

One additional major criticism of Colomb's views was adduced by Andreyev—that the British theoretician had overlooked the key trend of differentiation of naval-force types that had already begun in Colomb's time with the advent of the torpedo-armed destroyer, the first of a series of new weapon systems that threatened (and ultimately ended) the supremacy of the battleship.[54]

Andreyev drew the following conclusion:

> The place of the battleship as the main striking force in many cases was taken over by submarines and subsequently by aircraft carriers and this process of the development of naval forces is continuing (p. 62).

This was a most remarkable conclusion in that the submarine can in no real sense be credited with ever having replaced the battleship. Perhaps it was said to have done so just as lip service to the tenet of military doctrine that the submarine can adequately constitute the main striking force of a navy not only for holding the command of key maritime areas "in dispute" against a stronger enemy but even for gaining and maintaining a temporary command of the sea in some areas vital to the Soviet Union.

Even more remarkable was that, once he had credited the submarine with having succeeded the battleship at one time, he went on to state that the submarine in turn had been supplanted by the aircraft carrier. Taken in the Soviet context, this was heady stuff indeed for 1948! Captain First Rank Andreyev was not only denigrating the submarine in defiance of military doctrine but was also advocating the construction of aircraft carriers. And he was doing so to a readership of senior Army officers in an article that presumably represented the general views of the Navy. Remarkable indeed! This was more daring than even Admiral Alafuzov's article in the same Armed Forces' General Staff journal in August 1946. In it Alafuzov had dropped comments favorable to gaining a general command of the sea that he had included in his largely identical April-May 1946 *Naval Digest* article and replaced them with comments extolling aircraft carriers and elaborating his zones-of-defense thesis. Yet for all Alafuzov's outspokeness, he had not ventured to diminish the importance of the submarine vis-a-vis the aircraft carrier.

All this strengthens the speculation, voiced earlier, that the never-released postwar issues of *Naval Digest* contained a debate over the validity and desirability of establishing a general command of the sea. Furthermore, general command of the sea was to be acquired basically by building a superior force of attack aircraft carriers, the ultimate goal of Soviet naval development. The appearance of such a pro-carrier statement by a senior naval officer in *Military Thought* suggests that, as of 1948 at least, the idea was not only ascendant in the Navy but was being insistently urged on the Army and Party by the naval leadership.

Andreyev ended his article by alleging both that the United States had "adopted a law in October 1945 requiring the development of a navy superior in forces to those of all of the other countries of the world together" and the (more supportable) claim that the United States was "exerting itself to establish a network of naval and air bases all over the world." (p. 64) The implication seemed manifest that the Soviet Union should match, if not exceed, this effort—or provide the Navy with enough "floating air bases" to compensate for having so few overseas bases.

Mahan's Command-of-the-Sea Views Criticized. The second of the four articles on British and American naval doctrine attempted to discredit Mahan's theory of command of the sea.[55] Carrying the polemical title, "The Reactionary Nature of American Naval Doctrine," the article alleged that the United States had set the goal of gaining a general command of the sea (gospodstvo na more) that would give it "a commanding position in the world." Andreyev's claim that the United States was building a navy greater than those of all of the rest of the countries of the world combined was repeated, although in substantially modified form. The United States was said to be aiming at "a navy superior in its power to any adversary or any coalition." This navy, averred author Captain Second Rank Kulakov, would be kept "concentrated in a single strike force assigned the mission of gaining command of the sea." The command-of-the-sea theory as a whole was roundly condemned as essentially imperialistic, even racist, and as one propounded by Mahan and being propagated at the time by Walter Lippman as essential to American security at sea.

If taken at face value, this article was just a routine anti-American propaganda piece. However, its theme and timing (during a lively debate on command of the sea) suggest otherwise. More likely it was intended to underpin a postwar Navy campaign to incorporate the limited command-of-the-sea concept into Soviet military doctrine.

The Soviet School's Limited-Command Theory Denounced. The third of these four articles was signed by a well-known Russian naval historian, Rear Admiral Piterskiy and appeared in *Military Thought* in July 1949.[56] Entitled "American Views on the Role and Missions of a Navy in War," the article portrayed the United States as bent on gaining general command of the sea and of the world itself with aircraft carrier task forces. He also asserted the "absolute impossibility of the United States' gaining a general command of the sea as long as its adversary has submarines and aviation." (p. 75)[57] Piterskiy described U.S. naval strategy for general war in terms implying that it had been designed explicitly to overcome the Soviet Union's naval opposition at sea. The U.S. Navy would, in general, aim at nothing less than the destruction of the Soviet Navy in order to gain an "undivided command of the sea." (p. 81) In particular, Piterskiy implied, it would thwart any Soviet efforts to apply the limited command-of-the-sea concept by applying a basic principle which the U.S. Navy had adopted of concentrating forces in key areas "and in strength several times superior to that of the enemy." (p. 80) More specifically, even in Soviet home waters (where the Soviet Union planned to provide strong forces and a good base infrastructure in peacetime to establish "zones of permanent command"), the small combatant ships stationed there would not be able to oppose the carrier strike forces effectively enough to "make the operations of large combatants difficult, even in direct proximity to the coast" of the Soviet Union. (p. 77)[58]

In effect, Piterskiy seemed to be advocating that the limited command-of-the-sea concept be dropped as inadequate and a dangerous delusion. The Soviets should rely on the existing light forces (mainly submarines, aircraft, and fast surface-craft) plus the few available large combatant ships to deter or weaken U.S. naval forces as much as possible until the Soviet Union could build strong fleets of aircraft carriers to match those of the United States. This view, in its essentially fleet-in-being nature for the short-term, (basically Old School for the long-term) seemed to counter the evolving composite Soviet School strategy that had produced the limited-command concept in its effort to synthesize the most applicable tenets of both the Old and Young Schools.

Piterskiy's article also was noteworthy for giving a second inkling in the postwar era of the fleet-against-the-shore versus fleet-against-fleet theory of naval strategy noted first in Eremeyev's article in the June-July 1945 issue of *Military Thought*. This strategy was to be fully explicated for the nuclear era by Gorshkov in *Izvestia* on 19 May 1963. Admiral Nimitz, then U.S. chief of Naval Operations, was accurately quoted as having said that "the function of a navy is the projection of military power onto the territory of an enemy." (p. 77)

Corbett's Views on Command of the Sea Criticized. The fourth and final article on command of the sea, available in the Soviet open literature of the 1948-1949 period appeared in *Red Star* in August 1949 over the signature of another established naval historian, Captain First Rank Mil'gram.[59] It employed the same highly polemical style of the *Red Star* article of seven months earlier by Captain Second Rank Kulakov, which had attacked Mahan and the U.S. command-of-the-sea doctrine. Mil'gram's article, entitled "The Insolvency and Reactionary Nature of British Naval Theory," attacked Colomb, Corbett, and British command-of-the-sea doctrine in general. The use in the titles of both of these *Red Star* articles of "Reactionary Nature" to separately describe U.S. and British naval doctrine suggests that they were intended as companion pieces.

According primary attention to Sir Julian Corbett's modifications of Colomb's theories on command of the sea, Mil'gram derided the former's conclusion that the ultimate aim of warfare at sea was to gain full and permanent command of the sea, even at the expense of all other missions, including cooperation with the ground forces, protection for the transit and debarkation of amphibious landings, and protection of communications.[60] Mil'gram most notably professed to view command of the sea as only a means to the end of supporting the Army's coastal flanks rather than an end in itself for gaining a general command of the sea to ensure the success of other missions. Unlike Andreyev's 1948 article in *Military Thought*, Mil'gram did not spell out for the less sophisticated readership of *Red Star* that the end sought was just a limited command of the sea for long enough to conduct individual Army-flank support operations.

Corbett's views were condemned on both theoretical and evidential grounds. His theoretical views were held to be fallacious for their "idealistic basis," for allegedly being "divorced from historical development," for their "metaphysical dogmatism," and for attempting "mechanically" to transfer precepts of "the Manufacturing Period to the present." Mil'gram cited the Spanish-American and Russo-Japanese Wars as events contemporary to Corbett but whose lessons the latter allegedly had ignored.

Moreover, Corbett was said to have been wrong in his 1911 prediction that the British Navy would be able, in the coming war, to gain command of the sea by exerting control over "all general maritime communications," as Corbett was quoted as having expressed it. "Such an aim," Mil'gram observed, "of course was not achieved." Due to their "erroneous doctrines," British naval efforts in preparation for the war had been "falsely directed," the failure to have prepared antisubmarine forces being cited in this regard. As a result, the battleships and cruisers of the Grand Fleet remained "virtually inactive" (at Scapa Flow) and protected by "coastal installations, minefields, and light surface forces." Any such employment by a stronger navy of the fleet-in-being principle, Mil'gram opined, was predestined to fail due to the submarine threat. That he may have been using a foreign surrogate to criticize a Soviet predisposition at the time in favor of a fleet-in-being strategy is suggested by the fact that near the end of his article, Mil'gram asserted that the ideas of Colomb and Corbett were being "revived again and again abroad in works on the problems of a contemporary navy." He added in a polemical style typically Soviet:

> The striving for absolute "gospodstvo na more," for undivided "komandovanie morem," runs like a red thread through the speeches of the incendiaries of a new war who are dreaming of establishing their command worldwide.

As has been noted with regard to other Soviet writings, it is normal procedure for naval and military authors to avoid censorship by attributing to foreign sources ideas or events in the Soviet Union. While the charge was not so patently false as to be obvious, it was sufficiently exaggerated as to suggest to informed readers that Mil'gram was really referring to a situation at home. An underlying aim of this and the companion piece on the "reactionary nature" of the American command-of-the-sea theory might have been to pressure the neo-Old School proponents. This school wanted to build a navy with the intent of eventually gaining a general command of the sea. But if they gave up their long-range aims, they could lend more support and credibility to the limited "command-of-the-sea" doctrine that was deemed necessary for the time being as the least incredible of the available alternative strategies.

Mil'gram's article also contained several noteworthy remarks about the Army, the implications of which merit consideration. First, he accused Corbett of having divided strategy into naval strategy and military-ground strategy, and, by use of such a bureaucratic gambit, had managed to pit the Navy and Army against each other. Again, in the context of the very frequent use of foreign surrogates by Soviet military and naval writers, the suspicion is warranted that Mil'gram was referring to an Army-Navy interservice rivalry within the Soviet Defense Ministry. Judging from the tenor of Mil'gram's charge and from similar situations previously described in the Soviet military and naval literature, Mil'gram appears to have been implicitly criticizing those in the Navy (and perhaps a few senior officers in the Army) who favored a separate naval strategy. This strategy would be a way of ensuring that the Navy could pursue the independent naval missions of defeating the enemy's naval forces first to gain general command of the sea (at least in the peripheral seas) before undertaking the conduct of other missions, especially for cover and support of coastal ground forces.

A Postwar Stalinist Carrier Construction Program? There is no direct, reliable evidence that the Soviet Union ever programmed the construction of any aircraft carriers in the Stalinist postwar period. But according to Shadrin,[61] a former Soviet naval officer, there was a program for the construction of at least four aircraft carriers approved no later than mid-1951 but cancelled by Stalin in 1952.[62] According to this source, a postwar Soviet naval construction program approved in 1947 was amended in 1950-1951 to add four or more carriers.[63] Shadrin also reported that in the fall of 1951 Admiral Kuznetsov told audiences of naval officers in Riga and Baltiysk that "in the not-too-distant future, the Soviet Union would start the construction of aircraft carriers" and that they would "enable us to operate in the open sea."[64] To his receptive listeners, including Shadrin at the Riga meeting, the mere fact that the Navy minister would make such a public announcement was interpreted by his audience to indicate beyond doubt that Stalin personally had given his assent to a carrier-construction program.[65]

According to the same source, construction of the first carriers was not scheduled to begin until after completion of several *Stalingrad*-class heavy cruisers—and these were said by Shadrin to have been only 50 percent completed in 1954.[66] It appears probable, however, that Stalin himself had deleted the carriers from the program in 1952—only a year after he had given the Navy at least oral approval for a carrier program once the *Stalingrad*-class cruisers were completed.[67] If true, this was a repeat performance of Stalin's late prewar initial approval and subsequent cancellation of carriers programmed to start only after the prior construction of a number of heavy cruisers. At any rate, Shadrin gave as the reasoning behind Stalin's cancellation of the carrier-construction program in 1952 that the Soviet Union lacked the "economics and time" that would be required— that "eight to ten years would be needed to build them and train pilots." It was also decided that it would be "better to have more 6,000-7,000-ton ships than [just] a few large [i.e., attack] carriers".[68] This last comment suggests that the carriers whose construction was reported to have been cancelled in 1952 by Stalin were attack carriers and that the program probably also included more than four light aircraft carriers of 6,000 to 7,000 tons.

In his memoirs, while talking about Stalin's unvarying lack of enthusiasm for building aircraft carriers, Admiral Kuznetsov added onto the end of a description of Stalin's cancellation of the 1937 carrier-construction program that "somewhat later" Stalin had personally cancelled first the large carriers and then the small ones.[69] This could conceivably have been a deliberately esoteric reference to Stalin's *postwar* (rather than prewar) cancellation of attack carriers in 1952 and of the 6,000-to-7,000-ton light carriers sometime later.

Insights from a 1953 History of Naval Theory. The last part of a three-volume work, *A History of Naval Art*,[70] which was prepared during Stalin's final years, appeared too soon after his death in March 1953 to have undergone any substantial revision.[71] In fact, it included a number of examples of the gross flattery that characterized the so-called Stalinist cult of personality.[72] Importantly for this study, this naval war college textbook had much to say about command-of-the-sea theory and other aspects of the Navy's official views on naval warfare at the end of the Stalinist postwar period.

The Classical Old School Views of Mahan and Colomb Criticized. The *History* tendentiously interpreted both Mahan and Colomb on command of the sea as only requiring an overwhelming superiority of forces concentrated in a sea or in a particular region of one. This misinterpretation seemed clearly enough to reflect the limited command-of-the-sea concept of the Soviet School of naval warfare. This rewriting of history minimized the obstacles to a weaker navy's winning a war at sea, particularly glossing over the fact that it is usually necessary to *fight* to gain command in any contested area at sea. (p. 7) As in the prewar period, the weakness of the Soviet Navy relative to its putative adversaries found its theoretical expression in the *History's* denial that the "general engagement" of classical sea-power theory and practice could ever recur.

Rear Admiral Piterskiy wanted to dissociate command-of-the-sea theory *per se* from Mahan and Colomb and the "colonialist" ends for which they allegedly had contributed the rationales. Therefore he claimed that the theory itself actually had originated three centuries before Mahan and Colomb while the "general engagement" had been taken over directly from the "ideologist of the Prussian-Junkers, the idealist Clausewitz." Ironically, considering that every effort was made to discredit Colomb's views, it was he who was cited as the authority who had made temporary command of the sea a viable concept.[73]

Falling back on a debating-point subterfuge that the Young School had used in the late 1920s, the *History* declared the command-of-the-sea theory of Mahan and Colomb to be unsound and unscientific because of its allegedly faulty methodology. No evidence was given to support this charge but since of course Marxist-Leninist methodology had not been used by Colomb perhaps it was considered to be an open-and-shut case for which any evidence would have been superfluous.

Methodology aside, the concept of command of the sea not only was said to be still valid but also to play a big role in naval warfare to "ensure the success of combat actions at sea." Of course, having here distorted the meaning of the term "command of the sea" to merely that of a local superiority of naval forces, the *History* may be seen to have misappropriated this time-honored term. In this way the concept would not be intolerably offensive to the Army, and ultimately would be expandable to embrace command of the sea, at least in the naval TVDs important to the defense of the Homeland against seaborne attack. It would also permit Navy publicists to discourse like the dominant sea power while obscuring the fact that they had set up a theoretical construct for the evasion of battle (except when unavoidable to protect Soviet shores from assault or to provide essential support to major operations of the ground forces).

The Classical Young School of Admiral Aube Criticized. In a short critique of the original French Jeune Ecole of Admiral Aube of the 1880s, the Young School was noted to have been essentially a cheap way out for a country whose economy could not afford to build a powerful navy of capital ships. This was claimed to have been perfectly correct under the circumstances but the emphasis placed on light, fast forces by the Young School was faulted for its one-sidedness in not realizing that a navy cannot carry out the missions likely to be assigned it unless it has "large ships as well as small ones."[74]

Young School Adherents of the Tsarist Navy. Interestingly, Admiral Stephan O. Makarov was claimed to have been the leading Russian Young School contemporary and follower of Admiral Aube in the last two decades of the 19th century. Remembered with respect for his writings on tactics, Makarov is favorably cited in the *History* for "warning against overestimating the importance of capital ships and the general engagement." (p. 8) Yet he is criticized for having entertained "the erroneous view" that a navy should be composed "only of small, unarmored, fast ships with powerful guns." (p. 17)

The Soviet School force composition being advocated implicitly was one between the Old and Young Schools at the point that large ships could be retained or even constructed—not to fight a major, decisive battle (at least not for the time being) but to provide support to light, fast Young School-type forces, particularly submarines and planes, that would constitute the main forces of a fleet. This conclusion is supported by a further comment that "Makarov viewed battle at sea not as a gunnery duel among a number of capital ships but as warfare of the heterogeneous forces of a navy." (p. 67) The word "heterogeneous" (besides its dictionary meaning of mixed) had come to imply in Soviet naval usage the need for big surface-ships including aircraft carriers allegedly (only) to afford "combat stability" to the main striking forces of the small, fast naval force types. Hence Makarov was praised gratuitously for this view attributed to him, that war at sea was a fight between all kinds of naval forces—not just capital ships. He was said to have been "far ahead of his contemporaries" in this and so to have made "an important contribution to the development of naval art." (Never mind that he had been criticized for having dispensed with capital ships entirely.)

Apparently speaking of the decade between Makarov's death in 1904 at Port Arthur and the outbreak of World War I, the *History* described as an insignificant group those officers in the Tsarist Russian Navy who "propagated another unscientific and harmful view of naval theory besides that of Mahan and Colomb"—that "battleships had lost their importance as the result of the advent of submarines, destroyers, and minefields." Obviously speaking of the unnamed Young School successors to Admiral Makarov in the Tsarist Navy, these anonymous officers were condemned for having opposed the construction of big ships. (p. 123) In the part of the *History* that treated the Russo-Japanese War, the same point was made somewhat differently:

> Admiral Makarov, being an opponent of the Anglo-American theory of "command of the sea" and understanding that the outcome of the war would be decided by the aggregate actions of the ground forces and the naval forces, knew better than the others how to evaluate the situation and assigned the fleet the mission of supporting the Army (p. 107).

Army-Flank Support and Maneuvering Bases. Similarly, a main conclusion drawn by the *History* from the Russo-Japanese War emphasized the importance of the Army-flank support mission:

> The experience of the Russo-Japanese War unquestionably showed that the final aim of war is achieved as the result of mutual cooperation by all services of the armed forces (in this case, by armies and navies).

> Mutual cooperation of the army and navy enabled the Japanese high command to effect a concentration and deployment of ground forces in the theater and to support the expansion of the system of basing of the Japanese Navy—which created favorable strategic and operational conditions for warfare on land and at sea (p. 107).

In additional examples of the recurrent mention of the Navy's allegedly primary mission for support of the coastal flank of the ground forces, von Tirpitz was criticized for his purported failure "to relate the conduct of military actions at sea to military actions ashore" and Corbett was similarly faulted for having "only formalistically acknowledged the existence of a *unified* strategy of the armed forces and indeed for having opposed naval strategy to military strategy." (p. 120)

While the implication in the above quotation that the Japanese Army captured one or more bases for naval use is false, use of the "favorable-conditions" expression is a common Soviet euphemism for "command of the sea." This quotation is particularly interesting for its allusion to "expansion of the system of basing" which may be read as an implicit reference to the recurrent theme that expansion of an inferior navy's zone of permanent command (largely by acquiring advanced bases) is the proper aim for naval warfare. This thought was implied in the above quotation by the historically inaccurate reference to the Japanese High Command's having employed ground forces to "support the expansion of the system of bases of the Japanese Navy." Gaining new bases almost automatically expands the sea area that a navy can bring under permanent command by virtue of a new forward (maneuvering) base from which daily combat activity in the forms of antisubmarine-warfare patrols, surveillance, minesweeping, etc., can maintain superiority in the vicinity of the base— provided only that the necessary naval forces are available.

Classical Command-of-the-Sea Theory Criticized and the Navy's Lobbying for Carriers Evidenced.

> The experience of the Russo-Japanese War showed the unsoundness of the reactionary Anglo-American theory of Mahan and Colomb, both in the matter of the aims of war at sea as well as with regard to the means and methods for its conduct. They asserted that the aim of war was command of the sea. Yet, in the course of the Russo-Japanese War neither of the belligerents viewed command of the sea as the aim of the war. Consequently, the actions of the fleets from the very first day of the war were directed not at warfare for command of the sea but at cooperation with the army—because precisely that led to the accomplishment of the aims of the war (p. 108).

Here we are implicitly informed that (as of 1953) command of the sea was still not considered the proper aim for the Navy—that support of the Army still had to be accepted as the top priority mission. To what extent the view was actually shared by the naval authors of *A History of Naval Art* or had been dictated by a tenet of the Soviet Union's unified military doctrine is not apparent from the *History*. However, we have Admiral Gorshkov's subsequent testimony in *Sea Power of the State* that the requirement rankled deeply.[75]

Evidence of the Soviet Navy's lobbying for construction of aircraft carriers appeared in the *History* so shortly after Stalin's death that its esoterically formulated pitch may be seen to have reflected the constraints on open advocacy for any program looked on with disfavor by Stalin. If indeed there had been a postwar program for construction of four aircraft carriers, Stalin himself must have cancelled it. The *History* contained two widely separated passages that may be seen as implicit advocacy of attack-carrier construction.

Immediately after condemning officers who opposed the construction of big surface combatant ships, the book made the not unwarranted claim that the Tsarist Russian Navy had taken the lead "in the development and practical employment" of seaplanes and aircraft carriers in the decade between the Russo-Japanese War of 1904-1905 and the outbreak of World War I in 1914. (p. 124)[76] Further on in the book is the surprising assertion that the design and construction of aircraft carriers and carrier aircraft had been accorded continuous priority in Navy planning. (p. 315) These two statements smacked strongly of the long-standing Navy line up until Stalin's death, that carriers had become indispensable for naval warfare. The implied message was that the Soviet "Government" (i.e., Stalin alone, for all practical purposes), should get on with building a number of aircraft carriers. Certainly no other evidence supports the claim that the Soviet Union had ever gotten around to the actual construction—or even to the keel laying—of one.

A Fleet-in-Being Strategy in the Early 1950s? In a paragraph purportedly describing "progressive" Tsarist Russian naval thinking before World War I, the *History* endorsed a strategy for naval warfare that lends itself well to the interpretation that it constituted a modernized and tactically offensive active fleet-in-being:

> In the Russian Navy arose the progressive idea of developing a defense-in-depth in a naval theater composed of fortified regions and mine-artillery positions. This served as the basis for a theory of battle in a previously infrastructured position in a coastal region with the cooperation of the heterogeneous forces and means of a navy (p. 124).[77]

Regardless of whether this was an accurate portrayal of Tsarist naval thought presented in the *History* as having been held by Makarov, the fact that such a description was given in a naval textbook at the end of the Stalinist postwar period and labeled as "progressive" provides some not inconsequential support for the conclusion that an active fleet-in-being strategy had been in effect in the early 1950s when the book was written. Moreover, further support is given to such a conclusion by what *A History of Naval Art* said about Sir Julian Corbett's views on the fleet-in-being strategy. Not only is this of intrinsic interest for this study but merits particular attention in view of the working hypothesis adopted at the outset of this chapter, namely that the Soviet Union, in the Stalinist postwar period, was following such a strategy along the lines formulated by Corbett. The *History* made the following substantive comments on Corbett's fleet-in-being concept:

> Besides the general engagement and blockade, Corbett recommended for achieving the aims of war at sea utilization of the "fleet-in-being" principle in combination with "small, active operations." He viewed this method for the conduct of war as a natural one for a weaker navy conducting a defense at sea (p. 121).

> However, the British [in World War I] utilized this method not only and solely when it was the weaker adversary but also when it was the stronger and was a member of a coalition and pursuing the aim of withholding its fleet to the moment of concluding peace.

The "active" aspects of a "fleet-in being" were its "small, active operations." Corbett understood this as employing what is called "auxiliary" forces and means against the main forces of an adversary. He assigned destroyers, submarines, torpedoes, and mines to these ["auxiliary" forces and means].

The fallacy of the method of "small, active operations" lies in its denial of mutual cooperation, which is the basis of military action . . . and also in its counterposing destroyers and submarines up against battleships and cruisers.

Despite the obvious groundlessness of this theory of Corbett's, the British Admiralty accepted the basic tenets of this theory as official doctrine in the First World War and mistakenly oriented the construction and combat training of its navy on it. For example, increasingly developing the construction of capital ships, the British did not give enough attention to the construction of light forces, which experience had shown were destined to play a major role in the war. Preparing to defend their sea communications against the enemy's surface ships, the British Navy showed itself to be completely unprepared for antisubmarine warfare—whose importance Corbett had underestimated. The experience of the First World War showed that the British Navy's doctrine as a whole did not withstand the test and suffered complete collapse (p. 122).

Several analytical comments are in order to test the evidence from the 1953 (first) edition of *A History of Naval Art* against our hypothesis that the Soviet Union under Stalin was following a fleet-in-being strategy, at least at the time of his death when *A History of Naval Art* was completed:

• While the *History's* description of Corbett's views on the fleet-in-being strategy was less explicit and informative than Admiral Alafuzov's article in the last issue of *Naval Digest* for 1946, both sources were recognizably talking about the same concept. This suggests that such a strategy may have been in effect throughout the Stalinist postwar period.

• The History failed to mention the gut distinction that Alafuzov's treatment had made—that the basic aim of a fleet-in-being strategy is to allow a weaker navy to keep the command of the strategically important regions of the key naval theaters "in dispute" and thereby deny the enemy free use for his own naval operations and shipping.

• Although the *History* describes the fleet-in-being theory of Corbett as one of obvious groundlessness, it is noteworthy that the only substantive criticisms either lacked definitiveness or were wholly irrelevant.

• The first was the criticism of small, active operations as "fallacious" on the grounds that they denied mutual cooperation and set light forces against the enemy's big ships. This likely was a way of saying that Corbett did not provide either for naval missions to be limited to those for Army-flank cover and support or for the big ships to function to support light forces. Whatever the intent, this was not a criticism of the fleet-in-being concept *per se* but just of the missions and tactics Corbett was said to have favored for implementing the strategy. In this regard, one is strongly reminded of the frequent criticism of the "general engagement" of Mahan and Colomb whenever it was expedient to criticize "bourgeois" theory (as is the case throughout the *History*), but doing so without discrediting the general command-of-the-sea theory which had been coopted to serve the limited Soviet ends.

• The second criticism was that the British had not commensurately increased the construction of light forces while expanding capital-ship construction. This was neither a valid criticism of British shipbuilding policy nor of relevance here. It obviously does not speak to the merits of a fleet-in-being strategy *qua* strategy.

• The third criticism regarding Corbett's reputed underestimation of antisubmarine warfare (and by implication the large number of "light forces" it necessitates) only concerns implementation rather than the strategy itself.

• The nature of the criticisms of the fleet-in-being strategy may be seen from the above to have been limited to the ways and means of its allegedly poor execution in practice. A reader gets the impression that if these details had been tidied up and if it were employed by a strong but weaker navy, as Corbett was said to have intended it (rather than by a stronger navy, as the Royal Navy in World War I), the fleet-in-being strategy could be expected to work like a charm! Whatever the intent of the description of Corbett's conception of fleet-in-being strategy and the British efforts to implement it, there seems to have been a detectable reluctance—similar to that exhibited with regard to the command-of-the sea concept—to damn it in perpetuity.

The Soviet School on the Relative Importance of Light Forces and Large Ships. In the final chapter of the *History* the lessons of World War I were summarized. One of the most important was formulated as a "sharp increase in the importance of light forces and submarines." Capital ships were said to have suffered only a relative loss of importance. The overall results for world shipbuilding were stated with general accuracy to be an increase in the rate of construction of light forces and submarines while the battleships and battle cruisers that had not been completed at the outbreak of war were said to either have been completed at a slow rate or "mothballed." As mentioned above, the "design and construction of naval aircraft and aircraft carriers" was said revealingly to have been accorded (continuous) priority in the Soviet Navy.[78] The Soviet School preference for combining light forces with big ships for support of the light forces was reflected in a statement that the heterogeneous forces of navies increased along with a relative increase in the light forces.

Additional Key Conclusions from the History. Ten other significant conclusions as to further changes in military strategy for naval warfare were averred to have been brought about by "the rapid development of combat forces and means" as well as their mass introduction into naval operations during World War I. As will be seen, none of these alleged changes were inconsistent with the working hypothesis adopted at the outset of this study's consideration of the postwar Stalinist period, that an active fleet-in-being doctrine was in effect.

First, the large number of naval forces involved were claimed to have made it impossible to achieve strategic aims by means of a single battle (i.e., by a Mahanian general engagement). Rather, war at sea was inaccurately claimed to have been characterized by "an increase in [the scale and number of] combat clashes and the further development of daily combat actions." The reputed increase in the number of small-scale (and hence indecisive) combat clashes and of daily combat actions was said to have necessitated organization of a "comprehensive and sophisticated system of successive and simultaneous combat actions." (p. 315)

Second, the experience of World War I was said to have demonstrated the necessity of providing "support" to every kind of combat action at sea, and in particular to "operations" [i.e., to those actions conducted outside a navy's "zone of permanent command of the sea"]. A frequently used euphemism for a limited command of the sea, "favorable operational regime," was employed to state that "the aim of daily combat activity was to create a favorable operating regime in the region of one's bases and coasts and also in the region of combat activity." (p. 316)

Third, the *History* summarized the missions seen as having been performed by navies in World War I, whether by daily combat actions (in coastal zones of "permanent command") or by operations (beyond those coastal zones). These missions were listed as:

(1) "Destruction of the forces of the enemy at sea;
(2) Cutting off an adversary's sea communications;
(3) Protection of one's own sea communications;
(4) Conducting amphibious landings;
(5) Gunfire and air support of the coastal flanks of ground forces; and,
(6) Laying of minefields and minesweeping." (p. 316)

It merits noting that the classical Mahanist method advocated by the Old School for gaining command of the sea by destroying the enemy navy was listed ahead of the *guerre de course* favored by the Young School.

The fourth of the lessons relevant to this study was that World War I was said to have brought the appearance of "the first efforts to organize the mutual cooperation of heterogeneous forces and the weakening of the adversary in the period of operational deployment by means of preliminary strikes." (p. 317)[79] The *History* continued in its conclusions to avoid use of the term "command of the sea," which it had been at such pains to discredit, although only superficially. It was still clear from the choice of the word for "weakening" [oslableniye] in the overall context of Soviet naval writings that the preliminary strikes were intended to perform the "force-equalization" function just in the areas of intended naval operations to provide the temporary superiority that the Soviet School theoreticians prefer to call "command of the sea in a region of a naval theater or even [just] in a sector of one."

A fifth point made by *A History of Naval Art* related to the methods employed in World War I for conducting the antishipping mission. These were listed as: (1) blockade; (2) action by surface raiders; (3) action by submarines; (4) laying minefields; and, (5) naval bombardment and efforts to bottle up ports. The third method was emphasized as a new and basic method for cutting off sea communications but was said to have revealed a major shortcoming in submarines' lack of mutual cooperation with the other forces of a navy. It was parenthetically indicated that the Russian Navy had recognized the problem during the war and had managed to effect a few exceptions, although no examples were given. Of particular relevance for later developments of the Navy under Gorshkov was the award of pride of place to the naval blockade as the leading method for the conduct of an antishipping campaign.

A sixth point elaborated on the nature of the blockade advocated. Warfare on sea communications in the First World War was said to have evolved a new method for carrying out the antishipping mission: "action [attack] along the entire length of the adversary's sea lines of communication" (rather than just a cordon or perimeter blockade of the ports involved, apparently). Also mentioned as new developments in the methods of naval warfare were the cooperation of naval aircraft with other naval forces against shipping, the shift to "systematic [daily combat] actions," and the efforts said to have been made to employ heterogeneous forces. Since these efforts did not amount to much, the fact that the authors of the *History* even mentioned them suggests that they wanted to imply the Soviet Navy's postwar preference for construction of big ships, including aircraft carriers, to support the submarines, as indicated by the "heterogeneous-forces" euphemism.

A seventh point of note in the conclusions of the *History* on the lessons to be learned from the 1914-1918 war was that the sea blockade, although it had not proved itself a "universal method for war at sea," had changed (from close or distant blockade) to a new form, one "echeloned-in-depth." This new form presumably was not unrelated to the new method described above of "action along the entire length" of an adversary's sea lines of communication but no effort to relate the two was made.

Yet an eighth point meriting mention was what the *History* said about "mutual cooperation" of navies and armies during the Russo-Japanese War. Alleging that at the start of the war "not a single navy was trained in mutual cooperation with ground forces," it was asserted that "during the course of the war practically all navies came to act together with [their respective] armies." This carried the implicit allegation that the main role of navies already had shifted significantly from fleet-against-fleet fighting for command of the sea to providing fleet-against-the-shore support for coastal ground forces—and hence to requiring command of the sea just as a means to the latter end. While "the naval forces of all states provided gunfire support to the coastal flanks of ground forces both on the offensive and on the defensive, the widest application of this type of combat action took place in the Russian theaters." (p. 12)

The importance of "mutual cooperation" (vzaimodeystviya) with the Army ground forces in coastal sectors is the proverbial Russian "red thread" throughout the *History*, appearing no less than eight times in contexts relevant to this study. Of particular interest is the *History's* criticism at its outset of the command-of-the-sea theory of Mahan and Colomb as having called for navies to act "independently" of the other armed services. (p. 67) From our earlier investigation of this subject it is clear that the Navy was forever having to assure the Army marshals and other field officers that—perish the thought— the last thing that would cross an admiral's mind would be any glimmer of a general command-of-the-sea doctrine involving missions independent of the Soviet ground forces or of any Navy lobbying effort to win Party approval of the outsized naval forces and budgets that would be entailed.

A ninth lesson of World War I was the conclusion that in actuality "naval battles had happened not as single, decisive general engagements" in accordance with the view ascribed to Mahan, but "as a sequence of clashes not coincident in place and time." The sea battles that had taken place in 1914-1918 were categorized into four classes: the "offensive battle at sea" (presumably only the Battle of Jutland, if even that, which in form was a "meeting engagement"; the meeting engagement (using the same term as for land warfare [vstrechnyi boi] and apparently the category intended to include the sequence of clashes mentioned above which was said to have replaced the single, decisive general engagement of Mahanian theory); the "defensive battle"; and the "battle on a fortified position or in a coastal region." (p. 318) The last category was the one presented as most typical of the Russian naval activity in World War I (although more true in the Baltic than in the Black Sea) and fits comfortably into the fleet-in-being hypothesis which involves an inferior Russian Navy striving to prevent its ships from being blockaded in port by holding the command of its port approaches and coastal areas in dispute by constantly "active" (i.e., offensive) tactics to defend "naval positions."

Finally to be noted as a tenth and last key point of *A History of Naval Art* for the investigation of postwar Stalinist naval theory in this chapter are two deprecatory comments about the view that World War I would be a short war. The first criticized both the Army and Navy commands on the German side for having "incorrectly oriented their forces for a short war." The second reference, which appeared in the final conclusions regarding the lessons of World War I, made the same point but in the context of four "substantiated facts indicative of a crisis in bourgeois military and naval theory" that allegedly had resulted in the complete miscarriage of "all the more important tenets of bourgeois military theory advanced on the eve of World War I by Schlieffen, Tirpitz, Foch, Mahan, Colomb, Corbett, and others." These were:

- "Failure of the prewar plans in the very first year of the war";
- "The error of having planned for a short war";
- "The positional dead end on the ground front . . ."; and,
- "The miscarriage of the Anglo-American doctrine of 'command of the sea' and of the German naval doctrine of 'small war.'"(p. 217)

The fact that so much emphasis was given to condemning the belief in the possibility of a short war, although made in the context of a lesson to be learned from World War I, seems likely to have been a surrogate for voicing concern that Soviet military policy in the last Stalinist years was trending to an eventual overdependence on nuclear weapons and the expectation that their great destructive power would necessarily make any third world war a very short war—with consequent neglect of the conventionally armed forces, including the Navy. It merits recalling that this same point had been made in 1948 by Captain First Rank Andreyev and apparently with the same motive.

Stalin's Negative Influence on Naval Art Denounced. In bringing the chronological exposition of developments in this chapter on the postwar Stalinist period to a close, it remains only to quote a comment by the eminent Soviet naval historian, V. Achkasov,[80] doctor of historical science:

> The achievements in the development of naval art could not, however, shield us to any degree against the errors and shortcomings committed under the influence of the [Stalinist] cult of personality in the working out of naval theory. The cult of personality hindered the progressive movement of Soviet naval art, miring it in a dogmatism alien to its creative spirit. The neglectful attitude of some naval-scientific workers to the study of the experience of the bourgeois navies was one of the manifestations of this dogmatism. The cult of personality also entailed errors in interpreting the course of combat actions at sea in the period of the Great Patriotic War.

> All of this, of course, could not but exert a negative influence on the theoretical work in the field of naval affairs. An important and responsible task confronts us under contemporary conditions—to liquidate completely the consequences of the cult of personality, to raise Soviet naval art to a new and higher level, and to enrich it with new principles based on the particularities of modern [that is, "nuclear-missile" in standard Soviet usage] combat actions at sea.

Further Analysis and Interpretation of Naval Theory, 1945-1953

The predominant role in naval warfare gained by aircraft carriers in World War II further convinced the Navy's leaders and its "official theoreticians" of the Navy's fundamental requirement for aircraft carriers if its surface forces were ever to be capable of fighting beyond the narrow coastal strip of 100 miles or so in which shore-based planes could provide fairly continuous air cover. This requirement was testified to by not only the two wartime chiefs of the Navy's Main Staff, Fleet Admiral Isakov and Admiral Alafuzov, but also by three of the Naval War College's most distinguished theorists, Professors Chernyshev, Belli, and Pavlovich.

Moreover, the Navy's case for aircraft carriers was made in the pages of the Armed Forces' General Staff journal, *Military Thought*, apparently by a naval aviator, Colonel Schner. In addition, the incomparable capabilities of aircraft carriers for defeating enemy naval forces, for supporting amphibious landings, and generally for gaining and maintaining command of the sea were spelled out in convincing detail by Captain-Lieutenant Razumnyi's account of the operations from 1941 to 1945 of the Japanese and U.S. carrier forces in the Pacific.

Such open advocacy of constructing aircraft carriers was no longer politically safe by the time Stalin died in March 1953, perhaps because the "Great Leader" had recently cancelled a postwar construction program for four carriers that he had initially sanctioned in deference to Admiral Kuznetsov's importuning. Nevertheless, the third volume of *A History of Naval Art*, published at that time as the official textbook on naval theory, contained clear if indirect evidence of the Navy's continuing desire for carriers: the Navy was claimed to have been first to employ such ships in wartime (in World War I) and to have never ceased designing and programming carriers for construction—implying that the blame for the Navy's still having *none* of the most important of all surface-ship types should be laid on shoulders other than those of the Navy's leaders.

Apparently resuming an unpublicized interwar theoretical discussion of fleet-against-the-shore operations as contrasted with the normally more frequent fleet-against-fleet actions, Captain Third Rank Eremeyev asserted in a mid-1945 article in *Military Thought* that World War II had brought a shift of the majority of naval operations to the former from the latter. That is, they had shifted from (major) sea battles and antishipping blockades to Army-flank cover-and-support operations, most notably to amphibious invasion operations.

Naval general engagements were acknowledged still to occur but were claimed to be of "ever decreasing importance in the general system of operations." Consequently, Eremeyev implied, gaining command of the sea (as the aim of general naval engagements and blockades in fleet-against-fleet operations) had changed from constituting an end in itself to being just the means to the end of carrying out fleet-against-the shore operations in support of the Army's coastal flank. Moreover, these operations only required gaining a limited "command of the sea" in contiguous Soviet seas by concentrating superior forces successively in selected regions of a theater of military actions just long enough for a given operation.

This formulation appears to be essentially a rationalization for avoiding direct contests of strength against the Soviet Union's far stronger naval adversaries of the post-World War II world. In effect, Eremeyev's formulation adapted for the Soviet School of naval warfare Admiral Castex's recommended strategy for the inferior of two strong navies unable to fight fleet-against-fleet battles with any reasonable prospect of success: that of resorting to fleet-against-the-shore strikes (i.e. "raids," in classical terms).

Despite the stated preference for fleet-against-the shore operations as the wave of the future and the assertion that command of the sea was just the means to the end of carrying out such operations, Eremeyev's statement of four cardinal advantages accruing to the side holding that command left no doubt but that gaining command of the sea in key naval theaters of military action, or at least in the key regions of them, whenever required for planned operations ranked high on the Soviet Navy's list of priority wartime operations. Notably, forcing the enemy to depend solely on submarines for high-seas operations was one of the four advantages that had obvious application to the Soviet Navy as the side likely to be constrained in such a manner.

The only other significant reference to fleet-against-the-shore operations turned up by research of the 1945-1953 period also appeared in a *Military Thought* article by a naval officer—four years after the Eremeyev article. Rear Admiral Piterskiy, a noted naval historian, accurately cited American Admiral Chester Nimitz as having stated that "projection of power onto the territory of an enemy" was *the* "function of a navy." However, it was not to occur until 1963 that Admiral Gorshkov publicly enunciated the view that this function, as a result of "the revolution in military affairs," should be considered the emerging main role of the Soviet Navy. This Admiral Gorshkov was to assert in an article in *Izvestiya* on 19 May of that year.

All in all, the available naval and military writings for the 1945-1953 period point consistently toward the Navy's continued advocacy of a Soviet School strategy of limited command of the sea. The strategy stipulated that the extent of effective sea control need not be overall or "general" but that it would suffice to concentrate a superiority of forces in the limited area of an intended wartime operation for just the temporary period of time required to conduct that operation. Implicit in this formula was that the duration of operations undertaken by an inferior navy such as the Soviet Union's, resorting to a limited command-of-the-sea strategy in one or more regions of naval theaters of military actions (TVDs), was restricted to the minimum period that might enable the enemy to reestablish his command in the region by bringing up stronger forces. (The importance for this purpose of having a "swing" strategy of bringing in reinforcements from other theaters was noted for the first time in Soviet naval writings.)[81] Consequently, Soviet naval theorists stressed that the time available for a given operation could be maximized by achieving surprise through deception and covertness.

At the same time, several of the leading naval theoreticians, most notably Admirals Alafuzov, Belli, and Panteleyev, made it clear that the Navy entertained no serious long-range ambition to contest for global command of the sea. However, they did look forward to the day when the Navy would be provided such large naval forces of the right types, especially attack aircraft carriers, to be able in any future general war to maintain the command of the key sea and ocean areas contiguous to the Soviet Union despite the concentrated opposition of the United States and other NATO naval forces— or, otherwise to at least be able to hold the command "in dispute" in such areas. It was apparent that the construction of aircraft carriers was being advocated solely on the basis of their potential use in the naval TVDs peripheral to the Soviet Union. Carriers would aid in eventually gaining and maintaining "strategic command of the sea" in those TVDs. Justification did not seem to stem from an intention eventually to challenge the general sea supremacy of the Western alliance throughout the "World Ocean" but from a need to protect the Soviet Union from seaborne attack.

It was this preferred alternative of gaining command of the sea limited to just the peripheral seas that seemed to be clearly reflected in Admiral Alafuzov's several articles in 1946. The Naval War College chief stated and repeated for emphasis that the essence of naval warfare and naval strategy was to gradually expand one's "zone of command" (or of established or permanent command) until it embraced the entire naval TVDs concerned. He argued that, with proper advance preparation, a weaker navy could maintain the "command" of an extended coastal zone. He added that a stronger adversary would be forced increasingly to fight to win command in a Soviet coastal TVD and that it might require an enemy years of fighting to wrest command from Soviet forces. In other words, Alafuzov was asserting that the four Soviet fleets' capabilities for holding the "command" of Soviet home waters in dispute, even against the more powerful non-Communist world navies, would be increasing in the years to come.

Alafuzov also refuted the main argument employed by the Young School adherents ever since the late 1920s to prove the proclaimed invalidity of the command-of-the-sea doctrine. The argument ran that, because (allegedly) the two operational manifestations of command of the sea prescribed by Colomb and Mahan (the general naval engagement and the sea blockade) had been proven to be no longer valid, therefore the command-of-the-sea theory itself must be *ipso facto* invalid. Alafuzov claimed that the general engagement had been replaced by two complementary forms of naval warfare: "daily operational activity" for maintaining command of the sea within one's coastal "zone of established command" (to enable one to carry out assigned missions in that zone); and especially planned operations for gaining command of a new area initially or for expanding it subsequently (as well as for defeating enemy attempts to reestablish command in one's zone of established command). He explicitly rejected the view that the fact that the forms for gaining command of the sea (general engagement and blockade) had changed with the advent of new weapons systems meant that the basic command-of-the-sea principle had been invalidated.

In an article in the Armed Forces' General Staff journal, *Military Thought*, of August 1946, Alafuzov even took pains to disabuse that journal's senior military readership of the belief previously shared by both the Old and Young Schools that success could be achieved in a war at sea by following a strategy that established systematic evasion of battle as the norm. Rather, he stressed that the outcome of a war at sea would require actual fighting to maintain command of the sea in Soviet coastal zones of established command and that the command often would not be achievable without accepting battle that, as he put it with tactful indirection, would "cause losses to the enemy."

However, Alafuzov considered a force-equalization strategy impracticable, doubtless due to the great disparity of forces faced by the Soviet Navy. It will be recalled that, although Professor Belli favored building up the Soviet Navy so it could implement such a strategy, he had acknowledged in a June 1940 article that the German Navy then suffered too great a disparity of forces to use such a strategy against the British Navy.

In this same *Military Thought* article, Alafuzov also set out in detail a new concept involving three concentric "zones of defense" extending out from Soviet shores. In the Near Zone, just offshore out to about 100 miles, Soviet coastal craft could operate under land-based air cover and so gain and maintain the "command." The Far Zone, which extended farther out to sea beyond the Near Zone for 150 to 200 miles more, was intended primarily for operation of large surface combatant ships with limited air support and hence capable only of attempting to hold command of the sea "in dispute." Beyond lay the Open-ocean Zone, the almost exclusive domain of Soviet submarines, intended mainly for conducting warfare against merchant shipping.[82]

The Naval War College head, whose institution traditionally is expected to take the lead in the creative revision of outmoded doctrine, also commented on "the increasing role of aircraft carriers" in oceanic theaters, noting that their appearance in contemporary navies had "markedly increased the radius of action of naval air power." This remark made it appear likely that Alafuzov was an advocate of building attack aircraft carriers for the Soviet Navy. Furthermore, aircraft carriers are *the* naval-force type *par excellence* to fight for gaining and maintaining command of the sea; submarines are inherently limited to keeping the command "in dispute" by helping to deny unhindered use of the sea to an adversary but cannot by themselves ensure effective use of the seas for their own side. Alafuzov both favored aircraft carriers and believed in the gaining of theater-wide command of the sea as the proper goal of Soviet strategy for the naval side of any major war. This provides sufficient evidence for concluding that he saw the construction of attack aircraft carriers as a necessary means to the end of building a Navy that some day could expect to be able successfully to at least hold command of the sea "in dispute"— if not to gain command for itself against the powerful Western naval powers—in the maritime areas critical for defense of the Soviet Homeland against seaborne attack.

Rear Admiral Belli remained as staunch an advocate of limited command of the sea in the postwar period as he had been earlier in his formulation of Soviet School tenets. Nevertheless, he too showed signs of favoring the construction of a navy that eventually would be able to at least hold command of the sea in dispute over the full extent of the key sea theaters peripheral to the Soviet Union. Most notably, he argued, at the Naval Scientific Conference held in March 1946 at the Naval War College in Leningrad, that the main reason for the assumed invalidity of the general command-of-the-sea doctrine was that the Soviet Union lacked the productive capacity to build the big-ship navy that would be required to implement such a strategy. The seeming implication in this formula (also stated by Penzin) was that the general command-of-the-sea doctrine was not invalid *per se*. It was merely unsuitable in the postwar Stalinist period for a navy so inferior to its probable adversaries in any future war at sea that it would have been unrealistic in the extreme to have based Soviet strategy for such a war on any conceivable combination of surprise, tactical proficiency, or force-equalization-by-attrition methods.

In the prewar period, Professor Belli had surreptitiously brought limited command of the sea in from the cold by the back door after having ejected it from the front with a stream of loud invective. He did this by means of his two-part prescription of providing "preliminary support" to major operations as well as the normal "direct support." The outspoken Admiral Alafuzov scorned such subterfuge and in 1946 stated candidly that "special measures" would have to be taken to reduce a stronger adversary's forces in the intended region of operations *before* undertaking major operations (that is, "preliminary support" must be provided). That these measures of support for an operation were tantamount to gaining a limited command of the sea was made explicit by Captain First Rank Evseyev in an article in the *Naval Digest* at the end of 1946.

In a 1948 article in *Military Thought*, Captain First Rank V. Andreyev considered at length the support requirements that the Navy was required to give to Army coastal operations. Parallel with this, he maintained (on the basis of numerous historic examples) that command of the sea should not be viewed as an end in itself but rather as the means to the end of gaining temporary command in a TVD, or in a region of one, (only) when necessary to support (primarily Army-flank) operations. Among the examples cited was the 1940 German Navy's operation in seizing Norway. At the time Professor Belli had defended that operation against charges of "adventurism." However, instead of drawing the conclusion that Belli had drawn, that the Norwegian operation proved that no command of the sea was required prior to launching a major operation, Andreyev resourcefully brought that operation within the bounds of Soviet School theory by concluding that the German Navy had in actuality gained temporary (or limited) command of the sea (by its provision of support) for the operation.

Unlike Evseyev, who, in late 1946 (as described above), had equated providing adequate support for an operation with gaining a limited command of the sea, Andreyev, two years later, turned the formula around. He criticized the Young School for having taken the position that direct support (in the course of an operation) would suffice, rather than realizing the "necessity for gaining command of the sea as one of the methods of preliminary support (before the start of an operation)." Yet, whether preliminary support was viewed as a prerequisite to gaining command of the sea, as Evseyev saw it, or gaining command of the sea as one of several necessary kinds of "preliminary support," as Andreyev did, the results were the same in establishing a requirement for adequate sea control.

Andreyev gave particularly clear evidence of being mainstream Soviet School in his views by his evenhanded criticism of both the Young School and the Old School. It will be recalled that the Evseyev article in 1938 (that had heralded the birth of the Soviet School) had been characterized by its impartially virulent denunciation of both the Old and Young Schools.

In what was probably the most significant of his several thought-provoking observations, Andreyev asserted: "The place of the battleship as the main striking force in many cases was taken over [since Colomb wrote in the early 1890s] by submarines and subsequently by aircraft carriers. . . ." This was a revelation not only for its claim that the aircraft carrier had become the main striking force of navies (and seemingly for urging acceptance of this view by Army and Party leaders), but also for its assertion that the submarine was considered to have had held this role for a time but then had been superceded by the aircraft carrier.

The *Red Star* article in January 1949 by Captain Second Rank Kulakov was, on the surface, a routine, polemical exaggeration of the "imperialist threat." On closer inspection the article was notable for its allegation that the United States had set itself the goal of gaining a general command of the sea that, if achieved, would give it "a commanding position in the world." Taken in the context of the times, when a debate over the validity of command-of-the-sea theory was going on in Soviet military and naval circles, the article seemed calculated to contribute to a Navy lobbying campaign in the postwar period to replace the military doctrinal tenet that the Navy should only provide the (minimal) support required "in the main directions" of Army-flank operations with the (more force-intensive and costly) limited command-of-the-sea strategy.

A voice opposing the Soviet School's advocacy of command of the sea was heard in July 1949 in a *Military Thought* article by well-known naval historian, Rear Admiral Piterskiy. He argued implicitly that a (Young School) "mosquito-fleet" strategy should be adopted until such time as the Soviet Union could build aircraft carrier forces to match those of the United States. Piterskiy, like Kulakov earlier in the year, alleged that the United States was aiming at gaining a general command of the sea with carrier task forces. He implied that those forces made the limited command-of-the-sea strategy, which the Navy was advocating, inadequate to prevent the destruction of Soviet naval forces in view of the "basic principle" of the U.S. Navy to concentrate its forces in the contested areas "in strength several times superior to that of the enemy." That Piterskiy's stand was reflective of a Navy campaign to win approval for a program for construction of aircraft carriers to contest with the U.S. Navy for holding command of the sea "in dispute" was to become apparent four years later with publication of the third volume of *A History of Naval Art* (which Piterskiy edited).

In his article in *Red Star* in August 1949, Captain First Rank Mil'gram returned to the staple assertion of Soviet School theoreticians that command of the sea should not be viewed (in Old School terms) as an end in itself but just as the means to the end of being able to create "favorable conditions" for the successful conduct of the Soviet Navy's assigned missions. Mil'gram specified the Navy's priority mission of supporting the Army's coastal flank but did not go into the more detailed aspects of the matter, as Andreyev had in his 1948 article in *Military Thought*. Andreyev said the command of the sea to be sought was merely limited sea control of a region of a TVD for just long enough to carry out whatever mission had been assigned— missions almost invariably associated with providing cover or support to the Army's coastal flank.

In particular, Mil'gram derided Corbett's modification of Colomb—that the ultimate aim of naval warfare was to gain "full and permanent command of the sea," even at the expense of "all other missions, for example cooperation with the ground forces, protection for the transit and debarkation of amphibious landings, protection of communications, and so on." Mil'gram's condemnation of Corbett's "erroneous doctrines" may have been aimed at neo-Old School advocates (like Rear Admiral Piterskiy appears to have been) of building strong forces of aircraft carriers to match those of the United States and so thwart its alleged aim of gaining global command of the sea.

The third and final volume of *A History of Naval Art*, which Rear Admiral Piterskiy had edited and which (conveniently for our analysis) appeared at the very end of the 1945-1953 period, reveals a great deal about Soviet naval views at the close of the postwar Stalinist era. It reflected a head-in-sand approach to the necessity, accepted by the Soviet School theoreticians, to be ready to accept battle with the putatively stronger adversary in Soviet home waters. Instead, Soviet naval views seemed to return to the pre-Soviet School systematization of evasion of battle that was common to both the Old and Young Schools. By a flagrant misinterpretation of the basic tenet of Mahan and Colomb (on the inescapable necessity to either destroy or blockade an adversary), Piterskiy maintained that they only advocated a limited command-of-the-sea doctrine. The *History* grossly exaggerated the chances of a much weaker navy to win a war at sea by avoiding the unpleasant fact that it is usually necessary to fight the stronger adversary— even for limited "command."

However, this appears to have been intended as merely a short-term expedient. More important for the long term was the example of the French Young School of Admiral Aube in the 1880s as a combined foreign navy and historical surrogate. Piterskiy's *History* appeared to be lobbying for the Soviet Union, now that it had grown strong economically, to eschew such cheap solutions as the French Young School had attempted and as the Soviet Young School had advocated by building only light naval forces, and instead to build aircraft-carrier forces of sufficient size as to be able in due course to hold command of the sea "in dispute" against the U.S. Navy. In his 1949 article in *Military Thought*, Rear Admiral Piterskiy had advocated just such a shipbuilding policy to enable the Soviet Union to pursue precisely such a limited command-of-the-sea strategy. One may reasonably surmise that Piterskiy was already well along in editing the *History* when he wrote the *Military Thought* article.

At any rate, the fact that a senior naval officer was responsible for expression of such views in both the closed and august forum of the theoretical journal for the Armed Forces' General Staff and in the openly published textbook for the education of Soviet naval officers leaves little doubt of the official status of the views expressed as constituting the authoritative stand of the Soviet Navy.

The remarkable thing about it was the implicit optimism and the opportunism with which the Navy abandoned its long-fought campaign to gain doctrinal acceptance over Army opposition for even the Soviet School's limited command-of-the sea doctrine. (That would only have required the construction of small aircraft carriers to provide air cover and reconnaissance for peripheral-seas operations.) It expanded the limited-command theory considerably to one for building the numerous large carriers necessary to fight against the U.S. Navy. Stalin was known to have favored the then head of the Soviet Navy, Admiral Nikolai Kuznetsov and, at the latter's importuning, quite possibly to have approved a construction program of aircraft carriers by 1947. Whatever the case, it is certainly fair to conclude from Piterskiy's 1949 article in *Military Thought* and from his 1953 edition of *A History of Naval Art* that the Navy, in fact, was preparing the necessary theoretical justification for the anticipated construction of aircraft carriers by a strong, if "inferior," navy and their use for a neo-Old School strategy of attempting to hold the command "in dispute."

The *History* provides solid evidence of what seemed apparent from Professor Belli's formulation of the limited command-of-the-sea thesis from 1938 to 1940—that the concept was readily expandable should circumstances ever permit. By 1949, when Rear Admiral Piterskiy's article appeared in *Military Thought*, the time apparently seemed propitious to the Navy to do so, as indicated by the contents of that article.

The *History* is standard Soviet School fare, with the same evenhanded criticism of both the Old and Young Schools. Yet it is notable how skillfully the *History's* neo-Old School strategy of aiming at holding command of the sea "in dispute" with aircraft-carrier task forces after the U.S. Navy manner could be grafted onto the body of Soviet School tenets with scarcely a lesion to reveal what major surgery had been performed. However, the *History* was not revised throughout to make it consistent with the expanded strategy—quite likely because it would have been premature to do so since the *History* was intended as a textbook for educating Soviet naval officers and hence had to basically reflect the strategic tenets applicable for the near term.

Patently, the neo-Old School strategy of fighting the U.S. Navy to place command of the "World Ocean" "in dispute" was something for the future, when and if a sufficient number of attack aircraft carriers could be built, manned, trained, and brought into operation to enable the Soviet Navy to fight the U.S. Navy at sea. In the interval of the several decades that such an ambitious program would require, some interim strategy was obviously needed. Was this to continue to be the limited-command strategy for which the Navy had lobbied so long and hard to gain its acceptance by the Army and Party? Or was it to opt for a tactically "active" fleet-in-being strategy such as Piterskiy had recommended in his 1949 *Military Thought* article?

(Piterskiy had asserted that any wartime effort to implement the limited-command strategy would only lead to the destruction of the Soviet Navy inasmuch as the U.S. Navy's established strategy provided for keeping its forces concentrated in strength far superior to any possible concentration of Soviet naval forces.) It would seem that the choice had been made (or perhaps just reaffirmed?) for a near-term "active" fleet-in-being strategy— pending development of a carrier navy able to fight to hold the command "in dispute." Accordingly, it is appropriate at this juncture to go back and review the evidence developed for the 1945-1953 period on Soviet views on the "active" fleet-in-being strategy.

Admiral Alafuzov, in a *Naval Digest* article at the end of 1946, seemingly advocated that the Soviet Navy strive to hold command of the sea "in dispute" in zones of command on naval positions. It was hypothesized for testing against the subsequent evidence that Soviet military strategy for warfare at sea from 1946 to 1953 was one of a modernized, tactically offensive fleet-in-being in the sense that Corbett attributed to Nelson, of an inferior fleet kept actively in being in order to exploit its general power of holding such command "in dispute."

Of the three pieces of evidence that subsequently developed, the first was a 1948 article by Captain First Rank Andreyev criticizing the early Old School advocates for their insistence that the Navy must have a sizeable enough battle force of capital ships to hold command of the sea in Soviet home waters "in dispute" before any active operations for carrying out the Navy's assigned missions could be conducted. Andreyev maintained, in effect, that even a much weaker navy could gain temporary "command of the sea" in some sea regions and exploit it to conduct at least some of the normal missions of a navy. In this advocacy of "active" operations by the inferior navy, Andreyev came close to describing a fleet-in-being strategy.

The second bit of evidence was quite tenuous. This was contained in an article by Captain First Rank Mil'gram which appeared in *Red Star* in 1949. It involved the seeming use of a foreign-navy surrogate condemning Corbett's account of the British fleet-in-being strategy in World War I and the likelihood that Mil'gram had been implicitly criticizing Soviet adoption of such a strategy. The only supporting shred of evidence was Mil'gram's associated complaint (and a possible foriegn naval surrogate) that Corbett's views were being "revived again and again abroad in works on the problems of a contemporary navy."

The third piece of evidence to support the hypothesis that the Soviet School of naval strategy was tantamount to an "active" fleet-in-being strategy came in 1953 in volume 3 of *A History of Naval Art* and was more substantial. The Tsarist Russian Navy had the "idea of developing a defense-in-depth in a naval theater composed of fortified regions and mine-artillery positions." This was said to have "served as the basis for a [Soviet] theory of battle in a previously infrastructured position in a coastal region with the cooperation of the heterogeneous forces and means of a navy," and was termed "progressive."

Also, the *History* commented on Corbett's fleet-in-being concept in favorable (i.e., non-polemical) terms that seemed to present the concept in a manner tailored for the Soviet Navy of the period: ". . . for achieving the aims of war at sea Corbett recommended utilization of the 'fleet-in-being' principle in combination with 'small, active operations.' He viewed this method for the conduct of war as a natural one for a weaker navy conducting a defense at sea . . . Corbett understood this to mean employing what is called auxiliary forces against the main forces of an adversary. To these [auxiliary forces] he assigned destroyers, submarines, torpedoes, and mines."

True, the *History* went on to characterize Corbett's fleet-in-being strategy as one of "obvious groundlessness." However, all of the reasons that the *History* presented to support this allegation have been shown in the main text of this chapter to be either vague or irrelevant and to reflect a reluctance to damn the concept substantively.

On balance, the Soviet School of naval warfare closely resembled Corbett's concept of the fleet-in-being strategy. In particular, both extolled the virtues of "an active defense" to constantly harass a stronger enemy and so hold command of the sea "in dispute." As early as April 1939 Belli had adjured his fellow officers that "the defensive missions of the Navy must never be forgotten" and that even Soviet military doctrine's stress on the offensive must not be allowed to mislead them to "rule out a well organized defense." Moreover, ever since Frunze's time in the mid-1920s, the stress on an unceasingly "active" defense had been a tenet of the Soviet unified military strategy and hence mandatory for the Navy.

Finally, the *History's* choice of a description for Corbett's view of the fleet-in-being strategy as "a natural one for a weaker navy conducting a war at sea" seems to have been designed to neatly fit the Soviet Navy's situation. It seems too pat to be mere coincidence. It is not to be expected that the Soviets would admit publicly that they had adopted a "bourgeois" concept— but it seems to the author that the Soviet School strategy of 1945 to 1953 essentially was one of an "active" fleet-in-being. However, the available evidence is not sufficiently clear as to whether this strategy was in effect throughout the postwar Stalinist period (i.e., explicitly whether the "limited-command" theory of the Soviet School fit satisfactorily into such a strategy) or whether the fleet-in-being strategy was only introduced around the time in 1949 that Rear Admiral Piterskiy outlined such an interim strategy in his *Military Thought* article.

Notes

1. N.B. Pavlovich, review of V.F. Chernyshev, "Nadvodnye korabli v sovremennoi voine," *Morskoi sbornik* No. 10, October 1945, pp. 115-128.
2. Pavlovich had been a colleague of Chernyshev's at the Naval War College until the latter's demise in 1945, just prior to publication of *Surface Combatant Ships*.
3. The tasks carried out by aircraft carriers in World War II as listed by Chernyshev were: (1) "Torpedo and bomb strikes against ships at sea;" (2) "Strikes at bases and the ships in them;" (3) Reconnaissance; (4) "Anti-air defense of naval forces at sea;" and, (5) "Protection of convoys."
4. Pavlovich quoted Chernyshev correctly; see *Surface Combatant Ships*, p. 82.
5. Pavlovich, *op cit.*, p. 119.
6. Chernyshev, *op. cit.*, p. 25.
7. I. Schner, "Avianostsy i ikh rol' v operatisyakh flota," *Voennaya mysl'* No. 6, June 1946, pp. 77-82.
8. At the outset of the article mere mention was made of the fact that "special convoy or escort carriers" had been developed to provide antiair and antisubmarine defense of convoys.
9. Schner, like Chernyshev, did mention that at times battleships would have to play the supporting role of protecting the carriers against enemy surface ships.
10. In keeping with the article's previous emphasis on heavy carriers at the expense of light ones, Schner also implied in another passage that land-based aviation could provide adequate fleet air-support only in "limited sea theaters." (p. 81)
11. L. Eremeyev, "Angliyskaya literatura o voine na more" [British Literature on War at Sea], *Voyennaya mysl'* No. 6-7, 1945, pp. 168-175.
12. The annual cumulative listing of Soviet books for the year 1927 (*Ezhegodnik knigi 1927*) lists three monographs published that year by the Naval War College in Leningrad under the rubric "Warfare of Fleet Against the Shore in the World War." One of these monographs reappeared in 1937 under the title *On Operations of the Fleet Against the Shore in the Black Sea 1914-1917*. Moreover, V. Novitskiy noted in a 1935 article in *War and Revolution* that the concept of "against the shore" was interpreted very broadly, even to including "the land lines of communications." In 1940 a bibliography in the December issue of *Naval Digest* stated *re.* the fifth volume of French Admiral Raoul Castex's *Theories strategiques*, which was entitled *Sea Against the Shore* (1935), that Castex had taken a "continental point of view" that was "contrary to that of the British and American works [of Colomb and Mahan] which elaborated the theory for a sea power that held command with superior forces." This seemed to imply that Castex was recommending fleet-against-the-shore strikes for inferior fleets unable to conduct fleet-against-fleet operations. Finally, also in 1940, Professor Belli wrote that aviation had "shifted" sea lines-of-communication warfare "from the sea to the ports and land lines of communications." See *Naval Digest* No. 6, June 1940, p. 20.
13. The article indicated the appreciation that "bases are every bit as important an element of sea power as naval forces," citing Hanson Baldwin, the military editor of the *New York Times*, as the source for the quotation.
14. "The forces of a navy change theaters depending on the circumstances in the ground theaters, effecting a maximum concentration whenever it is planned to conduct ground operations and carrying out a maximum dispersion in the intervals between operations for support of the [favorable] regime established in each operational zone." (pp. 173-174)
15. V. Penzin, "Nauchnaya konferentsiya v voenno-morskoi akademii im. K.E. Voroshilova" [Scientific Conference at the K.E. Voroshilov Naval War College], *Morskoi sbornik* No. 3, March 1946, pp. 111-113.
16. Also the rapporteur, Senior Lieutenant K.V. Penzin is likely to have been a protege of Rear Admiral Belli and subsequently a close collaborator with him on several research and writing efforts, most importantly for the 1967 book *Combat Actions in the Atlantic and Mediterranean Sea 1939-1945*.
17. "The First World War, with its new means of warfare and with its daily combat activity, refuted the old theoretical propositions on command of the sea gained by a decisive engagement." (p. 111).
18. It is not entirely clear why Belli substituted "daily operational activity" for the customary formula of "daily combat activity," as employed by Penzin. The latter phrase referred to (and is still used to refer to) routine activities within one's own zone of sea control such as reconnaissance patrols, antisubmarine and antiair warfare, minesweeping, and defensive minelaying to ensure one's continued control. "Operations," by definition, are not routine, but special, and must be planned individually since they are to be carried out in areas in which command is either "in dispute" or held by the enemy. Belli may well have been trying to make the terminology consistent with the view that such routine activity is considered part of "operational art" rather than tactics.

19. Sviderskiy's choice of the "not denied" wording suggests that he may have been implying that conversely there had been no affirmation of the need for such big ships—and thereby to convey the conviction that the Soviet Young School in the late 1920s and first half of the 1930s really believed the airplane and submarine had made big surface ships too vulnerable to warrant building.

20. The term "heterogeneous forces" had come into Soviet naval usage to signify a surface fleet composed not just of small ships and fast coastal craft but major surface combatants as well, including particularly aircraft carriers in addition to battleships and heavy cruisers.

21. "The speaker noted as a characteristic of modern war that it was comprised of a number of successive and simultaneous operations, and also of daily activity for support of the operational regime." The fact that the speaker abbreviated the customary term "daily combat activity" to just "daily activity" may have been out of deference to the (short-lived) effort of Rear Admiral Belli and Admiral Alafuzov to substitute "operational" for "combat" in the term. (p. 112) See footnote 18 above.

22. "The 'Young School,' had thrown out the old theory of command of the sea and advanced the idea of the 'small war.' This zeal was understandable because it was essential to create forces for coastal defense at a more rapid rate." (p. 112)

23. "Admiral Alafuzov touched also on the most important problems broached in the reports at the conference. Analyzing a number of the theses of foreign authors—[Karl von] Clausewitz, [Sir Julian] Corbett, [French Admiral Raoul] Castex, and [German Admiral Otto] Groos—he demonstrated the purposefulness of these authors in creating not abstract theories of war but theories corresponding to the practical interests of their states." (p. 112)

24. I.A. Razumnyi, "Avianosnye soedineniya flota SShA v voine na Tikhom okeane" [The Aircraft Carrier Forces of the U.S. in the War in the Pacific], Morskoi sbornik No. 7, July 1946, pp. 61-81.

25. V.A. Alafuzov, "O sushchnosti morskikh operatsii," Voennaya mysl' No. 8, August 1946, pp. 15-28. (For naval zones of defense, see pp. 16, 17, 20-23.)

26. Thus, in 1966 then Defense Minister Marshal Malinovsky, in order to reassure Soviet citizens that they could sleep peacefully at night despite the threat of seaborne nuclear attack from aircraft carriers, revealed the existence of a "Blue Zone (or "Belt") of Defense" to counter that threat. Whether still called the Blue Belt of Defense, it appears to remain at least an element of the operative strategic concept for the seaward defense of the U.S.S.R. concept for defense against seaborne nuclear attack from aircraft carriers.

27. V.A. Alafuzov, "O sushchnosti morskikh operatsii," Morskoi sbornik No. 4-5, April-May 1946, pp. 6-26.

28. Alafuzov, Voennaya mysl' No. 8, p. 16. He added a sub-zone of this inshore zone by directly stating that: "Close inshore the power of seacoast artillery is added." In early 1946, an article in Red Star on Soviet military doctrine called for "several echelons of defense in depth" as a general principle to be observed in all branches of the military. Lt. Gen. F. Isayev, "Strategicheskoe iskusstvo Krasnoi Armii v Velikoi Otechestvennoi voine" [Strategic Art of the Red Army in the Great Patriotic War], Krasnaya zvezda, 20 February 1946.

29. The aircraft carrier, as a result of the widespread first perception of its role as an auxiliary, had not been held in the Soviet Union to be a "major surface ship" per se but rather a ship type "of special purpose." This distinction, which was also applied to amphibious ships, appears to account for Soviet claims, both before and after World War II, to have included surface warships of "all types" in the Navy's order of battle—but without ever having completed any of the aircraft carriers planned in 1937 and again in 1950.

30. V.A. Alafuzov, "Razvitiye povsednevnoi operativnoi deyatel'nosti flota," Morskoi sbornik No. 11-12, November-December 1946, pp. 11-21.

31. "However, daily operational activity can shift to being a defensive operation. This will take place whenever the occasional harassment by an enemy in our zone of permanent command begins to change into an operation directed at the liquidation of our command in a given zone." (p. 16)

32. "Daily operational activity not only fills the intervals between operations and continues during operations but constitutes an obligatory function of the Navy in peacetime. It protects the Navy, coasts, and sea communications against the surprise attack of an aggressor." (p. 16)

33. In the first of his three articles in 1946, Alafuzov noted that not only would there be some regions in which the enemy would have command and some in which the Soviet Navy would enjoy a favorable correlation of forces, but there would be other regions in which the correlation of forces would be about equal—a good paraphrase of Corbett's definition of a situation in which the command is "in dispute." Alafuzov, Morskoi sbornik No. 4-5, p. 14.

34. "A defensive operation is directed against an offensive operation by an adversary who has the mission of narrowing the zone of our permanent command. Furthermore, every defensive operation has the aim not only of preventing an adversary from accomplishing his mission but also of defeating him by exploiting the advantages which only the defensive can provide. Then, in view of the fact that

such an adversary has been weakened, the [Soviet defensive] operation can shift to the offensive and ultimately bring about an expansion of our zone of permanent command." Alafuzov, *Morskoi sbornik* No. 11-12, 1946, p. 16.

35. J.S. Corbett, *Some Principles of Maritime Strategy* (London: Conway Maritime Press, 1911). Reprinted by the U.S. Naval Institute Press, 1972, pp. 224-225.

36. A.K. Evseyev, "O strategicheskom razvertivanii flota v khode voiny" [On the Strategic Deployment of a Navy in the Course of a War], *Morskoi sbornik* No. 11-12, November-December 1946, pp. 22-45.

37. This likely is the same as the "A. Evseyev" whose name was signed to the article in the 28 August 1938 issue of the now defunct Navy newspaper *Red Fleet* in which the command-of-the-sea concept was publicly rehabilitated in apparent consonance with the decision to build a big navy whose nucleus would be battleships and other big surface ships, including aircraft carriers.

38. Yu. Panteleyev, "Borba za gospodstvo na more," *Krasnaya zvezda*, 16 January 1947.

39. It will be recalled that Admiral Alafuzov had criticized the force-equalization strategy as "impractical" in his *Military Thought* article of August 1946. This quite possibly accounts for the fact that Admiral Panteleyev described the substance of this strategy while avoiding its name.

40. V. Voznenko, I. Korotkov, and M. Skovorodkin, "Voyennaya strategiya v trudakh Sovetskikh avtorov, 1917-1967 gody" [Military Strategy in the Works of Soviet Authors, 1917-1967] *Voyennaya mysl'* No. 4, April 1967, FBIS Translation, pp. 83-103.

41. I. Eliseyev, "K voprosu o gospodstve na more" [On the Question of Command of the Sea], *Voyennaya mysl'* No. 6, June 1947. Comment: Not one of the issues of *Morskoi sbornik* for 1948 or 1949, or even up through 1960, has yet found its way to the West. The reason the Soviet Union has refused to provide copies even to the Library of Congress may well be that this debate on command of the sea (and the construction of the aircraft carriers necessary to implement a general command-of-the-sea strategy) took place in the pages of the *Naval Digest* and *Military Thought* during those 14 years. Quite possibly the substance of this debate is considered still so revealing of the intended eventual Soviet strategy for war at sea that the censors even now refuse to release these issues of a quarter of a century or more ago.

42. V. Shavtsov, "O gospodstvo na more" [On Command of the Sea], *Voyennaya mysl'* No. 7, July 1955. Shavtsov defines "strategic command" in this article (p. 11) as denoting "a favorable situation permitting the forces of the side enjoying it to successfully carry out their strategic missions either over the entire extent of a naval theater of military actions or in one of the theater's strategic zones, and this during the whole time required for carrying out one or a succession of such missions."

43. This was a formula taken from Colomb whose theories the Tsarist Russian Old School adherents had embraced about two years before Mahan in the 1890s. Colomb's *Naval Warfare* (1891) had been translated into Russian in 1894, while Mahan's *Influence of Sea Power on History* (1890) did not appear in Russian until 1896.

44. In addition, an article by Rear Admiral Alekseyev in a 1949 *Red Star* article for Navy Day made a revealing use of the term "command of the sea" (gospodstvo na more) for describing the Soviet Navy's great naval superiority in the Black Sea during World War II. Had the command-of-the-sea theory not been in reasonably good repute in the Kremlin as late as the end of July 1949 when the Alekseyev article appeared, it is most unlikely that any senior naval officer would have risked offending Stalin by employing the term in the press. Conversely, the fact that such a wholly unprecedented use was made of the term regarding the Soviet Navy in the Great Patriotic War may be taken logically to mean that the Party leadership did not find the term as offensive as did the Army (Rear Admiral N. Alekseyev, "SSSR— Velikaya morskaya derzhava," [The U.S.S.R.—A Great Seapower], *Krasnaya zvezda*, 20 July 1949).

45. V. Andreyev, "Psevdonauchnaya teoriya admirala Kolomba," *Voyennaya mysl'* No. 7, July 1948, pp. 49-64.

46. "Gospodstvo na more" was used but with the parenthetic note that the two other most frequent terms used with regard to general command of the sea—"vladeniye morem" and "obladaniye morem"— were synonymous with gospodstvo na more." Another synonymous expression for "gospodstvo na more"—one attributed to Admiral Makarov—is "komandovaniye morem," the first word being a direct Russification of "command."

47. "Deferring to foreign authorities, some of our 'theoreticians' [of the 1917-1925 period, who all were Naval War College professors] committed major errors. Under the guise of criticism of the views of Colomb, they tried only to update him somewhat but in actuality echoed him, asserting that if we did not have a large number of battleships and heavy cruisers with which we could hold command of the sea in dispute, we could not carry out any active operations since no results could be achieved without [such limited] command of the sea." (p. 57)

48. To take the most interesting example of Colomb's use of the "means-to-an-end" expression, he formulated a single exception to the principle which constituted the main theme of his book—that command of the sea must be gained before undertaking any other naval missions:

> If the population of one nation [in the Anglo-Dutch wars of the 17th century] had been greatly in excess of the other, and its land forces proportionately stronger, the ultimate aim of this nation might have been a military expedition. Conquest of territory might have been the aim of the war, and the command of the sea might have been looked at not as the end, but only as the means to an end.
>
> Conceivably, if the military power were immensely greater on one side than on the other, the more powerful nation might hope to end the war by that sort of sudden conquest, which, when undertaken on a large scale, is called invasion, and this without much care as to the permanent command of the sea. The attempt might even go further; the idea might be that the greatness of the force and the suddenness of its landing might achieve conquest and conclude the war with such speed as to render sea communications unnecessary and therefore to leave out of the question the command of the sea even for a time, the invasion being conducted by way of surprise or evasion. There are not wanting examples of this kind of operation, or attempted operation. . . . This is the case where the naval and military operations are separate, and where a purely naval war, however short it may be, is carried on simply to clear the way for the military operation which is to follow. (Colomb, *Naval Warfare*, 3rd ed., 1899, p. 108).

49. The Soviets argue that the Second Battle of the Philippine Sea in Surigao Straits in October 1944 is not properly considered a general engagement inasmuch as the U.S. naval forces were merely covering the landing on Leyte rather than seeking a general engagement. This flies in the face of the precepts of Colomb and Mahan, who defined a general engagement as just the actual battle between the belligerents' main naval forces (whatever their missions). Moreover, since that battle shattered the remaining naval forces of Japan and spelled the end of Japanese resistance at sea in World War II, it did achieve the aim prescribed by Colomb and Mahan—that of leaving the victor in the battle with an undisputed general command of the sea.

50. "The experience of the war [World War II] also demonstrated that in a number of cases, especially in limited theaters, the accomplishment of missions for gaining command of the sea was proven to be possible by the occupation of the coastal littoral by a ground army." (p. 60)

51. Since the Navy was left to make the final landward defense of its naval bases to delay the Nazi forces as long as possible, and since the Navy suffered heavy losses in ships and personnel when they finally evacuated their bases—especially that at Tallin—these facts were insults added to the injury of losing all their bases. Accordingly, Andreyev's observation is quite likely to have been, at least in part, a slap at the Army. There are quite a few implied criticisms of the Army on this score in Soviet naval writings.

52. "Of course, even in contemporary conditions, permanent command of the sea is better than temporary command, but to agree that the results achievable from a temporary command are worthless means to deny the facts." (p. 57)

53. Andreyev went on to make a statement that is analytically useful to demonstrate that the Soviets consider providing "support" (or "combat support") to be fundamentally a way of compensating for lack of a general command of the sea. Providing support temporarily provides forces supported with the additional covering or escorting forces required to ensure having superior forces in a given area long enough to conduct an assigned operation. Continuing his critique of the Young School, Andreyev stated: "Rejecting the necessity for gaining command of the sea as one of the methods of preliminary support (before the start of an operation), they tried to show that the successful outcome of an operation could be fully ensured by direct support (in the course of an operation)." (p. 57)

54. "The theoretical postulates of Colomb on the force structures of navies also have been shown to be unfounded. The evolution in the force structure of naval forces has continued uninterruptedly since the appearance of Colomb's research. During the course of the First and Second World Wars, the place of battleships and their role in the force structure of naval forces changed radically, first in connection with the advent of destroyers, then submarines and then also of aviation." (p. 62)

55. V. Kulakov, "Reaktsionnaya sushchnost' amerikanskoi voenno-morskoi doktriny," *Krasnaya zvezda*, 13 January 1949.

56. N. Piterskiy, "Amerikanskiye vzglyady na rol' i zadachi flota v voine," *Voyennaya mysl'* No. 7, July 1949, pp. 72-81. Piterskiy must then have been engaged in editing the three volume *A History of the Naval Art* which appeared between 1950 and 1953.

57. This formulation of Piterskiy's amounted to a specific application to the United States of the Young School view voiced just a year earlier in *Military Thought* by Andreyev that the advent of new types of weapons had ruled out all possibility for any country to gain an overall, global command of the sea in any future war.

58. It should be recalled that Captain First Rank Pavlovich had given a similar warning in an article on combat support which had been published in the November 1940 issue of *Naval Digest*.

59. N. Mil'gram, "Nesostoyatel'nost' i reaktsionnaya sushchnost' angliyskoi voenno-morskoi teorii," *Krasnaya zvezda*, 5 August 1949. Mil'gram, like Rear Admiral Piterskiy, was a well-known naval historian of the Soviet regime. But all of them, even the most noted "official theoreticians" of naval and military strategy, more often than not find it expedient to treat even the most serious subject matter polemically.

60. This was a tendentious interpretation of Corbett's main thesis that no "ulterior objectives" could be pursued without unwarranted risk by conduct of other missions until that for gaining command of the sea had been accomplished.

61. Captain Third Rank Nicholas Artamonov, or Nicholas Shadrin as he was known while in the United States, defected in 1959 from Gdynia, Poland. He had been assigned to train Polish naval officers there in the handling of the type of destroyer which he had commanded in the Soviet Baltic Fleet for over five years. After coming to this country, his *bona fides* as a reliable source of information on the Soviet Navy were certified in due course. This former Soviet naval officer disappeared in Vienna in December 1975 under still unexplained circumstances.

62. It seems well warranted to suspend judgment on the veracity of his report of a Stalinist postwar construction program, even though the reported renewal of postwar plans for carrier construction is consistent with the 1937-1940 planning, with Stalin's already having once given his consent, and with the Navy's (and especially Admiral Kuznetsov's) persistent efforts to have carriers built for the Soviet Navy.

63. U.S. Naval War College lecture, 19 March 1965. The evidence on the number of carriers projected as having been four is not to be found in any of Shadrin's seven annual lectures at the Naval War College nor even in his Ph.D dissertation at George Washington University, "Development of Soviet Maritime Power," but was obtained in a telephone interview with Shadrin by this writer in 1967. In that phone interview Shadrin stated that it was certain that Stalin had acquiesced for a time to the Navy's postwar importunings for construction of at least four carriers. Shadrin noted that it would have been typically Stalinist to have tentatively approved a carrier-construction program at the urging of his naval advisors but without personally committing his own prestige to the program until its success had been "demonstrated by life itself."

64. N.G. Shadrin, "Development of Soviet Maritime Power," unpublished Ph.D dissertation, George Washington University, 1972, p. 84.

65. Telephone interview from Munich to Washington, D.C., with Shadrin by this writer, 22 January 1967.

66. U.S. Naval War College lecture, 19 March 1965.

67. U.S. Naval War College lecture, 27 October 1961.

68. U.S. Naval War College lecture, 19 March 1965.

69. N.G. Kuznetsov, "Pered voinoi" [Before the War], *Oktyabr'* No. 11, 1965, pp. 142-143.

70. *Istoriya voenno-morskogo iskusstva*, v. 3 (Moscow: Military Press, signed to press 17 September 1953). Edited by N.A. Piterskiy.

71. Chapter I (pp. 1-52) contains critiques of both the Old School views of Mahan and Colomb and the French Jeune Ecole of Admiral Theophile Aube that were written by Captain First Rank R.N. Mordvinov and Captain Second Rank V.I. Achkasov. The remaining three chapters, which bring the *History* up through the end of the First World War, were prepared by Captain Second Rank I.N. Solov'yev with the advice of nine other naval officers most notably Major General D.I. Korniyenko, Captains First Rank G.M. Gel'fond and N.N. Mil'gram and Captain Second Rank K.V. Penzin.

72. Also, this is the only Soviet military book to be found that does not give the date on which the manuscript was submitted initially for a review and censorship—a likely sign of an effort to obscure the fact that the book had been prepared under Stalin's rule.

73. "Colomb . . . distinguished between command of the sea when it was assigned as an ultimate goal and when it was gained only as a means for achieving some future aim." Napoleon's desire to control the English Channel for just six hours to invade England was cited as a hypothetical example of "temporary command of the sea." The Anglo-Dutch wars were given as the alternative case when gaining command of the sea was the ultimate goal of war because such command gave control of the other's sea routes and hence of the shipping on which the economies of both depended. This was a tendentious interpretation of Colomb in that it did not go on to relate that he held that the strategy of assigning command of the sea as the ultimate goal was correct while showing by innumerable examples that pursuit of what he termed "ulterior objectives" without first defeating or blockading the enemy to gain command of the sea almost always led to disaster.

74. "Together with the imperialistic, reactionary theory of Mahan-Colomb at the end of the 1880s and the start of the 1890s of the 19th century, there arose another anti-scientific bourgeois theory called the "Young School" whose country of origin was France. . . . The unsoundness of this "school" lay

in its one-sidedness. It is known that only the aggregate of all combat means and a combination of the various types of combatant ships (large and small) can lead to the successful carrying out of the missions with which navies were charged in the Machine Period of warfare. The practice of combat actions at sea has shown that such small ships as destroyers, submarines, torpedo craft, etc., can carry out only limited missions in war." (p. 14)

75. Gorshkov, . . . Morskaya moshch' gosudarstva [Sea Power of the State], 1976, p. 296.

76. The "aircraft carriers" referred to were three float-plane tenders, at least two of which saw action in World War I. One in the Baltic apparently never became operational but two in the Black Sea Fleet did operate with that fleet to provide air cover and even conducted several fleet-against-the-shore bombing raids against Turkish ports on the Black Sea.

77. "Heterogeneous forces" refers nominally to surface ships, submarines, and aircraft while "means" implies weapon systems and equipment. In practice, as mentioned earlier, it is often used to specifically imply large surface combatant ships, particularly aircraft carriers.

78. Previously it was claimed that the Tsarist Navy had taken the lead in "the development and practical employment of seaplanes and aircraft carriers." While there was considerable truth in this (as explained two footnotes ago), and a grain of truth in the above claim concerning the postwar period (Soviet interest in the German aircraft carrier *Graf Spee* and quite possibly a plan cancelled either just before or after Stalin's death to build four or more aircraft carriers), the claim to have accorded priority to their construction seems scarcely warranted. It is conceivable, however, that the statement was true in the partial sense that, while the Navy had always wanted aircraft carriers, it had never been possible to overcome Army opposition long enough to hold Party approval for the length of time required to develop the much improved shipyard facilities required to build the carriers whose construction had been approved. (pp. 314-315)

79. Earlier in the *History*, in an analysis of the Russo-Japanese War and the advent of the seeming fleet-in-being concept of war in a mine-artillery position, it was claimed that as early as 1905 "the idea of preliminary strikes had been advanced already."

80. V. Achkasov, "Tvorcheskiy kharakter Sovetskogo voenno-morskogo iskusstva" [The Creative Nature of Soviet Naval Art], *Sovetskiy flot*, 28 July 1956.

81. This was done in Captain Third Rank Eremeyev's article in the June/July 1945 issue of *Military Thought*. It noted the importance of interfleet transfer of naval forces in order to concentrate sufficient forces to gain local sea superiority. The stress on "frequent and substantial regrouping of fleets and their transfer from one theater to another" has not appeared subsequently in quite such explicit form but has been remarked frequently enough to warrant the conclusion that it constitutes an important part of the Soviet Union's thinking about war at sea in general and about the methods for gaining a limited command of the sea in a given region of a naval theater of military action.

82. "In the mid-thirties Commander Belli formulated a limited 'command-of-the-sea' concept. . . . After World War II, this concept was widened into a concept of three zones. The closer to the shore an attacker came, the greater degree of command-of-the-sea the Soviets could exercise," Former Soviet naval officer Nicholas G. Shadrin, "The Soviet Navy," address to the U.S. Naval War College, 20 May 1975.

VII
The First Round Against Khrushchev-
Zhukov Won by the
Soviet School, 1953-1956

The Evidence and Some Partial Analysis

A Mid-1950s Reconsideration of Carrier Construction. Nick Shadrin (Nicholas Artamonov) reveals in his Ph.D. dissertation[1] an insider's knowledge of the Soviet Navy—he was commanding officer of a destroyer in the Soviet's Baltic Fleet from a few years before Stalin's death in March 1953 until his defection in 1959. Artamonov (alias Shadrin) has provided an account of the Soviet regime's reconsideration in the mid-1950's of the desirability and feasibility of building aircraft carriers and carrier aircraft as a delivery system for atomic bombs. Shadrin's authority is Admiral Gorshkov's generalized account of possible nuclear weapons delivery systems applicable to the reconsideration of the carrier option which Shadrin claimed took place in the mid-1950s.

> The Party and Government did not spare efforts but devoted considerable time to studying the problems in detail, clarifying and comparing the various points of view of Navy and Army specialists, scientists, and designers, analyzing the experience of the war and the possibilities which had been opening up in connection with the accelerated progress in science and technology. (p. 106)[2]

Artamonov added to the above quotation from Gorshkov that: "Consideration was given to the composition of the future navy and what forces— surface, submarine, aviation, or any combination of them—should represent the 'main striking forces' of the future Navy." He immediately provided what he considered to be the relevant context:

> Apparently, as to the nature of a future war, i.e., whether nuclear or conventional, there was no problem, for it was assumed that it would be nuclear. Special consideration was given to capital ships. The Soviets "knew that the sun had set on battleships as far back as the Battle of Midway in 1942," and, according to Gorshkov, "the replacement of long-range guns in surface ships with artillery using nuclear ammunition and even missiles would not make them any less vulnerable or suited for employment in a nuclear war as a primary naval strike force." The Soviets also concluded that "the process of the sun already setting on aircraft carriers as well had begun and that the process was irreversible." The Soviets became convinced that "seeking ways in which to employ them (aircraft carriers) as a primary strike force in the armed struggle at sea had no future." (p. 107)[3]

Without a break, Artamonov added: "The rejection of the attack carrier as the main striking force of the future Soviet Navy was made in the atmosphere of a strong belief that the era of the general erosion of surface naval forces had begun." Artamonov's 1972 dissertation gave the careful caveat: "This, of course, does not mean the complete rejection of the surface ship . . . ." The construction of vertical-take-off-and-landing carriers, he added, could "not be excluded" but noted that the concept of operations of such ships would be "far from the attack-carrier concept." The dissertation further asserted: "It is safe to claim that no *attack* aircraft carriers will be built, that the Soviets have no great need for them."

Artamonov further noted the "Soviet skepticism" of the mid-1950s that he had experienced firsthand as to the viability of the attack-carrier concept for application to "a military conflict involving a major naval power" and expressed the view that such reservations were "largely justified." Finally, near the end of the naval section of his dissertation, Artamonov commented: "Although not a balanced navy in the Western sense, primarily because of a lack of aircraft carriers, the Soviet Navy appears to be not much disturbed by the fact."

In 1972, then Minister of Defense, Marshal A.A. Grechko, looked back on the immediate post-Stalin period. From the perspective of nearly two decades he observed that at that time "radical changes in military-theoretical views took place."[4] He explained that the introduction of nuclear missile weapons had necessitated "a fundamental reconsideration of [Stalinist] views on the character of a possible war, the forms and means of armed combat, and the role and significance of each of the services of the Armed Forces and of each of the branches of the services." (p. 24) This fundamental reconsideration of course involved the Navy's role and significance in the nuclear era and was reflected in the writings of Soviet naval officers and theoreticians.

Navy Calls for Release from Coastal Zones. In October 1953, seven months after Stalin's demise, there appeared in *Military Thought* an article by then Captain Second Rank (later Rear Admiral) N. V'yunenko. V'yunenko discussed the role of naval forces in joint operations and implied, inter alia, that gaining limited command of the sea in coastal waters was a prerequisite for any operations at sea for supporting the Army's coastal flank.[5] Although V'yunenko apparently thought it politic to avoid explicit mention of either command of the sea or aircraft carriers, he made some relevant points about each, specifically the following:

> For creating an advantageous correlation of forces and favorable conditions for the conduct of joint operations, the Navy normally will conduct independent operations for the destruction or weakening of the forces of an adversary. The aim of such ["independent"] operations consists of weakening the fleet of the adversary, to put his

surface ships and submarines out of action and [thereby] create conditions that exclude the possibility of any obstacles being placed in the way of the actions of our ground forces as well as of our naval forces. For the fulfillment of this mission [for "the destruction or weakening of the forces of an adversary"] there are normally employed surface ships (capital ships, cruisers, destroyers, and others), submarines, aviation and, in some cases, coastal artillery [all of] which can destroy or put out of action by joint strikes the ships of the basic forces of the adversary in their bases and at sea and thereby deprive them of the possibility of being employed for combat missions. The achievement of this aim creates favorable conditions for the conduct of subsequent operations by the forces of the Navy and moreover decreases the threat of an attack by the enemy on the coastal flanks of our ground forces. This has the effect of permitting the employment of greater [naval] forces in the main direction [of counterattack by enemy naval reinforcements] while ensuring with fewer forces the defense of the coast and the coastal flank [of the ground forces] (p. 23).

This passage reveals a very significant aspect of what the Navy considered was involved in establishing "favorable conditions" for subsequent naval operations and for conducting operations for cover and support of the ground forces in coastal sectors. V'yunenko listed both "in their bases" and "at sea" as the venues for destroying or weakening the enemy's naval forces. From this it is clear that the Navy desired that the scope of the requisite operations include striking the enemy in his bases rather than awaiting his appearance in superior force in the zones of Soviet naval operations. V'yunenko appears to have been advocating that the Navy be given *carte blanche* for strategic-scale offensive operations throughout any naval theater of military action rather than being limited to strategically defensive operations within the coastal zones directly involved.

To provide the requisite forces for such extensive operations would have entailed a shipbuilding program of large scope and long duration. Otherwise, the Soviet Union would not be strong enough to retain command of its peripheral seas and also keep NATO carriers out of those waters, let alone hold in dispute the command of the large oceanic areas from which carrier strikes could be launched against the Soviet Union. One may hazard the guess that V'yunenko's advocacy did not win many influential Army supporters since any great increase in the naval program implied both cuts in the Army's share of the defense budget and a higher priority for naval missions independent of the Army-flank cover and support missions.

Command of the Sea and Fleet in Being. The only evidence available regarding the status of the command-of-the-sea theory in 1954 appeared on Navy Day in articles by two Soviet admirals. Admiral Vladimirskiy merely used the term "gospodstvo na more" in describing Admiral Ushakov's 18th century success in wresting supremacy in the Black Sea from the Turks.[6] Rear Admiral Rodionov used the same term to assert that Germany had failed in World War I "to gain command of the sea along our coasts" despite having sent "a great number of her surface combatant ships and submarines against the Russian Navy."[7] This seemed to be intended to convey optimism that the Soviet Navy would be able to maintain command of its coastal waters even against U.S. carrier task forces. It may be recalled that both Pavlovich in 1940 and Piterskiy in 1949 had warned against making such an assumption. Whether Rodionov was contradicting Piterskiy and Pavlovich, or was taking recourse to surrogate advocacy of building strong enough coastal naval forces to constitute a sufficiently powerful fleet in being to dissuade U.S. carrier forces from planning to penetrate Soviet home waters in any future war was not apparent, although the latter explanation seems the more likely.

The mere fact that the term "command of the sea" was used in print may be taken as an indication that the concept still was an accepted one in Soviet naval circles. Rodionov indicated that the area in which the German Navy in World War I failed to gain command of the sea was not the entire Baltic or even the Gulf of Finland. He specified that it was limited to Tsarist Russia's coastal waters. This implies a claim that Tsarist Russia had at least succeeded in holding command of her coastal waters "in dispute," perhaps signifying that a "fleet-in-being strategy" had been employed to good effect then and could be again.

Limited Command-of-the-Sea Theory for the Nuclear Era. The year 1955 saw publication of an article that was to prove seminal for subsequent development of Soviet naval thought.[8] Entitled "On Command of the Sea," it appeared in the July issue of *Military Thought*,[9] the theoretical journal of the Armed Forces' General Staff. Signed by an unknown and possibly nonexistent Captain First Rank V. Shavtsov, this long article was so exceptionally informative about the nuclear-era military strategy for a war at sea that the Navy was advocating or perhaps announcing that its salient arguments unquestionably warrant presentation in some detail.

Most likely because the article appeared in a restricted-distribution publication rather than in the open literature, it was the most candid exposition of Soviet naval thinking since Admiral Alafuzov's revelations concerning the Soviet zones of defense in the August 1946 issue of the same journal.[10] The Shavtsov article had the further merit of being the first article available in the West to reveal some of the major results for Soviet strategy for the naval side of a general war since the advent of nuclear weapons.

Of greatest interest were two definitions of command at sea—one strategic and the other operational. They made the implicit admission that, while nuclear weapons were perceived as improving the Soviet Navy's chances for gaining "operational command of the sea" in (just) a region of a naval theater of military action for (just) long enough to carry out an intended mission, an enemy holding overall "strategic command of the sea" in the theater would always be able to transfer supplementary forces as needed to reestablish superiority in whatever region of the theater he found to be threatened. Thus, Shavtsov observed, the Soviet Navy cannot count on always being able to gain the command wherever it might be needed for the conduct of operations. Since these conclusions obviously are of central importance for this study, they will be set out as fully as given in the original article.

"Strategic command of the sea" was defined as follows:

> The term "strategic command of the sea" denotes a favorable situation permitting the forces of the side enjoying it to successfully carry out its strategic missions either over the entire extent of a naval theater of military actions or in one of the theater's strategic zones, and this during the whole time required for carrying out one or a succession of such missions (p. 11).

Correspondingly, "operational command of the sea" was defined in the following manner:

> The term "operational command of the sea" denotes an advantageous situation within the limits of an operational zone permitting the side enjoying it to successfully carry out a naval operation aimed at the accomplishment of an operational mission and making it impossible for the other side to oppose the operation effectively and bring it to nought (p. 12).

In the exposition of these definitions, it was first noted that "strategic command of the sea presupposes the existence of strategic [i.e., theater-wide] air supremacy." The requirements for gaining and maintaining "strategic command of the sea," which Shavtsov subsequently characterized as "a very difficult task," were stated as follows:

> The possibility of gaining and retaining strategic command of the sea depends directly on the correlation of forces present in the theater of military actions and on the feasibility of deploying these forces and of reinforcing them so as to enable them to mount a gradual but steadily increasing effort. It also depends on the strength and stability of the system of naval bases, on the security of the transportation lines for bringing supplies from the rear, and on the reliability of the intelligence and reconnaissance (p. 11).

Shavtsov also defined "tactical command of the sea." It was to be gained from "offensive" operations by establishing scene-of-action superiority of naval forces or from defensive operations by use of man-made defenses (i.e., minefields and coastal artillery).

The article went on to remark that "the gaining and retaining of strategic command of the sea requires time-consuming and costly preparation." Among such measures were five which were said to require advance preparation in peacetime:

- the creation of naval, air, and ground forces sufficient for carrying out the missions that may be assigned them and the stationing of these forces in the particular theaters of military action;

- the provision of sea and land transport required for carrying the various units of the Armed Forces and their materiel over the sea and land communication lines from one theater of military action to another; these transport means must make practicable an efficient and prompt execution of such movement and the threat of enemy attacks on them must be reduced as much as feasible;
- the construction of an adequate number of conveniently located naval bases and airfields;
- a suitable infrastructuring of the theaters of military actions; establishment of a strong defense of the coasts; an organization for the protection of navigation and air operations; and the creation of a system of surveillance and signal communications; and,
- the establishment of a shipbuilding industry and related industry adequate to replace . . . war losses and to gradually increase one's own forces . . . . (p. 11)

Shavtsov repeated, for emphasis apparently, that gaining strategic command of the sea is costly in terms of combat materiel. Consequently, he added, it may only be undertaken with the express authorization of the Supreme High Command. Such an undertaking would require the participation of different branches of the Armed Forces, the Long-range Air Force being mentioned specifically as another military service besides the Navy whose participation would be essential. Its role, the article stated, would be to deliver nuclear strikes at the "enemy rear."

If all of the above preparations were made in peacetime, Shavtsov asserted, the Soviet Armed Forces would be capable of carrying out the following five wartime missions to gain and maintain "strategic command of the sea" in the theaters in which such preparation had been made:

- destroy the enemy's naval forces;
- disrupt the enemy's basing system;
- enhance the Soviet system of naval bases;
- cut the enemy's lines of communication (i.e., both at sea and those ashore supporting enemy naval bases, or otherwise affecting the war at sea); and
- destroy the enemy's shipbuilding industry (pp. 11-12).

In a remarkably blunt and realistic statement, Shavtsov yielded a major point to Mahanian theory and thereby cut a theoretical Gordian knot that had defied the courage of earlier Soviet theoreticians: "Warfare for strategic command of the sea is aimed at making possible strategic naval and [not just] ground operations; therefore, this warfare must be undertaken before these operations take place." Previously, the hope had been nourished (more by the Army and Party leaders than by the Navy) that, by well-timed concentration of superior forces in a particular area, hit-and-run strikes against separate parts of the enemy's naval forces or against his bases could be carried out successfully before the enemy had time to concentrate the superior forces required to defeat such raids. This concept was retained in Shavtsov's article as a feature of "operational command of the sea." But by distinguishing between strategic and operational command of the sea,

Shavtsov was finally making it unmistakably clear to the Defense Ministry and Party leaders just how inadequate such a stopgap measure as limited command of the sea only in individual key regions of a theater would prove to be in wartime.

Shavtsov's assertion was that no "strategic naval and [coastal] ground operations" should be undertaken until after "strategic command of the sea" had been gained. That he realized its boldness, if not brashness, would seem to be evidenced by the pains he took immediately to reassure his military readers that lack of "strategic command of the sea" need not reduce the Navy to passivity and thereby expose the coastal flanks of the Army to unopposed seaborne strikes. At the same time he drove home the point that there really was no satisfactory substitute for "strategic command of the sea:"

> It must be noted that the gaining and retaining of strategic command of the sea is a very difficult task. One must therefore be prepared to fight at sea even when such command is lacking. As a matter of fact, experience has shown that the lack of strategic command of the sea does not make impossible naval actions of tactical and even of operational scope. However, in such a case, it will be necessary to gain and retain the operational command of the sea (p. 12).

Shavtsov also implied that there could be *no* operations of a strategic scale carried out prior to having gained "strategic command of the sea": "Depending on whether or not the missions required in any given theater necessitate strategic, operational, or tactical operations, command of the sea on a corresponding strategic, operational, or tactical scale will be required." (p. 11)

Shavtsov's assertion that the Navy must be prepared to fight at sea provided another dose of reality. It pointed out that the hope of devising a viable strategy for naval warfare that established evasion of a battle as its basis was fatuous indeed. His choice of the word fight was unusually direct and seemed to have been intended to make the senior Army officers on the distribution list for *Military Thought* think more realistically. Just what would it be necessary to achieve at sea in any World War III? Furthermore, the Navy must be given enough forces of the right types to be able to accept serious losses and still continue the war.

"Operational command of the sea" was, according to Shavtsov's article, to be manifested basically by a decisive superiority of one belligerent over the other (just) "in the zone of the main effort." As a rule, such a decisive superiority could not be achieved without a preliminary operation or operations to weaken the main enemy forces involved. Even when temporary superiority had been gained by such a preliminary operation, however, it was made abundantly clear that time was of the essence and reduced the type of missions that could be carried out to little more than hit-and-run raids:

Also very important for gaining operational command of the sea—especially when the strategic command is held by the enemy—are skillful concealment of our own operations, their proper timing, and the maximum possible reduction of their duration. . . .

Warfare for gaining and retaining operational command of the sea begins, as a rule, during a preliminary phase of the planned high-seas or coastal operation, and by the end of this phase the goals pursued by this warfare must be attained. Under modern conditions, the opportunity often arises during this preliminary phase of a planned operation for carrying out local actions aimed at weakening the naval and air forces of the enemy. . . . The execution of these local actions may be accomplished by making additional use of the very forces which have been assigned for conduct of the operation planned. Local actions aimed at weakening the naval and air forces of the enemy must be carried out shortly before the start of the main operation planned so as not to give the enemy time to compensate his losses by a redeployment of his forces (p. 13).

The author went on to note that diversionary deception could sometimes be carried out advantageously by the ground forces in coastal regions away from the planned zone of operations.

In an unprecedentedly blunt acknowledgment of the unique importance of full, general command of the sea, Shavtsov made the following assertion:

It must be kept in mind that, despite our best efforts to gain and maintain operational command of the sea, the enemy [who is considered by definition to hold the strategic command of the sea, or otherwise, operational command would not be being sought] will always be able eventually to concentrate superior forces in the planned zone of operations (p. 13).

And if this were not enough to make believers in "strategic command of this sea" out of the senior military and naval officers who read *Military Thought*, Shavtsov's next statement seemed calculated to do the trick:

Moreover, it is necessary to note that if strategic command of the sea is held by the enemy, operational command of the sea cannot always be gained in whatever zone would be desirable. When strategic command of the sea is held by the enemy, as a rule operational command of the sea can be gained only in our coastal regions (p. 14).

It was pointed out that Soviet coastal regions were the only areas "where our own naval and ground forces can be deployed," obviously a reference to the lack of aircraft-carrier aviation available to provide air cover to Soviet surface forces operating beyond the short operating radii of land-based fighter aviation.[11] The author went on directly to point out that operations beyond the "sea approaches to our littoral" can be carried out "only by submarines and aircraft." Shavtsov clinched his argument as to the irreplaceable value of "strategic command of the sea" with a final word on the subject that he must have hoped would sound irresistably attractive to even the Defense Ministry marshals:

If, however, strategic command of the sea is in our hands . . . it becomes possible to carry out any kind of operation throughout the entire theater of military actions (p. 14).[12]

In what sounds like a rationale for the post-Stalin development of the Soviet Navy as just a one-punch—a contest-for-the-first-salvo—force basically dependent on nuclear weapons for success in war at sea, the Shavtsov article explained an apparent Soviet expectation that tactical nuclear weapons held out real hope of being the great force multiplier that would enable the weaker Soviet naval forces to hold their own against the great NATO naval coalition, particularly for gaining the "operational command" by using nuclear strikes during the preliminary operations:

> The advent of nuclear weapons has opened more possibilities of gaining operational command of the sea when the strategic command is held by the enemy. If used effectively, nuclear weapons make possible the expeditious weakening of enemy forces deployed into a zone of operations. Thus, nuclear weapons make it possible to create a favorable correlation of forces and to attain operational goals before the enemy has time to augment his forces from other operational zones and so restore the previous correlation of forces (p. 14).

The *Military Thought* article went on to say that capital ships comprise "the most advantageous targets for nuclear strikes." It added: "It may be assumed that surface ships, just as before, will remain among the most important targets for attack by the forces trying to resolve the problems of gaining and maintaining command of the sea." (p. 15) Apparently this was intended to imply that submarines alone or submarines and land-based aircraft without surface ships—aircraft carriers in particular—could only try to gain and maintain command of the sea but with little if any prospects of success.

Submarines, on the other hand, were portrayed as relatively invulnerable to nuclear attack, particularly while at sea. Even while in port, proper dispersal was said to make it unlikely that a nuclear strike would affect more than a single submarine at a time—and the reassurance was proffered that a single submarine could scarcely constitute a very attractive target.

The Shavtsov article also provided some significant insights into the likely uses of Soviet submarines, airplanes, and surface ships in any future war at sea. This was done in the context of discussing what each of these three main types of naval forces could most advantageously accomplish in warfare for command of the sea. Taking submarines first, the article stated *inter alia*:

> The combat characteristics of contemporary submarines show much improvement over World War II. They are now substantially more self-sufficient; they can remain submerged for a much longer period of time; their surface speed and (still more important) their submerged speed have increased; and they can dive deeper . . . . Submarines are now able to attack a given target in a formation [i.e., aircraft carriers] without using their periscopes. While remaining submerged, they can detect minefields and other obstacles they may meet. Finally, a submarine can now serve as a platform for nuclear weapons which can be employed from underwater and from the surface.
>
> Thus, the appearance of nuclear weapons did not make the submarine lose any of its positive qualities. Quite to the contrary, as the result of a number of technological

advances, the range and . . . capabilities of the submarine have increased. Accordingly, it is warranted to assume that submarines will continue in the future to retain their advantages with respect to warfare on sea communications and will remain a formidable adversary of large surface ships in warfare for command of the sea.

Submarines, moreover, will be able to carry out a number of new tasks, including particularly to make nuclear strikes against distant naval bases of an opponent by employing missiles (p. 16).

The importance assumed by antisubmarine warfare for command of the sea was noted by merely averring that, as the result of all of the above-mentioned improvements in submarines, "the scope of warfare between the submarine and the antisubmarine surface ships will increase." The great value of the submarine to the Soviets as the weapon *par excellence* for holding command of the sea "in dispute" was indicated by an epigrammatic, if rather imprecise, implication that unless antisubmarine warfare could be brought abreast of the high state of the art of submarine warfare, Western navies would be unable to overcome the threat of Soviet submarines to the extent necessary to gain command of the sea: "There can be no question of gaining command of the sea without this warfare." (p. 16)

Turning next to Shavtsov's description of the tasks of aviation in gaining command of the sea, we read:

Aviation capabilities for warfare for command of the sea have been increased by the advent of nuclear weapons. Airplanes have become still more of a threat to large surface ships, both those operating at sea and those at their bases. Airplanes now can be employed very effectively for disrupting the system of naval bases of an enemy and for destroying the centers of his shipbuilding industry (which in warfare for command of the sea is one of the most important conditions for success). . . . An attack on a naval base with nuclear weapons at present can destroy it . . . to such an extent that it will be unusable for a long time. This means that naval bases have become very vulnerable at the present time . . . and the stability of the system of naval bases is one of the essential factors on which command of the sea depends (pp. 15-16).

In a brief statement in his article of July 1955 Shavtsov made the following claim about surface ships: "Surface ships will also participate actively in warfare for command of the sea by operating against submarines, by reducing the threat from enemy mines, and by combatting—in part—his aircraft." Ostensibly, no major role for surface ships was planned for the open oceans, since nothing was said about a surface-ship role against an enemy's large surface ships or against sea lines of communication. This silence on the open-ocean capabilities of large surface-ships was consistent with Rear Admiral Belli's advocacy in 1940 of light aircraft carriers for use just in the coastal regions of a theater to gain temporary command so as to permit the conduct of Army-flank cover and support operations.

The Shavtsov article contained an extremely revealing statement which seemed to reflect a Soviet appreciation in the mid-1950s, that the Soviet

Navy would be relatively ineffectual against NATO naval forces in a war at sea:

> In a war against a strong enemy who possesses . . . considerable naval forces, command of the sea can be gained only by a series of systematic actions. Command of the sea is to be gained as the result of warfare aimed at hampering the enemy's actions at sea, in the air, and on the ground, and [thereby] making these actions less effective, as well as by the destruction of the centers of the enemy's shipbuilding and aircraft-construction industries, of the supply bases of the enemy's naval forces, etc. Under the conditions of modern [i.e., nuclear] warfare, command of the sea must be gained through the combined efforts of the naval, air, and ground forces (p. 4).

This paragraph further clarified that the Soviets had redefined and adapted the traditional term "command of the sea" for their own purposes. They meant only gaining sea control in coastal areas plus trying to hold the command "in dispute" in key high seas and oceanic areas. The quotation above does not talk in Mahanian terms about a *superior* navy's defeating the enemy's naval forces (or blockading them) to gain overall command in a theater ("strategic command of the sea," per Shavtsov's definition). Rather, he talks in classical Mahanian terms of the strategy for an *inferior* navy of (only) trying to hamper enemy naval operations at every opportunity, by systematic operations.[13] The aim of such operations, it should be further noted, is only to make enemy operations less effective by "hampering" them rather than to bring them to a halt by defeating his naval forces. This, of course, is a sea-denial strategy, pure and simple—one reflecting a fleet-in-being strategy of merely trying to keep the command of the sea "in dispute" to prevent the enemy from having a free hand in using the sea approaches to the Soviet Union for his own purposes.

The article went on to reveal what appears to have been the real thrust of Soviet naval strategy in the mid-1950s with the observation that submarines are very effective against large surface-ships, "especially aircraft carriers" and against the sea lines of communication and "even when the command of the sea is held by the enemy." (p. 5) The foregoing comments combined with Shavtsov's remark quoted above—to gain "strategic command of the sea" would be "a very difficult task" suggest that the Soviets were harboring no illusions about gaining command of the sea in any of their main naval theaters in any future war. Furthermore, it suggests that they realized that at best they could hold the command "in dispute" primarily by means of the "basic striking force," the submarine.

The article subsequently made it appear that the Navy was advocating, with respect (just) to the maritime approaches to the Soviet Union, that Soviet military doctrine for the naval side of any third world war be revised. The doctrine should require gaining and retaining operational (or limited) command of the sea in those waters by exploiting the great destructive power of nuclear weapons:

. . . [T]he extended operational and tactical capabilities of the various services and arms of the Armed Forces warrant the assumption that a skilful employment of nuclear weapons with the support of the air forces and the ground forces can enable the Navy, although inferior to the enemy in large surface forces [that is, aircraft carriers, in particular], to expeditiously weaken the enemy and, exploiting the fact that light ships have the advantage of being less vulnerable to nuclear strikes, overwhelm him completely to gain the command of the sea along our coasts (p. 16).

Here the description of the strategy advocated indicates one that would employ the hard-to-blockade Young School forces of submarines, aircraft, and fast, light surface forces. If any large surface ships were to be involved, nothing was said about them in this context. This omission would seem to indicate beyond doubt that their role would be largely auxiliary, probably that of providing support and hence "combat stability" to the basic striking force of submarines, particularly in protecting them against ambush by enemy submarines in sortieing from base and supporting them by fighting to achieve a "breakthrough" of choke points to gain access to the open oceans.

Inasmuch as Soviet military doctrine traditionally demands that all forces be "active" (i.e., that they at least take the *tactical* offensive),[14] the World War III scenario had to include the tactical "offensive" by the Navy. However, all the quotation had to say on this score was limited to the single sentence: "Special preliminary operations will assume an increased importance, it is warranted to assume." In context, this may be fairly construed to mean that sinking U.S. or NATO aircraft carriers would be an essential prerequisite in any future war for maintaining a limited "command" in home waters.

Two points in Shavtsov's article lend themselves to the interpretation that the Army and Party leadership were being reassured by the Navy that money spent on naval forces, especially large ships, would not all be lost in one big shootout at the very outbreak of any third world war. In one place the Battle of Jutland in 1916 was cited as showing the difficulty faced by a belligerent desirous of bringing about the decisive "general engagement" of Mahanian theory. (p. 7) This sounded for all the world as though the Navy were saying soothingly: "Comrade marshals! Be of good cheer! We need not engage until advantageous to us!"

The second point reflected a longstanding dispute over whether gaining command of the sea was to be considered the end in itself that Mahan and Colomb had concluded history showed it to be. Or should it be viewed only as a *means* to the end of conducting the operations necessary to gain the aims of the naval part of a war? Shavtsov continued the dispute with a formulation that on first reading seems to deny the classical position. But on closer inspection the statement appears to have been calculated to give that impression without actually denying that command of the sea by destroying or blockading the enemy's naval forces must be made the initial aim of naval warfare:

> Command of the sea is not needed for itself but only because it permits a successful solution of the problems which in wartime confront the armed forces of a country in general and its naval forces in particular. Possession of command does not in itself automatically result in overwhelming the enemy (p. 4).

This dispute, which has been going on since the 1920s, centers around the basic difference between an Old School and Young School strategies. The Old School would strive for a general command of the sea employing the capital ships of the era; the Young School would only aim at gaining temporary superiority in limited areas whenever possible so as to carry out certain missions (before the superior fleet can send forces to regain the command) and to do so with the less expensive light forces of the era. The light forces of course are submarines and aircraft at present, while the aircraft carrier was, and remains, very much the capital ship of the times in the Soviet perception of the U.S. Navy.[15]

If the analyses of these two points are correct, it is likely of no little significance, as indicating such continued strong Army opposition to any command-of-the-sea strategy, whether general or "limited", that the Navy found it desirable to include such reassurances in the article. In this regard, as briefly noted earlier, the April 1967 article in *Military Thought*, by Major General Voznenko and others, implied that the Shavtsov article had ended a decade-long debate over command of the sea by achieving a consensus among the services on precisely the point discussed above as only superficially endorsed by Shavtsov—that command of the sea was not an end in itself— with the insincere implication that the less costly Young School strategy of only building a navy including small, fast ships to at least hold command of the sea "in dispute" would suffice for Soviet needs.

Another relevant point in Shavtsov's article was its claim that World War I had proved that it was possible for a weaker navy to retain the command of limited sea areas (even beyond strictly coastal waters), provided that proper defenses had been developed in terms of infrastructure and naval forces. The so-called wet triangle controlled by the German naval forces at Helgoland was said to have proven "the possibility of gaining and retaining command of a limited zone of the sea by a fleet inferior in strength to that of the enemy through an adequate organization of the theater of naval operations involved." (p. 7) The likely intent was for this to have conceptual relevance *in re.* the imminent threat of nuclear strikes from U.S. aircraft carriers from not far beyond coastal waters.

From the foregoing it may be concluded that the Shavtsov article constituted an extended and exceptionally clever formulation of the command-of-the-sea dispute. On casual reading it appeared to support the policy of Marshal Zhukov and Khrushchev of building a Young School navy of submarines, aircraft, and only small surface combatants, but actually it expounded and endorsed the Soviet School strategy. This strategy would require large surface ships, too, including aircraft carriers, to conduct the "special preliminary operations" against NATO's strong naval forces which the article said had assumed increased importance even for gaining "operational" command of the sea in Soviet home waters. That the strategy envisioned for employment of these forces was one of an "active fleet in being" intended to hamper NATO naval operations and thereby hold command of the sea in the Soviet Union's peripheral seas "in dispute" seems to be a well-warranted conclusion. In implicitly advocating such a strategy, Shavtsov's 1955 article both continued and elaborated the arguments for an "active" fleet-in-being strategy contained in the 1953 third volume of the naval textbook *A History of Naval Art.*

Aircraft Carriers as Viewed in the Second Half of 1955. To complete our review of the evidence from Stalin's death in March 1953 until the official announcement of Gorshkov's appointment as Navy chief in early January 1956, there remain only four articles to consider. They were published in the second half of 1955 and concern Soviet naval views on the general importance of aircraft carriers in naval warfare and on the type of carrier advocated, plus the Soviet view of the mission capabilities of carriers. Admiral Vladimirskiy, who authored the first article, appears to have been the head of the Naval Science Directorate of the Main Naval Staff and hence responsible for keeping naval theory abreast of technological developments. In an article for Navy Day published in 1955, he made it clear that the Soviet counter to the strike aircraft carrier would be land-based aircraft, submarines, and small, fast surface craft, all armed with antiship missiles.[16] Vladimirskiy gave no hint of the Navy's great desire to build aircraft carriers of its own.

However, in December 1955, *Red Star* carried an article on "Aircraft Carriers," by a Navy captain that, while dutifully calling attention to the Party line that carriers were vulnerable to nuclear weapons, pointed out the carrier's relative invulnerability to conventional weapons.[17] Moreover, the article emphasized that attack aircraft carriers constituted "the main striking force" of both the U.S. and British navies and seemed to imply that building attack carriers would really be the optimum solution for countering U.S./UK ships of that type.

Perhaps the construction of such costly and technologically difficult ships as attack carriers was not seen as a practical prospect at the time. The author limited himself to implying that Soviet naval shipbuilding should be directed to construction of a substantial force of light carriers, but ones that, at least, would be capable of employing offensive air-strike tactics against any enemy carrier forces bent on attacking the Soviet homeland.

In early September 1955, *Soviet Fleet* had carried an article ostensibly on British naval aviation.[18] However, it seemed to be a fairly obvious surrogate discussion of the Soviet Navy's views on the naval mission requirements which strike carriers could perform should the Army and Party ever acquiesce to construction of such ships. The article listed as "the most important tasks of aircraft carriers" the following three missions:

- striking at coastal installations, including naval bases and ports;
- destruction of surface combatants and submarines at sea and at their bases; and also,
- providing support to protect sea communications from attacks by submarines, surface ships, and aircraft.

The article further suggested in surrogate form that the construction of carriers was an active issue in Government and Party circles in Moscow.

Another article in *Soviet Fleet* two months later (mid-November 1955) asserted that the combat nucleus of the U.S. Navy was comprised of strike aircraft carriers and that they constituted its main offensive weapon system.[19] Clearly, considering all of the public discussion of aircraft carriers that had taken place in 1955 alone, the subject was under the intensive debate in Soviet Government and Party circles that normally takes place prior to major policy decisions.[20]

Further Analysis and Interpretation of the Evidence, 1953-1956

After Stalin's death and Malenkov's brief interregnum as Party secretary, the new Party secretary, Khrushchev, and his defense minister, Marshal Zhukov, made what Marshal Grechko was to describe nearly two decades later as a fundamental reconsideration of the Navy's role and significance for the nuclear-missile age based on "radical changes in military-theoretical views." This would seem to be putting a fine gloss on what was essentially an expedient move to cut the huge naval budget by cancelling the big-ship construction program and limiting shipbuilding to the much less expensive submarines. To rationalize this the fact was exploited that the "revolution in military affairs" had made it possible to make submarines a far more formidable weapon by powering them with nuclear reactors and arming them with missiles. As was footnoted earlier, Khrushchev himself acknowledged that he had a hankering to build aircraft carriers but that they were simply too expensive.

In face of the Khrushchev-Zhukov determination to reduce the Navy to little more than a large submarine force, one which they appeared to value largely for its deterrent role, Soviet School advocates of command of the sea, whether general or "limited," had to trim their sails accordingly—

particularly in public utterances. However, in the restricted-distribution, theoretical journal of the Armed Forces' General Staff, *Military Thought*, they were able to be somewhat more forthright. What can be learned in the West about Soviet naval thought for the 1953-1955 period (no issues of the professional journal *Naval Digest* have been allowed to reach the West) comes from two of the several issues of *Military Thought* that were smuggled out of the Soviet Union by Colonel Oleg Penkovskiy.

The first of these was the October 1953 issue which contained an article by then Captain Second Rank (later Rear Admiral) N. V'yunenko, who subsequently became one of Gorshkov's leading "official theoreticians," as Gorshkov has typified them. V'yunenko discussed naval operations for cover and support of Soviet ground forces on the offense or defense in coastal areas. He used his subject to imply the necessity of building the larger naval forces required to gain a limited command of the sea in Soviet home waters in order to successfully execute this Army-flank cover and support mission. Moreover, V'yunenko seemed to be lobbying his largely senior Army readership to gain a free hand for the Navy to go beyond the defensive operations involved in merely providing direct support "in the main directions" of Army-flank operations. He even wanted to be authorized to go beyond gaining "operational" command in key regions of theaters of military actions and be permitted to take the offensive against an enemy's bases and the ships in them. V'yunenko tried to support his advocacy (of measures long known to be unacceptable to the Party leaders and Army marshals who controlled defense policy-making) by arguing that the Navy would be better able to support Army coastal operations. However, even this appeal, in terms of the Army's self-interest, produced no apparent results.

The second of the two *Military Thought* articles available for the 1953-1956 period was a highly informative one by a Captain First Rank Shavtsov in the issue for July 1955. Entitled "On Command of the Sea," the very title is likely to have been enough to put its largely Army readership on its collective guard. Reading it should have engendered a mass apoplexy among the Army marshals who have dominated the General Staff and Ministry of Defense.

However, any Army readers who might have managed to suppress their ire and read through the long article with any degree of objectivity would have found a cogent and persuasive elaboration of the need for building a navy that would be able to contest command of the sea in key areas adjacent to the Soviet Union.

Shavtsov defined three separate degrees of command of the sea—tactical, operational, and strategic—and discussed the pros and cons of each. In a very telling fashion he made clear the inadequacy of the "tactical" command favored by the Army of merely providing support "in the main directions" to Army-flank operations. The "operational" (or limited) command long advocated by the Soviet School, although it required much stronger naval forces, was convincingly shown to be the minimum that the security of Army-flank naval support operations required. Even then, as Shavtsov made pointedly clear, the stronger enemy would always be able to send the additional forces into a given naval theater of military action to regain command.

The side retaining this "swing-strategy" option to regain the command at will was held by Shavtsov to hold "strategic" command of the theater(s) being contested. Shavtsov characterized gaining and holding the "strategic" command of a contested theater as very difficult and so costly that undertaking it could only be authorized by the Supreme High Command. To hold the "strategic" command, Shavtsov added, would require the support of other branches of the Armed Forces, particularly of Long-range Aviation.

Shavtsov detailed the requirements for "strategic" command, leading off with "a favorable correlation of forces," meaning that the Soviet Navy would have to possess enough ships of the right types to usually be able to concentrate a superiority of forces in any key theater. The "feasibility of deploying these forces" was Shavtsov's second requirement for "strategic" command and in all probability was intended to take into account the restricted access of the four Soviet fleets to the open oceans through the various geographic choke-points.

The third requirement was one essentially for additional combatant and auxiliary ships to permit a steadily increasing effort once a theater campaign had been initiated. A strong and stable system of naval bases was an obvious further requirement as was reliable intelligence and reconnaissance.

Shavtsov also listed secure lines of communication with the rear. He had done his homework well—most command-of-the-sea discussions concentrate on the need for superiority at the scene-of-action of battles and overlook this vitally important logistics requirement, or "second aspect of command" in Colomb's words.

Despite these formidable requirements for gaining "strategic" command in the key theaters in wartime, Shavtsov portrayed the advent of nuclear weapons as constituting a good reason to expect to find a way out of the dilemma posed by the great superiority of the NATO naval forces (and, implicitly, their attack-carrier striking forces in particular). While he presented nuclear weapons as a potentially great force-multiplier, he realistically limited his discussion to the advantages of using them to gain operational command. Eschewing an opportunity to make a pie-in-the-sky pitch for undertaking to annihilate all of NATO's main naval forces with nuclear weapons, Shavtsov restricted himself to the far more practical discussion of employing nuclear weapons to gain "operational" command long enough to ensure the success of any given Army-flank cover or support operation. Shavtsov made what appears to have been the single greatest contribution in the available Soviet writings—at least since Alafuzov in 1946—to the Navy's lobbying campaign to have limited command of the sea approved as part of the Soviet Union's unified military doctrine.

Shavtsov advocated building the forces required to maintain operational command in Soviet home waters so that Army-flank operations could be provided adequate cover and support against the NATO naval forces. Implicit would seem to have been a requirement for light aircraft carriers to provide air cover to Soviet naval forces operating beyond the 100-mile or so flight radii of shore-based fighter aviation.

Had Shavtsov advocated that Soviet Union prepare for contesting for "strategic" command, it would, with virtual certainty, have been interpreted by the senior Army readership of *Military Thought* as implicit advocacy of building a considerable number of prohibitively expensive attack aircraft carriers. Shavtsov judiciously limited the advocacy in his article to trying to win acceptance of the "limited-command" theory. In all likelihood, he appreciated the fact that there was not the slightest chance that the Army would accept a "strategic command" doctrine and that half a loaf would be better than nothing. Events were to prove that the Navy's plea in the Shavtsov article for even an operational-command capability was beyond what the Army was ready to accept in the mid-1950s.

Accordingly, Shavtsov had very little to say explicitly about aircraft carriers. He did mention that a trend had developed (in world naval construction) towards building not only lighter combatant ships but aircraft carriers too, since they "can be employed to protect other surface ships operating on the high seas." With this fairly light touch plus an implicit reference to the Navy's lack of light carriers for supporting fleet operations in Soviet home waters beyond the range of land-based fighter aircraft, Shavtsov discreetly dropped the subject of aircraft carriers. Thus, in listing the "time-consuming and costly preparations" that would be required in peacetime should the Party and Army ever elect to contest for "strategic" command of the sea, Shavtsov only listed (in first place) the need for sufficient naval forces to carry out the missions they might be assigned—but without explicitly stating a requirement for aircraft carriers or other particular types of ships.

On another subject even more certain to arouse the marshals' ire than advocacy of building attack aircraft carriers—that of acknowledging a requirement for the Navy to be assigned and prepared to conduct operations independent of the Army-flank cover and support missions—Shavtsov executed a theoretical ground-clearing operation in preparation for the day that the Navy could expand its limited "command" advocacy to one of "full" or "general" ("strategic" by Shavtsov's definition) command in key naval theaters of military operations peripheral to the Soviet Union. He took issue with the Army's long held view of the Navy as just its offshore arm and faithful assistant. He asserted that the proper aims of gaining "strategic" command should be not only to provide cover and support for Army coastal operations but also to enable the Navy to conduct strategic naval operations, apparently such as ones he had already listed for destruction of an enemy's naval forces and bases, shipbuilding facilities, and merchant shipping.

While outlining in full the potential advantage of "strategic" command of the sea, Shavtsov's article went to great lengths to reassure his readers that a limited or "operational-command" doctrine would be adequate to avoid the Navy's being condemned to passivity in the face of NATO's greatly superior naval forces, and consequent inability to perform the Army-flank cover and support missions. He pointed out that NATO's capital ships (i.e., primarily its attack carriers) would constitute "the most advantageous targets for nuclear strikes" while (Soviet) submarines, even while in port (if properly dispersed), would not make a lucrative target.

On the other hand, the great potential of submarines for allegedly holding command of the sea "in dispute" was pointed out by Shavtsov. In particular, he asserted that unless and until the state of the art in antisubmarine warfare were improved to match that of submarine warfare, the NATO naval forces would be unable to gain and maintain a general command of the sea.

The main role in modern warfare for surface ships was stipulated to be for antisubmarine defense. Perhaps due to the extremely limited antisubmarine capabilities of Soviet aviation at the time, the roles prescribed for aircraft in holding command of the sea "in dispute" were limited to attacking shore facilities and large surface ships. The vulnerability of naval bases to nuclear strikes from aircraft was especially emphasized. Also, the fact was noted that the exercise of command of the sea was greatly dependent on "the stability of the system of naval bases."

Notably, Shavtsov made no mention of any open-ocean role for surface ships. This bore mute testimony to the constraints on Soviet naval operations imposed by the Navy's lack of aircraft carriers. This lack necessitated limiting Soviet aspirations to merely attempting to retain command of the sea in Soviet coastal areas, to contest command of the sea for a few hundred miles beyond the coastal areas, and to merely hold in dispute the command of the open-ocean zone beyond the intermediate zone. An "active" defensive strategy was prescribed as the proper method for accomplishing these aims.

The Shavtsov article gave indication of trying to reassure the Party and the Army that money spent on surface ships would not be lost by their being sunk at the outbreak of a third world war. The feasibility of implementing the Navy's sought-after "limited-command" strategy without having to accept a disastrous general engagement against overwhelming odds was mooted and the Battle of Jutland cited to support this questionable thesis.

Moreover, Shavtsov professed to subscribe to the Army's view that gaining command of the sea could not objectively be considered an end in itself but only a means to the end of establishing favorable conditions for the performance of the Navy's (largely Army-flank cover-and-support) missions. Shavtsov accomplished this in an astute manner that avoided an actual denial that the initial aim of naval warfare must be to destroy (or blockade) an enemy's main naval forces. He thus avoided compromising this key tenet of Mahan and Colomb against the day that the Navy might again feel free to espouse a general command-of-the-sea strategy.

All in all, the Shavtsov article, while on the face of it supporting the Khrushchev-Zhukov policy of building only a Young School-style light-forces navy, actually was an exceptionally clever Soviet School formulation for an interim "active" fleet-in-being strategy as recommended for an inferior navy by classical sea-power doctrine. In this, it may now be further concluded that Shavtsov, like Piterskiy in his 1949 *Military Thought* article and again in the 1953 third volume of *A History of Naval Art*, further developed the Soviet School of naval warfare by advocating an interim fleet-in-being strategy aimed at gaining a limited "command of the sea" just for the duration and area of each scheduled operation. The long-range aim implicitly remained as spelled out in August of 1938 by Evseyev: a modified version of the classical Mahanian strategy of gaining a "full" or general command of the sea just in the theaters crucial for defense of the homeland with such naval forces as might be required to defeat the aircraft carrier task forces of the United States and other NATO naval powers.

The Army in all likelihood opposed the Navy's planning to gain "strategic" command of the sea in the key theaters as the goal of Soviet military strategy at sea (as had been espoused by Admiral-Professors Alafuzov, Belli, Piterskiy, and others during the Stalinist postwar period). Such opposition was indicated in an April 1967 article in *Military Thought* by Army Major General Voznenko and two Army colonels. It first implied that "a unity of views" finally had been achieved by 1955 in the Soviet defense establishment on a definition of command of the sea after a lengthy debate that had begun at the end of World War II. The Army authors presented a definition and description of command of the sea which took recourse to an old formula derived from Colomb, seemingly to make certain that Army opposition to either a "limited" or general command-of-the-sea doctrine was understood by the readership of *Military Thought*. This was done by reasserting the well-understood Young School formula that command of the sea should not be considered an end in itself (and hence the primary goal of naval warfare). Rather, command of the sea was viewed as merely a means to the end of enabling naval forces to carry out their other assigned missions (but not by battle to defeat the enemy's naval forces), primarily those of providing cover and support for the Army's coastal flanks.

This seeming Army opposition to the Soviet Union's adopting either a doctrine of aspiring to a limited "command of the sea" in regions of the key theaters of military actions or to an eventual "strategic" command throughout those theaters seems quite consistent with earlier Army opposition. The Army opposed both the Navy's being assigned any missions independent of the Army, and the large and expensive naval construction programs for big surface combatant ships that would be required for carrying out such independent missions. The Army probably assumed that the great expenditures involved in building substantial numbers of big combatant-ships would be taken in substantial part from its own share of the military budget (as had been the funds for the big-ship construction programs of 1937 and 1950). Hence, the Army may be assumed to have had a strong, if parochial, service interest in seeing that the Navy was not allowed to establish a doctrinal basis for justifying another big-ship construction program.

Notes

1. N. Shadrin [N. Artamonov], "Development of Soviet Maritime Power", Ph.D. dissertation, George Washington University, 1972.

2. Shadrin [Artamonov] quoted Gorshkov correctly, although in condensed fashion that did not indicate by ellipsis the inconsequential material excised (*Morskoi sbornik* No. 6, July 1963, p. 15). Earlier in his dissertation (p. 84), at the point where he related Admiral Kuznetsov's announcement to a 1951 meeting of ships' commanding officers in Riga that the Navy had been authorized the construction of an unspecified number of aircraft carriers, he footnoted that observation as follows: "This was the last time that the subject of aircraft-carrier construction was raised in such a definitive manner." This suggests that the reconsideration of the mid-1950s considered aircraft-carrier construction as just one of a number of options rather than as solely a matter of whether to build aircraft carriers.

3. Again Gorshkov was quoted correctly, this time from *Morskoi sbornik* No. 2, February 1967, p. 19.

4. A.A. Grechko, "Obrazovaniye SSSR i sovetskiye vooruzhennye sily" [Formation of the USSR and the Soviet Armed Forces], *Novaya i noveishaya istoriya* No. 6, November-December 1972, p. 24.

5. N. V'yunenko, "Sovmestnye operatsii i rol' v nikh voenno-morskikh sil" [Joint Operations and the Role of Naval Forces], *Voennaya mysl'* No. 10, October 1953, pp. 19-32.

6. L. Vladimirskiy, "Vernyi strazh morskikh rubezhei Sovetskogo gosudarstva" [Reliable Guard of the Maritime Perimeters of the Soviet State], *Pravda Ukraina*, 25 July 1954.

7. A. Rodionov, "Na strazhe morskikh rubezhei" [On Guard Over the Maritime Perimeters], *Vodnyi transport*, 24 July 1954.

8. V. Shavtsov, "O gospodstve na more," *Voyennaya mysl'* No. 7, July 1955, pp. 3-17.

9. The Shavtsov article is the one mentioned earlier as having been cited by the Army authors of a *Military Thought* article in 1967 for purportedly having achieved (after a debate that had lasted since 1946) an interservice "unity of views," on, in essence, a limited "command-of-the-sea" doctrine for the naval side of the Soviet Union's "unified military doctrine."

10. It should be recalled here that Alafuzov expounded the views that a weaker fleet still may normally enjoy the exercise of command of the sea over an extended coastal zone and that "the essence of war at sea in the final analysis consists of warfare for expanding one's own zone of permanent command so that it eventually embraces the whole theater."

11. Shavtsov observed, a page later, that a trend had developed in the major navies not only toward building lighter combatant ships but aircraft carriers too since they "can be employed to protect other surface ships operating on the high seas."

12. Some ten pages earlier, in his initial remarks, Shavtsov had spelled out the advantages of exercising command of the sea in a way that ignored all but those calculated to appeal to the Army: "The armed forces of a state that has gained command of the sea can break the sea communications of an enemy and make secure its own, can conduct overseas invasions of the territory of the adversary and prevent

landings on his own territory, can act systematically against the adversary's troops and targets along the coast by gunfire support, and can make it impossible for the enemy to conduct such operations." (p. 4)

13. Five pages later, World War II is said to have shown that warfare for command of the sea must be aimed at "the destruction of enemy naval and air forces or at hampering their activities with the purpose of creating favorable conditions for carrying out the missions of our own naval forces and of our own land forces operating in coastal zones." (pp. 9-10)

14. This traditional demand of Soviet military doctrine was quite accurately reflected in Shavtsov's statement which specified that such command of the sea as might be gained must be "actively" exploited. (p. 5)

15. This assertion is supported by a great deal of convincing evidence, but should not be construed to contradict the Navy's longstanding interest in aircraft carriers. Initially, aircraft carriers were desired mainly to provide air cover to Soviet naval forces operating in home waters but later to enable them to fight NATO's carriers for a limited "command of the sea," in the event of war, particularly to prevent NATO carriers from being used for strikes against the homeland or its ground forces.

16. L. Vladimirskiy, "Novaya tekhnika na korablyakh" [New Technology on Combatant Ships], *Komsomol'skaya Pravda*, 23 July 1955. "The counter to surface ships is the cruise missile launched from an aircraft, a submarine, or a small, fast surface-ship."

17. N. I Makeyev, "Avianosnye korabli" [Aircraft Carriers], *Krasnaya zvezda*, 15 December 1955. Aircraft carriers were classified as "heavy," "light," and "escort," the heavy type was said to carry a composite aircraft complement of strike, fighter, and antisubmarine planes.

18. I. Kudanov, "Angliyskaya avianosnaya aviatsiya" [British Naval Aviation], *Sovetskiy flot*, 7 September 1955.

19. V. Sokolov, "Bazovaya aviatsiya Amerikanskogo flota" [The Land-Based Aviation of the American Navy] *Sovetskiy flot*, 13 November 1955.

20. All of this discussion of aircraft carriers in 1955 tends to support the assertion from Artamonov's Ph.D, cited at the outset of this chapter, that whether to build aircraft carriers had been just one of the options considered in the mid-1950s review.

VIII
A Summation and Some Conjecture

The leading Soviet naval theorist of the 1920s, Naval War College President Professor Boris Gervais, advocated a classical Mahanist command-of-the-sea strategy for the weaker of two strong capital-ship navies. That is, the weaker navy should ensure that the command is held "in dispute" so as to make unfeasible or as difficult as possible the stronger adversary's use of the sea areas disputed. For the most frequent situation of the weaker navy finding itself blockaded in port, the German-style "small-war" tactics of gradual attrition would be employed. They were intended to reduce the blockading force by use of submarines, mines, coastal artillery, aircraft, and light surface forces in hope of weakening the adversary to the point of being "equalized." Then the blockaded major surface combatants could sortie to fight a general engagement with reasonable prospects of victory. These views formed the core tenets of what became known as the Old School of naval warfare.

It was readily apparent that even under the most favorable circumstances, a number of five-year plans would be required before the Soviet Navy could be built up to the two-thirds capital ship strength of the Royal Navy that Gervais held would be necessary to even hold the command of the Soviet coastal seas in dispute against the vastly superior British naval forces. So at Party direction, a "positional-war" strategy much more suited to the Soviet Union's stringent economic and naval circumstances was elaborated by Professor Mikhail Petrov, an Old School colleague of Gervais' at the Naval War College. This strategy involved establishing in key Soviet coastal areas what were termed naval positions (or mine-artillery positions, as they were more often called). In them were to be employed all of the light forces enumerated above. Petrov thought this strategy left much to luck and should only be tolerated as a stopgap measure. Gervais took issue with the view that such a strategy could be expected to defeat a strong enemy navy bent on an amphibious invasion of the Soviet Union. He maintained that it could only be expected to substantially weaken, not wholly destroy, the landing forces and so hopefully make it possible for the Army ground forces to finally defeat them ashore.

The real sympathies of Professors Gervais and Petrov manifestly laid with building a big-ship navy sufficiently strong to at least hold command of Soviet coastal waters in dispute against the major Western naval powers.

However, as the first decade of the Soviet Navy's existence drew to a close in 1927, Naval Commissar Muklevich warned his officer corps that classical command-of-the-sea theory was not at all applicable to the Soviet situation. The Battle of Jutland should no longer be taken as a model. Soviet security against the widely anticipated amphibious invasion of the Soviet homeland laid in working out the tactics for the Soviet Union's "small navy" to cooperate with the Army in executing a common war plan.

From late 1922 onward various Navy and even Army voices supported aircraft-carrier construction for the Navy. The Old School's Professor Gervais recognized that carriers were capital ships but held that they could not replace the battleship for gaining and maintaining command of the sea. Professor Petrov, after initially derogating the aircraft carrier, reversed himself in 1927 and proclaimed the carrier to be the ship type of the future.

As the period of the New Economic Policy ended in 1928 and the first Five-Year Plan was inaugurated, there arose a Young School of Soviet naval warfare opposed to the Old School of classical Mahanist command-of-the-sea strategic thinking of Gervais and Petrov. Composed almost wholly of recent students of the two professors (the former Tsarist officer, Captain First Rank V.A. Belli was the exception), it included most notably Aleksandrov, Dushenov, Ludri, and Yakimychev. The Young School argued that the advent of submarines and aircraft had made big ships obsolete or able at best to play a subordinate role of providing combat support to the light, strike forces. The Young School advocates criticized virulently their former mentors for their advocacy of a strategy of holding command of the sea in dispute with big surface ships. Their arguments, although based with some reason on the Old School's seeming lack of appreciation for the potential of submarines and aircraft, were intemperate, largely subjective, and politically motivated. Finally, in 1932, Gervais was coerced into publishing an abject recantation of his most strongly held views, particularly on the continuing validity of the doctrine of command of the sea, and Old School thinking was suppressed for the time.

From 1933 to 1936 the Young School dominated Soviet naval thinking. That school held both that submarines and aircraft could not be blockaded because they could pass under or over a blockading surface fleet and that they had replaced big surface ships as the main striking forces of navies. Hence, the Young School maintained that both the blockade and general engagement of big ships—the two forms of naval warfare advocated by Mahan and Colomb for contesting command of the sea—had become obsolete along with the theory of command of the sea itself. The value of light aircraft carriers for protection of the Soviet Union's vitally important coastal military shipping was acknowledged in 1934 by leading Young School advocate A.P. Aleksandrov.

Another view that gained ascendancy under the Young School was the insistence on providing submarines with the support of surface ships and aircraft for virtually all major missions, particularly when leaving or returning to port, when transiting choke points, and when making the main strike against the major combatant ships of a strong opponent. As Aleksandrov specified in two of his articles in 1930 and 1931, and Evseyev again in 1938, such support was explicitly acknowledged to be a surrogate for a command-of-the-sea strategy. This fact merits particular note because this limited-command surrogate was to be made subsequently into a tenet of the emergent Soviet School of naval warfare.

Such support was implied to require both big ships to deter or fight off any large surface forces of the enemy and smaller ships and craft to provide minesweeping and antisubmarine protection. It had two great but only implicitly acknowledged advantages, particularly in the eyes of the Army leadership. First, it provided support (or "combat support", as it began to be termed in the late 1930s) to the Army's coastal operations. This ensured that the Navy would remain a "faithful assistant" to the Army (rather than letting it go off on independent missions for gaining control of the key sea lines of communication). Second, it meant that the Army's share of the military budget would not be diminished while the Soviet Union built up a fleet of expensive big ships.

The several Tsarist-vintage battleships and cruisers that had been refitted and returned to service in the 1920s were not to be scrapped. Along with the destroyers and small ships and craft, they could provide the support deemed necessary for the main striking force of submarines at the several points in their mission profiles at which they would be most vulnerable to the adversary's main-battle and antisubmarine forces.

Yet, even while the Young School proponents were hailing the submarine and aircraft as the unblockadable means that had outmoded command-of-the-sea theory, if not the battleship, their condemnation of the former was usually reserved or evasive. From some of these rather half-hearted critiques of the operational forms rather than the substance of command of the sea, one gains the impression that the authors were hedging against the day that command-of-the-sea theory might again prove useful. This seems true despite the fact that by 1934 Aleksandrov felt free to assert that the command-of-the-sea concept had been fully discredited—especially since he had specified such discreditation as an essential precondition for the Young School to hold full sway.

For the mid-1930s, at a time when the Soviet Union had just begun to develop the basis for its current industrial capacity, the Soviet aim patently was, as Aleksandrov had put it, to build a primarily submarine navy. The implicit rationale for this was both to avoid the strain on the limited Soviet productive capacity that would be caused by an open-ended naval arms race (pursuing the Law of Numbers) and to exploit the greatly disproportionate costs to putative Soviet enemies of building sufficient antisubmarine forces to handle the large and growing Soviet submarine threat. Such a rationale for building and maintaining a large submarine force in the Soviet Navy was set out at length in a 1933 book by Ivan Isakov, A.P. Aleksandrov, and V.A. Belli, entitled *Submarine Operations*.[1] In his book, *Sea Power of the State*, Gorshkov found much of value in this book despite the advent of the nuclear-missile era.

In early 1937, Navy leaders and theoreticians briefly advocated heavy, attack aircraft carriers. This coincided with the formulation of the program for building a big-ship navy announced in 1938. Stalin did tentatively and temporarily concur with building four aircraft carriers to be laid down in 1942-1943 but the evidence suggests that they were all of light tonnage for employment in Soviet home waters, and after the program was announced, only advocacy of light carriers was voiced publicly.

The indictment of both the Young School and the Old School in August 1938 by a hitherto unknown junior naval captain (Evseyev) and the purge of many of the still surviving advocates of both schools presumably was deemed expedient by Stalin to clear the theoretical decks for the new Soviet School of naval warfare. This was accomplished mainly by Professor Belli, who, since at least 1926, had been a seeming stalwart of Young School conviction. He selectively chose those tenets from each school that he thought would be most usable for constructing the new strategy that had been peremptorily demanded by the Army political officer who served as Naval Commissar during the height of the Great Purge. Everything else was expediently rejected and renounced, including most of the Young School beliefs that Belli had advocated earlier.

The key tenets of the emergent Soviet School of naval strategy, as presented by Evseyev, Belli, and Pavlovich, may be summarized as follows:

1) Evseyev accompanied his virulent denunciation of both the Old and Young Schools by stating a basic premise of the evolving Soviet School. Without explicitly naming that school, he asserted that the advent of submarines and aircraft, far from weakening the command-of-the-sea doctrine as the Young School had maintained, actually had strengthened it. Evseyev asserted that all types of ships were to be built to enable the USSR to contest for command of the seas and oceans. He used the same hyperbole that characterized all Soviet pronouncements about the big "sea and ocean navy worthy of the Soviet [great] power" that the Soviets started in late 1937. In 1938 it was announced that the ships would be constructed under a new ten-year building program.

2) Belli reiterated the long-term goal of the Soviet School to be a strategy of force equalization. This strategy envisioned defeating a stronger naval adversary's main forces a part at a time until the attrition had weakened

the adversary sufficiently to allow the Soviet naval forces to seek out a general engagement with good prospects of victory. This would require construction of a big-ship navy that was not too inferior to its probable opposition, probably not more than one-third, to make a force-equalization strategy feasible. During the interval of at least a decade, when the required battleships, heavy cruisers, and aircraft carriers would be built, Soviet military strategy for a war at sea would be one of limited naval operations. They would be restricted to those for which adequate capital-ship support could be provided to the light naval forces of submarines, PT boats, and aircraft to ensure a superiority of forces in the intended area of operations just long enough for the planned duration of a given operation. This interim strategy accepted the fact that as long as the Soviet Navy was too weak to implement a force-equalization strategy, the missions that it could hope to achieve against much superior naval forces would be restricted to Army coastal-flank support, to antishipping, and to raids against enemy coastal installations (to attempt to hold command of the sea in key regions of any given theater of naval actions in dispute).

3) Professor Belli devised a two-stage method of providing combat support for naval operations that effectively, if surreptitiously, introduced a limited (but readily expandable) command-of-the-sea strategy into Soviet School theory. He accomplished this artful sleight-of-hand by stipulating that a prerequisite to any major naval operation must be to provide such preliminary combat support to a given operation as would cause sufficient attrition to the opposing naval forces that the Soviet forces available to give direct or simultaneous support to the operation would be adequate to overcome the remaining opposition. As a matter of practicality, and probably to avoid alarming the Army, the command-of-the-sea strategy and its concomitant general-engagement tactic were denounced as having been wholly discredited by the German Navy's successful operations for seizing the Atlantic coast of Norway in 1940.

4) However, Belli reserved the general engagement for the future use of the Soviet School but with the major caveat that it was not the sole tactic for defeating an enemy's main naval forces and hence not obligatory as in classical command-of-the-sea doctrine. As the preferred alternative tactic to the general engagement, Belli apparently had in mind the successive operations by which the force-equalization strategy of piecemeal attrition was (theoretically) to be implemented.

5) In what appears to have been little more than a face-saving formula for the submarine force and its Young School enthusiasts, Belli stated that different types of ships would play the leading role for different operations. Apparently neither submarines nor battleships were to be considered the main striking force. He further stated that submarines would be the main type for antishipping operations and would be accorded support by the other

naval forces while carrying out such operations. Having said this, however, Belli proceeded to gainsay it by adding that the best way to conduct an antishipping campaign would be by employing surface ships in joint operations with submarines and aircraft. Adding seeming insult to apparent injury, Belli asserted the necessity of also employing aircraft in any antishipping campaign to compensate for the limitations of submarines—such as being largely icebound in port in wintertime.

6) Belli made it clear that the Soviet School of naval warfare was giving appropriate consideration to protecting sea lines of communication—which in the Soviet context was largely a matter of protecting vital coastal shipments of war materiel and troop replacements for Army coastal operations. He noted also that aircraft carriers were of particular importance for this mission in "the far regions of a naval theater of military action which cannot be reached by shore-based aviation."

7) Belli implicitly drew attention to the importance for the Soviet Union of acquiring forward "strategic positions" for a war at sea, citing the great value of Norway as such. He emphasized that obtaining such strategic positions might prove to be one of the most important tasks of policy and strategy.

8) The interim aim of the Soviet School of providing combat support by other naval forces to the main type of naval strike forces conducting a given operation was actually to gain a limited command of the sea. Professor Pavlovich made this abundantly clear in the last relevant article published before the Nazi invasion in mid-1941. (In the 28 August 1938 *Red Fleet* article, Evseyev had verged on saying this—providing preliminary rather than just direct support to "one or another operations at sea, especially to landing operations," made it possible to achieve nothing less than gaining command of the sea.)

The composite Soviet School of naval warfare that resulted from Belli's eclectic work was not to be tested in World War II. Capital ships—including battleships, heavy cruisers, and aircraft carriers—would have been required to implement the force-equalization-by-attrition strategy prior to forcing a general engagement with the enemy's main force of capital ships (to at least gain full control of the Soviet Union's peripheral seas). These lay on the stocks uncompleted (or not even laid down in the case of the aircraft carriers) when the lessons of the Finnish War were digested in 1940 and the vast material and human resources being expended in the capital-ship construction program were diverted to meet the Army's demonstrated need for reequipment.

In *Soviet Naval Strategy* (1968) it was stated (in a long footnote at the outset of Chapter IV) that the evidence of a Young School dispute with the Old School was too persuasive to disregard—despite the repeated assertions of a former Soviet naval officer (Nicholas Artamonov alias Nick Shadrin) that the Soviet Navy had *always* wanted aircraft carriers and that the dispute of the two schools had not affected that longstanding desire or any other major policy issue of naval development. Additional evidence subsequently uncovered fully supports Artamonov's assertion that the Soviet Navy never gave up hoping for the eventual construction of aircraft carriers. However, the Soviet School of naval warfare that emerged as the dialectical synthesis of that dispute may be seen clearly to have critically affected the subsequent force structuring of the Navy, including Stalin's willingness in 1937 (and probably again in 1950) to include aircraft carriers in the Soviet shipbuilding programs. (Both programs were cancelled after two to three years).

The real significance of the Old School-Young School dispute seems to be that it accurately reflected the struggle between the Navy on one hand against the Army and Party on the other. At stake was the establishment, as a tenet of Soviet military doctrine, of a limited but elastic "command-of-the-sea" theory that was needed by the Navy to justify the construction of a large navy of capital ships, including aircraft carriers.

In a 1968 review of the 1965 book *Questions of Strategy and Operational Art in Soviet Military Works (1917-1940)*, a highly respected Army theoretician, Professor (Colonel General) N. Lomov, stated that as concerns the part of the book devoted to the strategy for a war at sea:

> The influence of two important factors affected the content of military-theoretical research and its subject matter in the field of naval art:
> (1) the divergence in the views of representatives of the naval and military services over general matters of military construction; and
> (2) the conflict of views between what were called the "Old" and "Young" schools concerning the missions of the naval forces in a future war and the character of the construction of the Soviet Navy.[2] (p. 105)

Similarly, in a 1980 book, *History of Soviet Military Thought*, the senior Army officer who authored it, stated that the two disparate viewpoints of the Old School and the Young School "were worked out in theory *and in practice* (emphasis supplied). Obviously the considerable historical research done in Soviet military theory by the Soviet author-historian, I.A. Korotkov, led him to the conclusion that the early debate between the two schools *did* have some practical consequences.

The lessons of World War II that most influenced Soviet naval theory during the war stemmed largely from the operations conducted by the navies of the Western powers and Japan. Due to the fact that Soviet naval missions, even that for a submarine anti-SLOC campaign against shipping, were oriented largely toward supporting the ground forces, the development of naval thought derived from the Navy's experience in the Great Patriotic War was limited primarily to the subject of support for the coastal flanks of the ground forces. Since this subject was not central to the Soviet School of naval warfare that dominated theorizing in the Navy, the impact of the

Navy's own experience on the development of naval theory was minimal. However, the oceanic operations of aircraft-carrier forces, amphibious forces, and antisubmarine forces of the major Western naval powers exerted a great influence on the evolution of Soviet naval thought in general and especially on the Soviet School of naval warfare.

Aircraft carriers were perceived by Soviet School theoreticians as the key ship type for naval operations beyond home waters—whether for fighting enemy naval forces to gain or maintain command of the sea in a given theater of military action, or in a region of one; for providing cover and direct support for amphibious landings; for conducting antisubmarine warfare for convoys and general protection of the sea lines of communication; or for the protection of other naval forces. Japanese-U.S. carrier warfare in the Pacific was interpreted as having demonstrated the Soviet School tenet that naval forces could successfully conduct active (tactically offensive) operations against stronger enemy naval forces provided only that the weaker forces could establish a superiority of forces in the intended area of operations and maintain it long enough to carry out what were essentially raids.

From a 1944 article on Soviet amphibious operations written by then-Rear Admiral Gorshkov about his extensive experience in commanding them over the preceding three years, it was apparent that the future Navy head had accepted the Soviet School views. Apparently Professor Belli had taught them to him at the Naval War College. This included the key Soviet School tenet that a limited command of the sea could be exerted (in just a given area for long enough to carry out quickly executed operations) before a stronger enemy could reinforce and intervene.

Professor Belli's Naval War College colleague, Professor Chernyshev, was first to publicly make the Soviet School's case for aircraft carriers as a requirement to provide air cover for the fleets at sea. He also persuasively justified requirements for other types of large surface-combatant ships. He did this in a book on surface naval warfare that appeared in 1945.

Chernyshev reflected the Soviet School's awareness that the submarine was limited in its mission capabilities largely to attacking merchant shipping and that the submarine is inherently incapable of replacing the aircraft carrier in the latter's multiple roles, particularly for contesting command of the sea. As Professor Stalbo was noted to have observed in the mid-1970s, the advent and availability of carrier strike and antisubmarine aircraft in "sea and oceanic theaters of military action" turned "a completely new page in the history of naval art."

After the end of World War II and throughout the second half of the 1940s, several of the leading naval theoreticians, most notably Admiral-Professors Alafuzov, Belli, and Piterskiy, made it apparent that the Navy did not necessarily entertain long-range ambitions to contest for full or global command of the sea in the Mahanian sense. Yet they certainly looked forward to the day when the Navy would be provided large naval forces of the right types, especially attack aircraft carriers. Then it would be able in any future general war to maintain the command of the key sea and ocean areas immediately contiguous to the Soviet Union, despite the concentrated opposition of the U.S. and other NATO naval forces, and be able to hold the command in dispute in a more extensive zone farther from Soviet shores. Apparently construction of aircraft carriers was being advocated just on the basis of their potential use in the naval theaters peripheral to the Soviet Union to aid in gaining and maintaining command of the sea in those theaters or to at least hold the command in dispute. The advocacy did not stem from any apparent long-term goal of eventually challenging the general sea supremacy of the Western alliance throughout the "World Ocean."

It was this preferred alternative of limiting command of the sea to the peripheral seas that seemed to be clearly reflected in Admiral Alafuzov's several articles in 1946. In these, the head of the Naval War College stated and repeated for emphasis that the essence of naval warfare and naval strategy was to gradually expand one's zone of command (or of "established" or "permanent" command) until it embraced the entire theater(s) of naval operations concerned. He argued that, with proper preparation, a weaker navy could maintain command of an extended coastal zone. He added that a stronger adversary would be forced increasingly to fight to win the "command" in a Soviet coastal theater of military actions and that it might take years of fighting by an enemy to wrest the command from Soviet forces. In other words, Alafuzov was asserting that the Soviet fleets' capabilities for at least holding command of the Soviet home waters in dispute, even against the more powerful non-Communist world navies, would be increasing in the years to come.

Alafuzov also refuted the main argument that had been employed by the Young School adherents ever since the late 1920s to prove the proclaimed invalidity of the command-of-the-sea doctrine: because (allegedly) the two operational manifestations of command of the sea prescribed by Colomb and Mahan (the general naval engagement and the sea blockade) had been proven to be no longer valid, the command-of-the-sea theory itself must be, *ipso facto*, invalid. Alafuzov claimed that the general engagement had been replaced by two complementary forms of naval warfare: daily operational activity for maintaining (a limited) command of the sea within one's coastal zone of established command (to enable one to carry out assigned missions in that zone); and specially planned operations for gaining the "command" of a new region of a theater initially or for expanding it subsequently (as well as for defeating any enemy attempts to reestablish command in one's zone of established command). He explicitly rejected the view that because the forms for gaining command of the sea (general engagement and blockade) had changed with the advent of a new weapon systems, the basic command-of-the-sea principle had been invalidated.

In an article in the Armed Forces' General Staff journal, *Military Thought*, of August 1946, Alafuzov even took pains to disabuse that journal's senior military readership of the belief, previously shared by both the Old and Young Schools, that success could be achieved in a war at sea by following a strategy that established systematic evasion of battle as the norm. Rather, he stressed that the outcome of a war at sea would require actual fighting to maintain command of the sea in Soviet coastal zones of established command and that the "command" often would not be achievable without accepting battle that, as he put it with tactful indirection, would "cause losses to the enemy." However, Alafuzov considered that a force-equalization strategy was impracticable, doubtless due to the great disparity of forces faced by the Soviet Navy. It will be recalled that, although Professor Belli favored building up the Soviet Navy so it could implement such a strategy, he had acknowledged in a June 1940 article that the German Navy suffered too great a disparity of forces at that time to use such a strategy against the British Navy.

In this same *Military Thought* article, Alafuzov also set out in detail a new concept involving three concentric zones of defense extending from Soviet shores. In the Near Zone just offshore out to 100 miles or so, Soviet coastal craft could operate under virtually continuous land-based air cover and so maintain the Near Zone as a zone of permanent command. The Far Zone, which extended farther out to sea beyond the Near Zone for 150 to 200 miles more, was intended primarily for operation of large surface combatants with limited air support. Expansion of the zone of permanent command to eventually include all of this intermediate or Far Zone was asserted by Alafuzov to be the main aim of naval development. Beyond lay the Open-ocean Zone. The almost exclusive domain of Soviet submarines, mainly for antishipping, the Open-ocean Zone is that area of the ocean in which, for lack of any substantial surface-ship or air-support operations, only sea-denial could be attempted to hold the command in dispute.

The Naval War College traditionally is expected to take the lead in the "creative" revision of outmoded doctrine. The college's head commented on the increasing role of aircraft carriers in oceanic theaters, noting that their appearance in contemporary navies had markedly increased the radius of action of naval air power. This remark indicates that Alafuzov was an advocate of building attack aircraft carriers for the Soviet Navy. Furthermore, aircraft carriers are *the* naval-force type *par excellence* to fight for gaining and maintaining command of the sea (while submarines are inherently limited to attempting to deny an adversary unhindered use of the sea but are inherently unable by themselves to ensure effective use of the seas for their own side). But Alafuzov both favored aircraft carriers and believed in the gaining of theater-wide command of the sea as the proper goal of Soviet strategy for the naval side of any major war. The two opinions warrant the conclusion that he saw the construction of attack aircraft carriers as a necessary means to the end of building a navy that some day could expect to at least hold command of the sea "in dispute"—or better to gain command for itself against the powerful Western naval powers—in the maritime areas critical for defense of the Soviet homeland against seaborne attack.

Rear Admiral Belli, although remaining as staunch an advocate of limited command of the sea in the postwar period as he had been publicly from 1938 through 1940 in his formulation of Soviet School tenets, also showed signs of favoring the construction of a navy that eventually would be able at least to hold command of the sea "in dispute" over the full extent of the key sea theaters peripheral to the Soviet Union. Most notably, he argued at the Naval Scientific Conference held in March 1946 at the Naval War College in Leningrad that the main reason for the assumed invalidity of the general command-of-the-sea doctrine was that the Soviet Union lacked the "productive capacity" to build the big-ship navy that would be required to implement such a strategy. This formula (also stated by Penzin) seemed to imply that the general command-of-the-sea doctrine was not invalid *per se*. It was merely unsuitable in the postwar Stalinist period for a navy so inferior to its probable adversaries in any future war at sea. It would have been unrealistic in the extreme to have based Soviet strategy for such a war on any conceivable combination of surprise, tactical proficiency, or force-equalization-by-attrition methods.

In the prewar period, Professor Belli had surreptitiously brought limited command of the sea in from the cold by the back door (after having ejected it from the front with a stream of loud invective). He had devised a two-part prescription—preliminary support for major operations, as well as the normal direct support. The outspoken Admiral Alafuzov scorned such subterfuge and in 1946 stated candidly that before undertaking major operations special measures would have to be taken to reduce a stronger adversary's superior forces in an intended region of operations. That these measures of preliminary support for an operation were tantamount to gaining a limited command of the sea was made explicit by Captain First Rank Evseyev in an article in the *Naval Digest* at the end of 1946.

In a 1948 article in *Military Thought*, Captain First Rank V. Andreyev gave lengthy consideration to the support the Navy was required to give to Army coastal operations. Parallel to this, he maintained (on the basis of numerous historical examples) that command of the sea should not be viewed as an end in itself. It was just the means to an end of gaining temporary "command" in a theater of military actions or in a region of one (just) when necessary to support (primarily Army-flank) operations. Among the historical examples cited by Andreyev was the German Navy's seizure of Norway in 1940 which Professor Belli had defended at the time against charges of "adventurism." However, instead of drawing the conclusion that Belli had drawn—that the Norwegian operation proved that no command of the sea was required prior to launching a major operation—Andreyev resourcefully brought that operation within the bounds of Soviet School theory. He concluded that the German Navy had in actuality gained temporary "command of the sea" (by its provision of support) for the operation. This, in effect, brought the Norwegian operation, which was restricted in both duration and geographic area, under the rubric of the limited command-of-the-sea concept that remains as the theoretical hallmark of the Soviet School.

Evseyev, in late 1946, had equated providing adequate support for an operation at sea with gaining a limited command of the sea. Andreyev, two years later, turned the formula around when he criticized the Young School for having taken the position that "direct support [in the course of an operation]" would suffice rather than realizing the "necessity for gaining command of the sea as one of the methods of preliminary support [before the start of an operation]." Yet, whether one chose to view preliminary support as a prerequisite to gaining command of the sea, as Evseyev did, or gaining command of the sea as one of several necessary kinds of preliminary support, as Andreyev had, the results were the same.

Andreyev gave particularly clear evidence of being mainstream Soviet School in his views by his even-handed criticism of both the Young School and the Old School. So, too, Evseyev's 1938 article (that heralded the birth of the Soviet School) was characterized by impartial denunciation of both schools.

In what was probably the most significant of his several thought-provoking observations, Andreyev asserted: "The place of the battleship as the main striking force in many cases was taken over [since Colomb wrote in the early 1890s] by submarines and subsequently by aircraft carriers. . . . " This was a revelation, not only for its claim that the aircraft carrier had become the main striking force of navies (and seemingly for urging acceptance of this view by Army and Party leaders), but also for its assertion that the submarine had held this role for a time but then had been superseded by the aircraft carrier. This patently inaccurate statement about submarines may well have been made as a mere debating-point concession to the widespread view among senior Soviet military officers that the submarine had become the main striking force of navies.

The January 1949 Red Star article by Captain Second Rank Kulakov, was on the face of it, just a routine polemical exaggeration of the "imperialist threat." On closer inspection it was notable for its allegation that the United States had set itself the goal of gaining a general command of the sea that, if achieved, would give the United States "a commanding position in the world." This article must be taken in the context of its times—i.e., during a debate over the validity of command-of-the-sea theory in Soviet military and naval circles. Thus the article seemed calculated to contribute to a Navy lobbying campaign in the postwar period to replace the military doctrinal tenet that the Navy should only be required to provide the (minimal) support required "in the main directions" of Army-flank operations with the (more force-intensive and costly) limited command-of-the-sea strategy.

A voice opposing the Soviet School's advocacy of (just) a limited command of the sea was heard in July 1949 in a *Military Thought* article by well-known naval historian, Rear Admiral Piterskiy. He advocated implicitly that an "active" fleet-in-being strategy employing submarines, aircraft, and light, fast surface-craft be adopted until the Soviet Union could build aircraft-carrier forces to fight those of the United States. Piterskiy, like Kulakov earlier in the year, alleged that the United States was aiming at gaining a general command of the sea with carrier task forces. He implied that those forces made the limited command-of-the-sea strategy, which the Navy was advocating, inadequate to prevent the destruction of Soviet naval forces, even if they remained in home waters. This was based on the view that the basic principle of the U.S. Navy was to concentrate its forces in the contested areas "in strength several times superior to that of the enemy." Piterskiy's stand reflected a seemingly successful Navy campaign to win Stalin's initial, if short-lived, approval for a postwar program for delayed construction of aircraft carriers, but one which, if Stalin in fact approved, was cancelled by him shortly before his death in 1953 (or promptly after it). The aim was to develop the Navy so that it could at least prevent the U.S./NATO naval forces from gaining and exercising sea control in Soviet home waters. The successful campaign was to become apparent four years later with publication of the third volume of *A History of Naval Art* (which Piterskiy edited).

In his August 1949 article in *Red Star*, Captain First Rank Mil'gram returned to the staple assertion of Soviet School theoreticians. Command of the sea should not be viewed (in Old School terms) as an end in itself; it was only the means to the end of being able to create "favorable conditions" (i.e., temporary command) for the successful conduct of the Soviet Navy's assigned missions. Mil'gram specified the Navy's priority mission of supporting the Army's coastal flank but did not go into the more detailed aspects of the matter as Andreyev had in his 1948 article in *Military Thought*. The command of the sea to be sought was viewed as a limited one for just long enough to carry out whatever missions had been assigned—missions almost invariably associated with providing cover or support to the Army's coastal flank.

In particular, Mil'gram derided Corbett's (inaccurately described) modification of Colomb, that the ultimate aim of naval warfare was to gain "full and permanent command of the sea," even at the expense of "all other missions, for example, cooperation with the ground forces, protection for the transit and debarkation of amphibious landings, protection of communications, and so on." Mil'gram's condemnation of Corbett's allegedly "erroneous doctrines" may well have been aimed at Rear Admiral Piterskiy and other advocates of building aircraft carrier forces sufficient to prevent the U.S. from achieving its alleged aim of gaining global command of the sea.

The third and final volume of *A History of Naval Art*, which appeared at the end of the Stalinist postwar period, reflected Piterskiy's earlier rejection of the Soviet School's theoretical readiness to accept battle with a stronger adversary in Soviet home waters. It seemed to return to the pre-Soviet School systematization of evasion of battle that was particularly characteristic of the Young School. It flagrantly misinterpreted the basic tenet of Mahan and Colomb (on the inescapable necessity to either destroy or blockade an adversary). Thereby it maintained that those two conceptualists of the "full" or "general" command-of-the-sea theory had only advocated a limited command-of-the-sea doctrine. The *History* grossly exaggerated the chances of a much weaker navy to win a war at sea by avoiding the unpleasant fact that it is usually necessary to fight the stronger adversary—even for a limited "command."

However, this appears to have been intended as merely a short-term expedient. More importantly for the long term was the use of the French Young School of Admiral Aube in the 1880s as a combined foreign-navy and historical surrogate. Piterskiy's *History* appeared to be lobbying for the Soviet Union, now that it had grown strong economically, to eschew such cheap solutions as that of the Young School (which by its nature traditionally had attempted to build only light naval forces) and instead to build aircraft-carrier forces of sufficient size and in adequate numbers to be able in due course to attempt to hold command of the sea "in dispute" in peripheral sea and ocean areas. The reader will recall that in his 1949 article in *Military Thought*, Rear Admiral Piterskiy had advocated just such a shipbuilding policy to enable the Soviet Union to pursue such a limited command-of-the-sea strategy. One may reasonably surmise that Piterskiy was already well along in editing the *History* and had shaped its main thrust on command of the sea when he wrote the *Military Thought* article. So is not surprising that the basic thrust of both were the same.

At any rate, the fact that a senior naval officer was responsible for expression of such views in both the closed and august forum of the theoretical journal for the Armed Forces' General Staff and in the openly published textbook for the education of Soviet naval officers leaves little doubt regarding the status of the views expressed as constituting the strategy preferred by the Soviet Navy. Its most notable aspect was the optimism it reflected that the time was ripe for the Navy to gain doctrinal acceptance over Army opposition for the Soviet School's limited command-of-the-sea concept. The Young School only advocated the construction of light aircraft carriers to provide air cover and reconnaissance for peripheral-seas operations. Instead, the Soviet School expanded the "limited-command" theory to one aspiring to a "strategic-command" justification for building enough of the large carriers necessary to fight to hold the command of the key theaters of military action "in dispute".

Stalin was known to have favored the then head of the Soviet Navy, Admiral Nikolai Kuznetsov. As mentioned earlier, Stalin appeared likely to have approved a construction program of aircraft carriers by 1947 to start in the mid-1950s. Whatever the case, it is certainly fair to conclude from Piterskiy's 1949 article in *Military Thought* and from the 1953 volume of *The History of Naval Art* that the Navy, in fact, was preparing the necessary theoretical justification for the anticipated construction of attack aircraft carriers. Furthermore, their mission was to contest for "strategic" command of the naval theaters of military actions peripheral to the Soviet homeland.

The *History* provides good evidence of what seemed apparent from Professor Belli's formulation of the limited command-of-the-sea thesis from 1938 to 1940—that the concept was expandable to a more extensive command-of-the-sea theory whenever circumstances permitted. By 1949, when Rear Admiral Piterskiy's article appeared in *Military Thought*, the time apparently seemed propitious, as indicated by the contents of that article, for the Navy to at least aim at "strategic command" of the key naval theaters of military action.

The rest of the *History* is standard Soviet School fare with the same even-handed criticism of both the Old and Young Schools that Andreyev had made in his 1948 *Military Thought* article. It is notable how easily the *History*'s recommended strategy of aiming at a "strategic" command of the sea in the key theaters of military actions employing aircraft-carrier task forces was added to Soviet School tenets. However, the *History* was not revised throughout to make it consistent with the "strategic-command" strategy. Quite likely it would have been premature to do so since the *History* was intended as a textbook for educating Soviet naval officers and, hence, had to basically reflect the strategic tenets applicable for the near term.

Patently, implementing a strategy of contesting against the U.S. Navy for strategic command of the key theaters of military actions was something for the future—when and if a sufficient number of attack aircraft carriers could be built, manned, trained, and brought into operation. In the interval of the several decades that such an ambitious program would require, some interim strategy was obviously necessary.

Was this to continue to be the "limited-command" strategy for which the Navy had lobbied so long and hard to gain its acceptance by the Army and Party? Or was it to settle for a tactically "active" fleet-in-being strategy such as Piterskiy had recommended for interim use in his 1949 *Military Thought* article? Piterskiy had asserted that any wartime effort to implement the "limited-command" strategy would only lead to the destruction of the Soviet Navy, even if it remained in home waters, inasmuch as the U.S. Navy's established strategy provided for keeping its forces concentrated in strength far superior to any possible concentration of Soviet naval forces. It would seem that the choice was made for a near-term "active" fleet-in-being strategy pending development of an aircraft-carrier navy able to contest for "strategic command" in the key naval theaters of military actions littoral to the Soviet Union.

Admiral Alafuzov, in a *Naval Digest* article at the end of 1946, adjured the Soviet Navy to hold command of the sea "in dispute" in zones of command on naval positions. From this it was hypothesized for testing against the subsequent evidence that Soviet strategy for naval warfare from 1946 to 1953 was one of a modernized, tactically offensive fleet in being in the sense that Corbett attributed to Nelson, of "an inferior fleet kept actively in being" in order to exploit its "general power of holding such command in dispute." Three pieces of evidence came to light. The first was a 1948 article by Captain First Rank Andreyev criticizing the early Old School advocates for their insistence that the Navy must have a sizeable enough battle force of capital ships to hold command of the sea in Soviet home waters "in dispute" before any mission-oriented operations could be conducted. Andreyev maintained, in effect, that even a much weaker navy could gain "temporary command of the sea" in selected sea regions and exploit it to conduct at least some of the normal missions of a navy. In this advocacy of active operations by the inferior navy Andreyev seemed to be describing a fleet-in-being strategy.

The second bit of evidence was quite tenuous. This was in an article by Captain First Rank Mil'gram which appeared in *Red Star* in 1949. It involved the seeming use of a foreign-navy surrogate condemning Corbett's account of the British fleet-in-being strategy in World War I and the speculation that Mil'gram might well have been implicitly criticizing Soviet adoption of such a strategy. The only supporting shred of evidence was Mil'gram's associated complaint that Corbett's views were being "revived again and again abroad in works on the problems of a contemporary navy." As the reader will have come to appreciate, ascribing developments at home to foreign sources is a standard method of the Aesopian communications employed by the Russians.

The third piece of evidence to support the hypothesis that the Soviet School of naval warfare was tantamount to an "active" fleet-in-being strategy came in 1953 in volume 3 of *A History of Naval Art* and was more substantial. The Tsarist Russian Navy's "idea of developing a defense-in-depth in a naval theater composed of fortified regions and mine-artillery positions" was cited. This was said to have "served as the basis for a [Soviet] theory of battle in a previously infrastructured position in a coastal region with the cooperation of the heterogeneous forces and means of a navy," and was termed "progressive." Also, the *History* commented on Corbett's fleet-in-being concept in non-polemical terms that seemed to present the concept in a manner tailored for the Soviet Navy of the period:

> . . . [F]or achieving the aims of war at sea Corbett recommended utilization of the "fleet-in-being" principle in combination with "small, active operations." He viewed this method for the conduct of war as a natural one for a weaker navy conducting a defense at sea . . . . Corbett understood this as employing against the main forces of an adversary what is called "auxiliary" forces. To these he assigned destroyers, submarines, torpedoes, and mines.

While the *History* went on to characterize Corbett's fleet-in-being strategy as one of "obvious groundlessness," the reasons given to support this allegation were all found upon analysis to have been either vague or irrelevant but to have reflected a reluctance to condemn the concept substantively.

On balance, the Soviet School of naval warfare seems to resemble very closely Corbett's concept of the fleet-in-being strategy. In particular, both extolled the virtues of an active defense to constantly harass a stronger enemy to keep him off balance and so hold command of the sea "in dispute." As early as April 1939, Belli had adjured his fellow officers that "the defensive missions of the Navy must never be forgotten" and that even Soviet military doctrine's stress on the offensive must not be allowed to mislead them to rule out a well-organized defense. Moreover, the stress on an unceasingly active defense had been a tenet of the Soviet Union's "unified military strategy" (and hence mandatory for the Navy) since Frunze's time in the mid-1920s.

Finally, the *History*'s choice of a description for Corbett's view of the fleet-in-being strategy as "a natural one for a weaker navy conducting a war at sea" seems to have been designed to fit neatly the Soviet Navy's situation. The Soviets would not admit publicly that they had adopted a "bourgeois" concept—but it seems to the author that by 1953 the Soviet School of naval warfare had come to be one of an "active" fleet-in-being.

With the Khrushchev-Zhukov switch not long after Stalin's death to a neo-Young School policy of building basically just a submarine navy, Soviet School exponents of a limited command-of-the-sea strategy found themselves silenced publicly in their advocacy. Only in naval-authored articles published in the two issues of the restricted-distribution theoretical journal of the Armed Forces' General Staff, *Military Thought*, that found their way to the West can one find continued reflections of the Soviet School's views.

The October 1953 issue of *Military Thought* contained an article on naval support for Army coastal-flank operations. Written by a Captain First Rank (later Rear Admiral) V'yunenko, the article implicitly argued for a limited command-of-the-sea strategy that would allow the Navy in wartime to strike directly at an enemy's naval bases to surprise the ships in them. This, in effect, was a plea for the Army to liberate its "faithful handmaiden" of 1941-1945 from its role of just providing direct combat support to coastal ground-force operations in coastal waters. The Navy wanted to greatly expand its role to allow it to make raids throughout the wartime theaters of military action.

The Army had a long-standing antipathy to giving the Navy sanction for operations independent of itself, quite likely because so doing would afford the Navy the requisite theoretical basis for demanding more surface ships (likely at the expense of the Army's budget). Not surprisingly, V'yunenko's argument appears to have fallen on deaf ears. This was so despite the fact that he had cleverly argued his case in terms of such raids being primarily calculated to give more support, although indirect, to the coastal operations of the ground forces.

The other particularly significant article on Soviet School theory that appeared in *Military Thought* during the 1953-1955 period was one published in July 1955. It was entitled "On Command of the Sea," and signed by a Captain First Rank Shavtsov. This article logically and persuasively argued that the Soviet Union would be amiss not to build the big ships so that it could eventually adopt a strategy for naval warfare that aimed at finally being able to gain and maintain "strategic command of the sea" throughout the key theaters of military action involved in the naval side of a general war.

Shavtsov showed the total inadequacy of merely gaining the "tactical command" of the area of an intended naval operation in support of the coastal flank of the ground forces. He went on to make it abundantly clear that "operational command" of at least a major region of a theater of an intended operation, even when nuclear weapons were to be employed by the Navy, was the minimum command required to yield a high probability of success for naval operations in support of coastal-flank ground force operations. Even then, Shavtsov concluded, the side that held the "strategic" command of a theater always retained the potential of bringing additional forces into any given region of a theater of military action to thwart the intended coastal-flank support operations of the Navy.

In effect, Shavtsov was arguing the inadequacy of an "active" fleet-in-being strategy. At the same time he was laying out for the senior Army readers of *Military Thought* the details of the "strategic command-of-the-sea" solution that the Soviet School of naval warfare recommended for the longer term. He made it clear that providing mere tactical support for ground-force operations in coastal areas, as then stipulated by military doctrine, could result only in failure. The costs for a viable "operational command-of-the-sea" strategy were indicated to be larger, better naval forces of the right balance of force types that would be capable of actually fighting and defeating an enemy's naval forces if they tried to interfere with the Navy's operations in home waters rather than evading them by hit-and-run raids. However, Shavtsov stressed that the Navy would not be reduced to passivity as long as it could gain and hold the "operational command." Nevertheless, he emphasized that the inability to gain the "strategic command" would limit naval operations to little more than raids.

Shavtsov admitted explicitly that it would be very difficult and costly for the Soviet Union to develop the necessary naval capabilities for gaining "strategic command of the sea" in the key naval theaters of military actions peripheral to the Soviet Union (let alone any thought at that juncture of gaining full or global command of the sea). He observed that such a major military program would have to be approved by the Supreme High Command and, in its operational execution, would require the support of the appropriate other armed services.

NATO aircraft carriers would be the main targets for the Navy's nuclear strike capabilities, with submarines perceived as having the major role in anti-carrier operations. While submarines could not replace aircraft carriers in their sea-control role, the former were portrayed as capable of denying command of the sea to NATO carrier forces by dint of sinking enough carriers to hold the command "in dispute" and so negating NATO operations.

Shavtsov stressed that shore facilities (in general) and naval bases were particularly vulnerable to airborne nuclear strikes. He presented the role of aircraft in sea control as attacking shore facilities and large surface ships. The latter were to constitute the primary antisubmarine platforms. No open-ocean role for surface ships was mentioned—implicit evidence of the constraint placed on the Navy's operations on the high seas due to its lack of aircraft carriers.

Shavtsov repeated Admiral Alafuzov's 1946 formulation of three concentric zones of naval defense and clarified their locations and the Navy's responsibilities. Shavtsov's article was couched in terms that gave the impression of being in line with the Khrushchev-Zhukov policy of building only a light-forces navy. In fact it was a rather ingenious Soviet School formulation for an interim "active" fleet-in-being strategy against the day when a more extensive command-of-the-sea strategy might be feasible. This concept was a logical development of the views expressed in 1949 and 1953 by Rear Admiral Piterskiy. It was also consonant with the basically Old

School prescription of Evseyev in 1938 of aiming, over the long term, to be able to gain and hold the command of the sea in the key naval theaters peripheral to the Soviet Union to defeat any NATO carrier task forces threatening strikes against the Soviet homeland.

By the mid-1950s the advent of nuclear weapons underscored the feasibility of producing suitable aircraft and submarine delivery platforms (including nuclear-powered submarines) for such weapons. Obviously these developments encouraged the Soviets to believe that an adequate capability for countering the threat of carrier-borne air strikes could be developed without the great delay, expense, and probable eventual failure of attempting to match or outbuild the NATO carrier task forces in a naval arms race.

A 1967 *Military Thought* article by three senior Army officers stated that a "unity of views" had been worked out by 1955 on a definition of command of the sea—gaining the command was not an end in itself (but just a means to the end of carrying out assigned missions). This suggests that the Army's long-standing opposition had not abated. The Army still would accept as doctrine no theory of command of the sea that would be more extensive than the "tactical command" for supporting ground operations in coastal sectors that Shavtsov had shown to be so inadequate. The Army had always maintained that it was sufficient for the Navy to do no more than achieve temporary superiority in the main direction of coastal operations of the ground forces. This was considered by the Army leadership and General Staff as adequate for the Navy to carry out amphibious landings, provide gunfire support, and perform other support tasks. As mentioned before, by sanctioning no more than this, the Army deprived the Navy of the requisite theoretical justification for building the substantial number of expensive large surface combatant ships, including aircraft carriers, whose great cost might well lead to a reduction in the Army's share of the military budget.

Finally then, what precisely were the tenets of the Soviet School of naval warfare theory that Admiral Gorshkov inherited when he officially took over the leadership of the Soviet Navy in January 1956? They may be summarized as follows:

(1) By 1953 the Soviet School of naval warfare favored by the Navy was one of an "active" (tactically offensive) fleet in being. This body of theory was not replaced or significantly altered until 1956 by the Khrushchev-Zhukov policy of building a largely submarine navy in pursuit of a neo-Young School doctrine.

(2) The "active" fleet-in-being concept favored by the Navy posited "an active defense" of uninterrupted harassment of a stronger, usually blockading, navy to prevent it from gaining and maintaining command of the sea; that is to hold the command in doubt, or "in dispute," so that the enemy could not carry out his own naval missions.

(3) The Soviet School operationalized this fleet-in-being concept of holding command of the sea in Soviet home waters "in dispute" employing a constant tactical offensive by adapting to naval use the military doctrinal tenets of "deeply echeloned zones of defense" for the "sea and oceanic" areas from which could originate seaborne threats to the homeland and to its ground forces in coastal areas. This involved establishing three concentric zones—the Near Zone, the Far Zone, and the Open-ocean Zone—which together extended out from Soviet shores right up to the coasts of potential enemies.

The Near Zone extended out from the coasts of the Soviet Union to the maximum range at which land-based naval fighter planes could provide virtually continuous air cover for fleet units—only 100 miles or so. In the Near Zone all of the Navy's forces could be brought to bear against any attempted enemy amphibious landings or naval shore bombardments or strikes. This would include the Navy's coastal artillery and missile batteries, defensive mine barriers, light, fast surface craft as well as larger surface ships, and all Soviet tactical submarines. In the Near Zone the Navy would hope to be able to maintain what it misleadingly termed "command of the sea," limited in geographical extent as it would be.

The Far Zone extended out to sea from the forward perimeter of the Near Zone to the maximum range from the homeland at which attack planes from enemy aircraft carriers could strike at Soviet ports, naval bases, coastal airfields, and other coastal installations of a naval and military nature. In this Far Zone only large surface ships, submarines, and the Soviet Union's long-range bombers and reconnaissance planes could operate. In this zone the Navy would attempt to fight and win control to the maximum of its relatively limited capability.

Finally, beyond the forward perimeter of the Far Zone lay the Open-ocean Zone, which embraced most of the "World Ocean" beyond the relatively narrow coastal strip of 400 to 500 miles included in the Near Zone and Far Zone together. In this Open-ocean Zone only long-range submarines and occasional long-range reconnaissance and bomber planes could operate to attempt to hold command of the sea "in dispute"—that is, to attempt to prevent the enemy naval forces from carrying out their assigned missions but with no thought of being able to conduct Soviet naval missions in the hostile environment of enemy sea supremacy.

Inasmuch as submarines are inherently incapable of more than sea-denial efforts to hold the command "in dispute" and cannot exercise command of the sea by themselves, and since the Soviet Navy had no aircraft carriers to take air power to sea, as essential for contesting for command of the sea and for maintaining that command by sea-control operations, the Soviet School of naval warfare could only set as its feasible aim that of expanding the Near and Far Zones gradually as new naval construction and circumstances might permit.

(4) This gradual expansion could be achieved in a combination of ways—by increasing the range of land-based fighter aircraft to provide fleet air-cover in a more extensive Near Zone, by acquiring forward bases, and by providing the Navy's large surface ships with improved antiair defensive capabilities. Seizure of advance bases at the outbreak of war would at least increase the Soviet Navy's "zone of temporary command" and, if the area could be adequately infrastructured with naval bases, airfields, defensive minefields, sonar installations, and shore command points, that "temporary" zone of command might even be made into a "zone of permanent command."

(5) The limited command-of-the-sea concept inherited by the new Navy commander in chief in January 1956 was a flexible one that had been formulated to be expandable in periods in which Soviet School tenets found official favor and the Navy provided with stronger, longer-range surface ships, including aircraft carriers. That school did advocate the construction of attack aircraft carriers, apparently primarily for use on the forward perimeter of the Far Zone to take on enemy carriers before they could launch strikes against the homeland. The Navy, particularly as revealed by Shavtsov's article, "On Command of the Sea," in the July 1955 issue of the Armed Forces' General Staff journal *Military Thought*, was attempting to convince the Army leadership of the inadequacy of building naval forces that could only gain "tactical command of the sea" in Soviet home waters for just long enough to provide naval support for Army coastal flank operations. To avoid condemning the Navy to passive impotence in the face of a concentrated attack by stronger adversaries, the Navy argued that it must be at least provided the forces required to enable it to gain and maintain "operational command" in the various key regions of naval theaters.

At the same time the advantages of "strategic command" of entire key theaters of military action were extolled as the sure way to success for mission accomplishment by the Navy. This clearly would require decades of construction of large surface combatant ships, most importantly attack carriers. In the interim, the Navy had to be content just to lobby for a force structure equal to gaining "operational command" of the really critical regions of the key naval theaters of military actions peripheral to the USSR.

These Soviet School tenets for the naval side of any general war were in place when Admiral Gorshkov entered upon his nearly 30-year incumbency as the commander in chief of the Soviet Navy. And from what we know of his study at the Naval War College under Professor, Rear Admiral Vladimir Belli, the chief architect of the Soviet School, and from Gorshkov's early writings, the new Navy leader had been converted to those beliefs long before he was chosen to head the Navy.

Notes

1. Although no copy of this book has found its way to the West, there are enough partial descriptions of its contents to piece together its basic nature with some confidence.

2. N. Lomov, "A Collection of Works on Development of the Theory of Soviet Military Art in the Interwar Period" [Sbornik trudov o razvitii teorii Sovetskogo voennogo iskusstva v mezhvoyennyi period], *Military-Historical Journal* No. 1, January 1968, pp. 101-107.

3. I.A. Korotkov, *Istoriya Sovetskoi voennoi mysli*, Nauka Press, 1980, p. 178.

4. "In the mid-'30s Commander Belli formulated a limited command-of-the-sea concept. . . . After World War II, this concept was widened into a concept of three zones and the closer to the shore an attacker came, the greater degree of command-of-the-sea the Soviets could exercise. . . . " Nicholas G. Shadrin, "The Soviet Navy," Address. U.S. Naval War College, Newport, R.I.: 20 May 1975.

Glossary of Soviet "Command-of-the Sea" Terms

Blockade, Naval—"Bottling up" an enemy's main naval forces in their bases. This is the only Mahanian alternative to the destruction of the enemy's main naval forces in a "general engagement" for gaining a general or "full" command of the sea.

Blockade, Close—Maintaining the blockading forces within sight (originally) but now within radar range of the bases to prevent the blockaded forces from slipping out to sea undetected.

Blockade, Distant—Maintaining the blockading forces out of sight of the ships in the blockaded ports. For example, the British blockade of the German Navy in World War II was conducted mainly at the exits from the North Sea, far from the German bases blockaded.

Command of the Sea, Holding in Dispute—Gaining enough control over the sea to at least deny its free use for the enemy's shipping and naval operations.

"Command of the Sea," Limited—Control of limited areas for just long enough to carry out a given operation before the stronger opponent can send in reinforcements to defeat the Soviet forces involved. Whenever the term "command of the sea" is used in the limited Soviet sense to merely imply sea control of a limited region rather than general of full command of the sea, it will be enclosed in quotation marks, both in this glossary and in the text.

"Command of the Sea," Operational—Sea control in a region of a naval theater of military action long enough to carry out an operation before the stronger opponent can send in reinforcements to defeat the Soviet forces involved.

"Command of the Sea," Strategic—Sea control of an entire naval theater of military action, which is the closest to a general command of the sea to which Soviet naval theory has so far aspired. Even gaining such strategic command of an entire theater of military actions does not ensure that a stronger enemy will not sooner or later "swing" superior reinforcements into the theater and reverse the results achieved toward accomplishing missions in the theater.

"Command of the Sea," Tactical—Sea control of only the local scene of action of an operation for the time scheduled for hit-and-run raids or other very brief surprise strikes. In effect, the Army-dominated Defense Ministry and Armed Forces' General Staff insisted throughout the 1917-1956 period that

the Navy only required a composition of small, coastal forces sufficient for gaining tactical control to support Army coastal-flank operations, usually just for making amphibious landings and for conducting coastal military shipping.

"Command of the Sea," Zone of—The area in which sea control is exercised or exercisable at any given time.

"Command of the Sea," Zone of Permanent—The area or region of a naval theater of military action in which the naval forces, bases, and other infrastructure are such as to reasonably ensure that sea control therein can be maintained despite the estimated maximum enemy opposition.

"Command of the Sea," Temporary—An area, region, or entire naval theater of military action in which sea control can be maintained in wartime until or unless the stronger adversary makes a concerted effort to concentrate sufficient forces from outside that area, region, or entire naval theater of military action to reassert its superiority therein.

"Favorable Regime of the Sea"—A euphemism for having established sea control by destruction of enough of the adversary's naval forces in the area, region or entire naval theater of military action to permit the conduct of an operation in the scheduled period before the adversary would have time to send in reinforcements in sufficient strength to defeat the operation.

Fleet-in-Being Strategy, Active—A defensive strategy of the potential offensive adopted by a weaker naval power for a fleet whose main naval forces are mainly held in port to avoid any general engagement but whose auxiliary forces (submarines, aircraft, and fast surface-craft) are employed for an "active" (tactically offensive) defense with the aim of holding command of the sea in dispute. This was the strategy for an inferior navy espoused by Sir Phillip Colomb and Sir Julian Corbett and the one seemingly adopted by the Soviet School of naval warfare.

Fleet-in-Being, Passive—A defensive strategy of the potential offensive adopted by either a stronger or weaker naval power in which a fleet is held in port or close enough to port not to be cut off. This strategy is employed as a deterrent against amphibious invasion or against attacks on coastal cities or installations. The aim is to persuade a stronger naval adversary to content himself at most with establishing and maintaining a blockade of the fleet in being. Professor Belli characterized this strategy as "a fleet in existence, a threat without strikes" because it proscribes accepting battle with the stronger fleet to avoid the risk of its destruction which would leave the country open to seaborne assault or to the imposition of a victor's peace terms.

Fleet-Against-the-Shore Versus Fleet-Against-Fleet—Two generic sets of naval operations whose nature is described by their names. The former dates back to at least the '20s and has been of particular importance to the traditionally weaker Soviet Navy because surprise raids against enemy bases is one of the few recourses against a superior naval fleet for a fleet too weak to accept battle in fleet-against-fleet actions.

Heterogenous Forces (raznorodnye sily)—Nominally refers to all of the main types of naval forces, submarines, aircraft, and surface ships but is frequently used to imply the need for large surface-combatants, particularly aircraft carriers.

Old School of Naval Warfare—A classical Mahanist full-command-the-sea strategy to be won by destruction of an adversary's main naval forces in a general engagement or two, or his blockade in port. This school was inherited from the Tsarist Russian Navy, particularly from Nikolai Klado. In the persons of Professors Boris Gervais and Mikhail Petrov of the Naval War College in Leningrad, it was dominant from 1917 until finally overthrown by the Young School in 1932.

The Small War at Sea, Per the Old School—A type of defensive naval warfare by a weaker navy that had two variants in the Old School theory. In the case of such a sharp disparity of forces that the gradual force-equalization tactics of causing the enemy gradual attrition until a general engagement was feasible had no realistic prospect of bringing victory, the aim of the weaker side was limited to hindering the stronger navy while the latter executed its missions but not expecting to prevent the enemy from accomplishing its aim. In the case of a weaker navy having at least two thirds as many battleships and heavy cruisers as its stronger opponent, the aim was to hold command of the sea in dispute to at least prevent the enemy from accomplishing his missions although without hope of being able to accomplish one's own missions. The Old School advocated this second case.

The Small War at Sea, Per Young School—A type of defensive naval warfare conducted by a much weaker side without capital ships. The less expensive auxiliary means of a "mosquito fleet" (submarines, aircraft, fast surface-craft, and mines) were employed. The aim was to deter a stronger adversary from attacking by "paralyzing" his will to fight through constant harassment in the forms of either raids and strikes against his naval forces, bases, ports, and coasts or against his weakest link (usually his merchant shipping), all the while avoiding any general engagement with his main naval forces.

Soviet School of Naval Warfare—An expedient synthesis of Old School and Young School tenets specifically designed to enable the Soviet Union to make effective use of the naval forces available in the late '30s and those projected for future construction. The Soviet School modified the Old School's full-command-of-the-sea concept to one of just limited "command of the sea" (that is, sea control). This limited command is to be gained initially just in regions of the key theaters of military action peripheral to the Soviet Union. This concept allows for expansion as more/forces and forward bases became available. The ultimate aim is seen as gaining "strategic command" of entire key theaters of military action peripheral to the Soviet Union. From the Young School the Soviet School adapted the former's greater appreciation for the capabilities of submarines and planes, including particularly the belief that the advent of such allegedly unblockable weapons platforms means that no naval power would be able to gain a full or general command of the sea. The Navy was to have heterogenous forces, that is, include both the light forces of the Young School and the capital ships, including aircraft carriers, of the Old School. However, submarines were to constitute the main striking forces and the capital ships were reduced from their Old School preeminence to merely providing combat support for the submarines.

Young School of Naval Warfare—Derived from the French Jeune École of the 1890s, the Young School eschewed command-of-the-sea theory in whatever form and aimed at exploiting allegedly unblockable submarines and airplanes as to deter stronger navies from blockading the Soviet Union. The Russian words for the Young School (molodaya shkola) can only be translated properly as such, not as "new school" as sometimes done.

BIBLIOGRAPHY OF
RUSSIAN-LANGUAGE SOURCE MATERIAL*

Alafuzov, V.A., "O sushchnosti morskikh operatsii" (Concerning the Nature of Naval Operations), MS Nos. 4-5, April-May 1946, pp. 6-26. (VI-228-27)

––––––– . "O sushchnosti morskikh operatsii", VM No. 8, August 1946, pp. 15-28. (VI-228-5)

––––––– . "Razvitiye povsednevnoi operativnoi deyatel'nosti flota" (The Development of the Daily Operational Activity of a Navy), MS No. 11-12, November-December 1946, pp. 11-21. (VI-228-30)

Achkasov, V. "Tvorcheskiy kharakter Sovetskogo voenno-morskogo iskusstva" (The Creative Nature of Soviet Naval Art), SF, 28 July 1956. (VI-232-80)

Achkasov, V.I., A.V. Basov, et. al., Boyevoi put' Sovetskogo Voenno-Morskogo Flota (Combat Course of the Soviet Navy), 3rd ed., 1974, 592 pp.(V-159-4)

Achkasov, V.I. and N.B. Pavlovich, Sovetskoe voenno-morskoe iskusstvo v velikoi otechestvennoi voine (Soviet Naval Art in the Great Patriotic War), 1973, 239 pp. (V-159-3)

Aleksandrov, A.P., "Podvodnaya voina v 1915 godu" (Submarine Warfare in 1915), MS No.6, June 1926, pp. 3-15. (I-18-28)

––––––– . "Kritika teorii vladeniya morem" (A Critique of the Theory of Command of the Sea), MS November 1929, pp. 3-27; February 1930, pp. 33-47; March 1930, pp. 1-16; and April 1930, pp. 27-45. (II-61-19)

––––––– . "Iz diskussii po dokladu I. Yakimychev 'Perelomnyi etap v razvitii metodov i sredstv v voiny na Baltiyskom more v voinu 1914–1917g'." (From the Discussion on the Report of I. Yakimychev "Transitional State in the Development of the Methods and Means for Conduct of War in the Baltic Sea in the War of 1914-1917"), MS No. 4, April 1931, pp. 30-40. (II-63-35)

––––––– . "Protiv reakttsionnykh teoriy na voenno-morskom nauchnom fronte" (Against Reactionary Theory on the Naval Science Front), MS No. 2, February 1932, pp. 28-58. (II-63-40)

*The Military Press of the Soviet Ministry of Defense should be understood to have been the publisher in all cases for which no other publisher is listed. Within the overall alphabetical ordering of the sources herein, multiple entries for any given source are listed in chronological order to afford an overview of each author's publishing history. The following abbreviations are used for the sources used most extensively: VM - Voennaya mysl' (Military Thought), MS - Morskoi sbornik (Naval Digest), KZ - Krasnaya zvezda (Red Star), SF - Sovetskiy flot (Soviet Fleet). For ease of reference each source is correlated with its initial appearance by a parenthetical listing of the chapter, page, and footnote number. Other listings may be readily determined from the index entries for a given author (e.g.: 228n30 - page 228, note 30.)

_____ . Review of articles of naval interest in the *Soviet Military Encyclopediya*, Vol. 1, MS No. 6, June 1932, pp. 148-156. (II-63-48)

_____ . "Voenno-morskie sily kapitalisticheskikh gosudarstv" (Naval Forces of the Capitalist States), MS No. 2, February 1934, pp. 17-54. (III-84-12)

_____ . "Operatsii na morskikh soobshcheniyakh" (Operations on the Sea Lines of Communication), MS No. 8, August 1934, pp. 18-63. (III-85-15)

Aleksandrov, A.P., I. Isakov, and V. Belli, *Operatsii podvodnykh lodok* (Submarine Operations), c1932. (III-84-1)

_____ . "Operatsii podvodnykh lodok protiv boyevykh korablei" (Submarine Operations Against Combatant Ships), MS No. 9, September 1932, pp. 7-42. (III-84-1)

Alekseyev, N., "SSSR - Velikaya morskaya derzhava" (The USSR - A Great Seapower), KZ, 20 July 1949. (VI-229-44)

Alagazin, A., "Sovremennye tendentsii morskoi aviatsii" (Modern Trends in Naval Aviation), MS No. 11, November 1925, pp. 89-104. (I-18-24)

Andreyev, V., "Psevdonauchnaya teoriya admirala Kolomba" (The Pseudo-Scientific Theory of Admiral Colomb), VM No. 7, July 1948, pp. 49-64. (VI-229-45)

"Avianostsy v sovremennoi voine na more" (Aircraft Carriers in Modern War at Sea), MS No. 5, May 1936, pp. 117-123. (III-85-21)

"Aviatsiya, morskaya" (Naval Aviation), *Sovetskaya voennaya entsiklopediya*, v. 1, 1932, pp. 139-150. (II-63-47)

Barjot, P., "Samoleti i avianosets" (Airplane and the Aircraft Carrier), MS No. 1, January 1938, pp. 99-110. (IV-137-7)

Basistiy, N., "Vrazhdebnaya ideologiya pod flagom neitral'nosti" (Inimical Ideolology Under the Flag of Neutrality), MS No. 3, March 1932, pp. 9-13. (II-63-45)

Basov, A. V., *Flot v velikoi otechestvennoi voine* (The Navy in the Great Patriotic War), 1979, 304 pp. ((IV-139-28)

Beigelin, K., "Sily vozdushnye i morskiye" (Air and Naval Forces), MS No. 11, November 1922, pp. 57-74. (I-17-5)

Belli, V. A., Review of V. P. Kalachev (ed) *Sovremennye boyevye sredstva morskogo flota* (Contemporary Combat Means of a Navy), MS No. 10, October 1933, pp. 144-147. (III-84-6)

_____ . Review of R. Gibson and M. Prendergast, *Germanskaya podvodnaya voina 1914-1918gg*, (German Submarine Warfare 1914-1918), MS No. 7, July 1935, pp. 156-158. (III-85-18)

_____ . "Osnovy vedeniya operatsii na more" (Fundamentals of the Conduct of Operations at Sea), MS No. 7, April 1939, pp. 13-24. (IV-139-49)

_____ . "Sovmestnye operatsii armii i flota" (Joint Operations of the Army and Navy), MS Nos. 17-18, September 1939, pp. 5-44. (IV-140-59)

_____ . "Pervyye operativno-strategicheskiye itogi voiny na more" (Initial Operational-Strategic Results of the War at Sea), MS No. 6, June 1940, pp. 8-21. (IV-139-53)

_____ . "Skandinavskaya morskaya operatsiya i ee uroki" (The Scandinavian Naval Operation and Its Lessons), MS No. 7, July 1940, pp. 39-53. (IV-139-56)

_____ . "Voina na Tikhom okeane" (The War in the Pacific), MS Nos. 11-12, November-December 1944, pp. 41-54. (V-159-7)

_____ . "Strategicheskiye desantnye operatsii" (Strategic Amphibious Landing Operations), VM Nos. 1-2, January-February 1945, pp. 30-38. (V-159-10)

Belli, V.A. and K.V. Penzin, *Blokada i kontrblokada* (Blockade and Counterblockade), 1967, 768 pp. (II-64-55)

_____ . *Voennye deistviye na Atlanticheskom okeane i Sredizemnom more 1939-1945gg.* (Combat Actions in the Atlantic Ocean and Mediterranean Sea, 1939-1945), 1967, 478 pp. (VI-227-16)

Blagodarev, S., "Malaya voina na Severnom more v 1914g" (Small War in the North Sea in 1914), MS No. 7, July 1927. pp. 15-26. (I-18-29)

Castex, Raoul, "More, susha, vozdukh" (Sea, Land, Air), *Voennyi zarubezhnik* Nos. 10-11, November-December 1937, pp. 22-23. (III-85-23)

Chernyshev, V.F., *Nadvodnye korabli v sovremennoi voine* (Surface Combatant Ships in Modern War), Leningrad and Moscow: Naval Press of the Peoples' Commissariat of the Navy, 1945, 159 pp. (V-159-15)

Colomb, Phillip, *Morskaya voina* (Naval Warfare, 1894 (A translation of the original work in English of 1890. (II-62-21)

"Desantnye operatsiye" (Amphibious Landing Operations), *Bol'shaya Sovetskaya entsiklopediya*, Vol. 21, 1931, p. 542. (II-62-33)

Dushenov, Konstantin, "K istorii voprosa o 'maloi voine' na more" (On the History of "the Small War" at Sea), MS No. 4, April 1928, pp. 29-44. (II-60-4)

Editorial, *Krasnyi flot*, February, 1924, pp. 19-20. (I-18-21)

Eliseyev, P., "K voprosu o gospodstvo na more" (On the Question of Command of the Sea), VM No.6, June 1947. (VI-229-41)

Eremeyev, L., "Angliyskaya literatura o voine na more" (English Literature on War at Sea) VM Nos. 6-7, June-July 1945, pp. 168-175. (VI-227-11)

Evseyev, A., "Do konsta razgromit vrazheskiye teorii v morkom strategii" (Eradicate Every Vestige of Inimical Theory in Naval Strategy), KF, 28 August 1938, pp. 2-3. (IV-139-10)

_____ . "O strategicheskom razvertivanii flota v khode voiny" (On the Strategic Deployment of a Navy in the Course of the War), MS Nos. 11-12, November-December 1946, pp. 22-45. (VI-229-36)

Gel'mersen, P.V., *Operatsii na zapadnykh teatrakh* (Operations in the Western Theaters), Leningrad: Naval War College Press, 1927). (I-62-32)

Gervais, B.B., "Osnovy voenno-morskoi strategii", Naval War College lecture excerpts of 1919-1921, published in 1965 under the same title ("Fundamentals of Naval Strategy") in *Voprosy strategii i operativnogo iskusstva v sovetskikh voennykh trudakh 1917-1940* (Questions of Strategy and Operational Art in Soviet Military Works 1917-1940), pp. 684-688. (I-17-11)

_____ . "Ocherk 5, O Morskoi Akademii, yeye nauchnaya deyatel'nost'" (Essay 5, Concerning the Naval War College, Its Scientific Work), Ms No. 12, December 1922, pp. 64-85. (I-17-6)

_____ . "Flot morskoi i flot vozdushnoi v sovremennoi voine" (The Sea Fleet and the Air Fleet in Contemporary War), MS No. 6, June 1923, pp. 198-206. (I-17-7)

_____ . "Osnovnye voprosy (K diskusii o 'maloi voine'" (Fundamental Problems [Toward a Discussion of "Small War"]), MS No. 12, December 1928, pp. 8-28. (II-61-15)

_____ . "Pis'mo v redaktsiy" (Letter to the Editorial Board), MS No. 3, March 1932, pp. 191-192. (II-63-46)

Gordon, L. and N. Mal'tsev, "Kreisera—avianostsy" (Cruisers - Aircraft Carriers), *Tekhnika i vooruzheniye*, No. 8, August 1936. pp. 50-61. (III-85-22)

_____ . "K voprosy ob avianostsakh" (On the Question of Aircraft Carriers), MS No. 4, April 1940, pp. 62-73. (IV-139-55)

Gorshkov, S.G., "Desantnye operatsii Azovskoi voennoi flotilii" (Amphibious Landing Operations of the Azov Military Flotilla), MS No. 4, April 1944, pp. 61-76. (V-159-11)

_____ . "Razvitiye sovetskogo voyenno-morskogo iskusstva" (The Development of Soviet Naval Art), MS No.2, February 1967, pp. 9-21. (VII-253-3)

_____ . *Morskaya moshch' gosudarstva* (Sea Power of the State), 1976, 464 pp. (II-61-17)

_____ . *Morskaya moshch' gosudarstva* (Sea Power of the State), 2nd rev, ed., 1979, 416 pp. (II-61-17)

_____ . "Voyenno-morskiye floty v voinakh i v mirnoye vremya" (Navies in Wars and in Peacetime), February 1972 through February 1973 less June 1972 and January 1973. (IV-138-18)

Grechko, A.A., "Obrazovaniye SSR i sovetskiye vooruzhennye sily" (Formation of the USSR and the Soviet Armed Forces), *Novaya i noveishaya istoriya* No. 6, November-December 1972, pp. 9-26. (VII-253-4)

Groos, Otto, *Ucheniye morskoi voine v svete opyta mirovoi voine*, 1930. Translation of 1928 German book *Seekriegslehren in Lichte des Weltkrieges*. (IV-140-57)

Henrikson, N., "Ob'edineniye vsekh sredstv dlya morskoi oborony" (The Uniting of All Means for Maritime Defense), MS No. 8, August 1925, pp. 111-122. (I-18-31)

Isakov, Ivan, "Avantyurizm germanskogo morskoi strategii" (The Adventurism of German Naval Strategy), MS No. 6, June 1943. (IV-40-60)

Istoriya voennogo iskusstva (History of Military Art), Vol. 1, O.A. Romistrov (Ed.), 1963, 528 pp. (V-159-6)

Istoriya voenno-morskogo iskusstva (History of Naval Art), Vol. 3, N.A. Piterskiy (Ed.), 1953, 335 pp. (VI-231-70)

Istoriya voenno-morskogo iskusstva (History of Naval Art), S. E. Zakharov (Ed.), 1969, 576 pp. (V-159-2)

Ivanov, L. and P. Smirnov, *Anglo-Amerikanskoye morskoye sopernichestvo* (Anglo-American Naval Rivalry), 1965. (III-84-3)

Korotkov, I.A., *Istoriya Sovetskoi voennoi mysli* (History of Soviet Military Thought), Nauka Press, 1980, 272 pp. (I-18-38)

Kotlovskiy, B., "Protiv reaktsionnykh teoriy v voprosakh boyevogo ispol'zovaniya podvodnykh lodok" (Against Reactionary Theory in Problems of the Combat Employment of Submarines), MS No. 2, February 1932, pp. 59-65. (IV-63-44)

Kotov, P., "Etapy razvitiya Sovetskogo voennogo korablestroeniya" (The Stages of Development of Soviet Military Shipbuilding), *Voenno-istoricheskiy zhurnal* No. 7, July 1982, pp. 53-58. (IV-139-27)

Kozhanov, I., "Sootvetsvovali li organizatsiya i metody maloi voiny strategicheskim zadacham nemtsev i obstanovke v protsesse razvitiya ot nachala do kontsa 1914 goda?" (Did the Organization and Methods of the Small War Correspond to the Strategic Missions of the Germans and to the Evolving Situation from the Beginning to the End of 1914?) MS No. 5, May 1926, pp. 100-114. (I-18-26)

Kudanov, I., "Angliyskaya avianosnaya aviatsiya" (British Carrier Aviation), SF, 7 September 1955. (VI-254-18)

Kulakov, V., "Reaktsionnaya sushchnost' amerikanskoi voenno-morskoi doktriny" (The Reactionary Essence of American Naval Doctrine), KZ, 13 January 1949. (VI-230-55)

Kuznetsov, N.G., "Rech' tov. Kuznetsova" (Speech of Comrade Kuznetsov), *Stenograficheskiy otchet XVIII s"ezda KPSS* (Stenographic Record of the 18th Congress of the CPSU), Political Press, 1939, pp. 477-480. (IV-139-24)

_____ . "Pered voinoi" (Before the War), *Oktyabr* No. 11, November 1965, pp. 134-171. (IV-139-24)

_____ . *Nakanune* (On the Eve), 1966, 344 pp. (II-63-52)

_____ . "Before the War" (in English), *International Affairs* No.12, 1966, pp. 93-144. (IV-139-26)

_____ . *Nakanune* (On the Eve), 2nd rev, ed., 1969, 376 pp. (IV–139–21)

Lomov, N., "Sbornik trudov o razvitii teorii sovetskogo voennogo iskusstva v mezhvoennyi period" (A Collection of Works on the Development of the Theory of Soviet Military Art in the Interwar Period), *Voenno-istoricheskiy zhurnal* No. 1, January 1968, pp. 101–107. (II–63–51)

Ludri, I., "Krasnyi flot v sostave vooruzhennykh sil respubliki" (The Red Navy in the Composition of the Armed Forces of the Republic), MS No. 10, October 1927, pp. 23–28. (I–18–37)

_____ . "O taktike malogo flota" (Concerning the Tactics of a Small Navy), MS No. 3, March 1928, pp. 14–22. (II–60–2)

_____ . "Istoriya otritsaniya gospodstva angliyskogo flota na moryakh" (History of the Abnegation of Command of the Seas by the British Navy), MS No. 11, November 1933, pp. 162–170. (III–84–9)

_____ . "Kh Vil'son — Morskiye operatsii v mirovoi voine 1914–1918gg" (H. Wilson — Naval operations in the World War 1914-1918), MS No. 2, February 1936, pp. 157–159. (III–85–20)

Makeyev, N.I., "Avianosnye korabli" (Aircraft Carriers), KZ, 15 December 1955. (VII–254–17)

Malinovskiy, Rodion, Accountability Report as Defense Minister to the XXIIIrd Party Congress, 1 April 1966, *Stenograficheskiy otchet XXIII s"ezd KPSS* (Stenographic Record of the 23rd Congress of the CPSU), Vol. 1, Political Publishing House, 1966, pp. 408–417. (II–60–12)

Mil'gram, N., "Nesostoyatel'nost' i reaktsionnaya sushchnost' angliyskoi voenno-morskoi teorii" (The Insolvency and Reactionary Nature of British Naval Theory), KZ, 5 August 1949. (VI–231–59)

Mor (pseudonym), "Voenno-morskoye iskusstvo i uroki morskoi voiny" (Naval Art and the Lessons of the Naval War), *Voennyi zarubezhnik* No. 9, September 1938, pp. 73–92. (IV–139–20)

Muklevich, R., "Desyatiletiye oktyabrskoi revolyutsii i morskoi flot" (The Tenth Year of the October Revolution and the Navy), MS No. 10, October 1927, pp. 3–13. (I–18–34)

Mus'yakov, P. I., "Flagman K. I. Dushenov" (Admiral K. I. Dushenov), MS No. 10, October 1963, pp. 52 and 76–80. (II–60–3)

Nauchnye voprosy na konferentsii VNO Baltmorya" (Scientific Questions at the Conference of the Military Scientific Society of the Baltic Sea), A. Aleksandrov (Ed.), *Krasnyi flot*, February 1926, pp. 97–98. (I–18–36)

Novitskiy, V. "Voenno-morskiye sily nachal'nyi period voiny" (Naval Forces in the Initial period of the War), *Voina i revolyutsii* No. 3, May–June 1935, pp. 46–55. (III–85–17)

"Ob' uyazvimosti lineinykh korablei pri vozdushnykh atakakh" (On the Vulnerability of Capital Ships Under Air Attacks), MS No. 1, January 1937, pp. 142-151. Translation from a Swedish naval journal). (IV–137–2)

Panteleyev, Yuri, "Bor'ba za gospodstvo na more" (The Struggle for Command of the Sea), KZ, 16 January 1947. (VI-229-38)

Pavlovich, N.B., "Boyevoye obespecheniye" (Combat Support), MS No. 11, November 1940, pp. 36-46. (IV-140-62)

_____ . Review of V. F. Chernyshev, *Nadvodnye korabli v sovremennoi voine* (Surface Combatant Ships in Modern War), MS No. 10, October 1945, pp. 115-128. (VI-227-1)

Penzin, V., "Nauchnaya konferentsiya v voenno-morskoe akademii im. K. E. Voroshilova" (Scientific Conference at the Voroshilov Naval War College), MS No.3, March 1946, pp. 111-113. (VI-227-15)

Petrov, M., "Morskiye pozitsii i pozitsionnyi boi" (Naval Positions and Positional Battle), MS, May-June 1919, pp. 18-47 and September-December 1919, pp. 41-74. (I-17-12)

_____ . "Vozdushnye sily v operatsiy na more" (Air Forces in Operations at Sea), MS No. 6, June 1923, pp. 178-197. (I-17-12)

_____ . "Zametki o taktike malogo flota (Notes on the Tactics for a Small Navy), September 1923, pp. 45-61 and January 1924, pp. 31-48. (I-18-13)

_____ . "Ob atake aviatsii v vstrechnom boyu na more" (On Attack by Aviation in a Meeting Engagement at Sea), MS No. 3, March 1924, pp. 38-51. (I-18-25)

_____ . "Morskaya pozitsiya" (The Naval Position), MS No. 4, April 1924, pp. 30-45. (I-18-14)

_____ . "Bol'she vnimaniya morskoi aviatsii" (More Attention to Naval Aviation), *Krasnyi flot*, April 1924, pp. 77-78. (I-18-19)

_____ . "Sovremennyi morskoi flot" (The Modern Navy), *Voennyi vestnik* No. 7, July 1927, pp. 12 and 14. (I-18-30)

_____ . "K postanovke voprosa o 'maloi voine'" (Toward a Formulation of the Question of the "Small War"), MS, February 1928, pp. 37-47; March 1928, pp. 3-18; May 1928, pp. 36-46; June 1928, pp. 3-20; and July-August 1928, pp. 8-21. (II-60-5)

Piterskiy, N., "Amerikanskiye vzglyady na rol' i zadachi flota v voine" (American Views on the Role and Missions of a Navy in War), VM No. 7, July 1949, pp. 72-81. (VI-230-56)

Razumnyi, I. A., "Avianosnye soedineniya flota SShA v voine na Tikhom okeane" (The Aircraft Carrier Forces of the U.S. in the War in the Pacific), MS No. 7, July 1946, pp. 61-81. (VI-228-24)

Rodionov, A. "Na strazhe morskikh rubezhei" (On Guard Over the Maritime Perimeters), *Vodnyi transport*, 24 July 1954. (VII-253-7)

Schner, I., "Avianostsy i ikh rol' v operatsiyakh flota" (Aircraft Carriers and Their Role in the Operations of the Navy), VM No. 6, June 1946, pp. 77-82. (VI-227-7)

Shavtsov, V., "O gospodstvo na more" (On Command of the Sea), VM No. 6, June 1955, pp. 3-17. (VI-229-42)

Shvede, E., "Razvitiye flotov kapitalisticheskikh gosudartstv za 20 let" (The Development of the Navies of the Capitalist States Over the Past 20 Years), MS No. 12, December 1937, pp. 113-126. (IV-137-5)

————. Voenno-morskoi flot Italii (The Italian Navy), MS No. 9, September 1938, pp. 90-103. (IV-137-6)

Smirnov, P.A., "Rech' tov. Smirnova" (Speech of Comrade Smirnov), MS No. 4, April 1938, pp. 8-9. (IV-138-9)

Sobelov, A., "Na poroge novogo etape Krasnogo flota" (On the Threshold of a New Stage in the Organization and Construction of the Red Navy), MS No.10, October 1924, pp. 50-51. (I-18-22)

Sokolov, V., "Bazovaya aviatsiya Amerikanskogo flota" (The Land-Based Aviation of the American Navy), SF, 13 November 1955. (VII-254-19)

Solonnikov, O., "Gospodstvo na more" (Command of the Sea), *Bol'shaya Sovetskaya entsiklopediya*, 1st ed., Vol. 18, 1930, pp. 270-274. (II-62-33)

Sovremennye boyevye sredstva morskogo flota (Modern Combat Means of a Navy), 2nd ed., I. Kalachev (Ed.), 1937. (IV-137-1)

Stalbo, K., "Avianostsy vo vtoroi mirovoi voine" (Aircraft Carriers in the Second World War), MS No. 1, January 1978, pp. 91-11. (V-159-16)

Stalin, I., "O nekotorykh voprosakh istorii Bol'shevizma" (On Certain Question About the History of Bolshevism), *Proletarskaya revolyutsiya* No. 6, 1931, pp. 3-13. (II-63-39)

Stepanov, M., "Sluzhba na flote . . .s 1900g" (Service in the Navy . . .Since 1900), MS No. 7, July 1977, pp. 72-73. (IV-140-64)

Stepanov, M.E., "Obespecheniye razvertivaniya podvodnykh lodok v khode voennykh deystviy" (Support for the Deployment of Submarines in the Course of Military Action), MS No. 12, December 1961, pp. 39-48. (III-84-10)

Stolyarskiy, S.E., "Vozdushnye sily v bor'be na more" (Air Forces in War at Sea), MS No. 3, March 1934, pp. 9-26. (III-84-13)

————. "Zadachi i metody operatsiyakh vozdushnykh sil v voine na more" (Missions and Methods of Operations of Air Forces in a War at Sea), MS No. 4, April 1934, pp. 9-19. (III-85-14)

Stolyarskiy, S.E. and J.F. Kireyev, "Morskaya aviatsiya kapitalisticheskikh gosudarstv" (Naval Aviation of the Capitalist States), MS No. 11, November 1935, pp. 108-122. (III-85-19)

Tukhachevskiy, M., "Strategiya organizatsii" (Strategy of Organization), *Voennyi vestnik* No. 28, 1924, pp. 26-29. (II-60-10)

Vladimirskiy, L., "Vernyi strazh morskikh rubezhei Sovetskogo gosudarstva" (Reliable Guard of the Maritime Perimeters of the Soviet State), *Pravda Ukraina*, 25 July 1954. (VII-253-6)

——————— . "Novaya tekhnika na korablyakh" (New Technology on Combatant Ships), *Komsomol'skaya pravda*, 23 July 1955. (VII-253-16)

Voenno-tekhnicheskiy progress i vooruzhennye sily SSSR (Military-Technological Progress and the Armed Forces of the USSR), M. M. Kir'yan (Ed.), 1982, 336 pp. (V-159-1)

Voronov, P.I., "Deystviya aviatsii na morskikh kommunikatsiyakh" (Action of Aviation on Sea Communications), MS No. 3, March 1944, pp. 52-69. (V-159-13)

Voroshilov, K., Accountability Report as Defense Minister to the 27th Party Congress, *Stenograficheskiy otchet XXVII S"ezd KPSS* (Stenographic Record of the 27th Congress of the CPSU), Political Press, 1934, 600 pp. (III-84-11)

Voznenko, V.I., Korotkov, and M. Skovorodkin, "Voennaya strategiya v trudakh Sovetskikh avtorov, 1917-1967 gody" (Military Strategy in the Works of Soviet Authors, 1917-1967), VM No. 4, April 1967. (VI-229-40)

V'yunenko, N., "Sovmestnye operatsii i rol' v nikh voenno-morskikh sil" (Joint Operations and the Role of Naval Forces), VM No. 10, October 1953, pp. 19-32. (VI-253-5)

Yakimychev, A., "Rol' vozdushnogo flota v morskom boyu" (The Role of an Air Fleet in Naval Battle), *Krasnyi flot* Nos 4-5, 1923, pp. 38-39. (I-17-7)

——————— . "Voina 'malym (slabym) flotam' i 'malaya voina' v epokhu parovoga flota" (War of a "Small[Weak]Navy" and the "Small War" in the Era of the Steam Navy), MS No. 9, September 1928, pp. 44-46. (II-60-9)

——————— . "Perelomnyi etap v razvitii metodov i sredstv vedeniya voiny na Baltiiskom more v voinu 1914-1917gg" (The Transition Stage in the Development of the Methods and Means of the Conduct of war in the Baltic in the War of 1914-1917), MS No. 3, March 1931, pp. 24-38. (II-63-34)

"Zet", Review of N. M. Lebedev *Ocherki gidroaviatsii* (The Story of Seaplanes), *Voennyi vestnik* No. 3, March 1924, pp. 44-45. (I-18-20)

Zof, V., "Mezhdunarodnoye polozheniye i zadachi morskoi oborony SSSR" (The International Situation and the Missions for the Naval Defense of the USSR), MS No. 5, May 1925, pp. 3-26. (I-18-23)

INDEX

A

E

Modern Combat Means of a Navy, 86, 137n1.
Mordvinov, Captain First Rank R. N., 231n71.
Moscow, 7, 77, 93, 159n15, 247.
Mosquito fleet, 155, 222.
Muklevich, R. A., 11, 18n35, 256.
Munich, 231n65.
Mutual cooperation with the Army. *See* Naval missions: providing seaward cover and direct support to coastal ground forces.
Mutual cooperation of naval forces, 116, 155, 171, 212, 213.

N

Napoleon, 146, 237n73.
Napoleonic wars, 193.
NATO, naval forces of, 9, 80, 81, 84n5, 158, 186, 218, 235, 241, 243, 244, 246, 249-252, 254n15, 263, 267, 274.
Naval Academy. *See* Naval War College.
Naval airfields, 73, 76, 120, 125, 127, 144, 145, 148, 156, 158, 160, 176-178, 182, 185, 189, 201, 275, 276.
Naval arms races, 46, 57, 58, 101, 257, 274.
Naval art, 31, 53, 99, 139n20, 141, 142, 153, 158, 232n80, 190, 215, 216, 222, 224, 230n56, 261.
Naval auxiliary ships, 15, 128, 176, 232n76.
Naval bases, 1, 2, 6, 11, 13, 17n2, 17n4, 26, 27, 31, 32, 36, 38, 53, 70, 72, 73, 95, 98, 111, 116, 117, 120, 123-125, 127, 129, 131, 132, 141, 145, 147, 148, 153, 157, 163-165, 167, 168, 181-184, 186, 188, 189, 197, 200, 207, 208, 212, 227n3, 227n13, 235, 237, 238, 242, 244, 247, 249, 272, 273, 275, 276.
Naval battle, 1, 2, 6, 7, 15, 17n7, 17n8, 17n9, 17n11, 18n35, 20, 23, 24, 26, 29, 33, 40, 47, 68, 70, 112, 113, 115, 124, 131, 144, 152, 154, 159, 165, 166, 174, 175, 178, 179, 186, 188, 199, 206, 212, 214, 216, 217, 219, 223, 230n49, 252, 264, 271.
Naval blockade. *See* Naval warfare: by blockade.
Naval bombardment of shore targets. *See* Naval missions: providing seaward cover and direct support to coastal ground forces.
Naval budget. *See* Defense budget, naval share of.
Naval commissars. *See* Naval ministers.
Naval construction: policy on, 5, 10, 12, 23, 30-34, 38, 43, 47n58, 66, 70, 170, 211, 223, 246, 247, 259, 268, 273, 276: programs for, xiii, xiv, 2, 8, 11, 34, 38, 59, 66, 81, 82, 84n12, 92, 103-109, 138n16, 157, 158, 191, 204, 208, 211, 216, 231n62, 235, 247, 253, 253n2, 258, 261, 267, 269.
Naval deployments, 36, 76, 120, 129, 130, 147, 148, 168, 182, 183, 188, 229n36, 237, 240, 241, 249.

113, 114, 120, 149, 175, 218, 220, 226, 228n26, 229n34, 251, 271; offensive, 21, 69, 71, 102, 125, 175, 248, 271; of evading battle/withholding forces, 1, 17n3, 67, 112, 113, 135, 145, 146, 156, 157, 167, 168, 175, 183, 187, 189, 205, 206, 209, 217, 219, 223, 239, 264, 268; stratagems for the weaker navy, 5, 29, 40, 65, 78, 123. *See also* Command-of-the-sea entries.
Naval theoreticians, 36, 71, 81, 84, 93, 99, 136, 137, 139n54, 141, 142, 172, 180, 192, 198, 199, 213, 216, 218, 222, 223, 229n47, 231n59, 234, 238, 248, 255, 258, 262, 267, 271.
Naval theory. See Naval science/theory.
Naval training, 24, 26, 30, 32, 45, 47.
Naval theater of military actions (TVD). *See* Theater of military actions, naval.
Naval War College, 2-4, 10, 12, 16, 17n7, 18n40, 20, 23, 37-40, 44-46, 50, 55, 59, 65, 83, 84n2, 86, 88, 89, 93, 110, 113, 136, 137, 137n5, 140n57, 151, 157, 169, 172, 186, 198, 218, 227n2, 227n12, 227n15, 229n47, 231n63, 231n66, 231n67, 231n68, 255, 262, 265.
Naval War College, U.S., 139n37, 277n4.
Naval warfare: to control the key SLOC, 1, 39, 42, 43, 65-67, 74, 96, 121, 157, 167, 203, 231n73; amphibious and counterlanding, 1, 3, 8, 10, 11, 13, 26, 35, 45, 93, 118, 141, 143, 144, 146-150, 154, 156-158, 166, 167, 186, 187, 195, 202, 216, 233; antiair, 6, 27, 74, 87, 137n2, 153, 162-164, 186, 227n3, 227n8, 227n18, 276; anti-carrier and anti-surface ship (ASuW), 3, 5, 73, 87, 96, 111, 113, 120, 122, 142, 144, 186, 227n3, 227n9, 241, 247, 262, 273, 274, 276; antisubmarine, 4, 35, 38, 52, 65, 70, 72, 76, 78, 79, 81, 86, 88, 117, 118, 120, 121, 123, 141, 143, 154, 156-158, 174, 186, 187, 208, 210, 211, 227n8, 227n18, 242, 251, 257, 262; by blockade, 1, 3, 8, 13, 17, 17n2, 17n9, 17n11, 21-24, 26, 28, 30, 31, 34, 35, 37, 39, 40, 43, 44, 51, 53, 61n18, 66, 68, 70, 72, 78, 81, 96-98, 115, 117, 119, 120, 122, 123, 143, 144, 154, 166, 169, 243, 245, 256, 263, 264, 268, 274; by counterblockade, 1, 4, 5, 7, 8, 17n3, 24, 26, 31, 33, 39, 44, 97, 117; nuclear, 195, 208, 212, 213, 227n18, 237, 241, 257; mine, 14, 39, 62n30, 65, 70, 111, 118, 120-123, 131, 139n52, 148, 149, 186, 187, 195, 208, 212, 213, 227n18, 237, 241, 257; submarine, 8, 18n29, 26, 34, 65, 69, 70-72, 77, 80, 83n1, 242.
Naval Warfare: the Basic Principles and Experience, 129, 192, 196, 229n43, 230n48.
Naval weapons: antiaircraft, 27, 81, 162, 174, 177; antisubmarine, 118, 122, 123, artillery, coastal, 4, 12, 14, 39, 43, 58, 66, 82, 141, 149, 184, 235, 237, 255, 261, 269, 275; bombs, aviation, 73, 74, 89, 124, 126, 141, 152, 163, 227n3; guns, ships', 1, 3, 24, 124, 126, 141, 152, 174, 175, 206, 233; mines, 12, 17n11, 68, 117, 118, 123, 181, 210, 226, 242, 255, 271; missiles, coastal, 275; missiles, cruise, 254n16; mine countermeasures, 118; torpedoes, 12, 68, 72-74, 151-153, 159n17, 174, 177, 179, 181, 182, 186, 189, 199, 210, 226, 227n3, 271; nuclear, 191, 215, 233, 234, 236, 241, 242, 244, 249, 272, 274; nuclear missile, ballistic, 191, 197, 246, 247.

The Naval Institute Press is the book-publishing arm of the U.S. Naval Institute, a private, nonprofit professional society for members of the sea services and civilians who share an interest in naval and maritime affairs. Established in 1873 at the U.S. Naval Academy in Annapolis, Maryland, where its offices remain today, the Naval Institute has more than 100,000 members worldwide.

Members of the Naval Institute receive the influential monthly naval magazine *Proceedings* and substantial discounts on fine nautical prints, ship and aircraft photos, and subscriptions to the Institute's recently inaugurated quarterly, *Naval History*. They also have access to the transcripts of the Institute's Oral History Program and may attend any of the Institute-sponsored seminars regularly offered around the country.

The book-publishing program, begun in 1898 with basic guides to naval practices, has broadened its scope in recent years to include books of more general interest. Now the Naval Institute Press publishes more than forty new titles each year, ranging from how-to books on boating and navigation to battle histories, biographies, ship guides, and novels. Institute members receive discounts on the Press's more than 300 books.

For a free catalog describing books currently available and for further information about U.S. Naval Institute membership, please write to:

Membership Department
U.S. Naval Institute
Annapolis, Maryland 21402

or call, toll-free, 800-233-USNI.